RELIEF ON THE HOOF

A volume in the NIU Series in

Slavic, East European, and Eurasian Studies
Edited by Christine D. Worobec

For a list of books in the series, visit our website at cornellpress.cornell.edu.

RELIEF ON THE HOOF

THE SEAGOING COWBOYS, THE HEIFER PROJECT, AND UNRRA IN POLAND

Eva Plach

NORTHERN ILLINOIS UNIVERSITY PRESS
AN IMPRINT OF
CORNELL UNIVERSITY PRESS
Ithaca and London

Copyright © 2025 by Eva Plach

All rights reserved. Except for brief quotations in a review, this book, or parts thereof, must not be reproduced in any form without permission in writing from the publisher. For information, address Cornell University Press, Sage House, 512 East State Street, Ithaca, New York 14850. Visit our website at cornellpress.cornell.edu.

First published 2025 by Cornell University Press

Librarians: A CIP catalog record for this book is available from the Library of Congress.

ISBN 9781501783890 (hardcover)
ISBN 9781501784644 (paperback)
ISBN 9781501783913 (pdf)
ISBN 9781501783906 (epub)

GPSR EU contact: Sam Thornton, Mare Nostrum Group B.V., Mauritskade 21D, 1091 GC, Amsterdam, NL, gpsr@mare-nostrum.co.uk.

For working animals everywhere

Contents

List of Illustrations viii

Acknowledgments ix

Note on Spelling, Translation, and Language xi

Introduction: Global Agents of Humanitarian Aid 1

1. UNRRA, Food, and Winning the Peace 12
2. The UNRRA–Brethren Service Committee Partnership 34
3. On Becoming a Seagoing Cowboy 52
4. Working Animals as Humanitarian Aid 76
5. The Making of "Relief Animals" 92
6. Cowboys and Animals at Sea 108
7. Bovines, Equines, and Humans in Poland 135
8. UNRRA and Animal Politics in Poland 160
9. Heifer Project Animals in Poland 177

Conclusion: Humanitarian Imaginaries 195

List of Abbreviations 205

Notes 207

Bibliography 277

Index 301

Illustrations

1. Polish children drinking milk with SS *William Riddle* in background — 83
2. SS *Cedar Rapids Victory* — 111
3. Seagoing cowboys — 114
4. Horses aboard the SS *Cedar Rapids Victory* — 115
5. Seagoing cowboys at work — 120
6. Cowboys in Gdańsk — 138
7. Unloading of horses in Poland — 143
8. Delivery of horses by UNRRA — 146
9. Delivery of horses by UNRRA — 147
10. Veterinarian examining UNRRA horses — 148
11. Delivery of horses by UNRRA — 149
12. Polish farmer from the Recovered Territories with horse — 158
13. Milking a recently arrived UNRRA cow on a farm near Gdańsk — 164
14. Children and cow — 186
15. Seagoing cowboys — 187

Acknowledgments

The subject of this book came to me quite serendipitously. I was poking around on the internet one day reading about animal welfare in contemporary Poland when I stumbled across Peggy Reiff Miller's Seagoing Cowboys website and blog. The site chronicles the remarkable story of American cattle and horses that were delivered as humanitarian aid in the years immediately following World War II. My curiosity was piqued. This book is the result.

My first thanks go to Peggy Reiff Miller. Peggy's grandfather, Abraham Reiff, traveled to Poland on SS *Pierre Victory* in 1946 as a Brethren seagoing cowboy. Peggy translated this direct and personal connection to the history of the seagoing cowboys into an impressive research project that has spanned more than two decades. Over the years Peggy has interviewed dozens of cowboys. She has recorded their stories and has assembled the world's largest private collection of photographs related to cowboy history. In my work I have relied on Peggy's deep expertise on the subject of the seagoing cowboys and the Heifer Project, and I have benefited greatly from her meticulousness and attention to detail. I thank Peggy for her careful reading of my manuscript and for her willingness to provide follow-up elaborations, corrections, and clarifications. Peggy and I have never met in person, but we evidently share a deep respect for some of the ideals that shaped mid-century humanitarian aid programs. It would seem that the heifers and horses that are the subject of this book continue to bring people together in unexpected ways.

A few graduate students from Wilfrid Laurier University played a small but important role in this project's earliest phase. Thank you to Stephanie Plante, Matthew Morden, and especially Rafal Stolarz (now Dr. Stolarz). Joanna Dobrowolska, a PhD student at the University of Illinois at Chicago, has been my research assistant since 2022. I am grateful to Joanna (and to her advisor, Keely Stauter-Halsted, who introduced us) for visiting Polish and American archives on my behalf during the COVID-19 pandemic and for being unfailingly professional, methodical, diligent, patient, and flexible over the few years that we have worked together. I could not have asked for

ACKNOWLEDGMENTS

a more talented and committed RA. I offer my thanks to Yelena Abdullayeva as well for an early reading of the manuscript and for the many conversations we have had over the years; these always leave me a little better informed. Thanks to Piotr Wróbel, too, for steady background encouragement, and to my terrific colleagues in the History Department at Wilfrid Laurier University. I would also very much like to thank the manuscript peer reviewers; I appreciate their enthusiasm, generous comments, and good questions.

A number of archivists and librarians facilitated access to the materials needed for this book, but a few stand out for going above and beyond: Jen Houser and Allison Snyder from the Brethren Historical Library and Archives in Elgin, Illinois; Wendy Chmielewski and Anne Yoder of Pennsylvania's Swarthmore College Peace Collection; Jason Kauffman and Eva Lapp at the Mennonite Church Archives in Elkhart, Indiana; and Annabella Irvine of the Slavic Reference Service at the University of Illinois at Urbana-Champaign. The staff at the Library and Archives Reference Desk from the United States Holocaust Memorial Museum facilitated digital access to material from the United Nations Archives when travel was not possible; this was a big help. Amy Menary at Wilfrid Laurier's Inter-Library Loans department has worked for years fulfilling one challenging request after another for me. I extend general thanks to the staff at the United Nations Archives in New York City as well as to the staff at the Archive of Modern Documents in Warsaw, Poland. Thanks to Amy Farranto, senior acquisitions editor, Northern Illinois University Press, and to Christine Worobec, series editor, Northern Illinois University Press Series in Slavic, East European, and Eurasian Studies, for their early interest in this subject. Thanks to Ellen Labbate of Cornell University Press for her work on the photographs. I would also like to thank Michelle Dusek Izaguirre, Vice President of Resource Development Operations at Heifer Project International, for the stimulating conversation and support.

I am grateful to my friends and to the different parts of my family in Kitchener-Waterloo, Toronto, and Ottawa for their love, support, and wit. Most of all I thank my husband Bob and our son Townes—both for asking about my book and for ignoring it. You make me keep things in perspective, always. What a privilege it is to spend my days with you.

Research for this book was supported by the Social Sciences and Humanities Research Council of Canada.

The title of the book is taken from an article titled "Heifers—Relief on the Hoof." This article appeared in *The Weekly Processor* on July 15, 1946. *The Weekly Processor* was published by the United Church Service Center in New Windsor, Maryland.

Note on Spelling, Translation, and Language

In this book I use the Polish spelling for the names of cities and villages in Poland except in the case of Warsaw; here I use the Anglicized form. I use Danzig instead of Gdańsk only when quoting from a source that uses Danzig. I also retain Polish spelling for the Polish currency: złoty. I provide the original Polish titles in parentheses after English translations of Polish institutions that are not well known but are important to the story that I am telling. I provide the Polish original in parentheses after the English translation in a few other cases, too, if I think that the precise Polish wording might be useful to researchers. All translations from Polish are my own, unless otherwise noted.

It is important to remember that humans are animals too, but I use the term "nonhuman animals" only occasionally. For the most part I use "animals" to refer not to humans but to the cattle and horses that are the main species featured in this book. I refer to animals as "she" or "he" rather than "it."

RELIEF ON THE HOOF

Introduction
Global Agents of Humanitarian Aid

Between 1945 and 1947, the United Nations Relief and Rehabilitation Administration (UNRRA) delivered approximately 286,000 horses, mules, and donkeys, along with 37,000 cattle, to countries whose livestock and agricultural lands had been devastated by Nazi and Nazi-allied aggression during the war. Additionally, UNRRA provided thousands of smaller animals, including sheep, pigs, rabbits, and poultry, to its target countries.[1] Poland was a primary beneficiary of the UNRRA livestock program. Czechoslovakia, Greece, and Yugoslavia also received UNRRA animals, as did, albeit to a lesser extent, Albania, China, Ethiopia, and Italy. The live animals complemented the more widely recognized forms of humanitarian relief that UNRRA provided, including grain, meat, nonperishable foods, clothing, farming equipment, and medical supplies.

Although UNRRA's animal deliveries were hardly sufficient to replace the number of animals lost, they marked a significant investment in postwar rehabilitation. The horses and cattle were especially valuable. Agricultural experts estimated that across Europe during the Second World War an astounding twenty-seven million cattle and eight million horses had been killed.[2] Postwar European recovery, food security, and the prevention of the social and political unrest that could be expected to follow hunger would be impossible to realize without replenishing the lost cattle and horses. UNRRA horses were immediately put to use as draft animals on agricultural fields while UNRRA dairy cows became producers of milk. Milk was the food that everyone in this period—humanitarian aid planners, politicians, and food scientists—agreed had unmatched nutritional value and ought to be fed to hungry people, children in particular. UNRRA animals were also used as breeding stock, and at least some of the cattle and horses in Europe today can trace their origins to UNRRA's postwar humanitarian relief program. As such, and in contrast to modern-day live animal maritime export, the animals were sent not *as* food—the intention was not to turn the animals into meat, or at least not immediately—but rather as the means to producing food.

Animals' inclusion in the broad category of "UNRRA aid" was by no means certain at UNRRA's inception. Shipping large animals from America to Europe—the horses and cattle came primarily from the United States—was expensive and logistically complicated. It also depended on securing a pool of competent livestock handlers, men who would accompany the animals on their trans-Atlantic crossings and provide them with daily care. Assembling such a workforce was a challenging undertaking, especially given that so many American men were still in the armed forces in 1945 and 1946. UNRRA found a solution in an unlikely place: the American peace churches. The Brethren Service Committee (BSC), a national agency of the Church of the Brethren in the United States, took on the job of recruiting the livestock handlers for UNRRA.[3] In undertaking this work, the BSC provided vital support to the operation of the UNRRA livestock fleet and played a key role in realizing the monumental ambitions of postwar agricultural rehabilitation.

The BSC recruited a total of 6,759 men to fill 8,851 available positions. Most of the recruited men made just one sailing as livestock handlers—or "seagoing cowboys," as they came to be known—but some made more than one trip. Each of UNRRA's 360 livestock sailings included seagoing cowboys. The seagoing cowboys were young and old and represented a range of social classes, professions, religious affiliations, and racial and ethnic backgrounds; they reflected mid-century America itself.[4] A significant minority—perhaps up to a quarter of the total—came from Brethren congregations and from the related peace church denominations: the Mennonites and, to a lesser extent, the Quakers.[5] This book focuses on this specific subset of seagoing cowboys, on those men who came out of a Christian milieu and shared the Christian values of the BSC that recruited them. It was also these men, as we shall see, who left a uniquely rich source base describing their experiences as seagoing cowboys and as agents of humanitarian aid provision.

In addition to recruiting and training men to work as animal attendants on the UNRRA ships, the BSC ran its own independent postwar humanitarian aid program called the Heifer Project. The Heifer Project collected heifers—young female cattle, usually under two or three years of age who had not yet given birth—to be delivered as gifts from Americans to people in designated receiving countries. The idea for the Heifer Project originated even before the Second World War had started, in the late 1930s, when the Brethren worked with the Quakers to deliver food aid to Spain during the Civil War. There in Spain the Brethren member Dan West had the idea that would evolve into the Heifer Project. Why hand out single cups of milk, West asked, when the whole milk-giving animal would be far more useful? The cow, according to the Brethren, was "the foster mother of the human race . . . one of the chief sustaining forces of human life."[6] By 1943 West's idea to ship living cattle as humanitarian aid was formalized into the Heifer Project and was adopted by the BSC as a national plan. What started out as the Heifer Project is known today as Heifer Project International, a global nonprofit that has received financial support from well-known organizations like the Bill and Melinda Gates Foundation.[7]

Approximately four thousand Heifer Project animals were on 13 of the 360 UNRRA livestock sailings. The men recruited by the BSC to work as animal handlers were present on all of the trips irrespective of whether the ship was loaded only with UNRRA animals or with Heifer Project animals in addition to UNRRA animals; the vast majority of the sailings included only UNRRA animals.[8] The Brethren's justification for running a live animal program was similar to UNRRA's: living animals delivered as aid gave the best value as relief commodities for the long term. As Fiorello La Guardia, UNRRA director from March 1946, said, "Grain and canned milk are relief . . . but a farm animal, with a future, spells rehabilitation."[9] The prosperity and rehabilitation imagined by contemporaries at this crucial postwar moment was dependent on the successful transfer, integration, and employment of horses and cattle.

The relationship between the tiny BSC and the UNRRA behemoth was mutually beneficial. For its part, UNRRA profited from the Brethren's ability to recruit and train reliable attendants to work on the UNRRA live aid ships. Without these men it would have been difficult to ship so many animals in such a short period of time. The Brethren, in turn, got free passage for "their" Heifer Project animals on the UNRRA ships and fulfilled their communities' desire to contribute directly to alleviating some of the suffering caused by the war. The Brethren would not have been able to afford to ship so many cattle otherwise. Herbert Lehman, Democratic governor of New York from 1933 to 1942 and UNRRA's first director general until his replacement by La Guardia, praised the BSC and the Heifer Project for making such a substantial contribution to the postwar relief effort. The Brethren-recruited cowboys, Lehman said, did "a splendid job not only as livestock tenders but also as representatives of their land and way of life."[10] They facilitated what UNRRA itself described as "the most important waterborne migration of animals since the time of Noah."[11]

According to George Woodbridge, an American member of UNRRA's European Regional Office in London and UNRRA's official historian, Poland received 151,400 horses and 17,000 cattle through the UNRRA program.[12] The horses and cattle arrived in Poland on 177 of the 360 livestock sailings that UNRRA made. In comparison, Czechoslovakia received 27,000 horses and approximately 5,000 head of cattle, while Yugoslavia received just over 23,000 horses and mules plus a small number of dairy cattle. Greece received 62,200 animals, the vast majority of which were mules, horses, and donkeys.[13] While available sources provide slightly different figures for the number of animals that each country received, they all show that Poland's share of the total was significantly larger than that of any other country.[14] That Poland was prioritized for livestock aid reflected UNRRA's assessment of this one country's enormous need and of its importance to the geopolitical interests of the United States, especially as early Cold War tensions formed. UNRRA was largely American-dominated from both a financial and a political perspective.

Poland's allocation of Heifer Project animals was similarly greater than other countries' during the UNRRA period: Poland received approximately eight hundred Heifer Project cattle from 1945 through 1947. Additional Heifer Project cattle arrived in Poland after the UNRRA period ended and until 1949 (the year the Brethren left Poland), bringing the total number of Heifer Project cattle delivered to Poland to 1,013. Czechoslovakia, Greece, Italy, and China received hundreds of Heifer Project animals each. Altogether, from 1944 to 1953 (so, again, well after the UNRRA period), the Heifer Project delivered almost seven thousand cattle to all destinations plus almost six thousand goats, hundreds of pigs and horses, and tens of thousands of chickens.[15]

We know very little about these animals or about the animal handlers that sailed on the UNRRA ships, just as we know little about the vast organizational efforts that brought the livestock programs to life. Similarly, the meaning and importance of the animals, from both the givers' and the receivers' perspectives, have not been studied in a systematic fashion or incorporated into other analyses of the period. This book addresses these gaps by providing an integrated history of the seagoing cowboys, the Heifer Project, the BSC, and UNRRA. In doing so, it speaks to a number of themes and subfields simultaneously.

One of these is the history of humanitarianism and food aid. As we know, the war was at least in part a battle for food and land resources, and Hitler's war aims included gaining control over the rich agricultural fields of eastern Europe. After the war, and largely as a response to wartime experiences, the pursuit of food security became a priority for policymakers. Postwar humanitarian aid programs were built on the premise that hunger was politically destabilizing and that food security offered the best hope for sociopolitical stability. Horses and cattle were key to agricultural production and therefore to alleviating food anxiety.

Despite the significance of animals to planned postwar recovery, they are seldom taken seriously in the literature about mid-century humanitarianism. Animals are rarely even named as a separate category in lists of the types of aid delivered. Instead they are too often subsumed by, and made invisible within, the category of "agricultural tools" as in this summary of aid deliveries: "3.5 thousand tractors, fertilizers, dairy cows, horses, seeds."[16] The well-used terms "relief animals" and "live aid" are arguably more descriptive, but even these combine animal species and thereby erase the differences between a chicken and a horse in terms of their contributions to agricultural development and to postwar rehabilitation. At any rate, the categories, statistics, and numbers both obscure and reveal the simple but important reality of live animal transport, which is that live animals can become sick and die along the path to becoming humanitarian aid. What this means is that the number of animals loaded at the starting ports in the United States was never the same as the number that arrived at the destinations. On some sailings animal deaths reached double-digit percentages, though the average was around 3 to 4 percent; for every thousand animals that left America, at least a few dozen (mainly horses, who are notoriously poor sailors and succumb easily to shipping illnesses) died during the ocean crossing. Sometimes animals became so sick that they died just hours or days after disembarkation. Long and arduous in-country transport routes resulted in further animal losses due to both death and theft, meaning, of course, that these animals never actually became the relief animals that program administrators wanted them to be.

In turning our focus specifically to the dairy cows and horses that formed an essential component of postwar aid programs, we see that the early postwar period was one of very active *animal* population movements and not just of human population movements. These animals were both objects and agents of a new mid-century globalization drive, and their inclusion in the postwar aid programs reflected the aspirations and successes (and failures too) of global cooperation. This is not a book about animals *in* war—a subject that has enjoyed a fair bit of scholarly and popular interest in recent years—but a story of how some animals' fates were determined *by* war and, more precisely, by plans for shaping the postwar global order.¹⁷ The UNRRA and Heifer Project relief animals came to occupy what we might call "transnational spaces, both mental and material."¹⁸ Animals' presence between borders and in global spaces mattered for practical reasons as well as for symbolic ones.

The histories of postwar humanitarian aid and of animals as aid converge in the collaboration between UNRRA and the BSC. I show how it came to be that an organization like UNRRA—massive, complex, highly bureaucratic, and ostensibly secular—found common cause and partnered, albeit in this partial and specific way, with the comparatively tiny and actively Christian BSC to move hundreds of thousands of animals from one continent to another at record speed. This book is about the interactions and sometimes surprising overlap between different expressions of mid-century humanitarianism and relief provision. The differences were not as great as one might expect.

But this is not just a top-down history of organizations big and small. Instead, in concentrating on some of the seemingly peripheral actors involved in delivering international aid—the seagoing cowboys—this work follows a general shift in the internationalism literature toward favoring bottom-up approaches to understanding the motivations and intentions of global humanitarian actors and agents and to unpacking the meaning and effects of relief programs at local levels.¹⁹ The seagoing cowboys—and specifically those who came out of peace church circles and who are the focus of this book—were unique international actors. Even as they embodied the privileges of UNRRA and of American economic and political power when they appeared on foreign shores, the men's identities were rooted in whole or part in their faith communities. It was as Christians that many of them answered the call of the BSC to help in the first place. In diary entries from aboard the livestock ships, in letters home from port cities, and in memoirs and interviews given weeks and even decades after the fact, the men described in detail how they did their work and what it meant to them to participate as they did in an international humanitarian relief effort.

The history I tell here is a layered one. It is partly American history, and it is partly global history. Yet ultimately the targets of the aid programs were national, and the circumstances of animals' lives unfolded in specific national contexts too. I follow the relief animals from the United States through to their final destinations in Poland. I focus on the Polish context because for both UNRRA and the Heifer Project, Poland was exceptionally important. The Poland program of UNRRA (in Polish it is rendered Administracja

Narodów Zjednoczonych do Spraw Pomocy i Odbudowy) was the largest of the European aid programs: UNRRA delivered approximately $471 million dollars' worth of aid, or 16 percent of the total amount allocated for country programs, to Poland. This did not include the considerable additional expenditure on Displaced Persons of Polish origin. The $471 million amount was well advertised: In Poland the UNRRA aid program was sometimes referred to simply as "471." Only the China aid program was larger, valued at $535 million.[20] The total amount of aid delivered to Poland measured two million long tons as of September 1947; this required well over a thousand ships.[21] Though UNRRA wound down at the start of 1947, it fulfilled deliveries of previously promised goods and animals well into 1947.[22] If ancillary costs related to administration and shipping are added to the Poland program, then its value rises higher still, to approximately $600 million.[23]

The first chapter focuses on UNRRA's creation during the wartime period. It outlines UNRRA's general relief priorities and goals during the busy two years that the organization was active and introduces UNRRA's "three Rs": relief, rehabilitation, and reconstruction. These were the concepts that guided the organization's actions and determined the types of aid that it would deliver. Contemporary thinking about food had changed by the time of the Second World War. The idea that food was a fundamental human right and that food insecurity was a global problem shaped how UNRRA conceived of its role and determined the types of aid it would provide. Chapter 1 also introduces the bases on which UNRRA made the decision to devote so many resources, especially animal resources, to Poland specifically.

The second chapter is about the relationship that developed between UNRRA and its supposedly secular model of humanitarian aid provision, on the one hand, and on the other the Christian humanitarianism represented by the BSC. The collaboration between UNRRA and the Brethren worked well for many reasons, not the least of which was that UNRRA itself used a rhetoric of Christian obligation and mission in its approaches to relief and, to some extent, in its conceptions of the international sphere. Chapter 2 also considers the place of animals in evolving humanitarian aid programming. For mid-century Christian humanitarians as for secular internationalists, animals embodied the hope for agricultural—and therefore broader socioeconomic—rehabilitation. Both types of relief providers were interested in stimulating longer-term independent development in addition to providing immediate assistance. This is why the considerable bureaucratic and logistical effort required to make the live animal deliveries was warranted. The rehabilitation of largely agricultural societies—such as those in Poland and in other parts of eastern Europe—was impossible without cattle and horses.

Chapter 3 traces the route that some of the men followed from their homes across the United States to the UNRRA ships. This chapter, based largely on records from the Brethren and Mennonite church archives and from the UNRRA archives, outlines how the BSC, the relief arm of a very small American peace church denomination, managed to provide the logistical support for the largest international aid program in the history of the twentieth century. Examined in this chapter are both peace church history and wartime history, including the history of conscription and conscientious objection in the United States. A small but revealing number of animal attendants on UNRRA ships had been Conscientious Objectors during the war. The peace churches had worked closely with one another during the war to advocate in favor of service options for drafted men, and this wartime collaboration in turn contributed to shaping the peace churches' cooperation in postwar relief projects. Moreover, the wartime period had provided the churches with a more profound sense of their common cause and had given them hands-on experience in effective community mobilization. After the war, the peace churches felt called upon once again to work in the international arena by organizing donations, charity, and aid on an unprecedented scale. The peace churches did this because they believed that humanitarian aid delivery fostered brotherhood and fellowship and that it reflected Christian duty and responsibility; as Dan West said, it constituted "a new testimony to our Master."[24]

The fourth chapter begins with cattle, the star species of the Brethren's Heifer Project and an important part of the UNRRA program. Cattle have carried both real and symbolic value in our world. This is largely because of female cattle's ability to produce an exceptionally nutritious milk that many humans like to drink, and therefore a key part of chapter 4 is about how cows' milk became a preeminent food relief product by the middle of the twentieth century. This chapter returns to the theme of food as a basic right, focusing on the right to milk specifically. It was during this period from 1945 to 1947 that milk became *the* symbol of united nations working together to nourish the hungry. Notwithstanding the importance of milk and cattle, however, horses formed a crucial component of UNRRA's aid program, too, and so the fourth chapter also considers this species' role in postwar rehabilitation.

The fifth chapter is about the logistics of the animals' transformations into humanitarian aid. It follows animals along their various stops in the United States and examines their encounters with public and private agencies, most notably with government bureaucracies and animal welfare activists. While it is true that large numbers of animals had been shipped across oceans before—for military purposes, mainly—the animals shipped during the UNRRA period were meant to live for the long term, and their bodies and moods needed to be suitable for work soon after landing. Relief animals were privileged and represented a different kind of investment, which meant that the incentive to keep them relatively healthy during their journeys was high. Yet none of this meant that the animals were insulated from the discomforts and dangers associated with travel. Indeed, it was the animals that bore the burden of realizing some of the humanitarian goals of the mid-twentieth century. The chapter ends just before the animals, now firmly in the category of "relief stock," boarded the ships that would take them to their destinations abroad.

The sixth chapter is about the cowboys' and animals' time aboard the ships that sailed from the United States to foreign ports. Cowboys' own descriptions of their daily routines with the animals highlight interactions between species that are frequently overlooked. Chapter 6 argues that nonhuman animals have interests and experiences that ought to be treated separately from human experiences.[25] In analyzing the choices humans make for animals, we can learn a great deal about collective values and priorities, and, as a result, we can develop a deeper understanding of specific historical moments and contexts. In this case what we see are, generally speaking, committed animal handlers working with what was sometimes substandard equipment and with infrastructure that was not always well suited to animal transport. It is also on the ships that we see the extent to which the UNRRA and the Brethren programs were intertwined: the cowboys hired by the BSC worked on UNRRA ships with Brethren and UNRRA animals essentially side by side. The arrangement was sensible and expedient, to be sure, and it also offers a symbolically rich example of the ongoing connections between mid-century secular humanitarianism and Christian charity.

In the seventh chapter, we reach Poland. The seagoing cowboys were among the first civilians to arrive in postwar Poland, a country that already by 1945 was under Soviet influence and whose government was increasingly dominated by Communists. Like the men, the newly arrived horses and cattle were witnesses to wartime destruction. Using UNRRA documents and Polish government records, chapter 7 describes what happened to the animals once they left the ships that had docked in ports along Poland's Baltic coast. This chapter examines the animals' encounters with the Polish state and describes their experiences during overland journeys to final destinations. Considered, too, is the geography of animal distribution and what it tells us about emerging political priorities and identities in postwar Poland.

Most of the cattle and horses delivered as UNRRA aid to Poland went to the so-called Recovered Territories. These were the lands that Poland gained in the west from defeated Germany, and the animals' presence there was integral to claiming and civilizing this sensitive new frontier, the so-called Wild West. This chapter provides a useful example of what "thinking with animals" can reveal about time and place.

In the eighth chapter, we move away from real animals who had needs and jobs to do and focus instead on animals as symbols. An underlying theme of this book is that specific animal species mattered in postwar humanitarian relief because of the tangible and practical role they played in agricultural renewal but also because of what they represented, both to the givers and to the receivers. This chapter traces the Polish government's shifting views of UNRRA, the Americans, and animal aid. The Communist-dominated government went from praising UNRRA and its animals to, by the end of 1946, criticizing the quality of the incoming horses in particular. Animals formed an easy target as so many of them arrived in the country exhausted, weak, and sick after their long trans-Atlantic voyages. Americans, the Polish Communists could claim, were obviously animal abusers. Such rhetoric contributed to an undoing of long-dominant associations in Poland between animal welfare, the west, and civilization, and it facilitated the drawing of new cultural boundaries between the Communist world and the capitalist one that would last for decades. In tracing this discursive evolution, chapter 8 situates animals in the broader story of the establishment of Communist rule in Poland.

Chapter 9 is about the Heifer Project animals in Poland. For a number of reasons, these animals—cattle almost exclusively—retained the privileges that had defined their journeys through the aid chain all along the way. This last chapter also discusses the visits that seagoing cowboys made to animal recipients' farms and shows how these visits connected givers and receivers. The chapter concludes with a brief description of the Heifer Project's evolution after UNRRA folded in 1947. I draw the line at the moment when the Heifer Project's cooperation with UNRRA ended and the cowboys either moved on to their postwar lives in America or, if they made additional trips as providers of humanitarian aid, they did so as representatives of the Heifer Project exclusively.

Overall, this book is about the animals and the aid programs that operated at mid-century. Animals played a crucial role in those programs and yet have been largely written out of analyses of postwar relief programming. The book is also about the seagoing cowboys who were central to animal aid delivery and yet have been mostly ignored in the big narratives that tell the history of this period. I bring these subjects together not only to tell these stories in their own right but also to give us new ways of understanding how various contemporaries understood relief and rehabilitation, agriculture, nutrition, and, of course, humanitarianism.

Chapter 1

UNRRA, Food, and Winning the Peace

Planning for postwar emergency relief, as a precursor to eventual reconstruction of ruined countries, started long before the defeat of the Nazis. In an early retrospective assessment of UNRRA's accomplishments, Major General Lowell Ward Rooks, the last of the three Americans who served as the administration's director, described UNRRA as having emerged from "a promise to the invaded lands and their people who were fighting for the common cause." This promise, Rooks continued, was to help those who had suffered in extraordinary ways during the war; it was a commitment that "once the aggressor's yoke had been lifted, the uninvaded lands would pool their resources to send food and medicines and clothing and other emergency supplies."[1]

Already during the war, the "liberation of Europe" was understood to include more than the military defeat of the Nazis. In other words, peace was about much more than a cessation of active conflict and a negotiation of relations between previously warring states; it was about managing the aftermath of war in the places where the greatest damage had been done, caring for people whose lives had been overturned by violence, and reestablishing the foundations for "normal" life.[2] British Prime Minister Winston Churchill had reassured occupied peoples as early as August 1941, just months after the German army's invasion of the Soviet Union, that eventual defeat of the Nazis would bring them "freedom, food, and peace."[3] The inclusion of "food" here is significant.

Shortly after Churchill's statement, and in preparation for the postwar period, twenty-six allied countries signed the Declaration of the United Nations. This 1942 Declaration consisted of a pledge by each of the signatories—those nations united in the fight against the Nazis—not to conclude separate peace treaties with the fascists and to continue the joint war effort until clear victory had been achieved. From the start the signatory countries recognized that their most pressing challenge in the immediate postwar period would be to provide relief, including emergency aid, to people and countries shattered by the conflict. The imperative would be to set up these countries as quickly as possible for self-sufficiency. By joint agreement, this assistance would be delivered by the United Nations Relief and Rehabilitation Administration, a temporary and new—and the first—agency of what became the United Nations in 1945.

UNRRA was formally established in Washington, DC, on November 9, 1943, when much of Europe remained under Nazi control and the western Allies had not yet landed on the continent. By this point forty-four allied countries (the so-called united nations) had signed the UNRRA Agreement, and the total number of member countries soon grew to forty-eight.[4] UNRRA was itself a recognition of the potential and the need for international cooperation among allies to address pressing transnational problems. These problems included, among others, evolving understandings of global security in an interconnected world, the potential and limits of mutual assistance, the importance of economic and sociopolitical links between countries, and the availability of mechanisms for solving conflicts or dealing with conflicts' aftermath.[5]

UNRRA was financially supported by all member states, and its existence relied, too, on political and moral support from those member states. This structure reflected the reality that no one country was capable of funding and providing all the aid that was required, but many countries cooperating together, across international boundaries, could hope to achieve the desired results. This was the new internationalism in action. UNRRA also modeled relatively new understandings of the role that governments and supranational bodies, as opposed to private charities and individuals alone, could and should adopt in mitigating the effects of war and bringing aid to the war-ravaged. UNRRA's task during its short active period from the war's end in 1945 to the date of its disbanding in 1947 was enormous and complex: It met unprecedented destruction with a response that was, too, unprecedented.

UNRRA became the world's largest peacetime supply and shipping organization, moving twenty-five million long tons of cargo around the world from its earliest shipments in 1945 to its last in 1947; this required six thousand ships and was more than triple the amount delivered after the First World War. The aid included food, clothing, large farm equipment (like tractors), small farm equipment (like shovels and hoes), and, of course, animals. All types of aid combined, for all destinations, came in at a cost of almost $4 billion.[6] This made UNRRA, as one contemporary journalist remarked, "the most ambitious humanitarian effort ever undertaken by mankind."[7]

Most of UNRRA's aid was directed at the eastern and southeastern European countries that had been under occupation by the Third Reich and its allies during the war (and which were most vulnerable to Communism in the immediate postwar era). Italy and Austria also received significant aid, however, and this despite their wartime cooperation with Nazi Germany.[8] Outside of Europe, China was the major UNRRA beneficiary. The states of northwestern Europe—the Netherlands, Belgium, France, Denmark, and Norway—though they too had been invaded and occupied by the Nazis, were determined to be capable of purchasing what they needed with more limited help. In addition, UNRRA operated Displaced Person (DP) camps in occupied Germany to aid victims of the Nazi regime who, at the end of the war and for a variety of reasons, found themselves in occupied Germany. Polish citizens formed the largest population group within the broad category of DPs.[9]

UNRRA paid for the aid that it provided out of general subscriptions made by countries that had not been invaded during the war. The amount that each country contributed to the general pool was set at 1 percent of the national income for the year ending June 30, 1943. The United States was the largest contributor by far, with $2.7 billion; this led, not surprisingly, to the perception that UNRRA was largely American. The United Kingdom contributed $624 million, and Canada was the third-largest contributor to UNRRA with $139 million. Together these three countries provided 94 percent of the total UNRRA budget.[10] President Harry S. Truman, who succeeded Franklin D. Roosevelt to the American presidency in April 1945, justified the high costs to the American people by emphasizing a simple humanitarian imperative: people were starving and dying and needed help. But President Truman also reminded Americans the debt they owed to Europeans for functioning as a first line of defense against fascism. The Europeans conquered by the Nazis, Truman said, had "kept the enemy from realizing the fruits of his early victories and from bringing his military might to bear upon our shores."[11] There were of course additional factors that made the UNRRA program appealing economically, politically, and socially to the Americans, as we shall see.

UNRRA and the Three Rs: Relief, Rehabilitation, and Reconstruction

Once the commitment to provide postwar aid had been made, UNRRA's first task was to measure precise needs in different contexts, to define the types of aid most urgently required in specific countries, and then to plan for how exactly to deliver relief in the form of food, medical supplies, clothing, and other essential goods, while also taking on the gargantuan task of caring for, repatriating, or facilitating the emigration of allied DPs.

None of these challenges and goals were in themselves brand-new; assorted relief programs had been operating in various countries during the war, and charities and private aid organizations continued to operate after the war as well. For example, the Council of British Societies for Relief Abroad had formed in 1942 as an umbrella body to coordinate wartime voluntary relief agencies. After the war dozens of independent groups—the Red Cross, the War Relief Services of the National Catholic Welfare Conference, the American Joint Distribution Committee, War Relief Services of the National Catholic Welfare Conference, and American Relief for Poland, to name just several—operated in various locations too.[12] Such groups often cooperated with private charity organizations in target countries as well, like Poland's Catholic Caritas, as long as the political situation permitted doing so.[13] In total over a hundred relief organizations and voluntary agencies contributed to the postwar relief effort in larger and smaller ways and operated either in cooperation with UNRRA, in a supportive capacity, or somewhat more independently of it, as circumstances dictated.[14] UNRRA itself recognized the importance of the voluntary agencies.[15] As Tehila Sasson has argued, cooperation between governmental bodies and voluntary aid organizations, so instrumental in the delivery of relief after the First World War (to Russia, for example), continued to mark humanitarian relief after World War II and throughout the rest of the twentieth century as well.[16] Ultimately, UNRRA took on a coordinating and lead role in the postwar relief effort and often replaced or absorbed smaller, preparatory, or temporary relief-giving bodies.[17] In such cases the agencies subsumed by UNRRA had to accept UNRRA's authority and abide by the general UNRRA rules that governed the distribution of aid; this included the need to maintain "political neutrality" in aid distribution.[18]

UNRRA had three priorities: to provide relief, to create the conditions for rehabilitation in its target countries, and to stimulate eventual reconstruction. Each of these terms, which were referred to collectively as "the three

Rs," was extremely broad and therefore open to interpretation even while there were attempts to delineate their meaning and scope.[19] Relief—immediate assistance through the provision of food aid—had been at the center of post–World War I policy approaches to crisis mitigation, and after the Second World War relief was similarly meant to address emergency food requirements and assorted pressing medical needs. At the same time, relief was considered a starting point only, a necessity in the short term but merely a stepping stone for more ambitious goals. The inclusion of rehabilitation as a policy priority was bold because it went beyond the delivery of immediate relief; it looked toward rebuilding people's lives and the societies and economies of which they formed a part. Taking steps toward restoring normality after a period of extreme disruption would ideally also shorten the amount of time that immediate relief aid would be required, as countries would more quickly acquire the material and financial resources to take over the work of welfare provision and help their own people. Rehabilitation, in other words, was about establishing a basis for longer-term recovery and setting up the conditions for eventual reconstruction (but not actually overseeing its implementation and development).[20] Reconstruction was thus the final phase of the UNRRA program as it was marked by countries' abilities to provide for themselves; reconstruction happened only once relief (food, basic supplies, and clothing, for example) and the tools of rehabilitation (like livestock and agricultural equipment) had been delivered and once UNRRA was no longer needed.[21]

One editorial in the December 30, 1946, issue of *Life* magazine summarized these priorities in a way that the average American reader would have understood easily: "Under relief you buy an indigent man a meal. Under rehabilitation you find him a job, perhaps repair the machinery in the factory where he works or prime it with raw materials, and leave him buying his own meals."[22] The logic was repeated by UNRRA itself. UNRRA's goal was to provide immediate assistance and relief, to be sure. But its goals were much broader still, aiming as it did to kickstart societies and economies; UNRRA's goal, that is, was "to help . . . the people to help themselves."[23]

The three Rs reflect UNRRA's own understanding of its goals and purpose while they also suggest how humanitarian aid at mid-century was interpreted in a broader sense. "Humanitarian" and "humanitarianism" are dynamic terms that have been evolving since their emergence in the west in the late eighteenth and early nineteenth centuries.[24] In the earliest days, "humanitarian" was used as a theological concept that invoked the human nature of Christ as opposed to Christ's divine origins. In the nineteenth century, the meaning of "humanitarianism" changed to emphasize empathy and an earnest desire to ameliorate conditions for (some) individuals or groups who needed assistance to survive or prosper.[25] "Humanitarian" also signified an understanding of the responsibility of the one to the many and in broad terms reflected a new "culture of sensibility" that was in evidence in the antislavery movement and even (in problematic and complicated ways, to be sure) in missionary work in colonial settings. Compassion and humanitarian sentiments soon came to be associated with civilization itself, with modern western understandings of social, political, and moral responsibility.[26]

Nineteenth-century humanitarianism was also associated with people who were concerned for the welfare of *all* sentient beings, human *and* animal. For example, the English social reformer Henry Salt founded the conspicuously named Humanitarian League in 1891 to advocate for a wide variety of "humanitarian reforms": of the penal system, of criminal law, of the education system, and of attitudes toward animals.[27] For animal welfare advocates in the late nineteenth century, a humanitarianism without the recognition of nonhuman animals' capacity to feel pain and suffer was no humanitarianism at all, and it belied contemporary understandings of civilization as well.[28] As Janet Davis has argued in her book on animal welfare in the United States, *The Gospel of Kindness*, early animal welfare advocates were motivated by a vision of global justice and a belief in the power of empathy, kindness, and decency to transform the world for both human and nonhuman animals.[29]

Moving into the twentieth century, however, there were still no precisely agreed-upon definitions of "humanitarian" and thus no shared understanding of what humanitarian programs ought to look like or who their specific targets or purveyors should be. In general, though, humanitarian impulses constituted a reaction to perceived suffering (and other than for a relatively small group of animal advocates, this referred to human misery and not to nonhuman animal suffering). Beyond that, the term "humanitarianism" referred to organized efforts to help individuals and groups affected by tragedies of various kinds and not of the targets' making—wars, natural disasters, or political revolutions, for example.[30]

That Nazi cruelties justified humanitarian interventions did not need an elaborate explanation; plenty of evidence had already accumulated during the war and had been revealed even more starkly after the conflict ended in photographs and documentary footage and through witness and perpetrator testimony. There was little debate that the people and places destroyed during the Second World War deserved massive levels of assistance from those countries that had avoided direct or acute destruction. The debate was focused instead on what a fully humanitarian approach to aid would look like.

That is where UNRRA's three Rs came in. UNRRA's humanitarianism aimed to be constructive and to improve human welfare in the longer term rather than only addressing immediate needs and providing temporary comfort; it included a transformative and future-looking element. Partly for this reason, modern humanitarianism, of the type that UNRRA practiced, differs from charity and philanthropy in that its goals are more ambitious and represent a much bolder intervention with longer-term implications. More fundamentally, modern humanitarianism has reflected a move away from understanding misfortune or mass hunger as a result of providence or in terms of individual failings. It reflects instead a belief in the notion of innocent victims caught up in the whirlwind of sociopolitical and economic forces, while it also suggests faith in principles of rational management and in the possibility of coming up with solutions to empirically measured challenges. It understands humans' interdependence and, with that, states' interdependence too.[31]

It would be difficult to deny that UNRRA fed hungry people, whether in their home countries or in DP camps, and this topic is well covered in the literature.[32] Analyses differ, however, in terms of whether one should celebrate or condemn UNRRA's overall record. The more optimistic evaluations of UNRRA highlight its tangible achievements in terms of meeting people's immediate needs; the very fact that people were helped is evidence that international cooperation could be effective. Critical assessments stress instead that aid distribution was simply inadequate and that the whole program was marred by financial waste, shocking levels of bureaucratic inefficiency, inequality, and unfairness. Critics also describe UNRRA as a profoundly flawed example of a postwar internationalism that tried but ultimately failed to reorganize the world in ways that would minimize the potential for new outbreaks of conflict.[33] UNRRA did not generate the conditions needed for long-term multilateral cooperation, collective security, peace, or prosperity. Perhaps the goals were just too ambitious. Or perhaps this was because UNRRA was (to borrow a word from scholar Jessica Reinisch) "reluctant" in its practice of internationalism. UNRRA continued to work in and through a nationalist framework, and national interests, both those of its strongest member states and those of the receiving nations, determined its vocabulary, terms of cooperation, methods, and scope.[34] This tension between nationalist imperatives and internationalism has formed one of the most important themes in the literature on UNRRA.[35] At the same time, this literature has itself expanded in recent years to emphasize a diversity of priorities, voices, and practices, even within a single period.[36] As we will see, UNRRA was far from the only humanitarian actor with an internationalist focus, even if it was the biggest, loudest, and best known.

UNRRA's Poland Program

UNRRA has a complicated place in Polish historiography because UNRRA had a delicate relationship with Poland and with other states that were becoming part of the Soviet orbit during the 1945 to 1947 period. Not surprisingly, the first monograph on UNRRA in Poland appeared not during the long years of the Polish People's Republic (1952–1989) but well after the collapse of the Soviet bloc, in 2018; this was Józef Łaptos's *Humanitaryzm i polityka* (*Humanitarianism and Politics*).[37] This is the most comprehensive book on the subject of UNRRA in Poland. Łaptos outlines the specific agreements, practices, problems, and successes that the program encountered throughout its relatively short life, and he also includes a detailed analysis of the aid given to DPs of Polish origin. Notably, Łaptos dedicates a few pages to the Heifer Project's work in Poland; this is the only discussion, however brief, of the Heifer Project in Polish scholarship.[38] Overall, Łaptos's approach to UNRRA is to see the organization first and foremost as part of the national history of Poland, and by extension of other recipient countries. Jacek Sawicki's *Misja UNRRA w Polsce: Raport zamknięcia (1945–1949)* (*The UNRRA Mission in Poland: Closing Report*) appeared just a year before Łaptos's book, and it has similar aims: to show how UNRRA operated in Poland specifically. Rather than a monograph, however, Sawicki's book is an annotation of a Polish summative report produced in 1949/50 that reflects on the organization's tenure in Poland.[39]

In treating UNRRA as part of Poland's national history, both Sawicki and Łaptos try to understand how UNRRA shaped Polish postwar reconstruction. Perhaps it is this very narrow national focus that makes each of these authors more sympathetic to UNRRA than those works that focus mainly on the less concrete internationalist ambitions that UNRRA had. Sawicki and Łaptos argue that despite its problems, both at the overall administrative level and on the ground in Poland, UNRRA's Poland program was effective. People loved and appreciated "Auntie UNRRA" and even decades later recalled her gifts with gratitude and warmth.[40] As Łaptos argues in his book, UNRRA allowed Poles to regain their dignity while it provided them with basic life necessities. This recognition of UNRRA's ability to deliver real everyday assistance is different from evaluating the institution as a whole, as an international body with goals beyond the provision of humanitarian aid to individuals and groups within one specific context.

Even though Poland received more aid than other European countries, according to George Woodbridge (UNRRA's official historian), this was still only a fraction of what the country actually deserved or needed; the scale of the destruction was that enormous. UNRRA aid in its various forms amounted to 22 percent of Poland's gross domestic product in 1946, which was the peak year of aid delivery.[41] Ira Hirschmann, friend and political ally of Fiorello La Guardia, calculated that Poland's total wartime losses were the equivalent of $50 billion.[42] Almost $200 million of Poland's total allocation went toward food alone, with the remaining amounts distributed across various other categories of essential goods, from farm machinery and tools for infrastructure repair to clothing and medicine.[43] Approximately $76 million went toward "agricultural rehabilitation," and this amount included the animal shipments.[44] Most importantly for our purposes, and as stated earlier, of the 360 live-aid shipments that UNRRA made during its tenure, almost half went to Poland alone. Eight of these came in 1945, 153 in 1946 (again, the peak year of aid delivery), and 16 arrived in 1947 when UNRRA was fulfilling previously made commitments but was not organizing new deliveries.[45]

Initial estimates of the size of aid required by each country, Poland included, were determined on the basis of perceived victimization levels and were calculated at the First Council Sessions of the United Nations, which were held in Washington during the war. Specific planning for country operations in Europe was done at the European Regional Office located in London. Then, in July 1945, an UNRRA delegation arrived in Poland to assess the country's needs more directly. Each aid recipient country ultimately signed an agreement with UNRRA that outlined the amount, terms, and conditions of aid; Poland signed its agreement on September 19, 1945, even though initial UNRRA aid had already been delivered to Poland that spring.[46]

Poland was particularly important to UNRRA, and especially to UNRRA's American backers, from a political and strategic perspective. Indeed, the creation of an independent Poland after the First World War was in some ways at the center of the new postimperial order. In large part because of its location between the Soviet Union and Germany, Poland's stability was crucial for European stability generally. But already by the summer of 1944, it was clear that Poland's emerging postwar political situation was volatile and complex and that the Soviet Union would exercise a greater or lesser degree of control over Poland and the other countries in eastern Europe that, as we now know, would go on to form the Soviet Bloc.

Though the London-based Polish government-in-exile was involved in the initial planning discussions with the United Nations, from July 1944 the existence of the Polish Committee of National Liberation, or the Lublin Committee, gradually and ultimately completely stripped the London government of its authority. The Lublin Committee, formed by Polish Communists and supported by Moscow, made it clear that it, and not the government-in-exile, would play the lead role in administering the liberated territories in Poland; it competed actively (if not fairly) with the Polish government-in-exile for international recognition and internal public support. The Lublin Committee became the provisional government of Poland from January 1945. Largely to appease western powers, in June the provisional government transformed itself into the Provisional Government of National Unity, a coalition between the Polish Workers' Party (the Communists) and the Polish People's Party (Polskie Stronnictwo Ludowe), which had been reestablished by the former prime minister of the London government-in-exile, Stanisław Mikołajczyk. Throughout 1945 and 1946, the Communists neutralized and marginalized the Polish People's Party and all other would-be opposition before orchestrating the victory of the Democratic Bloc (Blok Demokratyczny), a body that the Communists controlled, in the January 1947 elections. The year 1947 thus marks the date of the Communist takeover of Poland.

For the most part, UNRRA operated in Poland during this chaotic and complicated period when the establishment of Communist rule was still in the making instead of firmly settled. The context required walking a fine line between the Communists and the non-Communists. This was especially important given UNRRA's imperative to maintain neutrality; neutrality, and respecting countries' chosen political paths, formed an important if imperfect guiding principle in all UNRRA work, in Poland and elsewhere.[47] And yet despite the starkly contrasting views on the postwar order during this period, there was agreement by all sides that Poland ought to receive a great deal of UNRRA aid.

The UNRRA Mission to Poland was headquartered at 35 Hoża Street in Warsaw. It was not until 1946 that Polish authorities allowed regional UNRRA offices to be established as well; these had not been part of the initial agreement made between the Lublin government and UNRRA in 1945. Regional offices were set up in January 1946 in Katowice, Kraków, Łódź, Poznań, Gdynia, and Warsaw; a little later, in September, an additional regional office was established in Szczecin, a formerly German city in Poland's new western Baltic region. Together, these offices ostensibly facilitated more efficient aid distribution throughout the country.[48] Like many other organizations, however, UNRRA's Poland operation remained understaffed throughout its short life, as did UNRRA as a whole.[49]

The first UNRRA director general, Herbert Lehman, had appointed the Soviet ambassador Mikhail A. Menshikov to act as chief of UNRRA's Temporary Delegation to Poland from March 1945. Menshikov succeeded Dr. John P. Gregg, who resigned as delegation head shortly after his appointment and before even setting foot in Poland. The Communists had refused to grant Gregg a visa and favored Menshikov for the position of delegation head. Already here the delicate political situation in eastern Europe, especially the emerging Soviet dominance in the region, shaped how UNRRA operated, and this would remain a factor throughout UNRRA's existence. It was Menshikov who negotiated the formal agreement between Poland's provisional government and UNRRA, and it was Menshikov who outlined the country's specific relief needs. The first UNRRA delegates, including Menshikov, arrived in Poland in July 1945.[50]

Menshikov headed UNRRA's Poland delegation for just a short time, until September 1945, at which point he was replaced by the Canadian Brigadier Charles M. "Bud" Drury as mission head.[51] Menshikov was unpopular with Polish Americans, who were quickly becoming critical of the American government and of UNRRA for giving in to Soviet influence in eastern Europe so easily.[52] By this point, in the fall of 1945, it was even clearer than it had been just a few months earlier that the Soviets would play an important role in Poland for the long term. Drury took up his duties not long after the first UNRRA shipment arrived in Poland via the Baltic route in the fall of 1945 (rather than via a slower overland route, which was how the very first deliveries had made their way into the country in the spring). Drury was the first Canadian in the role of UNRRA mission head, and he would stay in this position until February 1947 when the American Donald R. Sabin took over; Sabin was in turn quickly replaced by M. E. Hays as acting chief of mission in May 1947. The Poland mission closed shortly after.

Drury, who would later become a Cabinet minister in the Liberal government of Pierre Elliott Trudeau in Canada, was a pragmatic leader during the longest and most critical phase of UNRRA's tenure in Poland.[53] Drury got on well with the Polish Communist authorities (which emerged, not surprisingly, as a source of worry for some Poles and Americans). Drury was also evidently very moved by the extent of Poland's wartime suffering. In a letter to the prime minister of the Provisional Government of National Unity, Edward Osóbka-Morawski, Drury reassured the prime minister of UNRRA's sympathy for the unique scale of Poland's disaster and of its determined commitment to Polish rebuilding.[54]

There was in fact much to do. It was Poland that had served as the first battleground of the war, and the country had suffered a particularly long and brutal German occupation from 1939 until 1945. Many of its cities had been ruined, meaning that infrastructure, communication, distribution, and transport networks—road, rail, and waterway—had been destroyed too. Factories had been stripped and wrecked. Postwar Poland had few goods to export, even though the country had been a major exporter of agricultural and forestry products in the prewar period, and as a result the country had no foreign currency with which to purchase essentials. While the revived postwar Poland lost land in the east to the Soviet Union, it gained territories (and with them substantial coal reserves) in the west as a form of compensation.[55] Coal production was essential to industrial development, and yet in the very early postwar era this potential could not be realized easily, as so many other problems needed to be solved first. By 1946 the situation improved such that Poland even contributed tens of thousands of tons of coal to UNRRA, which UNRRA in turn distributed to Yugoslavia (and a much smaller amount to Austria).[56]

And of course there were the demographic effects of the war: six million Polish citizens had been killed, and of this number, approximately three million had been Jews murdered in the Holocaust. This had many devastating effects. The loss of such a substantial portion of the population was also related to postwar labor shortages. Yet wages nevertheless remained low and were generally insufficient to allow many people to purchase much of anything on the open market.[57]

Agricultural circumstances in the new Poland were especially dire. The majority of Poland's population before the war had depended on agriculture for its livelihood. In the early postwar period, agricultural capacity was severely compromised.[58] One-sixth of all farms had been destroyed, meaning that farmers were not in a position to restart large-scale agricultural production.[59] In 1945 Poland's people were threatened with starvation.[60] Unexploded mines on agricultural fields remained a real threat in many areas, and in other places weeds had taken over planting fields. Agricultural machinery, primitive though some of it had been before the war, was either ruined or confiscated, especially in the areas around Warsaw, in the northeastern provinces of the Mazury region, in Białystok, and in eastern Pomerania.[61] The destruction was caused by wartime military engagements, to be sure, but also by the movement of enormous columns of Soviet troops—and the cattle, horses, and sheep that they had with them—en route to the USSR in the weeks immediately after the war had ended. This too resulted in the destruction of pasture lands, planting fields, trees, fruit orchards, and agricultural infrastructure. As they moved through Poland, the Soviets seized additional animals and hay reserves as well.[62] Seeds used to plant private vegetable gardens and to prepare pastures that in the next year would feed livestock were scarce, and so were the fertilizers, both natural and artificial, that were crucial to successful mass plantings.[63] Moreover, planting timelines on fields did not always line up well with people's return to their homes or their arrival at new homes, thereby compromising agricultural production in the short term further still. Building material for homes and barns was in scarce supply and yet was desperately needed.[64]

Livestock and draft animals (meaning animals that were strong enough to move heavy objects and to function, essentially, as tractors) had been killed in large numbers. A majority of the country's prewar horse and cattle population was gone, and the animals that were left were often in poor health and not fit for work or for breeding. There was a shortage of veterinarians too; only about a third of Poland's three thousand prewar veterinarians were in a position to practice their professions in the immediate postwar period. And yet without veterinarians, livestock diseases and agricultural renewal would be compromised further still.[65]

Physically, socially, and emotionally, the population was exhausted, gutted, and ruined. Millions of Poles had been in Germany as forced labor during the war and now needed to be repatriated and reincorporated into the new Poland. Others had been in various camps and, like the forced laborers, were awaiting reintegration or, indeed, emigration. Then there was the challenge of incorporating—psychologically as well as logistically—ethnic Poles from the eastern regions into other parts of the country, especially into the newly acquired and recently depopulated German territories. At the most fundamental level, early postwar Poland was forced to confront the "trauma of war": the psychological and social experiences of loss and destruction, and the lingering death all around.[66] Against this backdrop, too, was the raging civil war between Communists and non-Communists and, ultimately, between competing visions of the postwar future.

Food, Animals, and Security in the Postwar International Order

Undeniably, Poland needed many forms of aid very quickly, but the most pressing need was food, as the possibility of starvation, and the diseases that accompanied it, was a persistent concern for millions of people. As Marcin Zaremba has argued, fear of starvation was one of the most profound collective emotions of the postwar period.[67] Addressing immediate food shortages would save lives in the short term, to be sure. In the longer term, and in keeping, again, with the three Rs, UNRRA tried to go beyond only providing for people's immediate needs by establishing the bases for long-term food security in Poland. This two-pronged approach, as an UNRRA policy document stated, would "enable the liberated countries to stand on their feet again and to resume their normal production and trading function in the world economic structure."[68]

The provision of food aid in the aftermath of war was not of course unexpected or new, just as the recognition of hunger as a political problem predated UNRRA. The makers of the post–World War II order were very conscious of lessons learned earlier in the century when both wartime and postwar food crises in Europe had played an important role in shaping political outcomes.[69] The British naval blockade of Germany during the First World War was tied to waning support for the war effort in the Kaiserreich, for example, and, similarly, Austria's wartime and post–World War I "hunger catastrophe" (*Hungerkatastrophe*) was recognized as one of many factors in the Habsburg Empire's collapse.[70] There was a belief in the period after World War I that continued hunger throughout the fragile successor states in the east European region chipped away at political and social stability, and that programs to feed the hungry therefore had to move beyond providing basic sustenance. Aid programs were at least in part concerned with protecting "western values" and saving central and western Europe from the perceived threat that loomed just beyond the eastern borders of the region in Bolshevik Russia.[71]

In the period after the First World War, delivery of food aid to central and eastern Europe, and also to Russia, was provided by many small private and religious charities like, for example, the American Red Cross, the Polish Grey Samaritans, the American Polish Relief Expedition, and the American Friends Service Committee. Perhaps the most interesting of these was a group established by German Americans from South Dakota and called the American Dairy Cattle Company. In 1920 and 1921, this small relief program facilitated the delivery of over two thousand dairy cattle to Germany, America's erstwhile enemy in World War I.[72]

The greatest contributor of aid in the region after the First World War was the American Relief Administration (ARA) under Herbert Hoover. The ARA was formed by the United States government in 1919, and the American government also funded it. The ARA worked with several private charitable organizations to deliver and distribute many million tons of food to prevent starvation in Europe, and especially in hard-hit eastern Europe, Poland included.[73] From 1921 the ARA also worked in Bolshevik Russia, which was experiencing a famine in the context of an already brutal and disruptive revolution and civil war. During this period the so-called soup-kitchen model of hunger relief—emergency communal feeding at designated sites set up and supervised by international staff—predominated.[74]

The ARA fed millions of people. In total the ARA distributed four million tons of food and other basic goods across Europe. Well over a million children were fed by the ARA in post–World War I Poland every day.[75] In addition, the very existence of this organization reinforced an understanding of food's important place in the political realm and its potential to shape outcomes locally as well as at the international level; food, clearly, had the potential to be weaponized to pursue specific political goals. Hunger (and the diseases that inevitably accompanied starvation and malnourishment) was interwoven with broader security concerns for east-central Europe and ultimately for western Europe too. This is reflected in one of the underlying purposes of the ARA food aid program: to stop the spread of Bolshevism. Hoover's ARA reflected a belief that food would "win the postwar" by preventing the rise of extreme political movements.[76] Hoover—who had been born into a devout Quaker family and who, of course, went on to become the thirty-first president of the United States in 1929—believed that abundance would lead to stability and security and that its lack would ultimately threaten not just Europe but America too. He also believed that the ARA would give America the chance to style itself a moral leader in the world.[77]

These aspirations were not entirely different after the Second World War, and indeed the continuities in relief efforts after both conflicts are important. Hunger anywhere was potentially threatening. As UNRRA Director General Lehman said, "If these countries fall prey to famine and pestilence, there can be no security for any of us. Our responsibility is clear. We of the United Nations who have suffered least must take steps now to provide out of our resources the means to meet this desperate crisis. This requires supplies. Kind expression will not fill empty stomachs. You can't avert starvation without food."[78]

Postwar food aid policies were shaped, to be sure, by concerns about regional and global security and about politics and the economy. But they also reflected a shift in thinking that incorporated the new idea of "fundamental human rights."[79] Food was emerging as one of these fundamental rights. This was evident in postwar planning from the beginning. In his January 6, 1941, address to Congress, President Roosevelt outlined the Four Freedoms at stake in the war: freedom of speech, freedom of worship, freedom from want, and freedom from fear of aggression. Roosevelt defined "freedom from want" ambitiously as an "economic understanding which will secure for every nation a healthy peacetime life for its inhabitants—everywhere in the world."⁸⁰ Adequate food availability, which depended on stable agricultural production, was crucial to this. In short, as one scholar has stated, "The construction of a postwar international order began with food."⁸¹

By the Second World War, food policies reflected increasingly nuanced understandings of the relationship between food, individual bodily health, and broader national health. Nutritional science had come into its own as a field of inquiry by at least the 1930s, and during the earliest years of the war nutritional science research was used to calculate food needs for both armed forces and civilians. In 1941 the American Food and Nutrition Board established the Recommended Daily Allowances precisely for this reason: to provide reliable and standard measures of nutritional value that would guide food policies.⁸² The calorie—a measure of the energy content of food—was also part of this reshaping of food policies at the time.⁸³ The calorie "reduced food to a single number" and, significantly, made comparing foods possible, even across regions and time periods. This in turn made planning—by government, industry, or charities and other aid organizations—possible and intelligible.⁸⁴

At mid-century nutritional science was thus showing how different vitamins, minerals, proteins, and acids worked on the development of the body and the mind; not all food was "the right kind" of food, and some foods were simply better than others. Food had become so much more than an uncomplicated fuel for the body.⁸⁵ This in turn had implications for the related field of "hunger studies."⁸⁶ While starvation was problematic in obvious ways, substandard nutrition was increasingly understood as a concern as well. In short, both quantity and quality of food were important, so it was relevant to talk about undernourishment as well as malnourishment (a "qualitative nutritional deficiency").⁸⁷ And if food quality mattered in explanations of hunger and in assessments of its causes—if context and environment were significant—then it also mattered in proposals for its eradication. Perhaps the idea of "dietary determinism" (that "man is what he eats") could offer a way forward. Once hunger was understood as a biochemical condition caused by low-quality food or inadequate quantities of nutritious food, then it became a problem with a solution.⁸⁸

All of this justified a robust international relief system that, using supposedly objective criteria and scientific data, formulated food policies aimed simultaneously at eradicating hunger and contributing to the pursuit of postwar security. The joint Anglo-American Atlantic Charter from August 12, 1941, had pledged American support for the war in Europe (though of course the United States did not enter the war until December of that year) while it also looked ahead with optimism to a postwar future where the conditions for stability, economic prosperity, and satiety would be secured for everyone. In this the Atlantic Charter echoed Roosevelt's enumeration earlier that year of the Four Freedoms, the basic rights owed to all human beings.[89] At any rate, "freedom from want" was already familiar language in the United States from the New Deal era and its concerns about fundamental rights and security. When "freedom from want" was used by Roosevelt in 1941, it subtly prepared the nation for military involvement in the war; freedom from want would become one of the Allied war aims.[90] The meaning of "freedom from want" is perhaps best evoked in the well-known Norman Rockwell painting that shows an American family seated around a dinner table. The turkey that will form the main part of the meal that evening is at the very center of the painting. The caption reads, "OURS . . . to fight for. FREEDOM FROM WANT."[91] In 1943, the year the image was published in the American press, few Europeans could have imagined the luxury of a turkey dinner. Neither could they expect to eat this way in the first postwar years.[92]

Winning the peace in the aftermath of the Second World War depended, as it did in the aftermath of the First World War, on food.[93] Given a choice, people would gravitate toward the political regime that offered food security. As Roosevelt stated, "A man in need is not a free man . . . people who are hungry and out of jobs are the stuff of which dictatorships are made."[94] General Lucius Clay, the American occupation governor in Germany, similarly warned that a failure to understand this simple point would "pave the way to a Communist Europe."[95] At play were long-held stereotypes about the need to protect western Europe from the "contagion"—political, social, and sometimes even "racial"—that originated in the east. The narrator in the opening sequence of Canadian director Stuart Legg's timely film, *Food: Secret of the Peace* (1945), reinforces this point too: "The political stability of Europe and therefore of the world," the narrator says, "depends on food."[96]

That immediate food needs had to be met in order to avert imminent starvation, with its related political implications, was clear. Meeting these needs started with the delivery of millions of tons of food that could be consumed as soon as it arrived. UNRRA's "relief geography" was predictable and built on familiar assumptions; food aid helped "us" as much as it helped "them."[97] What had changed was the possibility—or the imperative—to do more and to help countries achieve longer-term food security. Reaching this goal depended largely on the ability to rebuild agriculture in what had been primarily agriculturally based societies in eastern Europe, Poland included, before the war. And horses and cattle were in turn crucially important to rebuilding agricultural capacity.

Prewar Poland's agricultural lands had been dominated by small peasant farms; almost all of them were under fifty hectares, and about a quarter were under two hectares. This was a general pattern across the central and east European region.[98] Typically, these farms depended on horse draft power rather than on mechanical cultivation. They also relied on farmyard manure, mainly from cattle, to fertilize agricultural lands and to maintain soil fertility, but without livestock there was no fertilizer for crops; artificial fertilizers were both expensive and difficult to acquire. The lack of adequate fertilization for the whole of the occupation period compromised soil fertility further still and resulted in sluggish agricultural production that, at the extreme, threatened the population with starvation. As the new food science was showing, both malnourishment (inferior nutrients) and undernourishment (too few nutrients) constituted troubling states of hunger.[99] This would lead to an inability to fight disease and infections across the country and perhaps beyond.[100]

Clearly, then, already during the war the Allies understood how important food, agriculture, and nutrition policies would be to a postwar economic, social, and political reconstruction agenda; food scarcity was threatening in the broadest sense, and world leaders therefore needed to tackle this problem together.[101] Important and initial steps toward developing a concrete food policy for the postwar period were taken by representatives from countries meeting for a United Nations Conference on Food and Agriculture in Hot Springs, Virginia, from May 18 to June 3, 1943. The Hot Springs Resolution adopted at the conference committed to the idea that "freedom from want of food" could and should be achieved, and that doing so would take unprecedented international cooperation of precisely the kind that the developing United Nations promised.[102] It would also take an extraordinary commitment by all countries involved to fostering research into nutrition and to promoting education about the best nutritional practices.[103]

The Hot Springs Resolution was not uncontroversial, however. Some members of the British and American governments feared what this commitment to providing food for "everyone" would do to the global economy, particularly if it became the responsibility of an independent organization to regulate food production, food prices, and food distribution; this looked like a potentially dangerous intrusion on governments' power while it also threatened to disrupt a system of global free trade and jeopardized plans for postwar reconstruction in the US and Britain in particular.[104] Nevertheless, the resolution had traction.

On the heels of the Hot Springs conference, on July 28, 1943, a young Pole named Jan Kozielewski, better known as Jan Karski, met with President Roosevelt at the White House. Karski had been working with the Polish underground and had been sent by Poland's government-in-exile, headquartered in London, to deliver a report to the American president about the extent of the Third Reich's brutal policies in occupied Poland. Karski's mission was also to relay news of Soviet maneuvering in Polish territories, to outline the activities of the Polish resistance as it tried to position itself against Soviet intrusion, and to rally American support for the Polish government-in-exile against the Soviets.[105] Roosevelt asked Karski a number of direct questions during the meeting, and Karski was given time to answer as he saw fit. It was during this meeting that Karski summarized the particularly dire situation for Polish Jews specifically, as is well known.

But Roosevelt also asked Karski two questions that seemed to have little to do with the human tragedies unfolding on what had been Polish territory. The first was whether Poland had in fact been a primarily agricultural nation before the war. Karski confirmed this. Roosevelt then asked Karski to further verify that the Germans had confiscated Poland's horses as part of their invasion of the Soviet Union in June 1941. Karski again confirmed the president's understanding. Karski recorded the details of this meeting with the American president in notes that he made just a week later.[106] In addition, Karski described details from the meeting during an interview in the late 1970s with the French director Claude Lanzmann for Lanzmann's monumental documentary *Shoah*; it is as a result of this interview in particular that the conversation between Karski and the president is familiar to so many.[107] What has struck some critics about the exchange is that Roosevelt seemed strangely preoccupied with such a seemingly minor issue—agriculture and the fate of Poland's horses—and was not overtly sympathetic to Poland and the Polish people generally or to the fate of Polish Jews specifically. In the end, Roosevelt looked as though he was more concerned about animals and wheat than the genocide of the Jews. Yet by the summer of 1943, President Roosevelt had known about the destruction of the Jews for quite some time, and so what Karski was saying on this subject was not exactly new.[108]

There is another way to understand Roosevelt's questions and preoccupations. Roosevelt's inquiries about agriculture and horses should be read in this broader context of relief planning for the postwar period and of agriculture's place in those plans. It was Roosevelt who had called the Hot Springs conference just a couple of months before this meeting with Karski happened. Roosevelt, moreover, was known to be an enthusiastic supporter of a "united nations" approach to solving problems.[109] Here was Roosevelt, seated across from Karski, mentally calculating Polish postwar agricultural needs, including the need for animal labor. Roosevelt seemed to understand at this moment what UNRRA would ultimately reflect through its aid program: that in addition to immediate food relief UNRRA needed to provide the means of achieving agricultural rehabilitation, and draft animals were crucial for reaching this objective. In its policy documents, UNRRA repeated this sentiment often: "The greatest harm to agriculture at the present moment is the loss of draught power which depends almost entirely on horses."[110]

Various UNRRA reports reflected on and provided details about different aspects of Poland's agricultural crisis. According to one report, 70 percent of the horses that had existed in Poland in 1939 west of the Curzon Line, which more or less followed the border with the Soviet Union, were gone after the war. And there were virtually no horses left in the territories newly acquired from Germany.[111] In total, UNRRA estimated that Poland west of the Curzon Line had lost over 2,500,000 horses either in battle, because of wider destruction caused by the war, or as a result of the requisitioning of animals by enemy armies. According to the Polish Ministry of Agriculture, approximately one million farms in Poland did not have a single horse.[112] The effects of this state of affairs on agriculture were bound to be devastating; the animals' presence or absence would directly affect economic development and security at the local level and, by extension, the regional and global ones too.[113]

UNRRA estimated that the delivery of one hundred thousand horses to Poland as part of its aid package would produce another hundred thousand horses in three years. Of these a little more than one third, or approximately thirty-eight thousand, would be old enough to work as draft animals.[114] Agricultural experts also estimated that, with the injection of adequate breeding stock in 1945, it would still take Poland twenty years to replace its horse population.[115] Acting immediately on addressing livestock shortages was necessary for the agricultural rehabilitation that formed such an important component of UNRRA goals.

The situation with cattle was also dire: UNRRA's estimates were that Poland had lost 60 percent of its prewar cattle and that it would take ten years to replace its cattle population.[116] Seven hundred thousand farms did not have even a single cow (a female of the bovine species who has produced at least one calf) and therefore no ready access to milk.[117] Yet as Stanisław Mikołajczyk, the leader of the Polish People's Party after the war who served as deputy prime minister and minister of agriculture, said in a 1946 speech, cows were "of the utmost importance to peasant life, and their loss meant ruin." He added that "the only way to increased wealth, better living conditions, and an improved level of nutrition" was to restock cattle herds in Poland.[118]

Reestablishing breeding programs and creating sustainable herds of both cattle and horses were clearly important for creating the conditions for socioeconomic stability in the short term and for building longer-term sustainability.[119] Animals would do in the postwar period what it had long been established that certain animal species were good at doing: creating the bases for thriving, settled, and stable communities.[120] As Dr. A. G. Wilder, the chief veterinarian of the UNRRA mission to Poland, said, "All the food in the world could be sent here and it would still only be a temporary measure, it would be eaten and gone. But livestock of any description sent to Poland is a foundation upon which to build a food producing machine which will stay here forever." For Wilder, moreover, the animals delivered after the war were destined to become "permanent living monuments" to the aid UNRRA had given Poland.[121] The animals offered "perpetual relief."[122]

UNRRA was not the only postwar international body to reflect these understandings of the importance of animals and agriculture to broader rehabilitation goals. While the wartime Hot Springs conference informed approaches to food and food relief after the war, it also laid the foundation for the creation in October 1945 of the Food and Agriculture Organization (FAO).[123] The FAO was a United Nations specialized agency that was separate from UNRRA while at the same time benefiting from UNRRA's work. It later received some of UNRRA's leftover funds, resources, and staff. The FAO was tasked with bringing together the latest information about food, agriculture, nutrition, economics, and trade in order to ensure an adequate and nutritious food supply for all of the world's people.[124] Unlike UNRRA's goals and mandate, which were short-lived and limited mainly to those countries that had been occupied by the enemy in the war, the goal of the FAO was more ambitious and broader: to eliminate hunger, to guarantee food security for all the world's people, and to improve nutritional standards by modernizing and improving agriculture.[125]

The commitment to food as a right "for everyone" was evident in Roosevelt's Four Freedoms, in the Hot Springs conference, in the establishment of the FAO, and of course in UNRRA. By this time, in the early postwar period, the "inhumanity of hunger" and "the right to eat"—to use phrases from Alice Weinreb's work on hunger in modern Germany—had become universally accepted positions, at least in theory. The starving bodies that had flashed across newspapers and film reels as concentration camps were liberated shocked the world and in turn reinforced and empowered the evolving commitment to food as a global human right: starving bodies had exposed what Weinreb refers to as a "violation of the 'rights' of the sufferer." This broader principle was ultimately included in the Universal Declaration of

Human Rights in 1948. In Article 25 the declaration recognized the right of every individual to "a standard of living adequate for the health and well-being of himself and of his family, including food, clothing, housing and medical care."[126]

At the same time that these ideas were circulating in the halls of international organizations and were on the minds of world leaders, the Brethren Service Committee was also reflecting on food and food relief at both the local and international levels. Ultimately, it was the Brethren Service Committee that provided the essential logistical support for UNRRA's agriculture program—a key component of which was the delivery of horses and cattle. Through the Heifer Project, the Brethren Service Committee also contributed its own small number of heifers to European rehabilitation. It is to the Brethren Service Committee that we now turn.

CHAPTER 2

The UNRRA–Brethren Service Committee Partnership

The Church of the Brethren, the Society of Friends (Quakers), and the Mennonites constitute the three historic peace churches in the United States. Each of these was and remains quite small. The Brethren numbered less than two hundred thousand in 1940, and its congregants at that time lived mainly in the Midwest and the eastern parts of the country. There were just over 1,000 congregations of the Church of the Brethren in the United States at mid-century.[1] At around this same time, there were approximately 120,000 Mennonites in the US, with "Mennonite" referring to a wide variety of spiritual and theological positions and including subgroups like the Amish and the Hutterites.[2] The Quakers, or the Religious Society of Friends (or sometimes just Friends), numbered 200,000 across the entire world at mid-century, with a little more than half of these in the US.[3]

The peace churches share a common origin story in that they all formed in Europe in opposition to Catholicism as well as to some of the ideas of the Protestant Reformation. The Mennonites came into being in the early sixteenth century and the Brethren in the early eighteenth century during the Anabaptist Reformation in what is now Switzerland, Germany, the Netherlands, and Austria.[4] They started coming to the New World in the eighteenth century to escape persecution in their homelands; the first Brethren landed in Philadelphia in 1719.[5] In simplest terms, the Mennonites and the Brethren believe only in adult confessions of faith; accordingly, they reject infant baptism practiced by both Catholics and some Protestants. The Friends emerged during a period of political turmoil in England in the middle of the seventeenth century. They believe, most strikingly, that the formal structures of religion are unimportant and that God has an unmediated relationship with each person.

The Brethren, Mennonites, and the Friends have been linked by their doctrinal pacifism and by a commitment to nonviolent methods to resolve conflict or achieve goals; they are collectively known as "the peace churches" for this reason. Pacifism, or "peace testimony," as members often refer to it, has been a defining feature of their religious and social practices since the beginning and remains important to this day. Expressions of pacifism have varied between the churches and even between congregations and branches of each church. But what is clear across the peace churches is that pacifism to some extent shapes congregants' relationship to the state. This was (and remains) no more obvious than during times of war.[6] Pacifists oppose the state's judgment about the need for military action and reject the state's ability to force people to fight that war.[7]

Moreover, the three churches have shared a commitment to humanitarian relief work and a conviction that helping others and alleviating suffering constitute crucially important components of religious devotion. This commitment to relief and charity-giving is reflected in the very name "Brethren Service Committee" (BSC); since the post–World War I period, "service" has formed a core element of Brethren identity. Arguably, this emphasis has to do with the persecution that the earliest members of the churches had themselves suffered and that had prompted them to seek refuge in the American colonies centuries ago. From their perspective it also reflects the simple and direct exhortation in Matthew 25:35–40 to feed the hungry, clothe the naked, and visit the sick.[8] Peace church members took this literally.

Dan West

By the mid-twentieth century, the peace churches were no strangers to relief work. During the immediate post–World War I period, from 1919 to 1922, the Brethren had already contributed almost $300,000 in humanitarian aid, with most of this amount going to Armenia. In addition, in 1921 the Brethren General Mission Board reported that the Brethren gave $130,000 to famine relief in China. The Brethren entrenched service work as part of their religious devotion and "washed the feet of the world" just as they washed each other's feet during special Communion services. The goal of Brethren relief work was also to soften the immediate effects of the state's choices on individuals.⁹ They did this in a context where hunger was increasingly interpreted not as a personal moral failing but as the consequence, either direct or indirect, of specific government decisions and policies that led to the availability of too little food or food that lacked nutritional substance.

The most formative experience for the Brethren in terms of relief provision was in Spain during the Spanish Civil War. It was in Spain that the stage was set for the Heifer Project and, in general, for the Brethren's expanded engagement in world affairs through humanitarian aid projects. In 1937 the Church of the Brethren received an invitation from the American Friends Service Committee to help organize a relief program in Spain. The American Friends Service Committee had been established years earlier, in 1917, as a relief-providing arm of the Quakers (though by this time the Quakers had been providing humanitarian assistance for decades already, starting in the Crimean War).[10] In September 1937, Dan West—a strong pacifist, onetime teacher, and very active Church of the Brethren lay member with a special interest in projects that involved youth—took up the Quakers' invitation and traveled to Spain on behalf of the Brethren in the role of "Peace Representative."[11] Over the course of a few months in Spain, from the fall of 1937 into the early winter of 1938, it became clear to West that Spaniards, both the Nationalists and the Republicans, were hungry. And though the volunteers with the Quaker-led project distributed what food was available, there simply was not enough to satisfy the need. The shortage of milk was felt most acutely and poignantly: those distributing the milk had the impossible task of deciding which child should receive some and which should not; children who looked like they had a better chance of surviving were generally prioritized.[12]

It was in this context that Dan West conceived of the Heifer Project. The humanitarian conversion narrative best associated with West is in a sense quite typical: stirred by his personal witnessing of human suffering, he was compelled to act.[13] West had heard what some of his coreligionists refer to as "the voice of God."[14] As the mythology goes—and this next part of the story is indeed a myth—it happened one day when West took a short break from his work in Spain and sat down under an almond tree. As he rested in the tree's shade, West reflected on the agony that war caused and on the limits of the existing structures of aid programming. His imagination turned to thoughts of home. West regretted that the milk of America—the cows of America—could not nourish the children of Spain. Or could they? What if living female cattle, raised by his people on those verdant fields of the American Midwest and elsewhere across the United States, could be shipped to families in need? What if the whole animal were to be provided as aid?

This thinking represented a radical revision of existing humanitarian practices that usually focused on provisioning finished food products and thus on the temporary relief of hunger. West reasoned instead that sending the whole milk producer would be more useful than sending just her milk. The quantity of milk given as aid by a single cow over a lifetime of pregnancies would be far greater than any quantity of milk that relief staff could collect, ship, and distribute in the moment. An average cow in the United States in the mid-1940s, according to West, produced approximately ten quarts of milk a day.[15]

There is no evidence in West's personal papers that he was sitting under an almond tree when the idea for the Heifer Project first took shape, despite the recurrence of this anecdote in published histories of West's life, the Church of the Brethren, and the Heifer Project.[16] Moreover, and perhaps like most good ideas, this one did not emerge all at once. Instead, what became the Heifer Project developed slowly during the few months that West was in Spain. West had first considered the possibility of sending cows to Spain while he was working with the Quakers in Nationalist territory. But it was West's visit to a hospital in Murcia in January 1938 that cemented his determination to send American cows as humanitarian aid to suffering people in Spain. In Murcia, then in Republican territory, West met a girl very ill with tuberculosis. The nurse told West that the girl would likely die and that only ample supplies of milk—which were not available—might yet save her and others like her. Upon hearing this West became determined to find a way to help.[17]

It would take a while for this determination to develop into a concrete plan, and the end result would ultimately be the product of many people's efforts. The compressed narrative that features a single decisive moment of inspiration in a bucolic setting under an almond tree nevertheless best accentuates West's central role in imagining what became the Heifer Project while it also reflects West's status as a larger-than-life figure in Brethren circles. Indeed, West's name remains a monumentally important one among Brethren today, and his volunteerism stands as a powerful expression of the service ethic that continues to animate the church and its congregants. In the existing literature on Brethren history, West is often described as "visionary."[18] Kermit Eby, who was a friend of Dan West, a minister in the Church of the Brethren, and a professor of sociology at the University of Chicago from 1948, called him a "so-called great of the earth," a "Brethren prophet," and a "modern mystic."[19]

The Church of the Brethren continued to work with the Quakers on relief provision in Spain even after West's departure from the country in early 1938. Once he was back to his regular life in the US, West started advocating for his plan. The original proposal to send milk-producing cattle to Spain specifically soon expanded with the advent of the Second World War and mounting evidence of critical food shortages in a number of countries; West's ideas developed along with the context. But even as he pressed ahead with the cattle plan, West also worked on a number of additional projects with the Church of the Brethren. Once the draft was announced in 1940, for example, West coordinated with other church leaders and the government on developing alternatives to military service for men who, for religious reasons, refused to participate in the war.[20]

In 1942 the Brethren approved in principle West's plan to ship relief cattle abroad, but it was not until early 1943 that the BSC, as the outreach wing of the Church of the Brethren, formally approved what by then was called the Heifer Project Committee of the Brethren Service Committee of the Church of the Brethren. In this way the Heifer Project—sometimes referred to as "Heifers for Relief"—became an official part of the Brethren's national plan.[21] The logic of the Heifer Project was described by the Brethren in the simplest terms: "A heifer provides milk (immediate food), a calf (to become another cow), and the heifer itself (more milk over a period of time), and soil rehabilitation (fertilizer)."[22] An important additional element of the Heifer Project plan was to breed the female cattle before shipping so that they would give birth soon after arrival; recipients would, in effect, receive two animals for the price of one, and the lactating cow would more quickly become a useful milk provider for the family that owned her. A similar preference for sending bred heifers would later be reflected in UNRRA's dairy cattle aid program as well.

The animals would thus facilitate an expanded and more robust approach to aid giving and would help lay the foundations for long-term self-sufficiency in target countries. This was part and parcel of the "rehabilitation" goal that formed one of the three Rs of UNRRA policy (the others being immediate relief and then eventual reconstruction). Moreover, for the Heifer Project (as for UNRRA), the animals would be given without regard for the political preferences of the receivers. This was already familiar from the Friends' approach to their Spanish program when they provided aid to both sides in the civil war; as the saying went, "milk knows no politics."[23] Kermit Eby reiterated this point using much the same language when he described the Heifer Project: "The program is rooted in the simple belief that milk knows no politics, that Communist babies are not born flying the hammer and sickle any more than ours are born computing compound interest."[24]

There was another significant requirement for Heifer Project animals specifically: that the firstborn female calf of every donated heifer be given away in turn to another needy family. This was called "Passing on the Gift."[25] Whether almost immediately or a little later (once a female calf was born to the animal that had been placed with a family), recipients thus "paid" for their gift. The animals themselves played a crucial part in this "cycle of giving"—or the "cycle of empowerment," as modern-day humanitarian agencies often prefer to call it.[26] This gesture was practical and useful, to be sure, and, in addition, the Brethren hoped it would build positive links between individuals in a given community while allowing people to preserve their self-respect and to feel like they were contributing to their own welfare. For West and the other Heifer Project enthusiasts in Brethren circles, it was also important that the donated living animals required active care from the receivers. The need to attend to the animals would bring dignity to people's situations while laying the foundations for self-sufficiency and reconstruction.[27]

The Heifer Project: "High Seas Service"

From the start, West and others believed that ecumenicalism would make the Heifer Project stronger and more successful.[28] The recent experiences of the peace churches working together in Spain (the Mennonites were involved in the Quaker-led relief project there as well) showed how productive that cooperation could be and arguably resulted in a growing recognition of the compatibility of the denominations' goals and beliefs; it gave each of the churches firsthand evidence of their ability to work together, and it cemented their identities as "peace churches." West thus reached out to other Christian denominations and invited them to join the Heifer Project. The Fellowship of Reconciliation joined first, in 1943, followed in 1944 and 1945 by the Quaker Rural Life Association, the Evangelical and Reformed Church, and the Catholic Rural Life Conference. In 1946 the Northern Baptist Convention, the Mennonite Central Committee, and the Methodist Committee on Overseas Relief all joined.[29] Joining the Heifer Project meant being able to name a representative to the Heifer Project Committee, and it also signaled a commitment to organizing heifer collections at the local congregation or church level and thereby contributing materially to the overall Heifer Project relief effort.[30] Despite this ecumenicalism and the fact that the Heifer Project received a degree of both moral and material support from other Christian denominations, it was a Brethren initiative, and the Brethren would maintain a lead role in it for several years. It was not until incorporation in 1953 that ties with the BSC were formally severed.

Until the war ended, however, it was impossible to realize the Heifer Project idea fully and to ship cattle across the ocean. In fact, no cattle would ever make it to Spain, the country where the idea was first conceived and to which West had hoped to send animals.[31] At any rate, throughout what would turn out to be the last part of the war, in 1944 and 1945, the Brethren were busy working on other relief programs. These included organizing nonperishable food aid drives, providing care for war orphans (in unoccupied France, for example), and collecting material relief like clothes and bedding for distribution to people who needed these items. As the war turned in the Allies' favor, the Brethren also did ministry work with German prisoners of war in Allied camps.[32] While these relief efforts were taking place, the Brethren were also working out the logistics of the plan to transport living animals from the United States to Europe. For this the Brethren needed (and so far lacked) ready contacts in target countries that could receive the aid they were offering.[33] Despite his work on a number of other Brethren initiatives, West remained part of the Heifer Project Committee during this period of building and organizing.

While logistical details related to the Heifer Project were still being worked out, the Brethren began spreading news of their plan throughout supportive communities across the United States. The plan was for heifers to be donated directly from supporters to the Heifer Project. Already by mid-1944—well before it was possible to ship cattle to Europe—the Brethren had approximately one thousand donated animals awaiting shipment.[34] The majority of animal donations would eventually come from rural Pennsylvania, Ohio, Virginia, and Indiana, and to a lesser extent from California, Idaho, Illinois, Iowa, and Kansas, in addition to smaller donations from many other states.[35]

To prepare for the day that European shipments became possible, the Brethren organized practice runs closer to home. The first such test run happened in the summer of 1944. From a stockyard in Nappanee, Indiana, eighteen heifers were transported by train to Mobile, Alabama, before seventeen of them (one was sick and was kept behind) were placed on SS *William D. Bloxham* and sailed to Puerto Rico, where a food and public health crisis was mounting.[36] The Brethren already had some experience in Puerto Rico. This experience came through their administration of the Martin J. Brumbaugh Reconstruction Unit, one of many Civilian Public Service camps that had been established during the war as part of the American government's alternative service program for Conscientious Objectors. Known as Camp #43, the Brumbaugh Unit operated in Castañer, Puerto Rico, and worked on a wide variety of projects designed to improve public health, medical care, and food access.[37] In this context the heifer shipment represents an extension of the Brethren's already strong commitment to providing relief in that specific location. With their gift of heifers to Puerto Ricans, the Brethren attached a note; the note read, simply, that "these producers of nutritious milk" were being given "in the spirit of brotherhood and service to our fellow men."[38] To this day the start date of that first shipment—July 14, 1944—remains an important one in the history of the Brethren and is considered the anniversary of Heifer International's founding. The second Heifer Project shipment to Puerto Rico came less than a year later, in May 1945, and there was also a shipment to Mexico plus two additional shipments to Arkansas. These first deliveries all happened before the partnership between the BSC and UNRRA had even started.[39]

These initial trial runs were celebrated as a great success. Important pieces were falling into place. The Heifer Project plan had the approval of the Church of the Brethren, and it had support from other Christian denominations. Donated heifers were accumulating in supportive communities. It was at this point, in 1944, that Michael Robert (M. R.) Zigler, the first executive secretary of the BSC from 1941 to 1948, contacted UNRRA with a proposal to include Brethren heifers as part of the general aid shipments that were just then being planned for Europe. Dan West, who worked with Zigler, had already established contact with Ollie E. Reed, the head of the Bureau of Dairy Industry in the US Department of Agriculture from 1928 to 1953. Reed gave West his general support for the idea of the Brethren donating heifers directly to the UNRRA program, but no concrete plans or promises had been made.[40]

Zigler received a similarly noncommittal initial response from UNRRA and was told that there were no immediate plans to include live animals in the aid shipments that would start soon after the war ended. The UNRRA country programs were still very much in the making. No one denied that including horses and cattle as part of the aid packages would allow UNRRA to best realize its rehabilitation plans. But it appeared to be too daunting a job, even for a vast organization like UNRRA. There were many reasons for UNRRA's hesitation. The first was that UNRRA, by necessity, had to focus on immediate relief first, and this meant providing inexpensive yet nutrient-dense food like grain; grains would ultimately account for almost half of the total UNRRA food expenditures for all countries combined.[41] During the planning phase, it was not clear how much of UNRRA's total available resources could be directed away from emergency food supplies and toward the provision of other types of aid instead. How much support UNRRA was able and willing to give to longer-term agricultural renewal remained an open question.[42] The right balance was difficult to set.

From UNRRA's perspective shipping living animals was logistically complicated, labor-intensive, time-sensitive, and expensive, and factoring losses in raised the costs of an animal aid program further still. The upfront purchase cost was in the range of $175 for a single Brown Swiss heifer and a little less for a Holstein-Friesen; bulls of these breeds (the ratio of female to male cattle shipped would be roughly thirty to one) cost considerably more at about $300.[43] Horses were cheaper to buy at about $78, but they cost more than cattle to ship to the ports, to feed, and to care for generally. They were also much more likely to get sick and die at some point along the way to the American port, at the port, or on the sailing from the US, meaning that they were a very risky investment from a financial standpoint.[44]

The Ocean Shipping Division of UNRRA, which would take responsibility for procuring the aid-carrying ships, also expressed reservations about launching what it viewed as an expensive, hazardous, and complicated livestock program. They raised several practical concerns. For one, animals had to be moved as quickly as possible from their point of origin to the ships so as to reduce loss rates, and the animals would need care along the route to the ports. Second, the arrival of draft animals at their destinations needed as much as possible to be coordinated with the arrival of other essential agricultural goods that UNRRA supplied in large quantities as well—like seeds, fertilizers, pesticides, and planting and harvesting tools—so as to be of maximum use in growing cycles. In addition to these arguments, there was yet another significant challenge: finding available and capable men who were willing to accept a several-weeks-long job crossing an ocean with animals that weighed hundreds of pounds each and that required around-the-clock attention. These men ideally needed some experience handling animals to protect UNRRA's investment and to ensure the success of its goals. UNRRA was also concerned that, given the contemporary job market, it might have to pay far too much in wages to the animal tenders, thereby raising the already high costs further still.[45]

But this was a dynamic and creative period, and assessments of needs, risks, and possibilities changed quickly. While logistical considerations in the United States tipped the balance away from running a live animal program, certain other practical and intellectual considerations favored it. The matter was open for discussion. For their part, agricultural specialists were telling UNRRA bureaucrats that, despite the challenges of sending animals abroad, they were essential for real agricultural rehabilitation, and UNRRA had already defined agricultural renewal as a key goal that would in turn spark other elements of rehabilitation. The argument was compelling.[46] In addition, UNRRA bureaucrats were becoming convinced that, from a social perspective, the animals would bring stability, rootedness, and a measure of normalcy to fragile communities; the animals constituted an important step toward broader reconstruction. To that end UNRRA's Technical Committee on Agriculture ultimately came out in favor of sending animals to war-destroyed countries. The director of UNRRA's Agricultural Rehabilitation Division, Edwin R. Henson, also pressed for the inclusion of draft animals and dairy animals in the organization's rehabilitation program.[47]

While different aspects of the livestock program were being discussed at the institutional level, the target countries were also pressing for livestock aid. Greece, for example, reported that it had lost 60 percent of its cattle during the war, and it argued that it therefore needed a sizable injection of breeding stock to build artificial insemination programs; these programs were themselves an important part of rebuilding livestock herds and animal-related industries (like the dairy industry).[48] UNRRA responded by facilitating a special shipment of six pedigreed bulls to Greece. The bulls came as a gift via the Heifer Project. The animals sailed from Saint John, New Brunswick, in Canada on May 14, 1945, on a Swedish ship called *Boolongena*.[49] Other target countries—like Poland—also made clear to UNRRA how important horses and cattle were to their rebuilding plans.[50]

In early May 1945, at long last, Edwin Henson of the Agricultural Division received permission from Roy F. Hendrickson, UNRRA deputy director general, Bureau of Supply, to move ahead with the livestock program. Henson immediately purchased six hundred head of cattle and six hundred mares. The United States Commercial Company of the Foreign Economic Administration, Office of Food Program, was in charge of procuring the animals for UNRRA at this time, though in October 1945 this body was liquidated and the Livestock Branch of the Department of Agriculture took over the job of animal procurement for UNRRA. The Livestock Branch would also eventually have the responsibility, along with UNRRA's Personnel division, of recruiting the veterinarians that would be responsible for animal care throughout the various stages of the process, including during the sailings.[51]

The challenge of where to find the livestock attendants remained, however.[52] During previous wars the Army Veterinary Service had either assigned enlisted men to attend to the animals aboard any given maritime voyage or hired civilian casual laborers to work as "horsemen."[53] UNRRA was of course not a military operation, however, and at any rate qualified military-age men were still enlisted in 1945. As such, UNRRA looked to voluntary agencies for a solution, and not surprisingly it very quickly turned to the BSC, which had already been in touch about the idea of sending livestock abroad. UNRRA contacted the BSC with a proposal: UNRRA would take Brethren heifers on its livestock ships without charge, and in return the BSC would recruit the cattle attendants that would accompany all livestock ships. The attendants would care for the animals—Heifer Project animals plus UNRRA animals—from port to port, and the animals would all travel together on the same UNRRA ships.[54] The men would be paid $150 for each trip, regardless of destination and regardless of how long the trip actually took. An agreement outlining these general terms between UNRRA and the BSC was signed on May 9, 1945 (and amended slightly in October 1945).[55]

More elaborate plans formed quickly after that, and a full-fledged UNRRA agricultural program that included the shipment of live animals tended by Brethren-recruited cattlemen was established. This partnership between the BSC and UNRRA lasted throughout UNRRA's tenure. Each side saw a benefit in the relationship. By functioning as what was essentially an employment agency for UNRRA, the Brethren gained free passage for their animals on UNRRA ships plus access to UNRRA's resources and contacts abroad. This tiny religious organization had hitched itself to an enormous global body with international political status and influence.

For its part, UNRRA left the recruiting of cattle attendants to a steady partner with administrative experience in aid provision and unusually good access to specific pools of available men: most notably those from the Brethren and related churches, and those from other Christian denominations that had joined the Heifer Project. To be sure, many of the recruited animal attendants would not be active Christians and would sign up mainly in pursuit of adventure or to earn fast money. But others, those who came out of religious milieux, were motivated by their faith and by the service ethic that was part and parcel of their local church communities.[56] Could UNRRA have shipped so many live animals without the BSC? Maybe, but skepticism about being able to recruit adequate numbers of men for the job had been identified early on as a key obstacle to running the livestock program. Even if large numbers of men had been demobilized quickly from the armed forces, many of them would likely have wanted to take advantage of the excellent in-country employment opportunities available to veterans. Robert Lintner, the chief of the Livestock Branch of UNRRA's Agricultural Rehabilitation Division, also feared that "the caliber of persons customarily employed to care for commercial shipment of livestock" was, as he said, often "undesirable."[57] The BSC seemed to offer a good solution to these concerns: the BSC wanted to do the job and to recruit the "right" kind of men, and it saw this work as so much more than simply fulfilling a contract.

What about the BSC? Could they have found another way to practice humanitarian aid giving? Could they have placed their animals with people abroad without UNRRA's assistance? The BSC did send four shipments of heifers to France and Belgium independently of UNRRA during the UNRRA period; in each of these cases, the recipient countries paid for the shipping.[58] But those countries where the need for animals was greatest, in eastern and southern Europe, could hardly afford to pay shipping costs for hundreds of animals. Besides, the cooperation with UNRRA allowed the Heifer Project to focus on animal procurement and placement without having to figure out the shipping logistics or costs on top of that. And organizing care for the UNRRA animals itself constituted humanitarian service. Ultimately, the UNRRA-Brethren partnership facilitated the mass movement of thousands of animals from one continent to another.[59] In late June 1945, two UNRRA ships sailed for Greece—SS *F. J. Luckenbach* from New Orleans and SS *Virginian* from Baltimore—with a full complement of BSC cowboys on board to attend to the animals. The UNRRA-Brethren partnership had begun in earnest.[60]

Mid-Century Humanitarianism and Christian Statesmanship

By the summer of 1945, both the Brethren's Heifer Project and UNRRA had come to the same conclusion: that shipping live animals from America to target countries was a necessary component of agricultural renewal and therefore of wider rehabilitation goals; it was a nonnegotiable element of humanitarian relief programming. Yet the BSC and UNRRA were two vastly different organizations. The one was a relief arm of a small American Christian church that was motivated by making a difference in the lives of others while fulfilling religious commandments to serve and give. The other was an enormous secular international body composed of dozens of countries from around the world, though dominated financially, administratively, and culturally by America. The practical reasons for this partnership are evident. But there were additional factors that explain how these two organizations saw common cause and came together as they did at this crucial postwar moment.

Part of the answer has to do with the role that Christianity played in mid-century humanitarian activism of all types and with the position that Christianity occupied in mid-century American identity more broadly. The United States at the time saw itself largely as a "Christian nation," and America's humanitarian impulse—including UNRRA's humanitarianism—was framed in Christian terms that would have been familiar to the BSC.[61] To some extent UNRRA had both evolved from and reflected Christian ethics.

In the speech he gave upon accepting the position of UNRRA director general in March 1946, Fiorello La Guardia used explicit Christian references when he talked about where the will to organize this massive relief effort had come from: "There is precedent for it [UNRRA] in the old scripture, in the new scripture, to love our neighbor, to aid the needy. That is not original. It just hasn't been carried out." La Guardia, an Episcopalian, liked a Christianity that was practical, busy, and helpful and that aspired to realizing the lofty goal of bringing "the heavenly kingdom" to Earth. He continued, "That is our call. That is all there is to it, to respond to that prayer. We then become a great army of mercy, great army, carrying out God Almight's [sic] response to the call for daily bread. . . . That is the mission of UNRRA, and that is the army I am going to lead." La Guardia's "army of mercy" would heal and build rather than kill and destroy; that was its "mission."[62]

UNRRA described its own cattle shipments, as we have seen, as following "in Noah's footsteps." This expression recalled the biblical ark from which the new world would be populated. In ancient times it was a flood that had led to rebirth, and in modern times "following Noah's footsteps" evoked the destruction that came as a result of war while it also looked optimistically toward peace and reconstruction in Europe and beyond.[63]

Others also made the connection between the contemporary humanitarian moment and the Judeo-Christian past. For UNRRA historian George Woodbridge, the organization embodied "the exhortation voiced long ago" by biblical prophets to protect the vulnerable and to show compassion for the weak. In his official history of UNRRA, Woodbridge drew on familiar biblical language to explain UNRRA's mandate: "Do right to the widow, judge for the fatherless, give to the poor, defend the orphan, clothe the naked, heal the broken and weak."[64] The Christian imperative embedded in UNRRA's mandate to "act humanitarian" was already familiar to Americans.

Contemporary American media reinforced the Christian bases behind UNRRA. In a *New York Times Magazine* article from the fall of 1947, the photojournalist and writer Gertrude Samuels suggested that UNRRA was nothing less than "a holy word."[65] At the end of 1946, as UNRRA was preparing to wind down, one *Life* editorialist reflected on what UNRRA had managed to achieve during its short tenure: "The American Christian knows, too, that the needs of his neighbors have a special significance. For, as Thomas Jefferson noted with pleased surprise, whereas the Greek philosophers had concerned themselves primarily with man's duty to himself, Jesus taught of man's duty to his neighbor. In UNRRA we had some promising answers to the question of Christian neighborliness."[66]

Harry S. Truman, who assumed the American presidency in April 1945, was himself praised by some contemporary religious leaders for his "act of Christian statesmanship" in supporting UNRRA.[67] The heads of seventeen Protestant denominations (including Baptists, Lutherans, Presbyterians, and Episcopalians) signed an appeal in February 1946 to the "Christian forces of our country" to continue funding aid programs like UNRRA. The church leaders encouraged the American people to write to their representatives and even to the president directly to signal their continued support for UNRRA. "Feeding a hungry world," the appeal read, "is too great a task for private agencies. It calls for action by the nation as a whole." The appeal went on: "The President has summoned our people to the sacrifices necessary to save millions in Asia and Europe from starvation."[68] Given the country's wealth, this responsibility fell to the United States first and foremost.[69] In a separate statement on the subject of aid, Rev. Dr. John Sutherland Bonnell of Fifth Avenue Presbyterian in New York City connected America's foreign policy choices directly to the words ascribed to Jesus Christ: "'I was hungry and ye gave me meat, I was thirsty and ye gave me drink, I was naked and ye clothed me.'"[70]

The appeal to Christian obligation is well reflected in the 1946 pro-UNRRA American propaganda film *Seeds of Destiny*. This film won the Oscar for the Best Documentary Short that year, and it was also shown in the summer of 1946 in Geneva at the Fifth Council Session of UNRRA when continued financial support for relief provision formed part of the deliberations.[71] *Seeds of Destiny* is just twenty minutes long, but it delivers a powerful message that reflects the Christian bases of the moment and warns against doing nothing. The title card that appears at the start of the film quotes a passage from the Bible: "A good tree cannot bring forth evil fruit, neither can a corrupt tree bring forth good fruit" (Matt. 7:18). The film shows dozens of images of war's harrowing effects, especially on children.[72] Flashing across the screen are children maimed by the war, children dying slowly of malnutrition, and children orphaned and alone after witnessing the murders of their families. The narrator warns that disregarding their obvious distress today could only lead to a new war tomorrow. Is there a young Einstein or Madame Curie in the crowds of children? Or is there a Hitler and a Mussolini? The narrator tells us that in providing "the plasma of peace"—vital relief goods—UNRRA is waging the "last battle" of World War II.[73]

The Christian influences in the Heifer Project are of course more obvious. The Brethren understood humanitarian relief as "a practical expression of the spirit and teachings of Christ" and as part and parcel of fulfilling fundamental obligations of Christian people to other people, whether Christian or not, wherever in the world they were. The BSC promoted the Heifer Project as a form of "creative citizenship and Christian testimony," a token of friendship and goodwill that transcended political divisions and national or ethnic boundaries as it strove to lessen the worst effects of war.[74]

Dan West himself referred to Brethren aid projects as "harness[ing] up our Christian faith to the world's needs." In a speech he delivered in 1993, Dan West's son Philip reflected on the Christian elements in the Heifer Project specifically; in effect the younger West answered the question of why the Brethren believed that heifers were so important. Heifers, the younger West said, "were more than animals"; they were "the reminder of Christian responsibilities, of sharing.... Heifers meant working together" to achieve a collective goal.[75] Professor and Brethren minister Kermit Eby similarly expounded on how the Heifer Project reflected something fundamental about Brethren Christian values: "Heifers, unlike bombs, are personal, particularly if you bring them up or sacrifice for them. Before they mature and become cows (giving their new host not only milk but the beginnings of a dairy herd) they become pets. Sent away to help the needy, a part of you goes along. Received by fellowmen [sic] in need, the Fatherhood of God and the brotherhood of man is reaffirmed."[76]

Christians, including the peace church members, had played an important role in the development of modern western humanitarian action, and these religious elements continued to be reflected in the postwar era. Mid-century humanitarianism—the UNRRA era—should not be read as a simple triumph of secular liberal internationalism and a wholesale abandonment of humanitarianism's Christian background.[77] Christians continued to play an important role in postwar humanitarianism, and powerful Christian inflections continued to exist alongside the new mid-century vocabulary of secular humanitarianism and liberal internationalism. As Samuel Moyn has argued, the "new" discourse about individual and collective human rights that started to unfold at this time, with its emphasis on basic rights to dignity, security, and opportunity, owes far more to Christianity and to religious humanitarian activism than we often recognize. The lines between the "old" way and the "new" were not so clear cut. Likewise, the commitment of UNRRA to political neutrality and impartiality in delivering aid (at least in theory) is often read as distinctly modern and as signaling a new era of relief provision. But we might argue instead and in addition that this choice reflects longer-standing ideas adhered to by some Christians about the "brotherhood of man" and "international friendship."[78] Quaker-Brethren cooperation in Spain had practiced this "neutral" approach to aid provision, for example, and in the aftermath of World War II the Brethren's Heifer Project was in favor of political neutrality in aid distribution as well.

The Economics and Politics of Mid-Century Humanitarian Aid

At the same time, relief programs formed part of the economic and political arsenal that helped establish the United States as a global leader after the war.[79] State actors understood the calculus that acting munificently in the present would yield benefits in terms of status, influence, and access to future markets.[80] Aid for Europe, in other words, could provide economic and other advantages for America if it were handled correctly. "Food is power," Senator and later Vice President Hubert Humphrey declared about American foreign assistance programs decades later.[81] This held true in the UNRRA period too.

Not surprisingly then, the US Congress stipulated specific conditions for the forms that American aid contributions could take.[82] Congress insisted that the aid chain begin in America and that the overall aid program provide concrete benefits to American companies, agricultural and otherwise, as they pivoted away from wartime to peacetime production, while also providing jobs for American workers and returning soldiers. International aid programming would absolutely have to serve American national interests. Far from having been devastated by the war, the American agricultural sector experienced a huge wartime boom and was therefore in a uniquely strong position to sell its surplus—grain and animal—after the conflict ended. In fact, the war years were seen as ushering in a kind of second agricultural revolution in the United States. Mechanization of farm labor in the US also decreased the demand for horses while it increased agricultural yields. American food production in the immediate postwar era rose by one-third compared to the prewar period. America had an abundant supply of grain and other foodstuffs, most notably dairy products, that it could sell through the UNRRA program.[83] The American approach to aid provision reflected an American approach to farming, diet, and food generally: a focus on volume and diversity.[84]

It was not just the American agricultural sector that benefited from UNRRA. Railroad companies like C&O experienced a significant rise in business too after they were engaged by UNRRA to move relief supplies (including animals in addition to food) to American ports.[85] Ports boomed as well. The main UNRRA port was at Newport News, Virginia, and for a time this location was known as "the largest waterfront stockyard" on the Atlantic Coast of the United States.[86] Newport News was well connected by railway to the Midwest (from which many animals traveled) and was conveniently situated along the Atlantic coast for Europe-bound trips. It had been a major embarkation depot for supply, troop, and horse shipments already in World War I and World War II, meaning that much of the required infrastructure for animal transport was already in place there.[87]

Newport News started accepting animals for the UNRRA program in February 1946, several months after the very first animal shipments had started. SS *Carroll Victory* was the first ship to sail from Newport News to

Poland. Until March 1947 Newport News sent out a total of 175 animal-carrying ships to various destinations, and at its 1946 peak two and even three ships with a total of between 1,500 and 1,600 animals were sent out from this one destination every twenty-four hours.[88] Even at the time, the work accomplished at Newport News was a source of pride for UNRRA. A BSC satellite office was established at Newport News as well so as to be best able to administer the cowboys and coordinate with UNRRA. By May 1946, with many months yet left to go in the Brethren-UNRRA partnership, approximately forty thousand horses and fifteen thousand cattle had been sent abroad from Newport News.[89]

Other ports sent out UNRRA animals too. The major ones were in Savannah, Georgia; Baltimore, Maryland; New Orleans, Louisiana; Houston, Texas; Portland, Maine; and Montreal, Canada.[90] Shipyards worked to capacity, and in general the shipping industry flourished in this immediate postwar period. The UNRRA program accounted for most of this growth, but, even earlier, lend-lease was an important factor as well, as was the army.[91] G. Ben and Sol Levinson's Levinson Livestock Company, with a four-thousand-acre farm along the C&O Railroad in Virginia, profited from improved business, too. The Levinsons built a modern thirty-acre terminal stockyard next to Pier X in Newport News, where UNRRA animals were stocked before they were loaded onto the waiting ships; the stockyard could hold a few thousand animals at a time.[92] Henry Lintner from the UNRRA shipping division praised the Levinson yard, which included a chute to the loading area at the pier, as "the most efficient system in any port in the nation." The whole enterprise created jobs for the local economy too.[93]

From an American economic perspective, then, it made sense to buy livestock in the US and ship the animals to Europe rather than buying "surplus" animals from somewhere closer to the countries that needed them. Even in a Europe generally so overwhelmed by war, there were arguably more convenient options than packing hundreds of live animals onto a ship and sailing across the Atlantic. In fact some relief horses did come from Iceland and the United Kingdom, and many more horses and cattle came from Denmark.[94] The Danes had a large surplus of horses (mostly the Jutland breed) in part because during the war, when their access to oil was cut off, they had to rely on horses over tractor power, and then, after the war, they no longer had use for the animals. UNRRA paid the Danes about three times what it paid for American horses and directed about forty thousand of them to Poland from 1946 through 1949, albeit without the American seagoing cowboys aboard the ships.[95] Short maritime trips in part explained why the Danish horses were healthier and stronger when they arrived at their destinations.⁹⁶ Other animals, like mules, came from Italy as surplus from the US and British armies; the mules were shipped to Greece and Yugoslavia. It was UNRRA's European Regional Office in London that handled these smaller livestock purchases of animals in Europe for Europe.⁹⁷ Generally speaking, and in keeping with postwar American political and economic priorities, UNRRA, working with other agencies and especially with the Department of Agriculture, purchased the animals from American farmers, American livestock companies, or American breeding associations.⁹⁸

The aid program, including the animal aid program, was therefore sold as being good for American business in the short term and in the longer term, too, as Europe's economic rehabilitation and political stability would ideally translate into attractive markets for American goods. The economic argument was a key part of the pitch. "You can't do business with a graveyard," wrote a journalist in Virginia's *Highland Recorder* as part of an explanation as to why America should devote such substantial resources to UNRRA.⁹⁹

Yet arguments about maximizing economic advantages and amassing political capital through aid provision needed to be made carefully as they were so obviously self-serving, even if it was American economic and political strength that had enabled expressions of "Christian generosity" in the first place. There was also an emotional element at play here. The period after the war's end gave rise to a new and powerful "transnational 'emotional community'" into which both Christian and secular actors could imaginatively place themselves.¹⁰⁰ Collectively, Americans empathized and "felt bad" when viewing images of suffering (as shown in *Seeds of Destiny*, for example) and were thus motivated to help strangers across the world. Emotional responses to the brutality of the war produced new ways of understanding one's relationship to people all over the globe and created new connections between "us" and "them."¹⁰¹ Relief furnished what Arthur Bliss Lane, American ambassador to Poland, called in his memoir "a great spiritual bond" between givers and receivers and between the recipients and "Western civilization."¹⁰² This marked the start of what some recent scholarship has referred to as a "diplomacy of sympathy."¹⁰³ To some extent it was these feelings that had sparked the creation of UNRRA and the Heifer Project in the first place.

In the next chapter, we explore Brethren motivations for mid-century relief work in detail while we also trace the process by which men became seagoing cowboys. The chapter is about the wartime American circumstances that produced these men. Given that recruiting the cowboys was the responsibility of the BSC, and not of UNRRA directly, the chapter is largely about the Brethren.

CHAPTER 3

On Becoming a Seagoing Cowboy

In the autumn of 1944, the Brethren Service Committee purchased property in New Windsor, Maryland, and set up what would become an important center for humanitarian aid and material relief. Despite the town's small size—its population was only about five hundred people—New Windsor was transformed in the immediate postwar period into an unusually busy place with a distinctly global outlook. From early 1946 the seagoing cowboys program was managed primarily from New Windsor, as was the Heifer Project. The selection of cowboys, the organizing of cowboy crews for the various UNRRA shipments, and the coordination of heifer deliveries all happened there. The Brethren's Material Goods program, through which donated goods were collected, sorted, packaged, and distributed to individuals and communities in need, was also based in New Windsor and formed a vital aspect of the Brethren's commitment to crisis response and service.[1] Other Protestant relief agencies had a presence in New Windsor, too.[2] Ultimately, thousands of pounds of clothing, food, and other relief materials were shipped abroad from this one Maryland town, with the value of these donations on the order of several millions of dollars.[3]

Managing the Brethren's Material Goods program required a base staff of dozens plus many volunteers; volunteers came to the New Windsor Center from across the United States to help prepare the goods for shipment abroad. Some of these volunteers were Brethren college students, and some were the wives of seagoing cowboys who were going or had gone on an UNRRA sailing. Occasionally men from the Civilian Public Service (CPS) also volunteered time to the program. From 1944 to 1946, New Windsor was the home base for a Brethren-managed unit of the CPS, and the men assigned to the unit were billeted in repurposed college dormitories located on the grounds of the center (even though their work involved soil conservation projects off the Brethren campus). Other volunteers were just regular people who chose to take time away from their everyday jobs to contribute in some way to postwar humanitarian efforts. Some volunteers stayed for months, but many came for just a short period, perhaps for only a couple of days or a couple of weeks. The volunteers were typically billeted in the old college dorms.[4]

New Windsor was also occasionally the first stop for men who had been selected as cattlemen, provided that they were scheduled to sail from nearby ports in the northeastern states and that they had ample time for such a detour. Those men who made it to New Windsor were immediately absorbed into the rhythms of the center: they too sorted and packed donated clothing and contributed to the community's maintenance by helping to prepare meals. Some of the men also worked on nearby facilities that were being used as holding centers for the relief animals before they were shipped abroad.[5]

Irrespective of the specific work they did at New Windsor, volunteers participated in the various social, cultural, religious, and educational activities organized at the center. One popular event was a speaker series that featured men who had already been abroad as cattle attendants who were willing to share their experiences with those waiting for their sailing call at New Windsor. In general, cowboy accounts describe this period staying in a small Maryland town as a socially exciting and religiously stimulating time, with some cowboys even telling of budding romances with women who were volunteering at the center.[6] All of this activity meant that New Windsor became in the postwar period an important crossroads that linked people, places, and ideas.[7] But how did the men come to find themselves in this position, and how did they become seagoing cowboys in the first place? It is to this question that we now turn.

Calling All "Christian Gentlemen"

Though the seagoing cowboys were recruited, processed, and managed by the BSC, they were formally employed and paid by UNRRA.[8] The standard payment of $150 was reasonable but not extravagant given that the average annual income for a single male residing in either urban or nonagricultural regions in the United States was approximately $1,000 just after World War II.[9]

Cowboys and would-be cowboys had no direct contact with UNRRA, however; they were, in effect, subcontractors hired by and answerable to a third party, the BSC, and thus the BSC, rather than UNRRA, became the men's primary point of reference. There was at least one UNRRA-appointed supervisor per ship (SS *Mount Whitney* was so large that it sailed with three supervisors); this was a managerial position that paid twelve dollars per day. The earliest shipments, in the spring and summer of 1945, did not include a specially designated foreman, but by September UNRRA requested that the BSC designate at least one cattle tender per sailing to work under the supervisor as a "foreman tender" who would act in a leadership capacity; the number of foremen depended on the ship type and size. As an incentive, foremen cowboys were awarded a payment of $250 for the trip instead of the standard $150 that cowboys received. Veterinarians were also included in each sailing; a senior veterinarian earned almost seventeen dollars per day and junior vets fifteen dollars per day.[10] Sending veterinarians with animal shipments was routine and had been practiced by Americans during the wars as well.[11] The cowboys' wages were collected from UNRRA by Brethren program administrators at New Windsor and were then distributed to the men upon their return to the United States.

Round trips would normally last from four to six weeks, but occasionally they could take three months or longer if the ship needed repairs, if the weather was severe, or if some unforeseen problem arose, as sometimes it did. The actual length of the trip did not affect the lump sum payment, so men took a bit of a risk by signing up; their daily pay went down as the trip length grew. Meals and lodging on the ship were covered, of course, but UNRRA did not pay for the cattlemen's journeys to the American port of sailing or back home from that port. The total cost of these trips obviously depended on where the men were coming from and how close they were to the sailing port, and some men admitted that they could scarcely afford these costs up front.[12] UNRRA did, however, give a maintenance allowance of $2.50 per day for the regular cowboys (more for supervisors and veterinarians) while the men waited in port to ship out, and indeed sailing dates could be unpredictable, so the amount paid varied quite a bit.[13] All together the cowboys, supervisors, and veterinarians formed an expensive part of UNRRA's agricultural program.

More than anything else, it was the war that determined which types of men were eligible to take on the position of cattle tender. Some of the men who might normally have been interested in doing this work either were still in regular military service in 1945 and 1946 or were employed in vital military and defense industries. Men had to have been discharged from active military service before they could even consider signing up. There were a couple of additional categories of qualified men: those who had been too young or too old for conscription and so had never been in the war, and those who had farm deferments or ministerial deferments and had never been in service. The last eligible category included men who had been Conscientious Objectors during the war. These were men whose religion decreed that war is "contrary to the will of God," that killing humans in all instances is wrong, and that helping others constitutes an important expression of faith. The majority of Conscientious Objectors came from the three historic American peace churches: the Brethren, the Mennonites, and the Quakers.[14]

From these pools of available men, the BSC chose who they would hire; the BSC handled the advertising as well as the selection of the men.[15] The BSC recruited from their own denomination, but, given how numerically small the Brethren were and given the ecumenicalism that was part of the Heifer Project from the start, they also recruited from those other denominations.[16] The final number of cowboys who came from specific religious groups is difficult to determine precisely, however. Despite the fact that each cowboy was issued a record card when he signed up with the BSC to work on the UNRRA ships, the cards were not always filled out completely or accurately, especially when it came to supplementary information like religious affiliation rather than essential details like name, address, and sailing route and date. Even when men had a strong religious affiliation to give, it was sometimes not marked on the record card. At other times recorded affiliations were distant, stretched, or tenuous. In the end, seagoing cowboys who came from the peace churches may have formed up to a quarter of the total number of men.[17]

Nevertheless, all of the cowboys, whether from the peace churches or not, were recruited by a self-consciously Christian organization—the BSC—and operated in a broadly Christian American context that understood mid-century American humanitarian activism at least partly in Christian terms.[18] Recruiting strategies reflected these Christian foundations in that quite often the BSC placed advertisements for livestock handlers in the religious press; ads appeared in newspapers and magazines associated with specific Christian denominations.[19] The Brethren weekly *Gospel Messenger* and the Mennonite *Gospel Herald* were two such periodicals. The BSC also advertised the program through notices posted on Brethren college campuses.[20] The men recruited for the very first sailing—to Greece in the spring of 1945—had responded to one such notice posted on a bulletin board at the Brethren-affiliated Manchester College in North Manchester, Indiana.[21] Other college student recruits came from institutions like Oberlin, Ohio State, the University of Tennessee, and Elizabethtown College in Lancaster County, Pennsylvania. These college men, some of whom were pursuing preministry programs, saw the cattle-boat trips as an opportunity to expand their knowledge of Europe's postwar problems and the international political context more generally. Some of the Mennonite men were also motivated by the fact that, before the war, there had been a large minority of German Mennonites in Gdańsk, the port city where many UNRRA ships docked. The trips offered an opportunity for these men to connect with aspects of Mennonite history.[22]

Recruitment happened in direct and personal ways as well, within congregations, and it was not uncommon for men to learn about the seagoing cowboys program through word-of-mouth recommendations from family, neighbors, and friends. Harold McNett, for example, was seventeen years old and had just graduated from high school when he got an unexpected call from someone he knew from church asking if he would consider becoming a cattle attendant; Harold made the decision that same weekend and soon enough found himself sailing for Poland.[23] The BSC liked the word-of-mouth approach to recruitment, as this made it more likely that the men were coming from sympathetic religious and social milieux, even if these were geographically distant from one another. Peace church communities were strongest in Pennsylvania as well as in the Midwestern states of Ohio, Indiana, Illinois, and Kansas, and not surprisingly many of the peace church cowboys came from these states. Sometimes several male members from one family signed up together, making the experience a truly familial one. Other times surnames revealed men's membership in (and the popularity of the seagoing cowboys program among) specific faith communities if not the same congregations. As one supervisor remarked, "For a long time every relief ship leaving this harbor had a 'Yoder' on it."[24] Yoder was a common surname throughout Brethren, Mennonite, and Amish circles.[25]

To recruit the several thousands of men it needed to staff the UNRRA ships, however, the BSC had to look beyond its own and related Christian denominations, and it did so by running advertisements in a wide assortment of newspapers from across the United States, many of them rural and local. The BSC also ran radio announcements that enticed men to apply for the job.[26] In the end the majority of cattle-boat crews were composed of regular men who may or may not have been religiously affiliated. The seagoing cowboys were a diverse group of men. According to one description, they included "farm boys from Pennsylvania, rodeo men from Texas high schools and college teachers from the Mid-West, ministers from many denominations, wealthy farmers who can afford to hire help for a few months, [and] city men who claim farm experience" (but who sometimes did not actually have it).[27]

Cowboy Dwight Smith broke down the composition of his Poland-bound crew: "8 high school students, 7 ex-servicemen, 3 farmers, 2 ministerial students, 2 factory workers, 1 horse dealer, 1 auctioneer, 1 truck driver, 1 CPSer, 1 taxicab driver, 1 run away, 1 college Prof., 1 chip builder."[28] Smith himself had only just recently finished high school. This geographic and social diversity in the cowboy group was recognized by UNRRA too. As one UNRRA report read, "Home addresses were from nearly every state in the Union, truly as comprehensive a cross section of American life as could be found."[29]

Experience working with animals and a willingness to do manual labor were explicit requirements for the job of livestock attendant. But a man's ability to do this type of work was presumed rather than spelled out in any detail, much less verified; it was consistent with the work that men (especially those from rural communities) normally engaged in anyway, had done at some earlier point in their lives, or were just expected to know how to do. There was therefore little need for an elaborate training program. One cowboy expressed his personal view that the right attitude and a willingness to learn and help were really the most important qualities that cowboys could bring to animal care in this context. For this particular cowboy, religious commitment was also important to doing the job well. His message to prospective cowboys was a reminder of just how closely work and religion would be intertwined in some of the men's daily activities aboard the ships: "You cannot pray unless you work. Seagoing veterans [cowboys who had made earlier trips] . . . watch you work and measure your religion by your perspiration."[30]

A typical help-wanted advertisement from 1946 spelled out only the essential details when it asked men to become livestock attendants on UNRRA ships. It stated that the length of the trip away from home would be between four and six weeks, that the pay was $150, and that applications ought to be made through the BSC. Typically, ads also gave the eligible age range as sixteen to sixty.[31] In the earliest postwar months and into 1946, the youngest men in this age range did in fact become cattle attendants (as long as they had their parents' permission, like Harold McNett did). Later in 1946, however, program administrators, reacting to some problems with some of the youngest recruits, raised the minimum age to eighteen.[32] Besides, as the draft ended and the pool of available labor grew, it became less difficult to recruit interested men. The increased availability of men was also reflected at the other end of the age range: *Gospel Messenger* reported in late 1945 that the maximum age of eligibility had been lowered from sixty to fifty. And yet despite this, there were plenty of cowboys who were in fact older than the maximum, showing that the stated age limits were sometimes simply ignored.[33]

Responses to the BSC's appeal for recruits were strong and reflected a wide array of motivations. Some men were enticed by a combination of good pay, adventure, and a genuine desire to participate, even in a small way, in an international humanitarian aid project. For some of the youngest men in particular, the appeal of becoming a seagoing cowboy was rooted in a sense of adventure and a desire to leave American shores for the first time to explore a bit of the world.[34] Well-known theologian Harvey Cox relayed that when he was still in high school he was "inebriated with adolescent wanderlust" and therefore jumped at the opportunity to sign up as a cowboy. Cox sailed to Poland in 1946 and would forever consider his time at "Robert Hart University" (Cox sailed on a Liberty ship known as SS *Robert W. Hart*) as having given him opportunities for unprecedented personal growth.[35] For others, the appeal included a chance to make friends and socialize with men from the same faith group: "Our motives were mixed—adventure with Christian service," said Albert J. Meyer from Sterling, Ohio, who was just sixteen when he was part of a group of Mennonite cowboys (thirty-two in all) that accompanied 834 horses to Poland in the summer of 1946 on SS *Stephen R. Mallory*. (Meyer went on to complete a PhD in physics at Princeton.)[36] Some saw it as a chance to learn more about the war and the world the war had created, and for others it was about feeding hungry people and doing their part to "help" in what seemed like an unprecedented moment of need. But even the actively religious men were not what one might describe as typical missionaries who set out to win religious converts.[37] Cowboy Lawrence W. Shultz addressed the question of proselytizing using plain language: "The people in Poland want bread and not stones to rebuild their church houses."[38] At any rate, as the cowboys knew, their status as would-be missionaries or international humanitarian actors was only going to be very temporary and partial, tied as it was just to this one specific experience that would see them spending only a short time in the target country.

The BSC understood that men signed up for a variety of reasons. From their perspective what ultimately mattered most was a man's "good moral character."[39] The Christian bases of moral character were assumed, as was Christian men's unique suitability for the type of relief effort that the postwar moment demanded. This message came through in the help-wanted advertisements that the BSC placed in newspapers. One advertisement called openly for "Men with character and Christian principles."[40] Another ad published in *The Baptist Record* out of Jackson, Mississippi, stated boldly that what was "even more important" than sailing proficiency or experience handling animals was a "man's ability to conduct himself in a Christian manner so that friendship instead of enmity will result from his having been in foreign port cities."[41] Indeed, the BSC identified the potential for un-Christian behavior among some of the recruited cowboys as a key concern. As the ship's sailing date approached, recruiters became less selective about their hires, however, and at times filled crew vacancies at the very last minute if previously recruited men had to withdraw suddenly for personal reasons. One crew supervisor called some of these last-minute hires "water front boys": men of dubious character pulled off the street to fill an urgent and unexpected need.[42] (This type of recruiting was perhaps more in line with how animal attendants were hired for sailings of different kinds during earlier historical periods.[43]) According to one supervisor, these recruits sometimes showed "no appreciation of the position of the peace churches" and therefore threatened to create "disillusionment among the serious minded fellows who were expecting to be placed in the company of like-minded conscientious men."[44]

The incentive for the BSC to find the "right" kind of men for the job was thus significant, and the Christian inflections in the BSC's approach to recruiting were repeated at various stages of the process. In a follow-up letter to men who had expressed initial interest in the job (but who had not yet sent in all of their application materials), for example, the Brethren described openly what type of man they were looking for. The ideal cowboy would be "a Christian gentleman and a messenger of Good Will . . . actively committed to living his faith . . . tolerant, patient and sympathetic in every situation."[45] It was such men, the thinking went, who would be best able to exercise self-control and to resist the temptations that would arise during the trips.[46] In some administrative and planning documents, the seagoing cowboys were even referred to as forming part of a distinctly "Christian program of Relief and Rehabilitation." The use here of the capital Rs on "relief" and "rehabilitation" subtly recalled UNRRA's formal name and priorities. Devotion to God, family, and community was what ideally would motivate men to join the program in the first place and to thereby "give service" to other people—people who, program administrators noted, were part of a larger imagined Christian family.[47]

Even when versions of recruiting material and follow-up correspondence did not explicitly mention Christianity, the instruction to contact the BSC in New Windsor nonetheless signaled the seagoing cowboys program's Christian identity. Highlighting the BSC as the single point of contact for the seagoing cowboys program—as all recruiting material did, given the Brethren's exclusive control over recruitment—arguably left UNRRA's role just a little bit vague, just as it left vague the relationship of UNRRA to the BSC. Sometimes UNRRA appeared in the ads only as part of a description of where the men would be working: on "UNRRA ships carrying livestock."[48]

One specially recruited crew was radically unique. This was an interracial crew of African American, white, Latino, and Japanese American young men, thirty-two in all, plus two ministers and two veterinarians. All the men came from the Jim Crow South.[49] Despite objections from the BSC, UNRRA did not normally permit desegregated crews; at best African Americans were placed in all-Black cowboy crews.[50] Under some pressure to change its policy, however, UNRRA agreed to run this experiment with a desegregated cowboy crew. The men were assembled by the Fellowship of Southern Churchmen, an interdenominational and interracial coalition of southern Protestants devoted to "translat[ing] radical egalitarian theologies into action."[51] The Fellowship was led by the activist and educator Nelle Morton. Dr. Benjamin Mays, mentor to Dr. Martin Luther King Jr. and president of Morehouse College at the time, also played a role in setting up this experiment in what Mays referred to as extending "Christian Fellowship across racial lines."[52]

The recruiting process for this crew involved collecting formal and detailed written recommendations for all the interested men. References commented, in ways we could arguably describe as standard for the context, on men's "Christian character," but they also reflected on men's "ability to live and work intimately with men of different racial backgrounds." Remarkably for this specific crew, too, the referees provided plenty of evidence of the men's experiences in handling livestock; many of the applicants were in fact taking animal husbandry courses or were studying veterinary science, suggesting that the burden of proof for showing a range of relevant skills was higher for this group than it was for regular crews.[53]

The selected men ultimately sailed together on a Poland-bound ship, SS *Creighton Victory*, from Pier X in Newport News, Virginia, on July 4, 1946, with 214 horses and 590 cattle aboard.[54] During their sailing the men followed a special educational plan that focused on topics like Christian ecumenicalism, contemporary labor issues, the transformation of rural areas by modern technology, and world peace. In Poland the men bonded over their shared grief about war's destructive capacity and their sympathy for the people. This experiment was deemed a success by the Fellowship, the cowboys, and, ultimately, by UNRRA. Cowboy crews became formally integrated after that.[55]

Each man who was offered a job on an UNRRA ship as a cattle attendant had to undergo a physical exam. The exam was generally regarded as tough, and men had to pay for it out of their own pockets.[56] Men had to be free of communicable diseases, and certain medical conditions—epilepsy, asthma, and mental illness, for example—were reasons for rejection. In addition, men could not be less than five feet tall or more than six feet three inches in height, and "marked obesity" would also disqualify a man from the job. Immunizations for smallpox, typhoid, typhus, and tetanus were required. All men applying for the position of animal tender needed to possess a birth certificate and a social security number.[57]

Though there were a couple of voices advocating for women to become attendants, women were not in fact permitted to work on the UNRRA ships. As Ruth Steenburgh, secretary to John Nevin Sayre of the Fellowship of Reconciliation (an interfaith peace and social justice organization that was part of the Heifer Project), commented wryly in a letter to Dan West in May 1947, as UNRRA was winding down its operations, "I still can't help but feel that a boatload of bovines managed by such lovely (ahem) girls as we have here at 2929 [2929 Broadway in NYC, the address of the Fellowship's headquarters] would be an asset not only to the cows themselves but to the girls."[58] At any rate, to work on an UNRRA ship a person needed to become a nominal member of the Merchant Marine—then under the jurisdiction of the Coast Guard—and women were not permitted to be Merchant Mariners at this time.[59] The National Maritime Union, led by Joseph Curran, facilitated the special recognition that the men needed in order to allow them to do the UNRRA work; the cowboys carried Coast Guard papers. That this particular group of men, recruited and managed by the BSC, was acceptable to the Maritime Union was important; the union's approval came easily in this instance.[60] For their service in the Merchant Marine, cattle tenders were paid a penny per month as a formality.[61]

Men submitted their applications for a seagoing cowboy position directly to the BSC and specifically to Benjamin G. Bushong. Bushong was the main administrator of the cowboys program, and in this capacity he worked closely with UNRRA on sorting out the logistics that the movement of thousands of men and livestock animals required. But Bushong occupied many other roles as well. He was an active layman in the Church of the Brethren, a friend of Dan West, a dairy farmer from Lancaster County, Pennsylvania, and a member of the Pennsylvania Guernsey Breeders' Association who, as has been said about him, "knew cattle and the Brethren."[62] Bushong also served as the second executive director of the Heifer Project Committee. He occupied this role until 1951, well beyond the end date of the UNRRA–Heifer Project partnership.[63]

It was Bushong's name on the correspondence between the seagoing cowboys program and the men hired for the job. It was also Bushong's name on the notes of thanks that the men received at the end of their trips along with their payment.[64] Bushong's secretary was Carol Maxine Stine West, whose father, Ora W. Stine, played an important part in the Heifer Project's beginnings and its evolution through the UNRRA period (and beyond). Carol—who married Kenneth L. West (a distant relative of Dan West) in June 1947—handled the administrative details of the program at the New Windsor offices of the BSC.[65]

The initial letter that Bushong sent to men who had been hired as seagoing cowboys reflected the same Christian ideals that had guided recruitment efforts the whole way along. "It is the purpose of the Brethren Service Committee," Bushong wrote, "to be creative and Christian in all its endeavors, and in this effort your interests, thoughts and actions will be guided accordingly." Bushong continued by advising the new hires, "It becomes each member of your group to exercise a tolerant, patient and sympathetic attitude in whatever situation you find yourself. We must, first of all, practice brotherhood in our own group, then into all the world. Every attendant is expected to be a gentleman, and a messenger of good will. As such you are going forth in the name of Christ."[66] Bushong and the BSC appealed to men's sense of Christian service and (at least among the actively Christian recruits) assumed an understanding of the responsibilities the men owed to their faith and their religious communities—and not just to abstract notions of humanitarian relief—to do this good work. One Brethren cowboy named Wayne Brant said that, for him, the trip was in fact an expression of faith.[67] Being a cowboy was not just about usefulness and civic service and helping others; it was also about showing a supreme loyalty to God and about serving God through good works.[68]

But being a Christian cowboy from the peace churches was also about showing the state what those churches were capable of in this critical postwar moment. Participation in postwar relief efforts was a choice to incorporate the service impulse, publicly and consciously, into the peace churches' identity in a deeper way.[69] Cowboy Byron P. Royer recalled Bushong's instructions to a group of outgoing cowboys that was about to participate in the oath ritual at the Coast Guard Office before starting their work as cowboys. Rather than swearing an oath to the Constitution of the United States to do the assigned work, the Brethren chose (as was their custom) to "affirm" their commitment instead. Bushong reminded each man to be proud of his Brethren heritage as he made his affirmation and to carry himself at that moment—with pride and resolve—in the same way that "a soldier representing the United States" would carry himself.[70]

Seagoing Cowboys as Conscientious Objectors

Similar ideas about the need to fulfill obligations and to make sacrifices in ways that the times demanded had informed the peace churches' approach to wartime conscription. That the United States introduced a Conscientious Objector status during the war, and that peace church members could apply for this classification, is directly relevant to this history of UNRRA, the Heifer Project, and the seagoing cowboys. Of the almost 7,000 seagoing cowboys, 366 (or approximately 5 percent of the total) undertook their work on an UNRRA ship while they were still Conscientious Objectors. These men were part of the Civilian Public Service, the alternative service system established by the American government. An additional number of Conscientious Objectors joined the seagoing cowboys program *after* they had been released from the CPS, and others still joined the program as registered Conscientious Objectors who were nevertheless not in the CPS because they were on a farm deferment or because they were registered students.[71] All of this shows the extent to which the history of conscientious objection and the history of the partnership between UNRRA and the BSC (and humanitarian work more generally) intersect in revealing ways. The very fact that the government created a program for Conscientious Objectors—largely as a response to intense lobbying on the part of the peace churches—was incredibly important to those communities and shaped their conception of themselves as Americans both during the war and then, significantly, after.[72] That the peace churches ran most of the camps for Conscientious Objectors, moreover, provided the church administrators with additional experience in organizing and mobilizing their communities. This set up the peace churches for a quick transition toward a new kind of service once the war ended; to some extent it facilitated the Heifer Project and also the partnership with UNRRA that produced the seagoing cowboys program.

Each of the peace churches had long maintained an antiwar or pacifist stand, though there were differences in how each one interpreted pacifism and what obligations came with the definition, and there were even differences within denominations. Some Mennonites, for example, subscribed to a definition of pacifism that was based primarily on a literal reading of the New Testament. Jesus's directives to "love your enemies" (Matt. 5:39, 44) and to "put your sword back in its place" (Matt. 26:53) were (and are) taken literally by some Mennonites and applied on both the personal and the state levels. God's word and possessing a "Christian conscience" are, for many Mennonites, the final arbiter of right and wrong; the privilege of interpretation is neither the state's nor that of any single political voice. Others translated Jesus's exhortations differently and argued that they applied on an individual level only or that they would be relevant only in some future time when Jesus ruled the world. Still others, particularly Quakers, tended toward a nonliteralist but nevertheless firm commitment to "the spirit of biblical teachings on love and nonresistance."[73]

Regardless of the specific reasons for their opposition to war, it was this opposition that, in part, had driven the Brethren, Mennonites, and Quakers out of their European homes to what was called the New World centuries ago. In North America the peace church denominations were generally loyal to the state, which they regarded as a useful mechanism for maintaining law and order for the collective, but tensions developed when the state asked the peace church members to obey the state before obeying God. War was a time when, according to the peace churches, the state overstepped its authority by asking citizens to go against their firmly held beliefs. From the churches' perspective, the matter of conscientious objection was not addressed in a satisfactory fashion during the First World War, and though exemptions from military service were possible at that time, it was not entirely clear what the exemptions meant, and, at any rate, the alternative service options were loosely defined and extremely limited.[74]

The unresolved conscription issue during the First World War, plus the simple fact that wars undeniably caused pain and suffering, sparked the peace churches' interest in relief work. As we have seen, the American Friends Service Committee had formed in the context of the First World War, in 1917, to coordinate relief efforts undertaken by the Quakers. Quakers offered essential assistance to the war's victims. Similarly, the Mennonites organized relief through the Mennonite Central Committee. Shortly after the committee's founding in 1920, Mennonites worked in Russia, where a devastating famine was unfolding. During the interwar years and into the early part of World War II, the Mennonites also worked in England, France, India, Paraguay, and Spain.[75] As one prominent Mennonite explained, "Through relief service we are able to express our sense of responsibility for and our sense of unity with our fellow human beings. We feel that we need to bring food, clothing, and shelter to those in distress, but far more important than even such vital material assistance is the opportunity to share the burden of suffering of another, to aid him to recover his sense of self-respect and integrity, and to help restore a faith in love and goodwill through a practical demonstration of human sympathy and brotherhood."[76] These sentiments would be reflected in postwar relief work as well.

The Brethren, for their part, had participated in relief efforts organized by one of the other agencies (as in Spain where the Brethren worked with the Friends in the late 1930s) before the formal establishment of the BSC in 1941. With the creation of their own relief organization, the Brethren were ready to take on independent projects, and the first major one of these would be the Heifer Project. By the time of the Second World War, then, the three historic American peace churches had already developed skills in relief provision and had formed some important links with each other and with the government. These links would grow stronger still during the war when the question of Conscientious Objector status again came to the forefront.

With the announcement in 1940 of the Selective Training and Service Act, which ushered in the first military draft in peacetime in American history, the BSC, the American Friends Service Committee, and the Mennonite Central Committee together established a National Service Board for Religious Objectors (NSBRO). The role of NSBRO was to act as the point of contact between the various churches that had members opposed to military service while also functioning as the liaison between the churches and Selective Service (that is, the US government). Instead of having to deal with multiple religious organizations, the government dealt with just a single agency: NSBRO. For its part NSBRO represented an important next step in the peace churches working together on a common goal. Paul Comly French, a Quaker, well-known journalist, and antiwar activist, was the board's first executive secretary from the institution's creation at the end of 1940 through to 1947. M. R. Zigler, the first executive secretary of the BSC from 1941 to 1948 and the man instrumental in organizing the logistics of the Brethren's partnership with UNRRA, was the chairman, and Orie O. Miller from the Mennonite Central Committee was vice chairman (Miller and the MCC represented all Mennonite congregations in NSBRO as well as the Amish). Eventually, NSBRO would include dozens of other denominations (like Methodists, Catholics, and Jews, for example), in addition to its three founding churches.[77]

According to the Selective Training and Service Act of 1940, American men who fell between stipulated age ranges (the age ranges were adjusted once America entered the war) were required to register with their local draft board. Once drafted, there were five options: accept military service; apply for Conscientious Objector status and, if successful, agree to serve under military command in a noncombatant role, especially in medical units (I-A-O status); apply for Conscientious Objector status and refuse to serve under military command, opting instead to serve in the government-sanctioned alternative service program, CPS (IV-E status); apply for a deferment for farm work or for status as a full-time (meaning year-round) ministerial student; and, lastly, not even register with the draft board and serve a prison term instead (the majority of those who opted for this were Jehovah's Witnesses).[78]

Draft boards reviewed men's applications and decided whether requests for Conscientious Objector status were warranted or not. It was more straightforward for men from the historic peace churches, where nonviolence and conscientious objection formed a recognized and clear part of the teachings, than it was for men from other religions that permitted but did not require commitments to nonviolence, or for those whose opposition to war was ideological, political, and broadly humanitarian rather than religious (most such objections were on the extreme political left). In fact applicants were required to demonstrate that "religious training and belief" accounted for their objection to military service; the right to conscientious objection formed a part of America's commitment to *religious* freedom specifically. After all, President Roosevelt had named freedom of religion as one of the four "essential human freedoms" during his January 1941 State of the Union address to Congress, alongside freedom of speech, freedom from fear, and, as we have seen, freedom from want. Lewis Blaine Hershey, the director of Selective Service (all the way through to the Vietnam War), even if he may have been personally indifferent to the spiritual aspects of conscientious objection, nevertheless believed that the CPS system stood as an important example of American democracy and its respect for religious minorities.[79] The preamble of the United Nations Charter would similarly reflect a commitment to religious tolerance and its importance to maintaining "international peace and security."[80]

The most relevant Selective Service classification for the BSC was IV-E, which referred to alternative service under the CPS program. A total of 11,996 men were recognized as Conscientious Objectors with an IV-E classification. The classification entitled men to go into a CPS base camp and to do "work of national importance under civilian direction" as an alternative to military service.[81] The government supplied the camp site, the facilities, and the equipment needed for the work projects, but it was not typically involved in daily operations of the camp, and it did not compensate the men for their work, cover the costs of their basic necessities—food, utilities, clothes, bedding, and toiletry kits, for example—or give financial assistance to their dependents.[82] The majority of the camps were thus administered and supported financially by the Mennonite Central Committee, the American Friends Service Committee, and the BSC (though a smaller number of camps were maintained by other denominations too). Most of the men in the camps (almost 60 percent) were members of the peace churches; the Mennonites were the most numerous with over four thousand men or approximately 40 percent of the total. The Brethren constituted 8 percent of the men in CPS (over one thousand men), and the Friends 10 percent of the total number of men in CPS camps (or 951 men).[83]

By the end of the war, the three founding peace churches of NSBRO had contributed several million dollars to sustain men in the CPS program.[84] The churches explained these enormous costs in a couple of ways. The financial burden, they believed, would show the government and the American public just how many sacrifices church members were willing to make for their beliefs.[85] M. R. Zigler of the Brethren appealed to "every family of our brotherhood" and exhorted them to "recheck their giving to discover whether or not adequate testimony has been made." From Zigler's perspective, contributions to the financial costs associated with sustaining peace church men in CPS camps thus became "a testimony of appreciation to the United States government."[86] This would also ideally fend off accusations that decisions around conscientious objection had been taken lightly or that the men in CPS were spoiled and coddled while other American men died in the war effort. Instead, the peace churches hoped their management of the CPS camps would reveal that their members could be both American patriots—men who accepted fully that they had a national and collective obligation to fulfill—and pacifists simultaneously.[87]

Second, the peace churches argued that a church-funded and church-administered camp system would allow for the provision of religious, spiritual, and educational programming that reflected the values and priorities of the given denomination while creating a suitable social milieu for like-minded men.[88] In practice this meant that the camps served an explicit educational purpose. For example, "specialized schools" that focused on topics relevant to the denominations (like pacifism) were set up at select Brethren-managed CPS camps to fill men's leisure time.[89] M. R. Zigler specifically asked the men in the specialized schools to think in concrete ways about some topical questions: how to "wage peace" in times of war, how to build a just and peaceful world, and how to influence the development of a "Christian society of nations." Zigler's call "to settle disputes between nations and classes without going to war or using violent methods" echoed UNRRA's frequent references to cooperation between nations as one way to foster lasting peace.[90]

The men in the CPS were arguably well placed to contribute to postwar humanitarian aid programming. A special CPS unit designed to train men for reconstruction work in liberated territories was started as early as 1942, though opposition from politicians and the public to employing Conscientious Objectors as relief workers abroad thwarted the endeavor; the work was seen as too easy during wartime.[91] Once the war ended, sentiment changed, and so did the needs of the Heifer Project and of course UNRRA. Men who were still in the CPS who were interested in becoming seagoing cowboys could ask permission from Selective Service to leave the posting they were already in (meaning the CPS camp to which they were assigned), seek permission to transfer to a special CPS Reserve Unit (Camp #152), and take up work as a livestock handler on an UNRRA ship.[92]

Initially, Selective Service only considered a small number of men from CPS for a special posting with the BSC in the seagoing cowboys program: those who had joined the CPS during the one-year period from June 16, 1943, to June 15, 1944. In 1946, the rules were changed so that any man assigned to the CPS on or before October 31, 1944, was eligible to become a cattleman so long as he had completed at least eighteen months in the service.[93] These choices were made to limit the number of applicants in manageable ways and then to expand the number of eligible men when the need for greater numbers presented itself.[94] UNRRA and the BSC (as the day-to-day administrator of the seagoing cowboys program) were directly involved in negotiating for adjustments to the number of men released. For example, the director of UNRRA's Agricultural Rehabilitation Division, Edwin R. Henson, was the one who asked Col. Lewis F. Kosch, the assistant director of Camp Operations in the Selective Service System, to release more men from the CPS camps when more men were needed in 1946. Kosch was in fact willing to release another one hundred men, but only on the condition that Paul French, executive secretary of NSBRO, report back to Selective Service with confirmations that the men who had already been released for the program had in fact made the intended trips on cattle ships. Men who had been released from camps to work on the cattle boats but who failed to show up for those sailings would be reassigned to another CPS camp.[95] In the end, 366 CPS men were approved by Selective Service to join the CPS Reserve Unit and to leave the United States with the seagoing cowboys program.[96] Of these 366 men, 154 were Mennonites, 62 were Brethren, 46 were Friends, and the remainder were from other denominations, including the Methodists.[97] Of the 366, 91 made two trips as cowboys, 18 made three trips, 2 made four trips, and the remaining 255 made a single trip.[98]

Men in the CPS could also be discharged in the regular way, when their time came, and then they could go on to become cattlemen if they chose to do so; these men are not included in the 366 men that became seagoing cowboys while they were still in the CPS. Demobilization for Conscientious Objectors was initially slower than for those in active military service and happened in stages, with men over forty-five the first to be discharged. Like in the regular armed forces, general discharges were based on a point system and on calculations that took into account age, time served, and whether the Conscientious Objector had a dependent child. The very last discharges occurred a good year and a half after the war ended, in March 1947, when the last CPS camps closed and as UNRRA was concluding its aid shipments.[99]

The CPS was a formative and important experience for the peace churches. The peace churches had cooperated with one another during the formation and execution of the CPS, and the links (both personal and administrative) that were established in setting up and administering the CPS were quickly and usefully mobilized for new cooperation in the Heifer Project and in the seagoing cowboys program in the immediate postwar period. There was also the useful hands-on experience that some of the men received in their CPS postings—on dairy farms, for example, where the work was applicable to their new temporary positions as livestock tenders.

But most importantly, the experience of the CPS shaped the churches' understanding of their faith and of their position in American society. It also affirmed their potential to "do good" and cemented the view that "helping" formed a fundamental part of their faith. Relief work had to be handled carefully, and it needed to be undertaken for the right reasons; its primary purpose had to remain focused on helping people that needed the help. But relief work also increased goodwill and cross-cultural understanding, and it strengthened a sense of connection with others; it reflected the responsibility humans owed one another. Professor Henry A. Fast, vice-chair of the Mennonite Central Committee from the mid-1940s, contemplated the importance of the CPS to Mennonite development specifically. Fast summarized, "The CPS program has turned out to be a tremendous venture of Christian faith and Christian concern. . . . It is tremendously important now that men in CPS, as they begin to scatter, keep their vision clear, their faith burning with a steady flame, and their spirit of Christian love aglow with deep compassion and a keen sensitivity to the cries of human need. God has opened doors of opportunity to men in CPS and to the constituencies from which they come."[100] There were even remarkable suggestions that the best elements of the CPS could be rebranded after the war and used to create a new CPS: a Christian Public Service instead of the Civilian Public Service. The president of Bethel College, a Mennonite institution in Kansas, proposed this idea at a conference for directors of MCC-administered CPS camps in September 1945. President Kaufman referred to "the unfinished task of CPS" and looked ahead to the many "opportunities for service" that would exist in the postwar world.[101]

That the CPS remained significant in some circles after the war was perhaps shaped, too, by the other important work that CPS men completed during the war itself. Most notable here is the participation of thirty-six men from the CPS in the University of Minnesota Starvation Experiment. The experiment ran from late 1944 until the end of 1945, just as the magnitude of the food crisis in Europe was becoming apparent. Its purpose was to learn about the physical and psychological effects of starvation on the human body and about what diets might work best to "nutritionally rehabilitate" starving people. Men from the CPS who volunteered for the experiment had responded to ads that enticed their participation with the simple and direct question, "Will You Starve That They May Be Better Fed?"[102]

During the experiment the volunteers were semistarved under strict conditions for six months, such that they lost about a quarter of their body weight. The men's moods, motivations, preoccupations, and anxieties were carefully charted. Then they were rehabilitated over a period of three months.[103] Fifteen of the volunteers (42 percent) were from the peace churches, and others came from related Protestant denominations. The Minnesota Starvation Experiment, in turn, had a direct connection to the BSC (and by extension to both the seagoing cowboys program and the Heifer Project) through seven of its participants who later became seagoing cowboys.[104] In a more general sense, the connection also stemmed from a shared interest in the problem of hunger. In the summer of 1946, a Heifer Project office in Southern California republished an article by a participant in the Minnesota Experiment titled "How Does It Feel to Be Hungry?" The article, written by Harold T. Lutz, appeared in a Heifer Project newsletter called *Heifer Moos*. Lutz described what he experienced during the experiment and indicated how proud he was of work that, he wrote, "helped the government and other agencies make the best use of the food they are sending to starving people abroad."[105] The very fact that the Minnesota Starvation Experiment drew the interest of at least one Heifer Project office shored up connections between different contemporary approaches to "helping the hungry."

Ancel Keys of the Laboratory of Physical Hygiene at the University of Minnesota was the director of the Starvation Experiment. Keys's full scientific report on his findings would not be ready until 1950, when it was published as *The Biology of Human Starvation*. A preliminary manual that summarized the experiment's general findings was published in 1946, however. Titled *Men and Hunger: A Psychological Manual for Relief Workers*, it was published by the Brethren Publishing House in Elgin, Illinois.[106] A note titled "From the Sponsors" precedes the main text of *Men and Hunger* and was written by none other than M. R. Zigler of the BSC; Zigler was of course an important administrator in the Brethren's work with UNRRA on the seagoing cowboys program. In his note Zigler praised Keys's work for showing the psychological effects of "physiological need." As Zigler wrote, "Many of the so-called American characteristics—abounding energy, generosity, optimism—become intelligible as the expected behavior response of a well-fed people."[107]

Men and Hunger appeared as a tool for humanitarian relief workers to understand their subjects better and thus to do their jobs more effectively and with greater compassion. It gave imprimatur to what the manual's authors, Harold Steere Guetzkow and Paul Hoover Bowman, referred to as "the importance of ministering to the psychological needs of people in distress."[108] Bowman was himself a professional relief worker associated at one time with the American Friends Service Committee and more recently with the BSC. Guetzkow was a psychologist.[109] Their religiously inflected description of relief work—as "ministering"—is perhaps unsurprising given that the Church of the Brethren, the American Friends Service Committee, and the Mennonite Central Committee were all among the official sponsors of the experiment. The National Dairy Council was also a sponsor of the Minnesota Experiment.[110]

Of the three peace churches involved in the CPS, it was the Friends who expressed some reservations about postwar relief work generally and especially about linking it explicitly to expressions of faith. Already at the start of 1945, the Friends adopted the position that "relief work is not a vocation" and that after the war men from the CPS "should prepare themselves for their life-time vocation rather than for any short-term relief job." Part of the argument was that the men's value as relief workers would be all the greater only once they were experienced in their own professions.[111] In various statements issued toward the end of the war, the Friends were very clear about their opposition to relief work that was too technical and businesslike. They objected to using relief work for skills development as well; they did not want "human tragedy" to become a "training ground for persons wanting experience."[112]

Building the Crews

Once men accepted jobs as seagoing cowboys, the program office in New Windsor got to work assembling crews for specific scheduled sailings. Men could request to be with a specific group, with other men they knew from church or from school, or with men that were in some way part of their extended families or communities. Supervisors also had the ability to weigh in on the crew composition.[113]

Melvin Gingerich was the livestock supervisor on SS *Stephen R. Mallory*'s 1946 maiden sailing as a livestock boat to Poland. Gingerich had grown up on a farm in Iowa and had experience with livestock animals; he was thus especially well placed to oversee care for the more than eight hundred horses aboard his assigned sailing. At the time Gingerich worked as a professor in the Department of History and Government at Bethel College. He was also a committed Mennonite pacifist who later in his career would write about the history of the Mennonites, the CPS, and the various postwar relief projects in which the Mennonites were involved, including the Heifer Project and the seagoing cowboys program. As part of his research on the seagoing cowboys in the late 1950s, Gingerich sent short questionnaires to some of the Mennonite men who had worked on the UNRRA ships. Men provided basic biographical information and included reflections on different parts of their trips, including the sailings themselves and the time spent in the target countries. They answered questions about any problems that they, as Christians, had faced on their trip; how the trips contributed to their religious lives; and what "instances of Christian witnessing" (meaning prayer services or Sunday school, for example) they engaged in on the trip. These questionnaires, which run a couple of pages each, help inform what we know about both the seagoing cowboys program and the Heifer Project.[114]

Both UNRRA and the BSC were eager to have Gingerich (and men like him) occupy the supervisor's role on the live animal sailings. Members of Mennonite and related congregations also liked the choice and saw Gingerich as an exemplary role model for the younger men. In a memoir written in the late 1990s, Melvin's son Owen (later the world-renowned astronomer Owen Gingerich) said it was "the confidence the parents had in my father" that in part accounts for their willingness to allow their teenaged sons to become seagoing cowboys in the first place.[115] When Joe Byler, who would become the director of relief for the Mennonite Central Committee, learned that Gingerich would be leading a crew, he asked that his own son Delmar be included in the group.[116] Delmar would eventually sail to Poland on a special all-Mennonite crew that Gingerich organized. (As it would turn out, Gingerich's crew would be combined with another all-Mennonite crew that had been planned at the same time by Walter Oswald, a Mennonite professor from Hesston College.)[117]

Initially, the BSC had tried to find a "cowboy pastor" to accompany every animal shipment. The idea was that pastors would organize religious programming aboard the ships and act as counselors and role models for the cowboys. Recruiting for this specialized job was done through a letter from the BSC to over one hundred seminaries encouraging students of theology to apply for the position (some of the students did just that).[118] But it proved impossible to recruit the large numbers needed. This was yet another reason that Christian husbands and fathers of a certain age (like Gingerich, born in 1902) made excellent alternatives. Men like this, as Bushong himself said, would be sure to remind the younger men of the greater purposes implicit in relief work. After all, though the primary purpose of the trips was to facilitate getting essential material aid to those that needed it, a secondary goal, when possible, was to preserve a "Christian attitude and ideal in the livestock program" and in the postwar aid effort more generally. These relief trips provided a unique opportunity to build a sense of community among the Christian men on the sailings and to reinforce their collective values; they constituted an investment in the future of Christian aid-giving.[119]

Supervisors were expected to fulfill several roles simultaneously. Gingerich described some of these: "I have had to be the first aid man, public relations adjuster, spiritual counselor, personnel manager, efficiency expert, and farm hand."[120] Some supervisors took the initiative and prepared for their roles well ahead of time by communicating expectations to their crews well in advance, even before departure. Gingerich, for example, sent his crew detailed instructions and tips while the men were still waiting for the call to leave home. He even included a packing list, which recommended bringing work clothing and one old suit, a good padlock for the ship's locker, a song book, a magazine, a joke book, a game, and, of course, the Bible.[121] Martin Cohnstadt, another supervisor on a Poland-bound ship organized by the Fellowship of Christian Churchmen, specifically asked that the men in his group make some contribution to the recreational life of the collective by bringing games, magazines, or musical instruments.[122]

In his correspondence with his crew, Gingerich also reminded the men of the moral dangers they would face during the trip, and he tried to prepare them to withstand temptations that they were sure to confront.[123] Safeguarding and protecting the moral health of the young Christian cowboys was the most worrying part of the job for Paul Erb, editor of the Mennonite *Gospel Herald* from Scottsdale, Pennsylvania, and a supervisor on a 1946 sailing.[124]

For all these reasons and in all these varied ways, the BSC's seagoing cowboys inhabited a very different world from the one that the more familiar "American cowboys" inhabited. Though it is not clear who first used the name "seagoing cowboys," we do know that the men applied this name to themselves and that the contemporary press used it too.[125] The word "cowboy" comes from the Spanish *vaquero*. *Vaquero* describes a man whose job it was to ride horseback and manage beef cattle herds grazing across large tracts of land. *Vaquero*, in turn, comes from the Spanish *vacca* or cow; the cow as a species was introduced to the Americas by the Spanish. In the absence of adequate rail connections throughout much of the nineteenth century, cowboys were responsible for physically moving herds from Texas and other areas where land and cattle were plentiful to shipping points like those in Kansas and Missouri. From those destinations the animals would travel by rail to the populous northern states and meet the growing demand for meat.[126]

By the twentieth century, American cowboys had become the quintessential symbols of white American working-class masculinity, and this even though about a quarter of all cowboys were African Americans. Cowboys became the iconic men of the American frontier: tough and rugged horseback-riding individualists who valued freedom and independence and who obeyed few laws (but operated under a strict if opaque moral code).[127]

The cowboys recruited by the BSC, and particularly the smaller subgroup of men who were from denominations that worked with the Heifer Project, belied the American cowboy stereotype. Their farm experience, if they had it, tended to be on smaller dairy farms rather than on beef cattle farms, and this meant that they did not typically roam the American frontier in the way that "real" cowboys did. Besides, many of the recruits had never even ridden a horse and would have been lost on the frontier; the peace church men tended to come from the Midwest and the East rather than from the great open plains of the American West. The seagoing cowboys did not dress the part either; instead of cowboy boots and a cowboy hat, jeans, chaps, and bandanas, the Heifer Project cowboys wore regular work clothes and packed a suit, just in case, on their ocean voyages. They did not carry rifles or fight "Indians" in the battle for the American West in the familiar way portrayed in Hollywood westerns. And while we cannot say whether "most" of the seagoing cowboys personally eschewed violence and weapons or whether they rejected alcohol and cigarettes, we do know that the BSC leadership certainly did and that they encouraged all the men that they had recruited to do so too. The group of religiously motivated cowboys were the very opposite of the "drunken sots and beach combers" that the Brethren said usually made up cattle crews on ships.[128] These new cowboys were men who followed rules, recognized on-the-job hierarchies, and worked as part of a well-ordered team to achieve a collective goal and to "help." Their identities as Christian men had to a greater or lesser extent motivated their entry into the global public sphere in the first place (just as at various times women's sense of Christian duty challenged the separate-spheres ideology and facilitated their increasingly public roles).[129] Theirs was a forceful expression of modern peace church masculinity.

While seagoing cowboys were not typical cowboys, they nevertheless represented something quintessentially American. Even the name "seagoing cowboy" conveyed an adventurous and bold American spirt; the cowboys were different kinds of pioneers. UNRRA Director General Lehman had framed the success of UNRRA's live animal program as partly the cowboys' success; it was America, after all, that had made space for the religious convictions of the BSC and the peace church cowboys. When they crossed the ocean, the men sailed with American values, privileges, and freedoms in full view.[130] Each type of cowboy—the seagoing cowboys recruited by the BSC as well as the real and imagined cowboys of the American West—symbolized something of America's commitment to freedom: freedom of movement on the one hand and religious freedom on the other. The best-known seagoing cowboys (meaning the ones we have records for) embodied a Christian masculine identity that, while it did not make them media celebrities and the stars of Hollywood films, nevertheless transformed them into heroes at the local or community levels and brought positive attention to the churches from which they came. The men's stories, and the broader history of cooperation between the BSC and UNRRA, remain extremely important to the peace churches, the Brethren in particular, even today. The very fact that we know so much about the experiences of cowboys from the peace churches reflects this. Men talked and spoke frequently about their seagoing cowboy days upon their return to America. Their communities were attentive listeners.

Chapter 4

Working Animals as Humanitarian Aid

In the previous chapter, we saw how men became cowboys, and now we turn to examining how animals became aid. Just as there were concrete reasons for preferring certain kinds of men to work as seagoing cowboys, so there were specific reasons for selecting certain species for UNRRA's agricultural relief program and for the Brethren's Heifer Project. The answers are at once obvious and nuanced.

Cattle were one of the two main species included in the UNRRA livestock program and the only species included in the Brethren's Heifer Project. This choice had a lot to do with what cattle could offer recipients in a very practical way: female cattle were a source of milk, which had both economic and nutritional value, and male cattle were useful as light draft animals that were essential to restarting agricultural production in destroyed countries. While the Heifer Project did not deal in horses, UNRRA did send horses abroad, for the simple reason that horses were considered the most valuable draft animals. The agricultural reconstruction that UNRRA envisioned could not be achieved without them. The first several sections of this chapter are about cattle; the final one is about horses.

Europa and the Bull

Cattle are mammals that belong to the order Artiodactyla, meaning they have an even number of toes on each foot and walk on their hoofs. They are ruminant herbivores that are part of the bovid family (Bovidae); sheep, goats, and antelope are part of this family as well. Modern cattle are descended from a wild species of ox called the aurochs, which reached Europe a quarter of a million years ago.[1] In the fifteenth century, there were few aurochs remaining in Europe, with the last of the species concentrated, as it happens, in what is now central and eastern Poland, in the Jaktorów Forest in the Mazowsze region; the Polish Crown had given aurochs in the forest legal protection. The eventual extinction of aurochs, despite these protected lands, was the result of what are now familiar causes for species extinctions: habitat depletion to provide space for other species (in this case for domestic cattle pasture and human expansion), overhunting (notwithstanding the fact that the Crown had restricted hunting), and disease.[2]

The history of modern domestic cattle is intertwined with human history. Cattle had and continue to have economic value as work animals and as "moveable wealth," and cattle were one of the first forms of exchange that humans used.[3] Castrated mature male cattle, or oxen, were particularly valuable because they were strong enough to pull the plow that farmers needed to cultivate fields and develop agriculture. This animal species' reliable labor capacity in turn was one of the factors that allowed sedentary communities to develop. Though they were not as powerful or fast as horses, oxen were relatively inexpensive and easy to acquire. Cattle could also be slaughtered for meat once their ability to work efficiently diminished, and thus their utility lasted throughout their life cycle.[4] Female cattle in turn were prized (and even revered in some cultures) for their ability to provide "maternal nourishment" through their milk. Cattle manure, moreover, was vital for crop fertilization and therefore formed another crucially important factor in the development of agriculture. Cattle hides, too, proved useful for making clothes and shoes and other everyday items. For all of these reasons, cattle had come to signify "civilized life"; their presence was essential to the development of stable and settled societies.[5] The expression "civilization follows the cow" encapsulates these and other reasons for the enormously significant role that cattle have played in human history.[6]

Cattle's economic importance has been reflected symbolically over the centuries in art, literature, and myth. Indeed, it is a bull (an uncastrated male bovine) that is at the center of the founding myth of the European continent itself. The story goes that the Greek god Zeus was so enamored of Europa, a beautiful Phoenician princess, that he transformed himself into a gentle white bull and, using this animal form, charmed Europa. Europa's trust was misplaced, however, and as soon as the princess climbed onto the white bull's back, she was whisked away to the sea. Together Europa and the bull reached the island of Crete, and there Europa gave birth to three sons of Zeus, including Minos, the legendary ruler of Crete and founder of what is regarded as Europe's first advanced civilization. Minoan civilization spread from Crete across the Aegean into what is now mainland Greece, foreshadowing the later spread of civilizations even further north and west across the European continent. Ancient Greeks referred to these lands as "Europa"—and thus the continent came to be called Europe after Europa.[7]

This ancient myth of the continent's founding has been a part of European culture for centuries, and it remains well known to this day. Notably, *Europa Riding the Bull* is the name of a sculpture that sits in front of the European Parliament building in Strasbourg, France, and similar iconography appears in other European Union art and advertising. The Greek design on the two-euro coin features Europa sitting on a bull and recalls the ancient past that links "old Europe" with the new Europe represented by the European Union.[8]

Part of what makes the Europa-and-the-bull metaphor so enduring is its malleability. Scholar Ian Manners has suggested a distinctively postwar reading of the myth in which Zeus raping Europa recalls the violence of the Third Reich while it also evokes the idea of rebirth; Europe became a phoenix rising from the ashes of war. Just as Europa's ordeal with Zeus signaled a new beginning, so it was that the foundations for European unity began to take shape once the war's destructive force was subdued. An alternative reading of the relevance of the Europa myth, as Manners has also suggested, is to understand Zeus and the bull as the United States. America crosses the ocean, comes to Europe's rescue during the war, and liberates the continent from years of violence and oppression while showering it with gifts as it creates the conditions for a new and better life.[9] The bull brought peace, prosperity, and civilization.

Far away from Europe, on the other side of the ocean in the middle of the twentieth century, the Brethren had their own understandings of cattle's symbolic and concrete importance. Cows' ability to produce a constant supply of tasty milk, and thereby to deliver much-needed fat, protein, vitamins, and minerals (especially to children), cemented female cattle's high status in Brethren communities. Many Brethren were dairy farmers whose livelihoods depended on healthy cattle populations and high milk yields, and Brethren confidence in milk's nutritional value had largely motivated the formation of the Heifer Project. It was therefore no surprise that in rural communities in the Midwest, in the heart of dairy country, enthusiasm for the Heifer Project was very high.[10]

Like the Brethren, UNRRA, too, believed that the solution to postwar "hunger problems" rested with female cattle. UNRRA's strategy, as scholar

Frank Trentmann states plainly, "can be summarised in one word: milk."[11] Given this, we turn in the next section to the story of milk specifically, to examining how and why milk became so important to Americans, to the Brethren, to the Heifer Project, and to UNRRA.

Cattle and the Mid-Century "Gospel of Milk"

Milk is "fun to think with."[12] All mammals produce milk for their young. But humans are the only species that drinks the milk of another species and the only one that drinks it past the weaning stage. The human consumption of milk from other species developed in ancient times along with the domestication of milk-producing animals like cows, sheep, goats, and camels. The milk of these animals gave humans relatively easy and portable access to nutrition, which was especially important in times of scarcity. Milk consists mostly of water (85 percent), and the remainder is made up of fats, milk sugars (like lactose), proteins (like casein), and various vitamins and minerals.[13]

Conditions in America, particularly the availability of vast amounts of space for pasture lands, had long favored cattle, and dairying operations had expanded throughout New England and the Midwest as the United States formed. Moreover, cattle's status as "clean" animals in Judeo-Christian (and Islamic) traditions, and the relative ease with which cows could be milked, raised their value further still.[14] Milk thus became a nourishing American food staple.[15]

Preference for milk carried a nationalist element, too. Abigail Adams, for example, who was married to President John Adams, supported the colonial boycott of "foreign tea" as early as 1777 explicitly in favor of milk from local dairy cattle.[16] Milk was celebrated for its abundant health properties as well. In the mid-nineteenth century, milk enjoyed the status of a "liquid food," and some contemporaries referred to milk as "white meat" that would even bring wounded soldiers back to health. In other contexts, milk was known simply as "the chief food of sick folks."[17]

Milk in the early days was unpasteurized and came with risks, however: it spoiled quickly, particularly in warmer regions and in an era before reliable refrigeration was widely available. Far from healing the sick, milk could cause serious illness. Sometimes it was adulterated deliberately with cheap and dangerous substances by unethical traders eager to increase volume and thereby increase profits. In other cases, poor hygiene standards and improper handling could lead to milk being contaminated with dangerous bacteria, such as those that cause typhoid fever and scarlet fever.[18] Adulterated or spoiled milk was an important cause of infant mortality well into the nineteenth century. Some people, moreover, were unable to digest the lactose in milk and as a result were made sick when they consumed it.[19]

In addition, milk was initially available only when female animals were lactating, usually in the spring and summer months. This meant that for much of history milk was scarce and expensive, in addition to being occasionally hazardous. That changed in the late nineteenth century with the commercial availability of canned milk; the canning process took a natural product and prepared it in a controlled, regulated, and hygienic environment, thereby stabilizing supplies. Most importantly, the process of pasteurization killed harmful bacteria and disease pathogens. By the time of the Second World War, nearly all commercially available milk in the United States and Britain was pasteurized, making it consistently and reliably safe to consume.[20] This was revolutionary and made milk, as contemporaries frequently said, "pure."[21] The debate about milk as either a "white poison" or a "white elixir" had finally been settled very clearly in milk's favor.[22] Milk had become the king of foods.

Pasteurization and government regulation of milk production, including inspections of farms and milk-processing facilities, played a significant role in increasing milk's popularity, but other factors also contributed to its growth. Milk had influential backers. The National Dairy Council had been established in the United States in 1915, for example, with the intention of celebrating milk's nutritional value and recommending dairy foods to the public. During the First World War, the United States exported condensed milk to a hungry and desperate Europe, and this further raised milk's status as a unique food staple with awesome life-saving potential.[23] Herbert Hoover, head of the American Relief Administration and later president of the United States, regarded milk as an essential relief product.[24] The League of Nations also became a powerful champion of milk. Milk, a report from the League said, was *"the nearest approach we possess to a perfect and complete food, and no other single food is known that can be used as a substitute."*[25] Not surprisingly, dairy farms in both the United States and Britain expanded dramatically during the interwar period to meet consumer demand, and dairying operations became larger and more mechanized. All of this had profound implications for the lived experiences of cows as large-scale milk production paved the way for increased human interventions into cattle breeding.[26] Humans established cycles of impregnation, calving, and lactation, which required the relentless and physically demanding labor of cows.[27]

Nutritional scientists of course also played a central role in these developments that drove the popularity of milk. As we have seen, it was during the first few decades of the twentieth century that nutritional science started providing metrics for measuring and comparing the nutrients in different foods.[28] Leading nutritionists calculated that foods derived from other animal bodies, like milk and dairy, offered human bodies the best combination and range of vitamins (A and D), minerals, and amino acids that promoted "good" physiological growth and function.[29] The prominent biochemist and nutrition scientist Elmer V. McCollum called milk a "protective food," and he actively encouraged Americans to drink it in pursuit of good health. McCollum went even further and linked milk to wealth, modernity, and achievements in culture, politics, and social life; milk consumption was integral to civilization itself. According to McCollum, milk consumption explained why Europeans and North Americans surpassed Asians and "people of the Tropics" (who generally did not drink cow's milk) in a variety of measures, like lifespan, stature, and infant mortality.[30]

Nutritional science established that milk offered beneficial nutrients for all age groups. But milk was absolutely critical for children's development and essential for pregnant and lactating women as well. A 1927 study from the Rowett Research Institute—a prestigious international nutrition research center—found that poor children in Scotland who consumed half a pint of milk daily grew better and were healthier overall; real-world studies confirmed that milk was doing what science said it would do.[31] As a result, government-funded milk programs for children became popular on both sides of the Atlantic during the interwar years.[32] From 1940 the National Milk Scheme in the UK gave pregnant women and new mothers extra milk, and school milk programs that provided a daily dose of milk rose in popularity.[33] John Boyd Orr, the Nobel Prize–winning biologist and "crusading nutritionist" who led the Rowett Institute and was a strong advocate for milk consumption, would go on to become the first director general of the United Nation's Food and Agriculture Organization, which formed after the Second World War. He and Dan West—who of course had been motivated to start the Heifer Project because there had not been enough milk for children in Spain during the civil war—met on at least one occasion to discuss world hunger.[34]

For all these reasons, when Winston Churchill said over a radio broadcast during the Second World War that "there is no finer investment for a community than putting milk into babies," his listeners did not need further explanation or convincing.[35] By this time the "gospel of milk" had been preached for years in the US, the UK, and Canada—the countries that would go on to have the dominant roles in UNRRA—and people had grown accustomed to thinking of milk as a nutritious and essential health-giving food source. Here we return to one of the founding documents of the United

Nations: the Anglo-American Atlantic Charter from 1941, which, as we have seen, identified "freedom from want" as a fundamental right and as one of the ideals for which the Allied Nations were ostensibly fighting. Milk and the bovine bodies that produced the milk became *the* symbols of meeting this goal. The cow and her milk evoked material comfort; they were gifts from the prosperous and politically stable to the politically chaotic and to the war-ravaged. As historian Deborah Valenze has argued, milk had become "the emblem of the people's entitlement to basic sustenance."[36]

Milk and Children

The language of entitlement and fundamental rights was most evident when it was directed at children. The idea that children, as special victims of war, deserved relief before others was already reflected in the First International Declaration of the Rights of the Child, which had been adopted by the League of Nations in 1924. By the Second World War, the child had become a universal figure of innocence that evoked the brutality of conflict and illustrated the war's effects on the most vulnerable in society. Children inspired compassion, and their suffering constituted a special call to action.[37] This was well reflected in Herbert Hoover's 1941 pamphlet, "Can Europe's Children Be Saved?" There Hoover described children's enormous suffering and wrote of the Allies' obligation, as he said, to "prevent a holocaust of death and stunted bodies and minds" in what had been German-occupied areas.[38] In 1945 UNRRA Director Herbert Lehman also spelled out what was at stake by highlighting the needs of children in particular: "The future of the liberated Allied countries and their place in the family of United Nations depends in great measure upon restoration of strength and vigor of the child victims of World War II."[39]

That is where milk again came into the equation. Nutritional science had already established that milk was essential to children's development, such that milk shortages in target countries weighed heavily on UNRRA administrators from the beginning. Dr. H. A. Holle, the chief medical officer of the UNRRA mission to Poland, raised concerns that insufficient milk supplies in the country jeopardized the healthy development of the nation's children; this, in turn, threatened broader rehabilitation goals.[40]

Photographs reinforced just how important milk was to helping war-ravaged children. One such photograph was taken by the American photographer John Vachon. Since the 1930s Vachon had been part of the Farm Security Administration's very active photography unit. The Farm Security

WORKING ANIMALS AS HUMANITARIAN AID   83

Administration was an agency of the US government that had been created in 1937 as part of the New Deal; its goal was to alleviate rural poverty through the provision of loans to families in need and the establishment of assorted training programs and educational initiatives. Just after the war, Vachon was hired by UNRRA's Public Information Office, which included a Visual Information section, to document UNRRA's accomplishments in Poland specifically. Arguably one of the most iconic photographs from the UNRRA period was taken by Vachon (see fig. 1). It depicts three young children standing on the dock in Gdańsk in 1946 or 1947.[41] Each child has lifted a large cup of milk to their lips. The cow that has provided milk to these children has presumably just arrived from America on the ship that fills the background of the image. The ship connects the Polish children and the cups of "white elixir" that they hold in their small hands to the monumental humanitarian efforts of America and the United Nations.

The importance of milk to children was reflected in Brethren relief advertising too. In an article in a 1945 issue of the Brethren's *Gospel Messenger*, Dan West warned people against being stingy with heifer donations. He evoked the specter of starving children when he wrote, "The children who might be

FIGURE 1.   Polish children drinking milk, ca. 1946 or 1947. SS *William Riddle* in background. UN photo by John Vachon. UNRRA 4459, from the United Nations Relief and Rehabilitation Administration Collection, United Nations Archives.

saved by one heifer held back—their blood will be on your hands." West thus encouraged people in his community to give "all the heifers you can spare" to the Heifer Project, and he reassured his audience that a single animal "placed right" could save the lives of "ten babies this winter."[42]

Milk's unique importance to children was well reflected in other examples of the Heifer Project's advertising materials as well. In one pamphlet we see a drawing of a cow and three obviously hungry children approaching the animal. The accompanying text confidently tells the reader that a single cow gives enough milk to maintain twelve children.[43] Here the content of the illustration also reinforced a special imagined bond between children and animals; both were innocents at the mercy of the choices that others made for them.

The connections between cows' milk, children, and the postwar aid effort ran deeper still. Children were portrayed as the most deserving beneficiaries of life-giving aid, to be sure, but the Heifer Project also cast American children as potential givers of aid and therefore as providers of milk to foreign children. Even before the Brethren partnership with UNRRA was confirmed and before the war was formally over, the Heifer Project Committee published a short illustrated booklet called *Heifers for Relief: A Primer*. This booklet was designed to explain and promote the Heifer program to American kids specifically.

Heifers for Relief outlined the various ways that kids could raise money to purchase a heifer—a young animal that, like the kids themselves, was not yet fully grown but that nevertheless could still be useful. The text explained in straightforward terms why heifers were such important relief animals: "If children have no milk to drink, they often cough, and they get sick easily.... When children don't have milk it isn't easy to grow up to be tall and strong men and women." In the United States there were plenty of farmers who raised cows to give milk, the booklet told the kids; cattle were themselves evidence of America's unparalleled privilege in the world. But in other countries, especially those affected by war, farmers had either been killed or imprisoned and their animals had also been killed; as a result, kids there had no milk to drink. America, and American children, were thus uniquely well placed to share their plenty with the less fortunate: "Would you like to help send a heifer calf to hungry children across the ocean? Your heifer would grow into a cow and would give rich milk to make children strong and healthy." Starting a "Heifer Club" was the simplest way to raise money. The amounts that interested children needed to raise were spelled out clearly: a heifer calf cost between thirty and forty dollars, and an older heifer (one that was ready to mate and have a calf of her own) cost considerably more. Other contemporary sources put the average cost of a heifer at around $125 (though real value was sometimes as high as $500 for purebred and registered animals). Assistance in the task of raising money for this project could be given by a Sunday school teacher, a regular schoolteacher, or an older friend. Cash contributions directly to the Heifer Project in New Windsor were also welcome and, readers were informed, were an especially attractive option when the interested parties lived far from collection farms.[44] It is difficult to gauge how successful this specific project ultimately was, but the message it delivered was nevertheless revealing. It reinforced that the Heifer Project was a community affair that actively included children too while it also spoke to the transformative powers of milk.

One Species, Two Functions

American children sharing their abundant supplies of nourishing milk with less privileged children in war-devastated regions was both visually and rhetorically compelling advertising for milk and for humanitarian aid programming. Both the Heifer Project and UNRRA agreed about milk's value. Quite simply, milk provided a significant share of the agricultural population's "digestible protein," and it was a food source that was available all year long and not just after slaughtering fattened animals. The nutrients that milk provided were important for maintaining other animals' health, too; milk by-products were sometimes fed to animals like pigs that would later be slaughtered for meat. Milk was thus crucially important to the whole economy of rural households. UNRRA estimated that half of Polish farmers' income came from the selling of milk and dairy products. This money, which could be relied on to come in every month, even if just in small amounts (as compared to the larger profits from meat sales, for example), was typically used to cover regular household expenses, and access to this money raised the family's overall standard of living. In this way, cows were important for supporting the wider local economy and not just the family economy.[45]

All of this meant that the cattle breeds that would form part of the aid programs needed to be chosen carefully.[46] Yet it was not as simple as choosing the "heaviest milkers." In Poland and other similarly less developed rural contexts, cattle typically fulfilled two broad purposes simultaneously: the female of the species had to provide high milk yields, and the (castrated) male of the species had to be capable of working the land as a kind of alternative draft animal. This dual-purpose approach to cattle was, according to

UNRRA, "commonplace in the more primitive farming countries," which lacked a sufficient number of horses and, especially, tractors.[47] According to the Polish journal *Veterinary Medicine*, Poland's farmers would be inclined to send any smaller cattle breeds, and breeds unsuited to working in the fields, to the slaughterhouses (notwithstanding limits on animal slaughter after the war in certain regions). Farmers would simply conclude that the wrong breed was not worth the time, effort, and cost of maintenance otherwise.[48]

The Heifer Project preferred to send Holstein, Jersey, Hereford, and Guernsey cattle as part of their aid program; that these were the communities' own preferred breeds was in itself supposed to function as an affirmation of quality and utility. Holsteins in particular had been popular in Poland before the war as well. Cows from this breed were productive milkers. The males were known for having "strong constitutions"; they were good at turning feed into fats and protein and were husky enough to be useful for draft purposes. This quality was important in virtually all the target countries. Brown Swiss were popular for similar reasons. The Holstein-Friesian cross was also very popular as it was known to produce high milk yields.[49] Given that many cattle breeds that were common in the United States had originally come from Europe, sending these same breeds "back" to Europe posed no significant biological or environmental challenges (of the type that we have seen with subsequent live animal aid shipments from North America to African countries, for example).[50]

UNRRA generally sent the same breeds. As a bulk purchaser, UNRRA looked for cattle that were "representative of the breed in color and conformation" and with an optimal weight of at least eight hundred pounds. Ideally, it wanted heifers that had been bred to bulls of the same breed between nine and thirty-six months of age and that were due to calve within three to six months of delivery abroad; cattle have a gestation period of approximately nine months.[51] (For its part, the Brethren Service Committee specified an ideal of two years of age for heifers.[52]) The majority of the UNRRA cattle (58 percent) came from Wisconsin and Minnesota, and almost all of the Brown Swiss came from these two states plus Illinois.[53]

So it was that during this early postwar period, the cattle sent to Europe from America reflected specific historical developments and trends as well as contemporary assessments of need and assumptions about milk's nutritional value. Dairy cow bodies thus became food sources with broad economic value, to be sure. But they also became, as Michael Bresalier has said in reference to the general context of postwar food policy planning and relief programming, "political actors capable of influencing global security."[54] For these reasons dairy cattle's inclusion in UNRRA's relief strategy won widespread support from the American media, the public, and of course Congress.[55]

Consensus about the extraordinary nutritional value of cows' milk remained strong after the UNRRA/Heifer Project period ended. Milk remained a cornerstone of global food policy and public health initiatives well into the second half of the twentieth century. Its status as the leading nutritious food was even reflected in the logo that represented the United Nations International Children's Emergency Fund (UNICEF). UNICEF was a new UN body that started operations in December 1946, just as UNRRA was closing down. A Polish bacteriologist, Dr. Ludwik Rajchman, who had been a Polish representative to UNRRA and before that the director of the League of Nations Health Organization since its founding in 1921, was the first chair of UNICEF from 1946 to 1950.[56] From 1953 the UNICEF logo showed a child holding a cup of milk.[57] UNICEF shipped three million pounds of powdered milk (some of which constituted UNRRA leftovers) from the US to target countries in 1947 and beyond.[58] "The simple truth is that children of all ages need milk for their development," a UNICEF document declared in 1948, echoing earlier claims made by UNRRA and nutrition scientists more generally.[59] UNICEF's official historian even referred to UNICEF as a "'gigantic organizational udder': a proselytizer for milk, a worshipper of milk."[60] UNICEF also worked on developing native dairy industries that to some extent had been started by UNRRA and Heifer Project cattle.

Poland as a Horse Nation

Milk-providing female cattle were the quintessential symbol of the Heifer Program, for the reasons we have examined, and they formed an obviously important part of UNRRA live animal shipments. Time and again UNRRA reports about countries' agricultural, nutritional, and economic needs emphasized the importance of cattle and the milk that female cattle produced, and nowhere was this need quite as pressing as in Poland. As one typical UNRRA report concluded, "Without a cow the owner [of a Polish farm] is not considered to be a farmer in the full sense of the word. A peasant may not have a horse, but to be without a cow is looked upon as utter poverty."[61] Polish agricultural experts similarly referred to cows as "the most important beings in a farmer's everyday life"; the lack of cattle spelled ruination for Polish farmers.[62]

But cattle alone were not going to lead to relief and rehabilitation in Poland or in any other country where traditional farming practices predominated. Like cattle but in very different ways, the domesticated horse helped spread civilization and facilitated the growth of settled agricultural communities. In return for safety, food, and care, the horse submitted to human handlers and worked fields, provided transportation, and hauled heavy goods and people across significant distances. As "living machines" horses fulfilled roles that facilitated the economic activities of rural households.[63]

Horses are perfectly suited to agricultural work: they have a temperament and intelligence that make them good at following directions from humans, and their bodies are large and strong. In addition, they are able to move very quickly, are steady, and can maintain good traction. They also have amazing stamina and burn energy at an efficient rate.[64] Moreover, the fact that horses have traditionally been expensive to procure, use, and maintain accentuated the species' elite status and reflected positively on the owner's socioeconomic standing. The horse, while undeniably useful, symbolized both social position and power in a way that no other domesticated species did. For these reasons, as Ann Norton Greene says in her book about the horse's role in early American history, horses became "the natural aristocrats of the animal world."[65]

The war had destroyed Poland's horse population. This meant that in 1945 many farms were without a single horse to use for work in fields, in the distribution of produce, or for travel and communication between towns. Agricultural yields would be limited as a result, and Poland would be unable to feed its own people or, indeed, to produce livestock feed, and this loss would disrupt the human food chain. The number of horses that remained in Poland after the war were simply not sufficient to do the required work.[66] As the chief UNRRA veterinarian in Poland, A. G. Wilder, summarized, the loss of horses during the war resulted in uncultivated land after the war, which meant, in turn, "no crops to feed cattle, hogs, poultry, nor the home."[67] This threatened the entire relief and rehabilitation program, and UNRRA reports often repeated just how dangerous the low numbers of horses were to the entire rehabilitation project.[68] UNRRA ultimately delivered approximately 150,000 horses to Poland, far short of the need but a significant investment nonetheless.[69]

The low number of horses in postwar Poland was all the more worrying given the lack of mechanized cultivation in Polish agricultural practices. In short, there were few tractors in Poland, and those that did exist were old and functioned poorly. New tractors were expensive to purchase (if they were available for purchase at all), and the high costs of fuel and maintenance made them a less attractive option still. According to UNRRA estimates, there were only 1,500 tractors of various kinds in working order in Poland after the war; 1,500 tractors were the equivalent of 18,000 horses (with one tractor doing the work of twelve horses).[70] UNRRA therefore sent approximately nine thousand tractors to Poland as part of its aid packages, in addition to sending horses.[71] But recipients were not accustomed to the tractors, and they were sometimes slow to learn how to operate them. Moreover, machines broke quickly as a result of inexpert handling and then were rendered useless as spare parts were hard (if not impossible) to come by.[72] One settler in Poland's western territories recalled seeing valuable machines consigned to scrapyards because no one knew how to operate them. In some cases the machines were just abandoned and became toys for kids to play with and climb.[73]

The lack of tractors and horses in turn precipitated the need for relying on cattle to do farm labor, and this—using cattle as draft animals—consolidated an image of Poland as backward and vulnerable. Humans themselves sometimes became draft animals in the absence of other choices. As one UNRRA report stated, "It is a common sight in Poland to see whole families, obviously weakened from hunger, out pulling a plough or a cart for lack of farm draft animals. Or helping a single scrawny horse or cow to pull a two-horse wagon." Harnessing dairy cows for "tractive power" was a mark of desperation and, further, threatened to cut the cows' milk production by as much as half, thereby creating a host of other problems.[74]

The precarious state of Poland's agriculture and what this portended about its potential for broader socioeconomic recovery, as well as for political stability, was one of the most pressing problems that UNRRA's animal shipment program had been designed to address, as we have seen. And this was precisely what President Roosevelt had been concerned about during his wartime meeting at the White House with the Polish underground courier known as Jan Karski. It was clear to Roosevelt during that meeting with Karski, and then clear to UNRRA bureaucrats, that if UNRRA was serious about agricultural renewal, then it needed to invest in horses.

Beyond the important economic arguments for keeping horses, there were also decidedly less obviously practical arguments in favor of rebuilding Poland's horse population. Arguably, Poles and Poland had long had a special relationship with horses. In 1683, the winged hussars under King Jan Sobieski III organized an enormous cavalry charge and defeated the Ottomans at Vienna and, as the story goes, thereby saved Christian Europe from the Muslim threat at its doorstep. The memory of this battle, and of the horses' roles in it, lived on into the twentieth century. Though World War I had destroyed Poland's existing horse population, efforts to (re)establish breeding programs in independent Poland moved quickly. The period's greatest success was the Arabian breeding program at the Janów Podlaski Stud in the southeastern part of the country. Horses occupied outsized roles in interwar popular culture too. Many Poles even knew by name the horses of important historical figures from the era. For example, the beloved mare of Marshal Józef Piłsudski—hero of the Polish Legions and leader of the first postpartition independent Polish state that had been created in 1918—was Kasztanka, as everyone knew.

Poland's special love for horses was further reflected in stories about the lengths that some Poles went to during the war to protect their prized animals. Asking questions about animals' treatment during the war is a useful part of the social history of the era. Doing so can tell us about animal hierarchies, about which animals were worth taking risks for and which were not. We learn, for example, about Fliksier, an Anglo Arabian stallion born in 1920 who, in 1924, was selected to stand at the state stud. He had been bred with 1,320 mares since that time, and 924 living foals resulted from those pairings. During the war Fliksier was one of the few stallions that had been carefully and successfully hidden away from the enemy, which meant that he was still available to work as a stud after the war. UNRRA's Dr. Wilder described other stories of stallions that had been similarly concealed during the occupation or reluctantly given up to the enemy only to be stolen or bribed back. Wilder explained, "The love for a horse is one of the Pole's greatest emotions. It is truly said that a Pole will starve his family and go hungry himself that his horse may eat."[75]

UNRRA was well aware of the fact that before the war Poland had developed excellent breeding stock and that it had been well on its way to becoming a respected horse-breeding nation.[76] As a result, and in addition to providing horses that could work well as draft animals, UNRRA made some effort to kickstart postwar breeding programs in Poland (and elsewhere). It did this not only by delivering a number of horses that could reasonably fill this role but also by organizing lectures and demonstrations of the latest scientific developments in livestock breeding (targeting horses but also other species) and by facilitating expert partnerships to improve artificial insemination methods and breeding outcomes.[77] There were a total of fifteen state horse-breeding farms in Poland not long after the end of the war, but the hope was to increase that number substantially as quickly as possible.[78] UNRRA staff also inspected breeding facilities in Poland, including the farm where Fliksier worked, and lent professional advice to local breeders; this kind of international cooperation had long been part of breeding programs.[79] In January 1946 employees of the Requirements Branch of UNRRA visited state horse-breeding farms located in Leszno, Gostynin, and Walewice to find examples of what Poles considered an ideal horse type. The photographer John Vachon was part of this UNRRA delegation, and his job was to photograph the animal types that Poles preferred. The photos were meant to guide acquisitions for the remainder of 1946, when the bulk of UNRRA's rehabilitation aid would be delivered.[80]

Not surprisingly, during the postwar moment of crisis, the need for a large number of work-ready horses outstripped the need for high-quality breeding stock. In their communications with UNRRA, Poles specified a preference for, above all, dependable draft animals, "clean-legged" horses that could stand the rigors of labor.[81] Most of them, after all, would be pulling plows and farm wagons.[82] Poles also described wanting strong and "stocky" animals that would be relatively cheap to feed, could be expected to work for a good long time, and were "serviceably sound, gentle with no vicious habits, and without material blemishes or defects."[83] The ideal age for these horses was between three and eight years, and the ideal weight was between nine hundred and one thousand pounds.[84] These were a little larger and heavier than the horses that UNRRA supplied to Yugoslavia and Greece, but they were smaller and lighter than the preferred breeds in the US and western Europe. In the end the horses that UNRRA sent to Poland conformed generally with Polish requests. The majority were female horses, mares of breeding age, and usually not older than eight.[85] The most common breeds supplied to Poland by UNRRA were Percherons, Belgians, and Morgans.[86] The majority were obtained in the United States, but a small number came from Canada and Mexico.[87]

As we shall see, in the rush to assemble shiploads of horses quickly, ideals and standards were sometimes compromised, and as UNRRA itself admitted, "every common type" of animal that could conceivably "furnish the much needed horse power for the farms" was ultimately shipped abroad.[88] In the next chapter, we explore the logistics of horses' and cattle's transformation into "relief stock."

Chapter 5

The Making of "Relief Animals"

Finding, buying, and then preparing the relief animals for shipment required tremendous organization. The logistical challenges were not entirely different from those posed during the First and the Second World Wars, when hundreds of thousands of horses, mules, and donkeys from the United States and Canada were sent to the United Kingdom. Speed was of the essence. Numbers mattered. And the discomforts that the animals experienced during the shipments—and of course the dangers they faced on the battlefields—were simply accepted and understood as a natural part of the order of things. But unlike in wartime, the animals shipped during the UNRRA period were meant to live rather than die, and their bodies and temperaments needed to be ready for work and not for combat. They represented a different kind of investment. In this chapter we look at the process by which thousands of animals entered the aid chain in the immediate postwar period, whether that was as UNRRA animals or as Heifer Project animals, from point of purchase or donation to holding areas and then ultimately to the American ports. The chapter ends just before the animals, now firmly in the category of "relief stock," set foot on the ships that would take them to their destinations.

The UNRRA Animal Assembly Line

The demand for American agricultural products during the war and after was high. The United States was virtually the only country in the world that did not experience significant food supply problems during or after World War II.[1] Economically speaking, times were good in postwar America, and this was important when assessing support for humanitarian aid.[2] The thousands of cattle and horses collected in the US and delivered abroad as part of the Heifer Project and UNRRA were living symbols of this prosperous America.

UNRRA worked with the Department of Agriculture, and specifically its Inspection Section and the Assembly and Inland Movement Section, to procure the right kind of animals. UNRRA purchased its animals on the open market, typically either from large firms or from individual contractors with access to plenty of stock.[3] This procurement process, in some ways, was straightforward: UNRRA was a motivated buyer prepared to scoop up large numbers of horses and cattle and quickly move them on to the port areas. Sellers were plentiful, and the supply of horses was good, as the modernization and mechanization of farms in the United States meant that fewer animals were needed to do agricultural work. Motivated sellers wished to "liquidate holdings," as UNRRA described it.[4]

In other ways the buying process was anything but simple. The first challenge was finding sellers that could assemble a large number of the right kinds of animals very quickly. Next came the challenge of physically moving the animals at once across great distances; each animal weighed hundreds of pounds and needed to be cared for along each step on the route.[5] The animals' cross-country journeys to the ports were often long and complicated and came with risks to the animals' health.

There were several specific vulnerable points in UNRRA's animal procurement program, and the first of these was arguably at the point of purchase. Though UNRRA critics then and since have evoked examples of corruption and waste in the receiving countries, particularly in the increasingly Soviet-controlled east of Europe, there were rumors of "irregularities" involving the procurement of UNRRA aid at the point of purchase in the US as well. One interesting allegation of corruption came from a Polish agricultural expert at the Polish Embassy in Washington, Dr. E. Wiszniewski. Wiszniewski's job was to confirm the suitability of specific animal breeds for Poland's agricultural program. In 1946 Wiszniewski claimed to his superiors in Poland's Department of Agriculture that he had "secret information" about how UNRRA's livestock buyers were paying the sellers less than the established ninety-dollar maximum per horse but were nevertheless charging UNRRA the maximum amount. What this meant is that UNRRA received a lower-quality (cheaper) animal and that its designated buyers pocketed the extra money after using some of the supposed surplus to bribe the sellers and, later, the inspectors. It was these animals, already weak and sick, that were most likely to suffer and die on the ships that took them abroad or shortly after landing at their destinations. Wiszniewski did not say where he got this information, and his specific accusations cannot be verified. There is of course also the possibility that Wiszniewski's report to the Polish Ministry of Agriculture was politically motivated to show corruption and dishonestly in UNRRA and to make Wiszniewski himself look like a very conscientious bureaucrat watching out for Poland's best interests.[6]

We do have evidence, however, that UNRRA was well aware of corruption and dishonesty in the various parts of its procurement system and that it took some steps to mitigate problems. UNRRA warned its buyers to be on the lookout for assorted tricks and deceptions; some of the warnings broadly supported Wiszniewski's claims. UNRRA cautioned its buyers, for example, that unethical sellers would try to sneak sick animals into the group they were selling. UNRRA also warned buyers to be wary of prepurchase inspections that the sellers organized in dark barns; the lack of light could easily mask some signs of animals' poor health. Inspectors were directed to insist on good lighting conditions and to stop work early during the short days of winter. In other cases, UNRRA told its buyers to watch for vendors who placed too much straw or shavings on the barn floor; the absorbent and soft material would make it difficult to properly examine the animals' feet, meaning that lameness would be rendered less obvious. Lameness, weak ankles, and leg deformities were all reasons to disqualify an animal. Another deception involved vendors presenting horses whose teeth had been "worked on" so as to give the impression that the animals were younger than they actually were.[7] All things considered, bulk animal purchases were simply risky. In one instance a group of horses that had been purchased by UNRRA was found to have ticks. The horses needed to be first treated and then quarantined for ten days before ultimately being released for the program.[8] Though the ticks themselves would not have caused the animals' deaths, the need to quarantine meant longer confinement periods, and this, in turn, meant more physical stress for the animals and a greater chance of developing other illnesses that could conceivably lead to death. Again, it was the animals that were already weak or sick in the United States that had a low chance of making it alive to their destinations, especially given the normal challenges that long transport periods posed.

The animals that UNRRA ultimately selected and purchased were tagged and put in specially prepared holding yards to await shipment to the ports.

Under ideal circumstances this journey would start right away, immediately following purchase, and quite often that was in fact the case. According to the terms of the standard contracts that UNRRA's procurement agents signed with sellers, it was the sellers' responsibility to care for the animals until they reached the ports; the care was part of the purchase agreement. There needed to be attendants on the longer journeys, and provisions needed to be made for the animals to have rest stops and access to water and food during the trips as well.[9]

The selection, purchase, holding, and transport of the animals was regulated by legislation passed in 1944 that pertained specifically to animals designated for export.[10] It was the job of inspectors from the Department of Agriculture's Bureau of Animal Industry to ensure the health, humane treatment, and safe transport of these animals. Inspectors examined the animals at the point of purchase, at the holding pens, and then before they were loaded onto the waiting ships.[11] Vaccinations and inspections needed to be up to date before animals would be permitted to leave the country. Cattle, for example, needed to have been vaccinated at between four and eight months of age, and the vaccinations could not be older than twelve months; expired vaccines needed to be updated before export could be approved.[12]

In March 1946 the UNRRA Livestock Inspection Section came into being to help evaluate animals' suitability for the program. The UNRRA inspectors worked in an advisory and monitoring capacity only, however; the Department of Agriculture had the final say on matters related to animal purchase and export. Nevertheless, UNRRA inspectors hoped that they could influence decisions in some basic ways, and they tried to ensure that the animals considered for purchase met UNRRA specifications and conformed to the types of animals that receiving nations needed and wanted.[13] But assessing suitability and overall quality was difficult for everyone, especially at the speed required by an emergency humanitarian relief program.

Typically, UNRRA inspectors provided a summary of their assessment of the animals that had been presented at purchase points in reports filed with UNRRA. These reports were informational only, however, as, again, it was Department of Agriculture inspectors and not UNRRA inspectors that had the final authority to include or reject an animal. An experienced Department of Agriculture inspector could assess the health of approximately three hundred horses per day (and a smaller number of cattle due, mainly, to the method of assembling the animals). UNRRA records show that rejection rates were lowest in the earliest months of the program when the focus was on sending as many animals as possible quickly, and then again at the end of the program when there was a mad rush to send "everything," even, as UNRRA said, "the scrapings from the bottom of the barrel."[14] From August to

October 1946, United States Department of Agriculture inspectors rejected 15 percent of all horses that were presented to them for purchase; this means that 5,699 horses were rejected out of 38,159. UNRRA livestock inspectors believed that an additional 2 percent should have been rejected, but of course they did not have the authority to demand this. In a retrospective report on the subject of animal purchases, UNRRA argued that differences between their own assessments of livestock and the government's inspectors' assessments were "representative" of a broader pattern. UNRRA generally would have wanted to be even more selective and careful.[15]

The pressure to get the animal program going and then to move animals quickly through the various stages en route to the ports was immense. This was true for many reasons, including logistics and cost, but also because the Department of Agriculture inspection results were valid for only thirty days.[16] In practice the time between purchase and sailing varied for the animals, but the ideal was for it not to exceed a couple of weeks; delays were both expensive and hard on the animals, and animal illnesses, injuries, or deaths ultimately translated into another high cost for UNRRA. As it was, animals died at all of the possible stages during the American part of the process, from point of purchase to the ports.[17] The discovery of existing or new illnesses at the ports further complicated timelines as some of the animals needed to be moved at the very last minute into temporary hospital areas. As a result, planned sailings, with specific animal groups, needed to be changed at the final moment, and this was always complicated to organize.[18] Typically, too, sailings could be delayed because of a shortage of feed supplies, mechanical problems on the ships, or a lack of bottom cargo to complete the ship's load.[19] Sometimes delays and interruptions were entirely out of UNRRA's control, as when, for example, a May 1946 rail strike halted transport to the ports and therefore delayed sailings.[20]

The time pressures and the coordination challenges were especially enormous given that, at its peak, the UNRRA program moved up to ten thousand animals per week. One UNRRA report summarized the assorted logistical challenges that came with these high numbers like this: "The process followed in assembling livestock for export is very similar to the assembly line of an automobile plant. Once the process is started, it cannot be stopped suddenly without causing considerable financial and death losses."[21]

UNRRA and Animal Welfare

The functioning of the UNRRA animal assembly line was monitored—albeit completely unofficially—by the American Humane Association (AHA). The

AHA was a national animal welfare group with branches spread across the United States. Even before the US had entered the war, the AHA was already thinking about the war's effects on animals and was advocating in favor of banning the sale of horses (to any side) for military purposes (this did not happen).[22] A couple of decades earlier, in 1916, the association had founded the American Red Star Animal Relief program to provide assistance to animals used by the US Army during the First World War. The Red Star program remained active into the Second World War and funneled money and supplies to animal welfare societies working in Allied nations so that those groups could better tend to local animal victims of war.[23] After the Second World War ended in 1945, the American Humane Society got involved in a new project: monitoring and inspecting the transport, holding, and shipping conditions related to UNRRA's animal program. It was the AHA that had initiated contact with the Department of Agriculture's Bureau of Animal Industry and asked for permission to visit the UNRRA animal holding centers and loading ports.[24] The permission was granted, but the AHA was allowed to work in an advisory capacity only; it had no authority to implement its recommendations or to enforce any changes that it might have wanted.

Christian P. Norgord was the Washington representative of the AHA, and it was he who met with UNRRA to discuss what the relationship between the two bodies might look like in a specific sense. During these meetings, Norgord—who was also a professor of agronomy at the University of Wisconsin and an agriculture commissioner in Wisconsin—was assured that the humane treatment of animals was a priority for UNRRA. In fact, UNRRA representatives told Norgord that its staff had been directed explicitly to "prevent all inhumane treatment of animals."[25]

The AHA carried out inspections of UNRRA holding centers to test this claim. AHA inspector James M. Ross made a 1946 inspection of Rigby Yards, an UNRRA stockyard near Portland, Maine, managed by Charles and Frank Griggs. Ross reported that he saw plenty of good food for the animals, proper ventilation, roomy corrals in the holding shed, and comfortable walking surfaces that did not collect mud and that absorbed the animal urine adequately. Ross further reported that veterinarians from the Department of Agriculture were reliably on hand to look out for, and to treat, if need be, sick animals.[26]

Ross wrote a very positive assessment of UNRRA's stockyard in Maine and published it in the AHA's newspaper, *The National Humane Review* (which Ross also edited). "We found conditions as near perfect as it is given to man to make," Ross wrote. "Every care is taken to see that each animal is well treated, made safe and comfortable on the journey across the waters." The title of Ross's article in *The National Humane Review* reflected absolute confidence in UNRRA's high animal welfare standards: "Kindness and Comfort Paramount in Shipping Horses and Dairy Cattle Overseas to Replace Losses in Farm Animals." Ross was evidently very moved by the grand purposes of the UNRRA aid program, by the fact that, as he said, the animals would be "given homes" in war-ravaged countries, that they would "help people," and, lastly, that they would "have their part in restoring the necessities of life." Tellingly, Ross also referred to the UNRRA animal shipments as constituting "a hegira of mercy": a holy journey in which the resources required for civilized life were shared between friends.[27] Ross's use of Christian-inflected language was typical of American animal welfare activism (which had roots in nineteenth-century Christian evangelical social reform movements), as it was of contemporary humanitarian rhetoric more generally, as we have seen.[28]

The AHA did not question the choice to send animals across the ocean (just as the Heifer Project and UNRRA did not), and they did not problematize the notion of animals "as aid." Their understanding of nonhuman animals was entirely anthropocentric and answered the question of what animals could do for "us." Contemporaries used the terms "aid animals," "gift animals," and "relief animals" in uncomplicated, unproblematic, and overwhelmingly positive ways. We should not expect anything else for the mid-1940s. Even in the mid-1960s, *Our Dumb Animals*, the paper of the Massachusetts Society for the Prevention of Cruelty to Animals, actively supported the more modern incarnation of the Heifer Project, advised it on best practices in animal care, and published articles about the good work the organization was doing by sending relief animals abroad.[29] The Massachusetts Society's Livestock Department even funded the construction of a step-type livestock loading ramp at Logan International Airport in Boston to facilitate the Heifer Project's work. By the 1960s Logan had become a departure point for many Heifer Project animals destined to help "deserving people in foreign lands."[30]

Animal welfare societies of the immediate postwar period and beyond were composed of relatively conservative animal welfarists rather than radical abolitions who might have called for a revolution in relations between human and nonhuman animals. A broadly Christian worldview, which believed that God had created animals as lesser beings for human use, also informed the content of this activism. These animal welfare advocates showed themselves to be loyal supporters of UNRRA, of the government, and of "America's program of helping hungry millions in Europe."[31] Though it was "regrettable," according to AHA inspector James Ross, that "hardy and healthy horses must be taken from wide Western ranges, thrust into crowded box cars and sent on long journeys to seaports, thence dispatched abroad," this was a necessary sacrifice; one had simply to accept that some animals would die on these trips, despite good planning and the most conscientious care.[32] The greater cause—of providing humanitarian aid to humans in need—outweighed any concerns for animal welfare.

Indeed, even the best facilities and animal handlers could not mitigate the effects on the animals of long journeys to holding centers and from these centers to the ports; some animals did die on their way to holding barns, at holding barns, en route to the ports, at the ports, and then, as we will see in the next chapter, on the ships. At most what the AHA called for were improvements to general animal shipping laws in the United States. According to the AHA, the Department of Transportation rules did not adequately outline animal welfare standards in terms of watering, feeding, and resting.[33] Similarly, the AHA said, the concentration of diverse animal species and breeds from different regions (whether in holding barns or in transport rail cars) meant that diseases spread quickly, as the immune systems of animals from one area of the country could not easily handle diseases that affected animals from another part of the country. These "shipping diseases" already afflicted some of the animals even before they left the United States, which of course made animal deaths on the seas more likely. These deaths in turn jeopardized humanitarian goals. But these were relatively quiet recommendations and warnings and were not reflective of a concrete campaign for action and change in the present. The AHA seemed quite content to work within current structures and legal frameworks and to continue existing practices; it accepted the hierarchy established by humans in their perception of and treatment of nonhuman animals.[34]

Like the AHA, the Massachusetts Society for the Prevention of Cruelty to Animals concluded that UNRRA's animal shipments did not compromise the animals' welfare. The Massachusetts Society reported in *Our Dumb Animals* that though it had received a number of complaints and queries from the general public about the UNRRA animals, there was no evidence to substantiate concerns about mistreatment or negligence.[35] Any risks and problems that did exist were simply an unavoidable part of moving thousands of animals quickly across great distances and were justified by a belief in the inherent value of the effort itself; without cattle and horses, rehabilitation efforts in Nazi-devastated Europe would simply be impossible.

From Animals to Relief, the Brethren Way

There is no evidence that AHA inspectors ever visited any Heifer Project holding centers. In all likelihood such visits did not happen, as the Heifer

Project was a private affair, was not managed by the government, and was far smaller in scale than UNRRA's animal relief program. The Heifer Project cattle would only have been subject to the government inspections that were obligatory for all export animals. This constituted one important difference between how the UNRRA animals and the Heifer Project animals interacted with the state.

The differences in how each of these groups was transformed into relief animals began earlier still, however. While the approximately four thousand Heifer Project cattle shipped abroad during the UNRRA period became relief animals through donations, most of what UNRRA delivered as aid (including animal aid) had been purchased through the intervention of livestock procurement firms. That said, there were also some opportunities for American charitable and nongovernmental organizations to donate money to UNRRA, which UNRRA would then use to purchase animals (or other relief goods) and add to the overall relief effort. Resolution 14.9 of the UNRRA Financial Plan outlined the regulations that governed voluntary contributions from such organizations, and the logistics of this were overseen by the Contributed Supplies Branch, Bureau of Supplies.[36] One particularly large and notable donation came, for example, from the Polish-American Rebuilders of Poland Association, which had raised over $600,000 that was then used by UNRRA to purchase over eight thousand horses for the relief effort in Poland.[37] The advantages of this arrangement to the Rebuilders of Poland Association and other such groups were clear: UNRRA organized procurement and paid the considerable shipping costs.[38] Donations to UNRRA came from other organizations, too, such as from the Polish Supply and Reconstruction Mission in North America, whose head was the noted Pole and UNICEF founder, Dr. Ludwik Rajchman.[39]

Donations to the Heifer Project were different; they were made on a much smaller scale and were more direct, personal, and ultimately profoundly local. From its inception the Heifer Project made appeals for donations by running stories in peace church community papers like the Brethren's *Gospel Messenger*, *Brethren Missionary*, and *The Mennonite*; these were the same publications than ran "help wanted" advertisements for the seagoing cowboys program. These papers had a targeted and admittedly narrow readership, but at the same time they invited participation, through donations, in an enormous imagined global community. Posters at local churches also advertised the Heifer Project and appealed for donations from congregants. Sometimes, respected peace church community members made direct and personal pitches to church members asking them to give generously. Appeals often included the display of powerful photographic images of wartime ruin as a way to solicit empathy while also reminding people that their seemingly small individual actions could in fact make a significant difference and alleviate suffering abroad.[40]

Positive responses to these Heifer Project appeals reflected the faith that people had in their own churches and in the leadership of the aid effort; people believed that the Heifer Project would act as a competent custodian of their material and financial gifts.[41] And people did give generously. M. R. Zigler, the executive secretary of the Brethren Service Committee, estimated that a quarter of all Brethren heifers donated to the Heifer Project came from purebred stock, while the remainder was "good grade"; these were not farmers' rejected animals.[42] In fact, the Heifer Project even wrote to breeders of purebred cattle to solicit donations of the very best stock.[43] Philip West, Dan West's son (born in 1938), remembered going with his father to visit some of the Mennonite and Amish heifer donors in Elkhart County, Indiana. Some of those early heifers, the younger West recalled, "were better than some of our own cows. They had 'papers.'"[44] The generosity of donors was all the more remarkable given that donations to the Heifer Project came on the heels of the peace churches' substantial financial responsibilities in maintaining the Civilian Public Service camps during the war and the early postwar period.[45]

Even before there was a viable opportunity to send cattle to meet specific European needs, and before the partnership with UNRRA had formed, the Brethren mobilized their communities and began collecting animals for the Heifer Project. In addition to the national Heifer Project committee, local Brethren congregations maintained their own Heifer Project committees, and heifer donations often ran through those local committees. Donated animals came from individuals and from small and large peace church congregations, from other Christian denominations like the Methodists, and from service organizations or social-cultural institutions like the Lions and Rotary clubs and the Kiwanis club. They also came from school groups. Donors were responding to need in "hungry Europe" and were inspired by descriptions of deprivation and suffering and by the sense that they had the ability to make a positive difference in the lives of others.[46] For the Brethren, the act of donating itself formed a fundamental part of their devotion; time and goods were offered "in the spirit of Christian friendship and service to those in need."[47] Donors thus became an important part of mid-century relief.

The first calf donated to what would become the Heifer Project happened in April 1942 at a meeting of the Northern Indiana District Men's Work of the Church of the Brethren. This district, which represented forty-eight congregations of the Church of the Brethren, was the first one to support the Heifer Project, and in so doing it helped pave the way for the Heifer Project's formal adoption by the Brethren Service Committee the following year, in 1943.[48] That first calf was named Faith, and she had been donated to the program by her owner, the farmer Virgil Mock of New Paris, Indiana. There were many other people besides Mock involved in ensuring that Faith would eventually reach someone who needed her; raising this animal was part of a wider community affair. The calf's feed was donated by Ora W. Stine, mentioned earlier as an important figure in the Heifer Project and as the father of Carol Stine, Bushong's secretary in New Windsor. Faith was cared for by Ora's teenaged son Claire. Faith was thus one of the earliest "symbols of the idea behind the gift."[49]

Faith was put on the earliest Heifer Project shipment, which, as we saw, was to Puerto Rico in July 1944. Faith gave birth en route, and her calf survived. Reports indicate that she lived a comfortable life close to the ocean in Puerto Rico and was well cared for, as was her calf.[50] Hope, a two-year-old Holstein and another early donation to the Heifer Project (though she was not the only donated heifer called Hope), formed part of a shipment to Poland in 1946 on SS *William S. Halsted*, and she and another Heifer Project animal ended up at an orphanage not far from Warsaw, in Konstancin.[51] That the animals' fates are recorded in the documents is in itself remarkable, and even though we cannot know for certain whether these animals ended up with "happy lives," as the Heifer Project claimed, the assertion itself forms an important part of the Brethren humanitarian aid narrative. Securing good conditions for their animals—by which they meant standards of care that were similar to those that prevailed on American farms—was at once a part of their obligation and a measure of their success.[52]

Other donated animals came with special stories too. For example, the Quaker Stanley Hamilton of the Rural Life Association bought a yearling Guernsey heifer at an auction for $155 with the intention of dropping her off at a Brethren collecting farm and thereby donating her to the European relief effort. The young farmer who had sold the animal to Hamilton—"a German immigrant"—ultimately decided to tear up the check he had been given by Hamilton and to make the donation himself. It turned out that this immigrant from Germany was Jewish on one side and that he had left Germany shortly after Hitler had come to power. The *Gospel Messenger* article that reported on this story delighted in the evident interdenominational cooperation and empathy on display here: a Quaker, a partially Jewish German farmer, and the future recipient family of indeterminate "race or creed."[53] Another celebrated donation—"one of the greatest contributions to the heifer program yet," according to one observer—was one dollar that came from a young American man of Japanese descent who had recently been released from a tuberculosis hospital. This act was extolled by the Heifer Project administrators: "He is now working only for his room and board. Yet he shared one dollar. *That* is real giving."[54]

In addition to these at once modest and remarkable donations from individuals, there were group donations that flowed from grand and public gestures, often with the type of extravagant celebrity endorsements that we more typically associate with our own day. In one instance the Heifer Project Committee of Southern California put on a stage show at the Pasadena Civic auditorium. On May 7, 1946, stars such as Bob Hope, Rudy Vallée, and Jerry Colonna donated their time and talent to raise money for the purchase of heifers.[55] In another instance we see members of a specific congregation pooling their resources to make a group donation to the Heifer Project: the Lancaster Church of the Brethren in Lancaster, Pennsylvania, gave six heifers and a bull to their local donation drive.[56] Members of the First Baptist Church Sunday School in Weston, Massachusetts, collected enough money to buy one purebred Holstein heifer "for the relief of hungry youngsters in Europe."[57] St Paul's Catholic Cathedral in Boston raised a stunning amount of money—enough to buy 124 heifers at $125 each—to donate to the Brethren Heifer Project.[58] One particularly remarkable group contribution to the Heifer Project came in the amount of $482 from men who had become seagoing cowboys after having served for a period in the Civilian Public Service. This amount was especially significant, as one Heifer Project administrator wrote, "when you consider that the cattle boat trip was the first income most of these fellows had for a year and one-half to three years previous to the trip."[59]

Money was also raised at special livestock auctions. In February 1946, for example, Brethren and Amish farmers organized a sales barn for Poland specifically. Cows, horses, pigs, ponies, dogs, rabbits, roosters, and even "a magnificent team of Belgian mares" were all put up for sale along with vegetables, wagons, buggies, clothes, and home furnishings. There were five auctioneers who worked for free, and people scooped up animals and goods that they sometimes neither really wanted nor needed, often for extravagant prices, because they knew the money was going to the Polish relief effort.[60] Dairy cows—the recognized symbol of the Heifer Project relief effort—were especially prized, with each selling for $100 and up. An event like this, one pastor described, "is a social act, and an act of their religious freedom as well as of their religion. It is entirely of and by the people, and in their view it is for people in the name of God. It is a community act."[61]

Specific animals destined for the Heifer Project were also sometimes featured in newspaper articles. In one article we see Helga the Heifer posed between Victor Borge, an entertainer, and Mary Anderson, an actor. The two humans sit at a beautifully decorated dinner table at the Biltmore Hotel with Helga between them looking directly at the camera while munching on the lovely flower arrangement before her. The caption reads, "Bon voyage party given Europe-Bound Heifer." Helga's job, we are told, will be "to provide milk for starving children."[62]

The Heifer Project paid for Helga's expenses just as it paid for all other donated animals' expenses; these included food and care, as well as transport to the ports in the US (the transport fees ran at over ten dollars per animal). To feed a heifer cost approximately forty-five cents per day (or $3.15 per week); this amount provided for alfalfa hay, a lower-grade hay, plus a grain mixture. On top of this, the bedding straw cost was eighteen dollars per ton.[63]

The first leg of the Heifer Project animals' journeys after donation or purchase brought the heifers to one of many Heifer Project collection centers; these centers or farms were scattered throughout the country in approximately two dozen states. The Heifer Project suggested that communities or churches get together to send many animals to these centers at once; sending just one or two animals at a time was too costly, especially if the distances were significant.[64] The Heifer Project also advised sending someone from the donors' circle to accompany the animals to the collection farm, and it reminded donors of the importance of having the requisite health papers signed by the local veterinarian, the state veterinarian, and a federal inspector. If the animals did not have the legally mandated veterinary inspections and inoculations (against tuberculosis, shipping fever, and Bang's disease) it was possible (though not ideal) to have the shots administered at the collection center.[65] The animals would be moved again, this time to a holding center close to a port. For many of the animals, this was the farm of Roger and Olive Roop located near Union Bridge, Maryland. The Roop farm was just several miles from the Brethren Service Committee Center in New Windsor, only a couple of miles from the railroad, and forty miles from the docks in Baltimore.[66] The Roop farm was the main Heifer Project receiving and holding center; it was the last major stop before the cattle boarded the ships that would define them most clearly as "relief animals."

Roger and Olive Roop were members of the Church of the Brethren who had given 15 acres of their 130-acre farm to the Brethren Service Committee to use for the Heifer Project. The Roops had about twenty head of cattle of their own. In addition to the grazing land that the Roops provided, free of charge, to the Heifer Project, they also permitted the project to use a barn, pens, and a loading chute. According to the Roops, they had been motivated to donate their farm facilities to the Heifer Project because of the substandard conditions and chaos that they had witnessed during a visit to a similar animal holding center at the York, Pennsylvania, Fair Grounds; the Roops believed that they could provide far better facilities for the animals, with more space.[67]

The first cattle arrived at the Roop farm on July 31, 1945, even before the war against Japan had ended. By 1948 (so beyond the Brethren-UNRRA partnership), 3,600 animals had traveled enormous distances, from a total of thirty-one states, to this one farm in the eastern US before boarding ships bound for the world.[68] Not surprisingly, the initial fifteen acres of land that the Roops had provided proved insufficient to meet demand; the space was adequate for only about three to five hundred head of cattle at a time. The Roops eventually sold their own small number of cattle and rented their remaining property as pastureland to the Heifer Project. The rental agreement included use of the building and the equipment, and Roger Roop was hired as the farm manager. Either Roger or one of the volunteers, some of whom were not even from one of the denominations that were part of the Heifer Project Committee, picked up the animals at the train station and delivered them to their temporary homes on the farm. Smaller animal loads came directly to the farm on trucks and trailers.[69]

Roger organized the animals' stay at the farm and readied them for transport abroad. The Heifer Project paid for the expenses associated with the animals' stay at the farm, and it also paid for moving the animals from the farm to the embarkation point. Animals were also given medical care as needed by local veterinarians who occasionally gave their services without charge; all animals needed to be monitored regularly for diseases. Sometimes the donated animals were in a poor state indeed, though as Roop said, "That point should not be criticized too much because the person giving a poor quality animal may have made more of a sacrifice than the one giving a purebred suitable for the show ring."[70] The work of daily animal care was done by hired hands or by some of the seagoing cowboys who were temporarily billeted at the Brethren Service Center in nearby New Windsor, or even by some of the men from the Civilian Public Service unit who were also staying at the New Windsor complex.[71] Roger Roop summarized this pan-American effort of preparing the animals for shipment abroad with a little example: "An Illinois man [he was referring to one Wayne Keltner, who helped with the heifers on the Roop farm] fed California hay to Wisconsin heifers in Maryland."[72] Seagoing cowboys from perhaps another state still would eventually accompany these heifers to their final destination far away from American shores.

The length of time that animals stayed at the Roop farm varied, but the average was forty days.[73] The first shipment of Roop cattle left the farm in about a dozen rail cars (loaded with crushed corn cobs for bedding) and sailed from Baltimore on September 6, 1945, on SS *Zona Gale*, which had been used as a mule carrier during the war. The words that formed part of the dedication service that preceded this shipment reflected the bold ambitions of the Heifer Project; the animals were given so that "the spirit of brotherhood might come into the hearts of men . . . and bring a new dawn of peace."[74] Roger Roop accompanied this first group (and subsequent groups too) to the waiting ships at the docks in Baltimore.[75] The Roop farm stopped operating as a Heifer Project facility in 1948 when Roger Roop became sick with undulant fever.[76]

Last Stages

Final inspections of both Heifer Project and UNRRA animals were completed at the piers just before boarding to ensure that no sick animals were included in the group. These inspections were done through the Bureau of Animal Industry by professional veterinarians—port veterinarians, as they were referred to—and were required by law. A representative from the War Shipping Administration was on hand as well to monitor the process, and the AHA did spot checks of port conditions too. The AHA's assessment of animal welfare standards at the ports was not unlike its assessment of the holding centers and stockyards; they believed them to be quite satisfactory. This view was consistent with the association's generally positive impressions of animal welfare standards in the whole relief program. Inspector Ross from the AHA described impressive conditions and careful practices at the ports: nonslip flooring on the runways that led to the ships; good-quality lumber for the lodgings; and compartments that measured eight feet in length, thirty-two inches in width, and nine and a half feet in height. During one inspection Archibald MacDonald, chief inspector of the Animal Rescue League of Boston, described the conditions overall as "the best I ever saw."[77]

And yet what the AHA reported was not universally true or reflective of actual conditions. We know from other sources (such as cowboy diaries) that the piers were sometimes very crowded and chaotic. Given the numbers of large animals present in a relatively small space and the need to move them onto the ships very quickly, it is not surprising that sometimes the inspectors did not notice just how sick some animals were. Cowboy Jacob Wine, who was on a May 1946 trip bringing horses to Czechoslovakia (and docking in Bremen, Germany), speculated that sometimes the sick animals were loaded onto the ships anyway because to do otherwise would have made "the record look bad at the pier for them to die there." Animal deaths aboard the ships could be kept comparatively private and out of the public eye and could be attributed in vague ways to sailing conditions like rough seas and bad weather; deaths at the ports, in contrast, would have attracted too much attention and negative publicity.[78] It was these already sick animals that were, not surprisingly, the least well equipped for their trans-Atlantic journeys and most likely to die during or shortly after the crossings.[79]

Animals that did not pass the veterinarians' health inspections at this late stage and were in fact deemed unsuitable for shipment were moved into local holding pens that were organized according to what the animals' subsequent fate would be: a hospital stay (for cases of treatable infectious diseases and pneumonia), surgery (for abscesses in need of draining as well as for wounds and fistulae, for example), diagnostics or convalescence leading to likely recovery, sale (if a buyer could be found), or destruction (for animals that were in no condition to be sold alive for any purpose).[80] This became complicated after the UNRRA program end date approached; inspections of the very last groups of animals became less strict given that there were no "future shipments" in which recovered animals could be included. At any rate the forced sale of some of the animals would "bring little return," according to UNRRA, and so there was apparently little harm in including them on the shipments given that they were already at the ports.[81] The greatest cost, instead, was to the animals.

In his written reflections after the UNRRA program closed, Livestock Branch director Robert Lintner expressed frustration that animals sometimes failed health checks at this very late point in the process because, as he said, they had been badly cared for during their trips to the ports. Though the sellers were supposed to have provided attendants that would accompany the animals from point of origin to the ports, these attendants were on occasion "incompetent," according to Lintner. In addition, rail cars were often overcrowded and schedules sometimes poorly coordinated. This resulted in physically taxing train journeys and long periods of convalescence or even death for some of the animals. In other cases, Lintner said, the mandatory inoculations had been given "carelessly," and this caused abscesses to develop at injection sites, which led in turn to open sores and infections that had gone unattended for too long. According to Lintner, this showed that part of the problem was that the animals were considered to be "general cargo"; it took a while, even within UNRRA circles, for people to understand that the animals really did require special care and effort.[82] Lintner was of the view that throughout all stages of the program, cooperation and communication between UNRRA and Department of Agriculture inspectors could sometimes have been better. What was clear to everyone is that while good health at embarkation was no guarantee of a successful sailing, poor health at this last stage in the United States would almost always result in animal deaths aboard the ships.

CHAPTER 6

Cowboys and Animals at Sea

The species that formed part of both the UNRRA relief program and the Heifer Project had been selected, and the animals had been moved en masse to the port areas. The animal handlers had also been chosen and had similarly made their way to the ports. The ships, too, had been readied. The stage was set. The men and animals would meet each other for the first time at this point, aboard the UNRRA ships. The period when animals are in transit is typically opaque, and this is especially the case when it comes to ocean voyages; much of what happens on the oceans in terms of live animal transport has been and remains invisible.[1] To some extent this reflects our lack of interest in livestock animals and livestock caretakers as historical subjects as well as a presumed scarcity of interesting-enough source material.[2] Yet our case was anything but ordinary and uninteresting. The animals and the animal handlers were on special assignment, and their joint voyages were celebrated and well advertised. It was arguably Brethren and Mennonite Americans that followed the animal sailings with particular interest: It was, after all, the Brethren Service Committee that ran the seagoing cowboys program for UNRRA, and the BSC had recruited very successfully within Brethren and Mennonite circles. Additional cowboy recruits on the UNRRA ships came from Christian denominations that were actively involved in the Heifer Project too. These men were therefore particularly motivated to document their experiences—and document they did.

Some of the men kept diaries as they sailed the oceans, while others wrote detailed letters to loved ones back home, and others still prepared memoirs at some later point during their lives. Between 150 and 200 of them sat for interviews with the Brethren historian Peggy Reiff Miller during the last couple of decades. Then there were those who delivered talks to their coreligionists or reminisced at cowboys reunions over the years.[3] As reflected in Reiff Miller's work, the men's accounts are rich and, taken together, offer important and exceptional source material for understanding what it was like to be a seagoing cowboy during the very specific postwar moment. Cowboys' own words bring us onto the ships and into the animals' stalls in ways that other sources simply cannot, and in doing so they reveal the conditions of live animal transport during the mid-century's marquee relief effort. This chapter draws on a wide variety of these available sources to describe the hours and days that the cattle, horses, and cowboys spent together on the open seas. This chapter, in other words, is about the quotidian: the rhythm of the men's and animals' days together, their troubles and discomforts, and their pleasures too.

UNRRA Live Animal Transport

Plans to secure ships that could accommodate large numbers of animals that weighed many hundreds of pounds each and that could make many runs across the ocean quickly started even before the war ended. UNRRA worked with the Ocean Shipping Division and the War Shipping Administration to repurpose American military and merchant marine ships that had been used to move troops and supplies during the war. Retrofitting the ships to accommodate live animals was expensive—about $6 million in total—and was covered entirely by UNRRA.[4] Conversions took about three weeks per ship, and the technical skills needed were provided by the War Shipping Administration. The work consisted, in part, of building hundreds of stalls in the holds and on the decks and installing ventilation systems. Larger ships often had two rows of stalls and smaller ships just one.[5] Veterinarians were called in to advise on design, and the Bureau of Animal Industry, which was responsible for animal care in the UNRRA program, signed off on all conversions and approved both stall configurations and ventilation systems.[6] In the end UNRRA's livestock fleet consisted of just over seventy ships, though the exact number fluctuated depending on the point in the program.[7] At any rate UNRRA itself regarded this number as insufficient.[8]

Animals were transported—at a cost of about $185 per head of cattle—on two main types of ships: Liberty and Victory.[9] The United States Marine

Commission had authorized the construction of 2,710 Liberty ships from 1941 to 1945 to meet the immediate and emergency demands of wartime. The ships were designed to be built quickly (in just over two months) and cheaply. The Liberty was a small cargo and logistical support ship, with its primary purpose during the war having been the delivery of supplies to destinations where they were needed. Liberty ships were also used to transport mules and sometimes men.[10] The UNRRA relief worker Kathryn Hulme, who worked in UNRRA Displaced Persons camps after the war and later wrote a memoir about her experiences, was employed during the war as a welder in a shipyard in San Francisco building Liberty vessels and was known to have "signed" her work with a drawing of a small crocodile under a hatch end beam.[11] Of the almost three thousand Liberty vessels that had been built during the war, twelve were retrofitted for the UNRRA relief program, with each ship designed to carry from 335 to 400 animals, depending on the species. Each Liberty vessel also carried approximately four thousand tons of other cargo, which consisted of various other forms of UNRRA aid, from nonperishable food items to clothing. A special type of heavy Liberty vessel that had been used to transport tanks and crated planes during the war was also repurposed for the aid effort after the war; there were twelve of these heavy Liberty ships (known as Zecs), with each able to accommodate between 800 and 850 animals.[12]

Liberty vessels plus three retired army cattle ships were the first ship types used in the UNRRA program. The cattle ships were SS *F. J. Luckenbach* (with a capacity of 500 animals but no space for general cargo), SS *Mexican* (with a capacity of 625 animals plus cargo), and SS *Virginian* (the oldest ship in the fleet, having been used in World War I, with a capacity of 700 animals plus cargo). These ships first sailed as part of the UNRRA live animal aid program in late June 1945. Victory vessels began sailing a little later, in October 1945. The US had started building Victory ships in 1943 to supplement the Liberty vessels and to address some of the quality issues that had plagued the Liberty brand. Victory ships were larger and faster than the Liberty ships and could accommodate approximately 800 animals each, again depending on the species. In total, forty-one Victory ships were retrofitted for the UNRRA program. UNRRA generally used the faster and larger Victory ships when it could; these ships were expected to make approximately six round trips per year. A smaller type of Victory ship that carried animals only on deck sailed as well; there were five of these, and each had a capacity of two hundred animals.[13]

The largest ship in the UNRRA fleet was a C-4 class cargo vessel, SS *Mt. Whitney*, with a capacity of 1,500 horses or 1,600 cattle; this was enor-

FIGURE 2. SS *Cedar Rapids Victory*. Jacob C. Wine Collection from the Manchester University Archives and Brethren Historical Collection. https://www.manchester.edu/oaa/library/archives/DigitalCollections/seagoingcowboydiary.htm.

mous by contemporary measures yet very small by today's standards. *Mt. Whitney*'s inaugural sailing as a livestock ship was on July 28, 1946, from Newport News, Virginia. *Mt. Whitney* was also the fastest ship in UNRRA's fleet; return trips took about a month on *Mt. Whitney* as compared to up to six weeks for Victory vessels and two to three months for Liberty ships. Ultimately, the length of the trips depended, of course, on the exact destination, on the weather, and on factors that often had little to do with the ships themselves. Not surprisingly, cowboys generally found faster sailings more appealing, though of course they were not able to choose their ship type when they signed on to the seagoing cowboys program.[14]

The logistics of which ship would be used when and on what route were handled by the Ship Operations Section of the Ocean Shipping Division. The Port Reception Section serviced the ports and procured the supplies needed for loading all of the cargo, animals included, onto the ships.[15] Preparing the cattle crew for each sailing was the job of the Brethren Service Committee, as we have seen. The exact number of men required for each sailing depended on the type of vessel assigned to the given sailing, the number of animals on board, and the species being shipped.[16] The larger ships needed about twice the number of cattle attendants as the smaller ships; there were roughly thirty attendants for a loaded Victory ship and half that number for a Liberty vessel. On a sailing of SS *Woodstock Victory* that left Newport News for Gdańsk in March 1946, for example, there were 770 heifers and 79 horses aboard with 33 attendants to care for the animals, meaning that each attendant was responsible for about 26 animals, mostly cattle. The average number of animals assigned to each attendant was generally in the low to mid 20s.[17] Smaller sailings—like one in November of 1946—consisted of 16 seagoing cowboys and 331 head of cattle, or approximately 21 animals per attendant.[18] The large SS *Mt. Whitney* traveled with the largest number of cowboys: at least a few dozen. Whatever the exact number on specific sailings, the ratios were always far better than the ones commonly seen on modern-day livestock ships, which travel with very few animal handlers and leave much of the animal care to mechanized processes, and to fate.[19]

In all cases the arrival of the animals at the ports had to be timed for when space was available on the ships and when maritime schedules permitted. Coordination was difficult yet very important because the "living cargo" could not simply wait unattended for conditions to be right; animals needed constant care. The other major logistical challenge was ensuring that the attendants were ready to begin work as soon as the animals boarded the ships. The animals' and the men's arrivals at ports were affected by many factors including rail schedules and anticipated port space at the destination, and it depended too, of course, on port traffic in the United States and, again, on the weather.

Upon reaching the port, animals were given a final check and were directed one by one through a chute that led to a "flying box stall" or a "flying lift" operated by a crane; the crane then lifted the animals over the ship before quickly lowering them into position. This method was preferred over forcing the animals to climb a steep ramp onto the ship. While the livestock attendants did not participate in this process—the War Shipping Administration hired stevedores for this work—they did assist in setting up the animals' stalls in preparation for the voyage. Eighty animals could be loaded per hour if there were several cranes available.[20]

The American Humane Association, as we have seen, indicated that it was satisfied with what it described as the generally high animal welfare standards in place at the ports. But of course there were exceptions. Cowboy J. Olen Yoder from Indiana, for example, described a loading accident with one of the 744 horses that were supposed to sail on the Poland-bound SS *Clarksville Victory* at the end of 1945. According to Yoder some of the longshoremen—whom Yoder described as "foreigners and senseless"—forgot to secure one end of a horse crate: "When the horse was high over the ship it toppled backwards out of the crate, hit the rim around the hold opening on its middle. Then plopped over backwards again and down on the floor of upper tween! The poor horse jumped up—but no soap. Its legs went out in all directions, fell to the floor, sprawled out and died." The Bureau of Animal Industry investigated this accident, according to Yoder. An inspector had a "healthy conflab" with the loading crew and "condemned most of the crates."[21] There is no evidence that the American Humane Association was aware of or had investigated this specific case.

Daily Lives of Men and Beasts

It was unlikely of course that any of the nonhuman animals had ever been on a ship before this moment. But many of the attendants had never been aboard a ship either, and most were unlikely to have had any experience with ocean sailing; the ship and ocean environments were thus "unfamiliar and precarious places" to all of the species involved in the aid program.[22] Many of the men were struck first by what they could see from the ship's decks: the beauty of the ocean, the awesome force of the swells, the brilliant sunshine beaming down on the Azores, or the magnificence of the White Cliffs of Dover and Gibraltar. When, as sometimes happened, the ships made brief stops before their final destination to pick up additional UNRRA cargo (including, from time to time, animals), the men reflected excitement at having yet another new experience and glimpsing yet another part of the world that thus far they had only imagined.[23]

But the men also recalled the physical discomforts, for themselves and the animals, of being at sea for so many days and the need to adjust quickly to awkward physical conditions aboard the ships. The problems started from the very first day, when many of the men experienced seasickness and were therefore unable to perform the job they were there to do—care for the animals—or even to eat their meals (though generally they remembered the food as being quite good, varied, and plentiful on board). During this initial adjustment period, the men who were not seasick would have to cover for those who were; they picked up the slack and, as they said, learned their jobs all the more quickly. Cowboy Dwight Smith wrote in his memoir that there was a great deal of food left over during a sailing's earliest days because so many men were ill and had no appetite. This had some unexpected consequences for the animals. During Smith's sailing it meant that a cow quartered just outside the mess room door got the men's leftovers: "She ate whatever was put before her—beef-

114   CHAPTER 6

FIGURE 3.   Seagoing cowboys. From the diary of Jacob C. Wine, 1946. Seagoing Cowboy Diary, Jacob C. Wine Collection at the Manchester University Archives and Brethren Historical Collection, from the Manchester University Archives and Brethren Historical Collection. https://www.manchester.edu/oaa/library/archives/DigitalCollections/seagoingcowboydiary.htm.

steak, mashed potatoes, gravy, chocolate cake and all. She even drank the leftover coffee." Smith joked that "some farmer in Poland received 'coffee in his cream!'"[24] Here humans were cheered by the presence of a nonhuman species in their midst, just as the cow in this case was no doubt satisfied by the advantages that her proximity to humans provided, and by the interactions that they could have with each other.

Space on the ship was of course limited. The specially constructed animal stalls were located on the upper and lower decks and were described by cowboys as small, crowded, and uncomfortable. Ships simply could not reflect the best of animal confinement design that, by the 1930s, had become part of the milk- and meat-producing industries. While contemporary dairying paid ever more attention to optimal space distribution for working cattle as well as to the need for proper ventilation and the ability to regulate temperature, the UNRRA animal ships compromised—UNRRA would have said by necessity—on all of this.[25]

Typically, horses were "packed tightly against each other" in their stalls. The aim was to maximize the use of limited space, but it was also to prevent the animals from turning around and moving forward or backward; the intention was to make them more or less immobile for the entire voyage.[26] While horses can sleep standing up—in the wild this makes them less vulnerable to predators

FIGURE 4. Horses aboard SS *Cedar Rapids Victory*, 1946. Jacob C. Wine Collection at the Manchester University Archives and Brethren Historical Collection from the Manchester University Archives and Brethren Historical Collection. https://www.manchester.edu/oaa/library/archives/DigitalCollections/seagoingcowboydiary.htm.

because they can take off quickly when confronted with danger—they need to be able to move around in order to process their food properly.[27] The ship conditions were therefore far from ideal and resulted in colic and stress, as the cowboys themselves recognized and repeated many times in records of their experiences.[28] In contrast, cattle could lie down during the trip, and they tended to do so especially when the sea was rough. Cattle reacted to stressful environments by eating and drinking less and by acting what one cowboy referred to as "droopy."[29]

In general horses were known to be the most delicate travelers of all animal species because of how susceptible they were to colds, pneumonia, and other lung diseases; these illnesses were sometimes referred to in a generic way simply as "shipping fever."[30] In his official history of UNRRA, George Woodbridge paints a rather grim picture of what life was like for the horses aboard a particularly difficult sailing: "Conditions on the ships were bad. Most of the horses were standing in two or three feet of manure, their backs rubbing against ceiling fixtures." The threat of "spontaneous combustion from the piles of smoking dung" was a real concern.[31] Woodbridge's description is unusually frank and stands in marked contrast to his otherwise (sometimes overly) positive assessments of most other aspects of UNRRA's work. Perhaps he did not regard criticism of the animals' physical conditions as especially damning to UNRRA or to the international aid effort. And besides, as Woodbridge points out, from a financial standpoint UNRRA had an obligation to taxpayers to move quickly, to be responsible custodians of public funds, and thus to pack as many animals as could fit into a single sailing. The animals' discomfort was to be expected. Humans, not surprisingly, made choices for the animals according to human priorities; keeping costs down was a crucial one.

The cowboys recognized the massive logistical challenges that formed part of the UNRRA animal aid program, and they understood that sometimes the ships themselves undermined the main goal of their jobs, which was to deliver the animals safely to their destinations. They frequently described problems with the physical layout of the vessels: "Our ship wasn't built with horses in mind, and everything was unhandy," recalled one cowboy on a sailing to Greece.[32] Another cowboy, Byron Royer from Kokomo, Indiana, who sailed on SS *Zona Gale*, a Liberty ship, offered the following detailed description of what was wrong with the horses' stables: "The stables on the ship are not right. They are built so that a horse, when it is down, gets its back legs under the partition and its front legs out through the front of the stall, making it almost impossible for the animal to help itself. In addition to this, it is almost impossible to clean the manure out of anything except the back two or three feet." Royer marveled, too, at other construction choices. The floors of the stables were constructed out of first-grade lumber, for example, and this, he said, "makes the whole thing a mess. This lumber gets very slick from the manure and if the mare gets the least bit out of balance she goes down just like she would on ice. The floors should be made out of native timbers with crossbars, maybe, running in both directions."[33] Cowboy J. Olen Yoder had a similar criticism of ship design. In his memoir Yoder described how one horse on his sailing died because she got caught in an awkward part of the stalls: "This one must have been pushed or lurched forward—her head under the breast rail and probably broke her neck and died instantly."[34] At least in their diaries and letters, the men were not afraid to be critical of the choices made by UNRRA planners and ship retrofitters and to exert knowledge in a specific domain.

Moisture problems also plagued the horse stalls. Yoder described the stalls as "very foul and very damp. Moisture gathers on the metal beams and air ducts considerably. Alley ways and stalls are getting soaked making it very messy." The ship's renovated ventilation systems—at a cost of $20,000 per ship—was a part of the problem, according to Yoder: "Blowers force air into holds through the ducts and pipes above horses—instead of sucking the foul, hot air out. It is the most wrong-running affair I ever did see!"[35] The air quality was further complicated by the vast quantities of urine that accumulated in the hold. Although urine was pumped out as often as possible, there was always enough present to give off a strong ammonia that irritated the eyes of both the animals and the humans aboard.[36]

Owen Gingerich, who sailed on SS *Stephen R. Mallory* with over eight hundred horses, described how the two long and narrow aisles of horses in the hold created a dangerous work environment for the cowboys: "When I was filling their water buckets constant vigilance was required to prevent snappish horses from biting." Gingerich, though, was sympathetic to the animals: "But who can blame them? Snatched from their bucolic solitude, shipped by rail to a dockside corral, hoisted into a rocking ship, deprived of exercise, forced to stand with strange partners, and balancing ever more precariously as the manure built up under their hind legs, they had every reason to express frustration... Some of the horses were sick, and in the wilting heat and ammoniated atmosphere of the lowest holds, several died of suffocation." To make matters worse, Gingerich's ship ran into engine trouble shortly after leaving Newport News and therefore had to make a stop in Boston for repairs. In that short trip from Virginia to Massachusetts, several horses died. This at least precipitated some action; while the engine trouble was being sorted, modifications were made to the horses' environments to prevent additional deaths: "Long canvas air funnels were hung between the booms to force fresh air into the lower holds, three levels down near the center of the ship." The improvements notwithstanding, a total of sixty-five horses died on Gingerich's sailing.[37]

Relatively minor mechanical problems aboard the ships were not all that uncommon, and these had the effect of lengthening the trips and therefore extending the time the animals were confined to their stalls. Occasionally there was also a maritime accident or incident of some kind or other that further complicated a trip. A particularly close call came when SS *William S. Halsted*, a Poland-bound ship, collided with an Esso Camden oil tanker in November 1946 as it made its way from the port of Baltimore through Chesapeake Bay; there was a fire in the tanker, which in turn ignited the ship. All animals, human and nonhuman, were saved; the ship, however, needed to be repaired before sailing to Europe, and the animals had to be unloaded and then reloaded while the repair work was completed.[38] All told, only one UNRRA ship was destroyed completely during the UNRRA period, and that happened as a result of a mine in the Trieste harbor; all men were saved, but all animals drowned, and all cargo was lost.[39]

Unexploded mines were a particular danger in the Baltic Sea, and many cowboys described their anxiety upon entering this region.[40] Quite often mine sweepers preceded the cattle boats to ensure safe passage through dangerous areas, including harbor entrances, and typically the ships used local guides or pilots to help them navigate through the most hazardous areas.[41]

Some UNRRA ships were also equipped with a special protective system that was designed to kept magnetic mines from attaching to the ships.[42]

There was little margin for error given the importance of delivering aid quickly; the promises of mid-century humanitarianism were literally carried aboard these ships. The ships themselves were expensive, as were the general cargo and the animals too. And then there was all of the food that the animals needed while they were aboard the ships: tons of cattle feed, hay, oats, bran, salt, and water, plus straw for bedding. On top of that, there were the tools that facilitated the cowboys' work with the animals: thousands of feet of rope, wire clippers, dozens of manure forks, brooms, shovels and scrapers, and hundreds of buckets.[43] Often, ships also carried an extra thirty-day supply of hay and grain, which was stored below decks and distributed at the destination point; this was meant to address feed shortages at the destinations.[44]

There were other humans aboard the ships as well, notably the ship's regular crew, including a captain, sailors, and officers.[45] Both the supervisors of the seagoing cowboys and the UNRRA-appointed veterinarians enjoyed the privileges of officers aboard the ships.[46] While it was the supervisors and cowboys and not the regular crew that had responsibility for the animals' care, it was the ship's captain that had final say over everything that happened on his vessel. Cowboys came under the control of UNRRA only when they left the ship; while they were on board, they were answerable to the ship's captain.[47] This meant that in a very real sense, captains determined important elements of the cowboys' and the animals' experiences. The relationship between the two groups was described as positive overall: M. E. Hays, chief of the Agricultural Rehabilitation Division of UNRRA in Poland, reported back to Washington that the ships' captains had nothing but praise for the men from the Brethren Service Committee who worked as cattle tenders on UNRRA ships. And for its part the Brethren Service Committee, as the manager of the cowboys program, did not report any serious problems with the captains.[48]

There was at least one veterinarian per ship, or two for the larger ships with a greater number of animals. The veterinarians' work started even before any animals or cowboys set foot on the ships. Before sailing the veterinarians prepared and checked the adequacy of the ship's medical supplies, including the inventory of drugs; all veterinary supplies were purchased through the Emergency Procurement Section of the Bureau of Supply.[49] The veterinarians also conducted last-minute checks of the animals' health.[50] Once on board, the veterinarians directed the animal care with the aim of bringing as many healthy animals as possible to their destinations. This meant preventing the spread of illnesses, tending to sick animals, and of course establishing an optimal schedule for feeding and watering. Much depended on the veterinarians' skills, commitment to the job, and previous livestock experience. There were many attestations from the cowboys of attentive and careful veterinarians. As cowboy Harold McNett stated in an interview, from his perspective the vets "worked harder than anybody else I reckon you would say because they always had something to do."[51] But there were also examples of gross incompetence. Owen Gingerich, for example, described one of the veterinarians on his 1946 sailing on *Stephen R. Mallory* as spectacularly inept when he seemingly failed to recognize that one of the horses he was working on was already dead.[52]

Each veterinarian, if indeed there were two, was in charge of approximately half of the animals. Each toured his respective section every morning of the trip plus after lunch and then again in the evening just before bed. During these tours the veterinarians inspected the mucous membranes of the animals' eyes, nose, and mouth, and they looked for signs of congestion. They also took the animals' body temperature, especially if there were other worrying symptoms. Part of the veterinarian's job was to document any illnesses, and especially deaths, for UNRRA's records. The forms were filed with UNRRA.[53]

The veterinarians were also in charge of the cattle supervisors, who in turn both communicated the vets' instructions to the cowboys and enforced the vets' directives about what to feed and how much. This general structure—a veterinarian in charge of overall animal care and a supervisor who had direct authority over the men who performed the daily care rituals—was familiar from wartime animal shipments.[54] The supervisors and the veterinarians thus played very important roles aboard the ships, as their attentiveness and diligence, and their general rapport with each other and with the attendants, determined how the animals experienced their days. A good working relationship between a veterinarian and a supervisor could even compensate for a lack of experience in the cowboy crew; some cowboys themselves recognized that the "inexperienced tenders" in their group only added to the animals' stress.[55]

In setting the animals' feeding schedules, the veterinarians looked to UNRRA's Division of Agriculture, Rehabilitation Livestock Branch. The branch's general guidelines stated that the animals should be fed twice a day at least, morning and evening, and that they ought to be given fresh water three times a day. Horses were given bran, oats, salt, and hay (dried grass), while cattle were given alfalfa hay, timothy hay, salt, and a feed mixture. The veterinarians and the animal care crews were warned that they needed to guard against overfeeding and overwatering just as much as they had to look out for underfeeding and underwatering. All of these instructions, guidelines, and warnings were spelled out in a document called "Instructions to Veterinarians and Livestock Supervisors."[56] The food itself was provided via the Department of Agriculture and paid for by UNRRA.[57]

FIGURE 5. Seagoing cowboys at work. Photo by Ralph M. Delk in Edwin T. Randall, "More Values Than Many Sparrows," *Christian Advocate,* March 6, 1947.

Feeding the animals occupied most of the cowboys' time. Replenishing the food supply on any one deck was done using a winch to lift the bales of hay and straw and the bags of feed to the appropriate level. There were generally no troughs, so that both the grain and the water had to be delivered in cleaned-out buckets and placed in front of the animals. According to some of the cowboys, the animals would too often knock over these buckets; the cowboys of course had to clean up the mess. All of this was made more difficult, as the cowboys were quick to say, given the need to maintain one's balance while the ship rolled and pitched through the ocean waters.[58]

In his diary Arthur D. Meyer, a seventeen-year-old Mennonite from Wayne County, Ohio, who sailed on SS *Robert W. Hart* to Poland in the summer of 1946, during UNRRA's busiest period, described the feeding regime on board his ship. Meyer kept a diary while he was at sea and documented what he did. On June 29 he wrote, "Most of the mares gobble their oats undaintily. Some get their big noses stuck in the bucket and give the bucket and perhaps the ring a good toss. We must retrieve the equipment and start all over. A few horses must be coaxed to eat. Some evidently don't feel too well. The hold is very hot. I hope we can get on the high seas soon to get some cool ocean breeze for these animals. After the horses eat their oats, we water them, collect the buckets and rings, and spread hay in the aisles for munching."[59] The routine was repeated daily.

As much as cowboys' schedules were determined by the livestock supervisors' and the veterinarians' instructions, they were also shaped, more fundamentally, by the animals' needs and by their value as humanitarian relief—or, alternatively stated, by calculations of relief and rehabilitation needs. Everyone aboard the ships—veterinarians, supervisors, cowboys, captains, and sailors—understood that the animals constituted an investment that needed to be protected. As Nancy Cushing has shown in her analysis of animals on the First Fleet, the founding ships of Britain's colony in New South Wales in the late eighteenth century, livestock animals enjoyed an elevated status aboard the ships because they were so important to colonial ambitions: "Just as Noah's pairs of animals were to ensure that the human order could be re-established after the great flood, the First Fleet animals were to be the progenitors of animals which would allow British life to be transplanted onto a new continent."[60] The animals aboard the UNRRA ships carried a similarly enormous potential and responsibility: they would help reestablish the war-destroyed societies. In a more indirect sense—and if we accept the importance of agriculture to broader rehabilitation goals—it was the animals that would help realize the full potential of postwar humanitarianism.

To maximize this potential, heifers in both the UNRRA and Heifer Project programs (and sometimes mares in the UNRRA program) were typically bred before shipment so that they were pregnant en route from the United States and would give birth not too long after arriving at their destinations. This practice, it was hoped, would allow recipient farmers to get two animals for each one that left an American port. It was a question of efficiency and utility. Moreover, the recipients would get milk shortly after the female cattle arrived at their destinations and gave birth, thereby meeting local nutritional needs and providing economic benefit sooner rather than later. Lastly, increasing the number of animals as quickly as possible helped create a healthy and varied genetic pool for the long term.[61]

Timing the pregnancies and births was complicated, however. While cattle have a gestation period of around nine months, mares foal within a broader and less predictable range (though the average is typically 340 days).[62] Both

UNRRA and the Heifer Project considered "advanced pregnancy" a reason for disqualification from the aid program.[63] Yet miscalculations happened, and these resulted in animals giving birth on the ships rather than at their final destination. This carried with it significant risks for both the mother and the newborn.[64] In these cases cowboys had to learn very quickly how they could be most useful during births. They prepared spaces aboard the tightly packed ships, cleared newborn animals' mouths and noses of mucus, and collected the placenta to throw into the ocean. Successful births could bring cowboys and the ships' crews together in shared wonder. Melvin Gingerich remarked that even the hardest and roughest sailors were softened when they witnessed two colts born during a sailing to Poland.[65] Newborn calves would often be named by the cowboys. On Robert Ebey's fall 1946 voyage to Gdańsk, three newborn calves were named Bob, after Ebey himself; Mary, after Ebey's three-year-old daughter; and Joan, after the daughter of one of the other cowboys in the group. (A fourth calf died.)[66] Cowboys talked about the responsibility they felt in caring for the additional animals and the pride they felt when the newborns made it successfully to their destinations.[67]

Cows that had already freshened—that had already started producing milk because they had very recently given birth—were not initially eligible for shipment to Europe as the passage was determined to be too dangerous for them.[68] Later, as a sense of urgency increased, cows who were already lactating were sometimes shipped; the risks that this posed to the animals were simply accepted. This meant, though, that the cows needed to be milked on the ships, and this added another task for which the seagoing cowboys became responsible.[69] On the other hand, it also meant fresh milk instead of powdered milk for the cowboys, and this was always regarded as a great treat by the cowboys and the ship's regular crew.[70] That milk would be available immediately upon reaching the destination was, again, another enormous advantage.

Cowboys worked hard and were on call twenty-four hours a day for the length of the journeys: they were scheduled seven days a week from 6:30 until about 20:30, with most of the chores concentrated over a couple of hours in the morning and a couple in the late afternoon, but they could be summoned back to active duty at any time if a problem or critical situation arose.[71] There was also one night watchman (or sometimes two cowboys worked together) that made the rounds every hour and whose job it was to report any strange animal behavior or signs of illness—runny noses or eyes, for example—to the veterinarians.[72] While the objective conditions aboard the ships were far from ideal, the staffing levels were very good, and the care practices were designed to identify problems as soon as they started.

Reporting illnesses—or just irregularities in the animals' eating or drinking—formed a key and important part of the cowboys' responsibilities.[73] The men surprised even themselves by how quickly they learned to spot changes in the animals' health and how rapidly they adjusted to the daily work routines. As Mennonite cowboy (and Goshen College student) Kenneth M. Heatwole wrote in his diary about his July 1946 trip to Poland aboard SS *Lahaina Victory*, "If my darling would see the things I do such as wiping snot and pus from noses and eyes, etc. and could see the dirt on my hands with which we eat she'd probably faint."[74] It was all physically demanding and exhausting work, and sometimes entire crews remained busy the whole day and night long if there was a specific medical emergency.[75] Exceptional circumstances were often highlighted in cowboys' diary entries and reminiscences, and the anecdotes are told with a great deal of concern for the animals' well-being. "One of our horses was down again and we spent much of the day with it," Heatwole wrote.[76] Some supervisors made a point of telling would-be cowboys that they had to expect to work hard on the ships and to devote themselves completely to the animals; the cowboys quickly understood what it meant to say that "this is not a pleasure trip."[77]

Human-Animal Interactions

Some of the seagoing cowboys were from rural communities and had farming backgrounds, which meant that they were already familiar with the work they were asked to do aboard the ships. Providing food and water to animals, monitoring animal health, and cleaning animal living environments were usual chores. Agricultural backgrounds also meant that these men better understood how to conduct themselves around animals in general. Past experiences had taught them that it was usually more productive to work cooperatively with the animals, when possible, rather than to force them into compliance. At the very least, this meant that many of the men recognized that a sympathetic disposition made animals easier to handle and that this, ultimately, made their jobs simpler too. In the men's own dairying communities (if indeed they came from such communities), the belief prevailed that treating animals well—naming them and handling them with tenderness and affection—produced more and better milk and was therefore an approach grounded in good economics. This thinking reflected a longer tradition in farm communities: in the late nineteenth century, Wisconsin dairy farmers advertised the motto, "Speak to a cow as you would a lady!"[78]

Occasionally, cowboys encountered familiar horses on their sailings and expressed delight at having someone "from home" along on their journey.

John Nunemaker, an eighteen-year-old Mennonite from Goshen, Indiana, found his family's four-year-old mare, Queen, as part of a group of horses that had been assigned to him on his trip aboard SS *Queens Victory* that sailed from Newport News to Gdańsk in the summer of 1946. The ship carried a total of 770 horses and 27 livestock attendants.[79] Nunemaker's father had sold Queen at a Goshen auction earlier that year, and the new owner had evidently sold her too; she ended up in a lot of horses destined for the UNRRA aid program. "When I said 'Queenie' she nickered," Nunemaker remembered fondly after many years.[80] We cannot know for certain what Queen felt about this unexpected encounter, but it is well established that horses respond better to familiar handlers than to strangers and that familiarity reduces stress.[81] Nunemaker's affection for Queen reminds us that this can work both ways. It also suggests that the men's on-board emotional communities included nonhuman animals as well.[82] As we will see, this happened when the animals reached Poland, too: animals' very presence could soften some of the brutal effects of war and displacement.

In general, the seagoing cowboys who came from denominations affiliated with the Heifer Project favored cattle over horses because the cattle were easier to handle and because horses were simply not part of the Heifer Project; horses were not "Brethren animals" and were included only in the UNRRA shipments. Nevertheless, all the cowboys attended to both species. This made some cowboys a little cranky as the horses were, in a sense, "foreign" to them. And yet the fact that horses required a greater level of commitment and more involved care meant that the men wrote more frequently about this species in their letters and diaries than they did about the cattle, who, in comparison, needed less specialized attention. There was just a lot less drama around cattle. One attendant declared that after the trip he was well and done with "the horses business." "After all, we asked for heifers!" he complained.[83]

Horses were indeed challenging. They were poor travelers and afraid of loud noises, and they did not cope well with being in small and tight spaces or with being approached by strangers—especially loud, nervous, and inexperienced ones.[84] The cowboys generally agreed that it took greater skill to care for the horses, and yet many of the men simply lacked the confidence, knowledge, and experience that was needed for horses.[85] This inexperience, in turn, would have made the trips more stressful for the animals, too.

In their accounts cowboys discuss the various approaches that worked—or decidedly did not work—with the horses.[86] Here again the men subscribed to the belief that kindness and patience yielded better results than a stern attitude. "To be effective, one needed to get acquainted with the horses," wrote one cowboy.[87] The work with horses was so challenging that two of the Brethren cowboys, Russell Helstern and Ed Grater, prepared a short guide that they distributed to other cowboys who were about to make a trip on an UNRRA boat. Helstern and Grater's guide provided basic information about horses' eating and drinking habits but also tips for working with these animals in the very unique ship environments. For Helstern and Grater, what was important was for the cowboys to show "a natural love for animals" or, barring that, to use "a calm voice, with gentle treatment and manners, with no evidence of fear."[88] Dave Janzen, a German-speaking Mennonite from Ontario who sailed on SS *Frederic C. Howe* in 1946 as part of an all-Mennonite crew, adopted such an approach in working with what he called his "equine friends." There were nearly seven hundred horses on Janzen's sailing plus thirty cattlemen, two foremen, two veterinarians, and one supervisor.[89] These informal and unofficial tips had to suffice as training; neither UNRRA nor the BSC offered any formal hands-on training program that prepared the men for their daily work aboard the ships.

Familiarity between men and horses could make the animals calmer, but the length of the journeys and the discomfort that the ship environment created ultimately made the animals harder to handle. Art Meyer, the seventeen-year-old Mennonite introduced earlier, described the horses as "nervous, irritable, and high-strung from their travels to the ship and treatment while boarding. They kick, bite, whinny and snort. It's like running the gauntlet when feeding and watering the critters. Constant alertness and using the hose as a deterrent weapon seems to be our best protection."[90] Fear of being kicked by a horse was ever-present. A cowboy who sailed on SS *Luckenbach* with a cargo of almost six hundred horses gave voice to this fear: "I was really scared of them at first and walking down between a double row of waving heads who can bite each other across the aisle was a real task. . . . The most nerve-wracking job is hoeing out their stalls from behind. A horse is often quite a different personality fore and aft, and although I know both ends pretty well, it's the rear that causes the most trouble."[91]

A number of men were indeed bitten and kicked by horses who were exercising whatever little agency they had over their circumstances. "Some cattlemen will carry scars for a lifetime for not having discerned the moods of the horses, or perhaps having disregarded their moods or warnings," recalled cowboy Elmer Yoder. The mandatory tetanus shots the men got before sailing were intended to protect the men in these cases.[92] Mennonite cowboy Luke R. Bomberger, who sailed on a record nine relief ships, got an unexpected souvenir from one of his trips in the form of a scar from a horse bite.[93] It was similar for cowboy Jerry Liepert. As Liepert wrote, "I still carry a scar on my back from a horse that lifted me right off the deck. His teeth went right through my leather jacket."[94] Cowboy Byron Royer used a revealing war metaphor to describe such encounters between men and horses: the bitten men were "wounded in action."[95] There was really no comparable problem with the cattle. Horned cattle—which might well have proved dangerous to the handlers—had been deemed ineligible for shipment precisely for this reason. Any animals with horns were dehorned before shipment.[96]

Human and nonhuman animal tempers flared as the days wore on and as the total number of sailings on each ship increased; the equipment started to wear out, and everything became even less comfortable than it had been at the start. On his trip to Poland in 1946, Robert Ebey described deteriorating ropes, broken halters, damaged partitions between stalls, and breast plaits chewed through by horses.[97] Inclement weather and rough seas took their toll too. Sea storms and waves could be violent enough to heave animals across the decks (or in rare cases overboard) and could also topple tons of hay and straw or even break stalls and damage the ship.[98] All of this was compounded by winter conditions. Given that UNRRA's work needed to be done as quickly as possible within a very short time frame, animals were shipped in winter as well as in the warmer months. The risks associated with this choice were clear to many, and the decision to include winter shipping was by no means uncontroversial. The National Livestock Loss Prevention Board of Chicago, through its director, Dr. H. R. Smith, had even written to the secretary of state to protest the winter shipments of animals.[99]

A well-publicized incident helped make the case against winter shipping. A March 1946 sailing of horses to Poland was supposed to have lasted just under two weeks. The ship got stuck at sea for almost three weeks waiting out a storm, however; this resulted in enormous animal losses as many of the horses succumbed to pneumonia.[100] In other cases of bad weather—such as violent winds—ships would try to alter course to take the wind head-on and thereby create conditions for a smoother sailing that would be easier on the animals and, in turn, for the cowboys who throughout it all still needed to attend to the animals' needs.[101]

Numerous cowboys also worried about the manure accumulation aboard the ships and warned that this jeopardized all of the animals' good health. Manure could contaminate food and water, and it also generated masses of flies. Generally, manure was removed using the fire hose and seawater and was washed out through the scuppers. But given that the drains were narrow—often not even two by four inches down in the hold—they proved inadequate for the volume of manure that the animals produced and became clogged easily.[102] Again, the quick repurposing of the vessels as livestock carriers had not always allowed for optimal choices.

At any rate, manure was valuable as fertilizer for fields, and some of the cowboys from rural backgrounds knew that it would be useful in agricultural rebuilding efforts at the destination points and as a result was worth collecting. Sometimes ships did carry the manure on to their destinations instead of dumping it into the ocean, but this was largely at the captains' discretion.[103] Cowboy Warren Sawyer joked in an interview about his sailing to Gdańsk in 1946 that these trips were nicknamed "manure tours" because of the quantity of manure that the boats accumulated over the course of the sailings from America.[104]

On Death and Dying

Dying and dead animals were a unique challenge for cowboys, and the men often described animal deaths in their diaries and letters home. "Four more horses kicked off last night and today," cowboy J. Olen Yoder remarked in his diary on December 13, 1945, the second day of sailing from New York to Poland.[105] Animals that developed a serious illness on board the ships and were regarded as "beyond recovery" were euthanized (often with strychnine) by the ship's veterinarian. These on-board deaths, and even instances of serious illnesses, are perhaps the best evidence we have of animals' responses to conditions that their bodies found intolerable. The animals that died during sailings were thrown overboard, leaving no trace of their existence after the fact, other than on UNRRA balance sheets as a set of statistics.[106]

Throwing the bodies of large animals overboard—a horse can easily weigh half a ton—was no simple task. It was a bit easier if the horse died near an opening, and sometimes, if the men noticed an obviously sick horse during loading, they anticipated its death by placing it in a "convenient" stall so as to minimize the work that would later be required to throw the animal into the ocean.[107] Several men worked together to slip a rope around the dead horse's head and then to pull it into position so that the body could be hoisted (using a winch) above the deck and then swung overboard. The men who lifted dead animals by the winches were called "the pulling crew," and the work they did was called "towing."[108] The men knew not to throw animals overboard in the harbor, where patrol boats passed, but, as cowboy Yoder wrote, "out on the ocean any little or big thing won't be noticed."[109] When the large animal landed in the water, the men watched the body "bobbing up and down" as the ship sailed away.[110] They presumed that the dead horse would make "a meal for the sharks and scavengers of the sea."[111] But the men understood, too, that the dead animals represented "dead labor" and lost potential; the bodies reminded everyone how enormous the obstacles to rehabilitation were.[112]

Dead horses also became a labor issue. Cowboy Yoder reported that the ship's sailing crew was paid $1.05 extra per hour during "horse dumping," and as a result the sailors were not eager for the cowboys to do this work. But there was a countervailing pressure to save on operational expenses, and the captain preferred for the cowboys to do the dumping instead; the cowboys did not get paid extra, and, after all, the animals, whether dead or alive, were their responsibility. And often this is precisely what happened: the Brethren Service Committee men, and not the regular ships' crews, disposed of the animal bodies.[113]

Some of the very old ships lacked the equipment needed to move a dead animal from a stall located below deck, to the deck, and then overboard; cowboys in these instances reported having to cut up the animal on the spot and then to throw smaller body parts through portholes. This gruesome task was especially tough when the cowboy had grown attached to the animal that had been in his care, as evidenced by some moving descriptions of death and loss in cowboy accounts. Art Meyer wrote in his diary, "This morning our beautiful big roan mare went down, sick. This afternoon she died of pneumonia. What a pity, and when we were almost there. On top of this a bit later another bay mare went down also. After moving her and getting medication she too died tonight. We now have 67 mares left to bring through this ordeal. We'll do all we can to get them there!" Less sentimental cowboys took an entirely different approach to dead horses, as Meyer described: "Some of the fellows have cut rawhide from the dead animals, have tied rope to it and are dragging it through the sea water to 'cure' it. They hope to use the hide to make things later."[114]

Deaths were frequent and not unexpected, and cowboys often observed in their diaries and memoirs that some animals arrived on the ships already sick; these were the ones most easily weakened further by the conditions aboard the ships and therefore the most likely to die. For example, cowboy John Gingerich, who described himself as an experienced horse tender, reported that on his trip on the SS *Wesley W. Barret* to Gdańsk in April 1946 "most" of the 833 horses were already sick before sailing from Baltimore harbor: 13 died during the loading stage alone, 85 died en route, and, amazingly, another 15 dead horses were unloaded in Gdańsk harbor.[115] Cowboys reported that veterinarians were regularly giving out sulfa tablets to the horses to try to keep whatever infections they might have had under control and to keep the death count as low as possible.[116]

The Brethren Service Committee, based on reports it received from the cowboy supervisors, in turn reported the high death rates to UNRRA.[117] The ships' veterinarians also submitted reports to UNRRA that detailed the various animal illnesses that were carried on board or that developed during the sailings and that sometimes resulted in death. The reports were matter-of-fact. One report from the veterinarian on SS *Mt. Whitney* that had sailed from Newport News on January 24, 1947, to Gdańsk stated that 79 of the 1,462 horses on board had died, most of them after a heavy storm that hit the ship on the first two days of February: "We attribute the majority of deaths to exhaustion and collapse of the previously sick animals as a number of them had influenza previous to shipment."[118]

Equine influenza (or "horse flu") and pneumonia were particularly pernicious problems; as many vets and cowboys confirmed, these infections circulated in the waiting lots before the horses even boarded the ships.[119] One *New York Times* article reported that almost five hundred horses died in 1946 while awaiting shipment in the Atlantic Coast Line Terminal in Savannah, Georgia; most of the deaths were caused by pneumonia.[120] The men knew all too well what the problems were and repeated them many times in their accounts. Winter sailing was hard, they said, and pneumonia rates were typically highest when the temperatures were low. Rough seas and forceful waves made animals feel unwell and often required them to be tied, as too much movement could lead to injuries. But increased immobility, the men knew, was stressful for the animals. Bad weather meant, too, that voyages became longer than expected, with animals confined indoors for the duration; this only further increased the risk of illnesses spreading throughout the group because of poor ventilation on the ships.[121]

Ship veterinarians were clear, too, that it was the very fact of sailing that made an illness of one kind or another "probable." There was little research at the time on animals and seasickness, but as one veterinarian theorized, the physical strain of bracing themselves in the holds (generally but especially during rough sailings) contributed to animals' stress and overall weakness. While cold weather was clearly a problem, in the summer, heat stroke was a persistent threat too. Vets treated heat stroke with a saline solution and glucose (plus water poured over the body of an overheated animal), but it was often not enough. Minor surgery happened occasionally, as did deliveries and abortions. Veterinarians commonly had to deal with abscesses, too; vets placed tubes in the trachea to help horses with labored breathing that was being caused by pressure from the abscesses. They routinely gave both intravenous and oral drugs aboard the ships: sulfathiazole was administered intravenously and sulfanilamide orally.[122]

None of this was news to UNRRA, which, as we know, had fully expected livestock losses in its animal aid program. The imperative to assemble and deliver animals quickly trumped everything else, and there was little they could do or were willing to do to improve the outcomes. As the August 1945 issue of UNRRA's *Monthly Review* stated plainly, "In shipping livestock by sea a percentage of loss in transit is to be expected."[123] From the start experts had estimated that losses would hover around 10 percent overall given that the shipping was planned for the whole year and not just in the better-weather months; that these losses would be expensive (UNRRA did not insure the animals or the other cargo that it shipped) was accepted.[124] In the end, as George Woodbridge states in his history of UNRRA, the livestock shipments had an overall loss rate of 3.8 percent.[125] This rate referred to the maritime part of the journey only, and as such it did not account for what happened to the animals before they boarded the ships or immediately after disembarking; these are significant omissions. In one UNRRA report, the total number of horses who died somewhere between being sold to UNRRA and the moment of loading at one of the American ports is given at over eleven thousand or 7 percent. The losses for UNRRA cattle in the US were 2 percent. Losses were heavier or smaller depending on the sailing.[126]

Moreover, aggregate loss rates that count all species together hide a couple of key factors. First, the aggregate numbers conceal the fact that horses tended to die in much higher numbers than cattle: in some reports the sailing loss rate for horses was 4.6 percent as compared to 1.5 percent for cattle.[127] Second, they obscure the significantly different loss rates on different sailings. Peggy Reiff Miller has calculated that on some sailings total loss rates could be under 1 percent whereas for others that rate could jump into the double digits, especially when loads were composed mostly of horses and the sailings happened during especially cold and rough weather.[128] Generally, the faster Victory vessels had a lower loss rate, whereas the slower Liberty vessels had a higher loss rate.[129] In other words, the type of ship that an animal ended up on mattered a great deal to his or her experiences and, ultimately, to the chances for survival, as longer voyages were more difficult for the animals to bear.[130]

At any rate, losses on individual sailings that were significantly below UNRRA's stated average of 3.8 percent were celebrated as an accomplishment. When SS *Mt. Whitney*, which departed Newport News in 1946 with 1,499 horses, reached Gdynia eleven days later with 1,459 horses, Dr. Wilder, chief veterinarian of the UNRRA mission to Poland, praised the posted 2.8 percent loss rate. Losing only forty horses, he said, was "very satisfactory."[131] Wilder made regular trips to the ports of Gdynia, Gdańsk, and Szczecin to inspect the animals that were being delivered and to record the deaths that had occurred during the crossings.[132] Like UNRRA bureaucrats generally, Wilder understood that horses were simply more susceptible than cattle to respiratory diseases on board the ships and that cattle generally did better in the hot and poorly ventilated ship conditions. According to Wilder this was the cost of running the livestock program.[133]

Cowboys generally adopted this line of thinking too. While they typically regarded the deaths as regrettable, what really worried them was the possibility that their sailing might post a loss rate that was higher than the average and that this would reflect poorly on the whole crew.[134] Even the American Humane Association, which was involved (even if somewhat passively) in monitoring the UNRRA livestock program, considered losses within a certain range quite normal and acceptable; the greater cause—delivering animal aid to war-ravaged contexts—justified some nonhuman animal deaths.[135]

These loss rates perhaps become starker when the percentages are translated into actual numbers: For example, during the ten-month period from September 29, 1945, to July 28, 1946, a total of 59,438 horses were shipped to Poland alone, and of these 4.4 percent—or 2,600 animals—died. That means that 65 horses died every week in just this one program and just on the ocean sailings themselves. A total of 19,281 cattle arrived in Poland during the same period, and of these 184 (or 0.9 percent) died.[136] A willingness to accept these numbers reflects a belief that animals existed to serve humans and were inherently expendable. Those animals that could not tolerate the conditions they encountered simply became part of livestock program accounting; their deaths had been factored in from the beginning. The animal deaths were measured in economic terms and in terms of impact on investment rather than on animal welfare per se.[137] Arguably, too, the loss rates reflected cultural attitudes toward waste more generally, whether that was food waste, resource waste, or indeed animal waste. Evidence suggests that the Americans and the British differed in this regard. British officials commented disapprovingly on the extent to which postwar American food policies, for example, were driven by food surpluses in the United States, and they were dismayed at how much food waste the Americans generally accepted as normal in shipping or, indeed, in everyday life. The British also believed that Americans' postwar horse surplus meant that austerity and frugality did not need to drive (and therefore did not drive) policy choices.[138] Though we cannot directly compare American and British approaches to animal shipping (the British did not run an animal aid program whether as part of UNRRA or separately), the remarks about an American willingness to accept "more" waste does speak to the favorable economic situation in the United States at the time.

Religious Devotion and Leisure Time

After their work with the animals was completed, some of the religious cowboys tried to make time for devotion. The frequency of religious services depended largely on the overall composition of the specific cowboy group and of course on the men's willingness to participate in prayer services. Many cowboys also remember that the type and frequency of prayer were determined by the supervisor, who was the one who often took a lead role in organizing both Sunday and midweek services, chorus groups, and Bible study. On a sailing of SS *Mt. Whitney* to Poland, for example, one Rev. Bury held Gospel preaching services in the mess hall every night (except for the first night) and prayer meetings in the stables at Christmas.[139] On the Gingerich-Oswald Mennonite crew, there were regular devotional and religious services in addition to organized recreational programs.[140]

Participating in religious services aboard the ships with like-minded men was very important to many of the cowboys. Accounts describe these moments as heightening the men's feelings of community and faith and their commitment to helping those in need. Livestock attendant E. S. Rowland from Hagerstown, Maryland, described his trip to Poland on SS *Mexican* in November 1945 as ultimately having given him "more faith in God, more of a desire to do relief work and a greater hope for the outlook of our Church of the Brethren abroad and at home."[141] Cowboy Robert Ebey said after his fall 1946 trip to Poland with a load of heifers that the experience had sparked in him a desire "to preach peace with more earnestness."[142] In contrast to the busy outbound trip, the more relaxed return journeys to North America offered far more opportunity for general "Christian fellowship," as some of the men liked to refer to it.

On the return voyages, the major job entailed washing out and cleaning the animal stalls. In a particularly evocative description, Owen Gingerich invoked the labors of Heracles and the cleaning of the Augean stables to convey what an awesome amount of work the scrubbing of manure-encrusted stalls entailed.[143] Sometimes the cowboys also applied creosote to the pens to both disinfect and preserve them. And at other times captains came up with additional work for the cowboys to do (though they were not supposed to demand it). The cleaning of the ships could also be done at the destination port, as ships were occasionally used to transport troops back to the US and space needed to be prepared for the men.[144] The goal was for all the ships sailing into American ports to be ready to take on a new load of animals and goods as quickly as possible. Once the necessary work was done, the return trips afforded plenty of time to play "cards, checkers, [and] chess" and to read.[145] Daniel Hertzler, who had sailed in December 1945 on SS *Park Victory* to Poland with a crew composed of sixteen Mennonites, ten Brethren, one Methodist, one Baptist, and one Presbyterian, said it was "probably the longest 'do nothing' experience I would ever have."[146] One Canadian cowboy described his return voyage as being all about "eating, sleeping, reading, playing games and argue [sic] with the Americans, trying to convince them that King George is not the dictator of Canada."¹⁴⁷ And while some men complained about the small sleeping spaces—a fifteen-foot-by-twenty-foot room for twenty men—others highlighted the comradery that developed between men living in such close proximity.¹⁴⁸

Cowboy crews were also encouraged during this free time to focus on "self-improvement"—studying a map of the world, building models, singing, participating in discussion groups, and learning new skills.¹⁴⁹ Melvin Gingerich remembered his men enjoying study evenings where the topics included the history of Denmark (where their ship had made a stop) and the history of UNRRA itself. Some ship captains gave the cowboys tours of the vessel if time allowed and taught them a little bit about sailing. Other cowboys worked on their physical fitness and spent time in the improvised ship gymnasium, which had been set up in the ship's hold (where until recently baled hay had been stored.)¹⁵⁰ Others took the time to record their experiences in diaries or letters home. By design the cattlemen's mess was kept open at all times so as to facilitate writing as well as game playing and other social activities.¹⁵¹

Throughout their time on the ships, both outbound and inbound, cowboys and the regular ship's crew had minimal direct or planned interaction with each other. The regular sailors were physically separated from the cowboys (they occupied a different part of the vessel) and from the relief animals. Some of the religiously minded cowboys observed the great emotional gulf that separated them from the regular crew, whom they regarded as generally vulgar and coarse.¹⁵² Owen Gingerich referred to the ship's sailors as "hardened young men not much older than we, whose vocabulary was salted with the f-word, used several times in every sentence and often creatively inserted mid-word, in participial form. They were obsessed with sex in every waking moment and probably in every dreaming moment as well."¹⁵³ Some of the sailors "had contracted venereal disease during shore leave," Gingerich revealed. And in one instance, according to Gingerich, the penicillin that would normally have been given to the sailors to treat an infectious condition had gone missing; Gingerich said that he and some other cowboys suspected "Doc Solar," one of the ships' veterinarians, of having removed it to sell on the black market.¹⁵⁴

Some of the Mennonite cowboys went so far as to say that conditions on the ships were "intolerable" because of the presence of "immoral sailors."¹⁵⁵ Too many of the sailors, according to one cowboy, were "slaves to alcohol."¹⁵⁶ Nevertheless for some of the preachers and ministers, their work with UNRRA as seagoing cowboys provided a singular opportunity to get to know (even at a distance) "a cross section of life" aboard the ships; this allowed them to better understand laymen's lives.[157]

Cowboys' willingness to describe their experiences in such rich detail means that we have an unprecedented opportunity to hear about what happened aboard the livestock ships, how the animals fared on their trips, and how they were cared for and why. Moreover, by stepping aboard the ships we can best grasp the degree to which the UNRRA and Brethren initiatives were enmeshed. While the sailing arrangements and the ships' layout reflected pragmatism and efficiency, they also embodied mutual purpose and served as striking symbols of the era's intersecting values, of a moment when secular humanitarianism and Christian charity converged in meaningful ways.

Chapter 7

Bovines, Equines, and Humans in Poland

The first UNRRA deliveries destined for Poland arrived at the Soviet-controlled Black Sea port of Constanza in Romania, where there was a reloading base for a unit of the Polish army. This was in the early months of 1945. From Constanza the shipped goods—emergency food, clothing, and basic agricultural supplies, but not yet animals—were reloaded onto dozens of train cars that traveled the long distance to Poland. It was a dangerous route. Military escorts accompanied the shipments starting in August 1945 to try to minimize the theft that had grown all too common along the way.[1] These initial Black Sea shipments had started even before the Potsdam Agreement had been signed in the summer of 1945, and before the USSR, which was tightening its grip on Poland and the other east European states, had granted visas to the UNRRA team to enter Poland. Foreign UNRRA employees did not arrive in Poland until July 1945.[2]

Though Constanza was not an ideal solution given the port's limited docking and storage capacities and its distance from Poland (it could take several weeks for the aid to reach Poland along the terrible transport routes), it was the best option in this early period when the use of the Baltic for maritime transport was not yet safe. The Baltic waters needed to be swept for mines, and scuttled warships that blocked the path to the Polish port cities had to be removed. The ports needed to be made accessible and operational.[3] In total, twenty-eight ships arrived at Constanza in the summer of 1945, and three docked at the port of Odessa (again, without animals aboard); the last of these shipments reached the Polish border in January 1946.[4]

The first UNRRA cargo ship to dock in Poland arrived at the port of Gdynia in early September 1945.[5] There were no animals aboard this shipment, however, as the infrastructure at Gdynia (and at the other major port of Gdańsk) still needed additional repairs, and a trained dock workforce that could handle the incoming animals and the masses of relief goods was not yet ready either. The first UNRRA animals finally docked at Gdańsk at the end of September 1945. SS *Virginian* had sailed from New York with just over three hundred heifers, about a dozen bulls (intact males), and approximately four hundred horses aboard.[6]

Ultimately, UNRRA used three Baltic ports for its shipments to Poland; it was the Baltic that connected the new Poland to the postwar world. A total of 770 UNRRA ships docked in Gdynia, and a smaller but still very large number—409—docked in Gdańsk; 33 docked a little west along the Baltic coast in the port city of Szczecin. Most animals arrived in Gdańsk.[7] The grand total was 1,243 shipments of various types of aid (including animal aid) to Poland.[8] The peak level of aid delivery—54,500 tons a week—was reached in June 1946. Just over a quarter of the total aid that Poland received came in the second quarter of 1946. UNRRA's operations wound down in 1947, but scheduled aid shipments, including relief animals, continued to reach Poland well into the year.[9] The number of animals that arrived on any given day varied and depended largely on the size of the incoming ship: the largest ship carried over a thousand animals and the smallest just a few hundred. Many aid ships did not carry any animals at all.

Almost 40 percent of the UNRRA aid that Poland received consisted of emergency food provisions that would be consumed almost immediately. The country also received thousands of mechanized vehicles to facilitate the recovery of its transportation and communication infrastructure. Vital medical equipment and clothing formed an important part of UNRRA shipments as well, as did large quantities of DDT that would control the rat population and thereby prevent the growth of a typhus epidemic.[10] As we know, too, about half of the three hundred thousand living animals shipped by UNRRA to all possible destinations went to Poland; a majority of these were horses.[11] There were also several hundred Heifer Project cattle that arrived in Poland on the UNRRA ships. All of these animals had been cared for by the Brethren Service Committee's seagoing cowboys.

The Cowboys' First Impressions

The seagoing cowboys, or the *morscy kowboje* as they were called in Polish, were among the first civilians to see and experience postwar Poland. Sometimes the cowboys were ashore in Poland for just a very short time. Their length of stay in the country depended primarily on maritime schedules and on the sailing weather, and this was generally true for other destinations as well.[12] But whether their stay was long or short, most cowboys saw enough of Poland to carry lifelong memories of a country ravaged by war. The cowboys conveyed their understanding that Poland was a special victim of Nazi Germany and that its people had endured extreme suffering during the war.[13] UNRRA thought so too. This understanding accounts in part for why Poland received more aid, including more animals, than any other country in Europe.

The unique scale of destruction along the Polish coastline and in the coastal cities had an immediate impact on the cowboys. The damage was evident already as ships approached the Baltic ports after having made their passage through the English Channel and the Kiel Canal. Cowboy Glenn Rohrer (who signed up for cowboy work after his time in the Civilian Public Service) described his first glimpses of Poland, of seeing "bombed docks and the tops of sunken ships" as he approached Gdańsk.[14] The sea was littered with metal scrap and ship masts (though as the cowboys said, even these compromised waters did not stop some of them from enjoying a swim!).[15]

Incoming ships were greeted by hundreds of people. Art Meyer described in his diary the moment of his ship's arrival: "All was a confused scene of excitement as the gangplank went down. The people look thin, ragged, unhealthy and sad. They are desperate for candy, food and cigarettes. It appears that the real medium of exchange is not money but cigarettes, which will buy most anything—cameras, binoculars, souvenirs, etc. The extreme poverty of these people shocks me. They appear to be much worse off than the Germans we saw along the Kiel."[16]

These early impressions were reinforced by what the men saw in Gdańsk itself. According to cowboy Gerhard Friesen, "The wreckage and ruins in the port gave a sorry sight, but nothing compared to what we were to see later in the city of Danzig [Gdańsk] itself."[17] Friesen wrote about the "wrecks of cannon" that dotted the city, and he described abandoned war equipment strewn across what had once been busy (but were now largely abandoned) streets. Moreover, the Russians, Friesen said, picking up on early reports of the Red Army's storm through the east en route to Berlin and then back again after the war ended, had stripped the city clean and had taken away everything and anything valuable. The Soviets had also taken agricultural equipment and livestock (including horses) back to the USSR, which further undermined Polish farmers' ability to till fields; this exacerbated the humanitarian crisis further still. According to Friesen, Gdańsk was "a heap of ruins made so by the Russians ten days after they occupied it. It was pure vandalism or revenge, so we are told."[18]

Mennonite cowboy Dwight Smith describes taking "an overcrowded trolley" from Nowy Port, where his ship had docked, to the center of Gdańsk.

The city, he said, had been "totally levelled." "Children were playing in the rubble," Smith wrote, "and older people were sorting through the bricks to find wood that could be used for fuel." Smith and his friends then found "a Polish boy" to show them a battlefield near the city. "We found wreckage everywhere. We crawled through wrecked tanks and armored cars, operated the guns, and searched for souvenirs."[19] When Smith and his friends stumbled across the corpses of two German soldiers, they "left in a hurry."[20]

Owen Gingerich and a few of his fellow cowboys had quite the scare when they happened upon a helmet with a skull still inside. They also found live ammunition lying about and were generally struck by the war's ferocity as well as by the resulting poverty and desperation of the people. For Gingerich this cemented his pacifism: "It vividly reinformed my previously theoretical abhorrence of war and gave me great sympathy for the plight of the Polish people."[21] Other cowboys made similar remarks: that witnessing war's destruction up close further deepened their convictions "concerning the way of peace."[22] Desperate conditions surrounded the men in Gdańsk. "It smelled of rotting garbage and acrid smoke," Harvey Cox wrote in his autobiography.[23] "There is filth everywhere," cowboy Yoder reported, and he explained that this was in no small part because sanitation and public water

Figure 6. Cowboys in Gdańsk. From the Daniel J. Peacock Collection, Swarthmore College Peace Collection, Swarthmore, PA.

systems had been demolished. Yoder continued, "Hopeless! Can't see what makes people go on living amid such ruin and despair."[24] There was also at least one visit to the Stutthof concentration camp.[25]

In rare cases men who hoped to see more of Poland still—or to continue on to other parts of Europe—could choose to "jump ship," as it were, with little more than blind faith that UNRRA would arrange a spot for them on a later sailing. UNRRA was clear about not condoning these actions and told the men that it would assume no responsibility for getting them home if they missed their scheduled departure.[26] More typically, if the scheduled departure date was set for many days into the future, men could freely explore parts of the country away from the coast. For example, cowboy Kenneth Heatwole described in his diary traveling on a double-decker bus in 1946 all the way from the coast to the ruins of the Warsaw Ghetto. Heatwole recorded his reactions: "My heart was nearly torn to pieces. . . . I was reminded of Jeremiah wailing over Jerusalem. . . . But not only was there not one stone left upon another the stones were broken & rent in twain. There were acres and acres of just bricks. No ruins were left standing at all. And where are the 350,000 Jews that lived there? . . . The Germans allowed no one to leave and then blew up the place!"[27]

While some of the men were too distressed by evidence of violence to discuss what they had seen, others felt an obligation to share their reflections. Their communities back home in America were keen to listen to them. Part and parcel of affirming that the Heifer Project and the Brethren Service Committee—and of course UNRRA too—were doing good and useful work was in proving that the scale of human suffering had been mammoth and that the need for aid was great, too. There was a purpose to telling these stories. People's misery warranted the men's—and their communities'—time, effort, and expense. As such, some of the men (and again, provided there was time for this) launched into additional relief work as they waited for their return sailing. Warren D. Sawyer, for example, volunteered for three days with the Danish Red Cross serving food at a makeshift soup kitchen that operated from the back of a truck.[28] In this way some of the cowboys became more typical humanitarian agents, even if only very briefly, while they worked in-county and interacted with the locals. For most cowboys, however, encounters with locals were generally casual and incidental, occasioned, for example, by handing out small gifts, gum, or candy to children they met on the streets. Cowboys also met locals at restaurants or at street markets where they went to buy souvenirs.[29] Or, as happened in December 1945, men from a sailing on SS *Morgantown Victory* mingled with locals when they attended a Catholic mass on Christmas Day. Two men from that same sailing gave up the special Christmas dinner that was being offered on their ship and invited two local Polish children to take their place instead.³⁰ In some cases, and as we will discuss in chapter 9, seagoing cowboys were also taken on tours of animal holding barns and of some of the farms where both UNRRA and Heifer Project animals had been placed.

Whatever their specific experiences, many of the men were struck by what they regarded as the "moral" effects that the war had had on the Polish people. One cowboy reported being surprised by the gender role subversions he witnessed: young women in "long trousers and old coats [were] working where men should be," and he marveled at the fact that "a good supply of sturdy stock of men just isn't seen here."³¹ Harvey Cox described the "oily pimps" that sidled up to him and his two friends on their walk through the rubble-filled streets of Gdańsk "whistling the way they had heard sailors do at women, describing the voluptuous shape of their ladies-for-sale with hand motions and gestures." Cox could not stand the "charred wreckage, hungry children, sadness and chaos" and faked a hangover when his friends wanted to go ashore the next day too. "Was this the Europe I had looked forward to seeing?" he asked. Cox was tortured by what he had witnessed. "I sensed a new object for my disgust and revulsion: the war. The war had done this."³²

For others the period spent in a port city far from home provided license to take risks and act like someone different. Cowboy Heatwole wrote frankly in his diary about what he viewed as the disturbing behavior of some of the other cowboys with whom he traveled: "Also most of the cattle boys came in with alcohol on their breath. Even, I'm sorry to say, the Mennonite boys. Everyone seems to drink Vodka (the most powerful liquor). The American Bar has almost become the embassy. The whore houses have been frequented by our number too. Why must men behave like brutes and devils when they get away from home."³³

Of course, the Brethren Service Committee that had recruited the men warned against what it referred to as "un-Christian" behavior during the relief trips.³⁴ It is difficult to gauge how frequently these supposed moral transgressions happened among the cowboys, and not surprisingly the men who left accounts (and who are the focus of this book) do not describe their own experiences with drinking or sex. Instead, what do appear frequently are descriptions of the black market that thrived in every port town. The men knew that cigarettes were a valuable currency in the black market and that they could be traded for just about anything. Though the Brethren Service Committee associated smoking with immorality, temptation, and financial imprudence, a number of men describe packing cigarettes with them on their trips to trade for souvenirs like military medals and war-related materiel, for example, or relics from churches that had once belonged to the German Mennonites of the region.³⁵

For his part, cowboy supervisor Melvin Gingerich voiced his objections to this practice, reminding the men that they were on a service mission to "help" rather than to "exploit" desperate people.³⁶ For those that abstained, the enthusiasm that others exhibited for the black market, and that the locals in turn showed for the cigarettes they were being offered, made an enormous impression. "To see a people so sodden in the nicotine habit and in such a desperate condition economically, politically, and spiritually gives one a feelings of hopelessness," a Mennonite cowboy reported after his trip to Poland.³⁷ Witnessing this desperation up close itself justified the humanitarian interventions the cowboys were making.

The Animals' First Impressions

While the brutality of war was everywhere in evidence for the cowboys, back at the ports the animals, too, quickly felt the burden of having arrived in a war-ravaged place. Dozens of men were needed to unload the newly arrived animals: a single Victory ship required approximately one hundred stevedores. These numbers, however, were difficult to secure, especially in the earliest postwar months, and so labor shortages contributed to the overall chaos in the port areas.³⁸ Then when sufficient bodies could be found, the work was still slow, as the newly hired animal handlers were obviously weak and hungry, or they lacked experience with livestock and did their work inefficiently.³⁹ The infrastructure problems at the port made unloading more difficult still. At the Nowy Port dock area in Gdańsk, there were wet and muddy surfaces, which made it more likely that the newly arrived horses would slip and fall and possibly break a leg. In addition, there were scraps of steel and other debris strewn about, and there was inadequate fencing to keep the animals contained. Though the Polish authorities worked to address these problems, improvements took time.⁴⁰

At the extreme and during particularly busy periods, the unloading of the animals could take days, even though livestock had priority in the unloading order. One cowboy described the "ruined port buildings, tracks, cranes, and piers" as complicating what had once been relatively simple tasks.⁴¹ In addition, and especially with the earliest shipments, it was sometimes unclear who was responsible for caring for the recent arrivals (the government had ostensibly contracted private companies to do this work), and this meant that animals were too often left without proper care for long periods.⁴²

Even the ships' captains and crews, who had no formal or direct responsibility for the animals aboard, understood very clearly that the already-fragile health of the cattle and horses was compromised further during the unloading period.⁴³ Master J. B. Oliver of SS *Norwalk Victory* was so outraged by the inefficiencies he witnessed that he wrote to UNRRA directly to complain. Oliver counted five horses who died after the ship arrived in Gdynia and another fourteen that were taken off "in sick and dying condition" because of the inadequate care they had endured on the docked ship. According to Oliver the animals were given insufficient food and water while the unloading process took place, and those of them on deck also faced lengthy exposure to the elements.[44]

Animals were typically lowered from the ship in a wooden crate held by an "elevator" that swung high in the air. When the animals reached dry land after being released from these "flying stalls," they were frantic with fear and eager to shake off their confinements. Others refused to leave the crate and needed to be coaxed out, gently or roughly as the situation demanded.[45] The language barriers between the animals and the Polish dock workers were felt immediately. One cowboy described the futile attempts of Polish handlers to corral newly arrived horses and to communicate with them: the Polish-language horse commands and standard Polish hand gestures could not be understood by animals who either had been wild until very recently or had thus far only heard and responded to English commands and American-style hand signals.[46] Americans typically used "woha" to command a horse to stop, for example, whereas Poles said "grrr." The language barrier slowed down the entire process and contributed to a generally hectic environment.[47]

Each newly arrived UNRRA animal was branded on its back with the UNRRA name; the branding, as one of the cowboys observed, was sometimes done by women.[48] Along with other cowboys, George Willoughby had the chance to watch this work. He wrote about it to his wife, Lillian, commenting that "miraculously 'UNRRA' was forever a part of that cow."[49] The branding would advertise the UNRRA program for the short term and, as UNRRA hoped, would serve as a long-term reminder of the aid that had come to Poland from the United Nations.[50]

There were some touching scenes on the docks at this point. Waiting cows needed to be milked, and this milk was distributed to the hungry people that always lingered near the ships.[51] Sometimes women came with their children and milk buckets in anticipation of just such an opportunity.[52] It happened occasionally that the women were even permitted aboard the ships to milk the cows themselves.[53] Then there was the moment when people met their newly arrived animal for the first time. Will Keller, the radio operator on SS *Park Victory*, described what he saw: "A ship's boom swings up and out of a hold and over to the dock, lowering another animal container. Out staggers a sick cow, head hanging down, frothing at nostrils and mouth. Given extra injections by Vets. Old man and old woman waiting nearby come forward. Old man places rope around cow's neck; old woman covers cow with blanket. Man leads cow away as old woman walks alongside hugging and petting cow."[54] No doubt cowboys relished providing this

FIGURE 7. Unloading of horses in Poland. From the Daniel J. Peacock Collection, Swarthmore College Peace Collection, Swarthmore, PA.

evidence that the animals they had shepherded across the Atlantic were going to the neediest of the needy and that they were doing some good.[55] This, after all, was what the cowboys' work was all about.

What was fortunate for humans was not always experienced in positive ways by the animals, of course. Animals that were obviously near death as they were removed from the ships represented a different kind of opportunity for the waiting crowds. One cowboy recalled a case in which one of the sick horses "went down" during unloading and proved unable to get up again. The "starved Poles" wasted no time: they "fell upon the hapless beast and within minutes had butchered and cleaned it."[56] The flesh of an already-dead horse should not be consumed for food, and so the hungry people killed the animal themselves, drained the blood, and distributed the meat—even though chevaline was not a standard part of the Polish diet during normal times.

Cowboys also reported hearing rumors about recipients who slaughtered their newly received cattle as soon as they returned home to their farms. This was despite the fact that there were bans at specific times and in specific regions against the slaughter of animals for meat. UNRRA, too, did not intend for its animals to be turned into meat immediately.[57] Yet reasonably enough, keeping animals to work fields and to reestablish herds felt less pressing in the short term than feeding hungry families. "I suppose this is just natural," wrote one cowboy in his reflections about this.[58] Though the animals were not sent *as* food, they nevertheless became food in some instances; the humanitarian programs' intentions for the animals were secondary to people's immediate needs.

Another cowboy who arrived in Poland with 750 horses describes witnessing the locals seize and kill a "mean-spirited" horse that had just been removed from the ship. They hit the animal between the eyes with a sledge hammer, cut it up, and, again, immediately distributed the meat.[59] The skins of recently dead animals like this one could then be delivered to raw leather processing facilities, and in this way the Poles would earn a little money.[60] These were rogue actions, to be sure, and they were possible only in moments like this, when routines were still in the making and oversight was limited or at least inconsistent. But these examples also remind us that locals did not hesitate to act in their best interests when given the opportunity. Though the horses that the locals slaughtered in these examples were not being used as intended, their bodies did, broadly speaking, deliver aid and offer relief.

Animal-State Encounters

That the reality on the piers was sometimes different from plans that UNRRA had made was not surprising. UNRRA focused its energies on getting the animals to the target countries, and for many reasons the organization was less able to determine what would happen to them once they arrived at their destinations. Formally, control over UNRRA aid, in all its forms and in all destinations, transferred to the receiving government from the moment it landed; this was standard practice and had been agreed to as a general principle from the earliest planning days. What this means is that responsibility for the aid shipments that arrived in Poland fell to the Provisional Government of National Unity, which was the result of a coalition-type agreement between the Communists and the non-Communists from the summer of 1945.[61] It was the Polish government, and not UNRRA, that made decisions about how to collect and distribute incoming goods and animals. This arrangement made good logistical sense: relying on local governments and local people relieved UNRRA of the need to staff and organize the distribution and, more importantly, to determine what resources were needed where.[62] The arrangement, moreover, provides a useful reminder of how much room there was in this postwar moment for national priorities and agendas to determine important details about international aid programs.

At the same time, however, UNRRA was supposed to ensure that all aid was being distributed in accordance with Resolution 6, which forbade discrimination based on race, religion, or politics; aid was also not to be used as any kind of political weapon.[63] UNRRA thus maintained the right to have observers and advisors in the recipient countries in order to confirm that its rules were being followed. As such, representatives from UNRRA were on hand when ships came to port (though their presence was limited to a monitoring role), and the representatives also had the right to conduct spot checks related to the distribution and use of UNRRA goods. They made visits to holding yards and toured recipient farms as well.[64]

The first direct contact between all incoming animals and the Polish state came shortly after the animals' arrival through Ministry of Agriculture veterinarians who greeted the arriving ships.[65] Each ship was required to produce a health declaration that would be filed with the ministry; the declaration included the name of the sailing ship; the number of animals that had arrived, divided by species and type; the inspection date; and the veterinarian's attestation that all of the animals had been examined and declared healthy or unhealthy for specific reasons. It was these veterinary reports that determined where the animals would go next. The Ministry's Representation for UNRRA Affairs at the Ports of Gdynia and Gdańsk (Przedstawicielstwo do Spraw UNRRA na Porty Gdynia i Gdańsk) attached a summary to the veterinarians' inspection reports too. These summaries repeated some of the information that was in the veterinarians' reports (the name of the ship and the number of animals that had arrived, most notably) and included a brief reflection on the quality of the incoming animal shipment as a whole: "healthy" or "in a bad state" or "average."[66]

The inspection process needed to be handled quickly so that the animals could be moved along to their next destinations. The pressure to work fast in turn led to objections from the Polish veterinarians, who argued that the considerable time pressures undermined their abilities to make accurate and confident assessments. Veterinarians complained, too, that the crowded and chaotic conditions at the ports meant that they could not really inspect every animal properly. Nighttime unloading compromised the inspections further still, as the darkness easily obscured some health problems (lights were eventually added to the port areas to improve visibility).[67] These problems with rushed inspections were already more or less familiar from the American context.

Cattle and horses that did not look like they could recover from whatever ailed them (some of the arriving animals were unable to walk, for example) failed these preliminary health inspections. Prognoses were reflected in the documents that the veterinarians filed with the ministry and could read, simply, "unsuccessful" or "unsuitable for work." These animals were

FIGURE 8. Delivery of horses by UNRRA, 1946–48. Reference code 3/3/0/11/441. Collection: Socjalistyczna Agencja Prasowa, Narodowe Archiwum Cyfrowe. https://www.szukajwarchiwach.gov.pl/jednostka/-/jednostka/9743659.

slaughtered. Some were directed to vaccine-producing plants; one such plant produced a vaccine for erysipelas, a common bacterial infection found in pig populations. Alternatively, the sick animals were sent to state veterinary facilities for use in teaching; the exact destination depended on the type of illness and needs at the moment.[68]

Animals that did not pass the initial inspection but that looked like they had a reasonable chance of being nursed back to health were moved through the system in a modified fashion. There were a couple of main options. The first was to sell the animals to institutions (like schools, for example) that had the means to provide more complicated care and that did not desperately need either the labor or the milk (whichever the case may have been) of this one newcomer. In these cases, the recipient institution had to attest to the fact that the given animal's health problems had been clearly communicated and that the institution would not hold the ministry responsible if the animal's health status worsened or if the animal died. The

FIGURE 9. Delivery of horses by UNRRA, 1946–48. Reference code 3/3/0/11/441. Collection: Socjalistyczna Agencja Prasowa, Narodowe Archiwum Cyfrowe. https://www.szukajwarchiwach.gov.pl/jednostka/-/jednostka/9743659.

receiving institution also had to provide a general care plan for the animal that included proper veterinary attention. For its part the ministry made medicines available to the new owners of unhealthy animals for a very low cost. The recipients also had to agree not to use sick animals for work until recovery was complete.[69]

The second option for animals that did not pass the initial veterinary inspection was a stay at a clinic that was run by the Veterinary Department of Poland's Ministry of Agriculture.[70] The veterinary clinic in Gdańsk opened in April 1946, on what is now called Haller Avenue, and clinics also opened in Gdynia, Szczecin, and Sopot.[71] Between 10 and 12 percent of all arriving horses were sent to the Gdańsk clinic alone. As we know, Poland received many more horses than cattle from UNRRA, and horses ended up

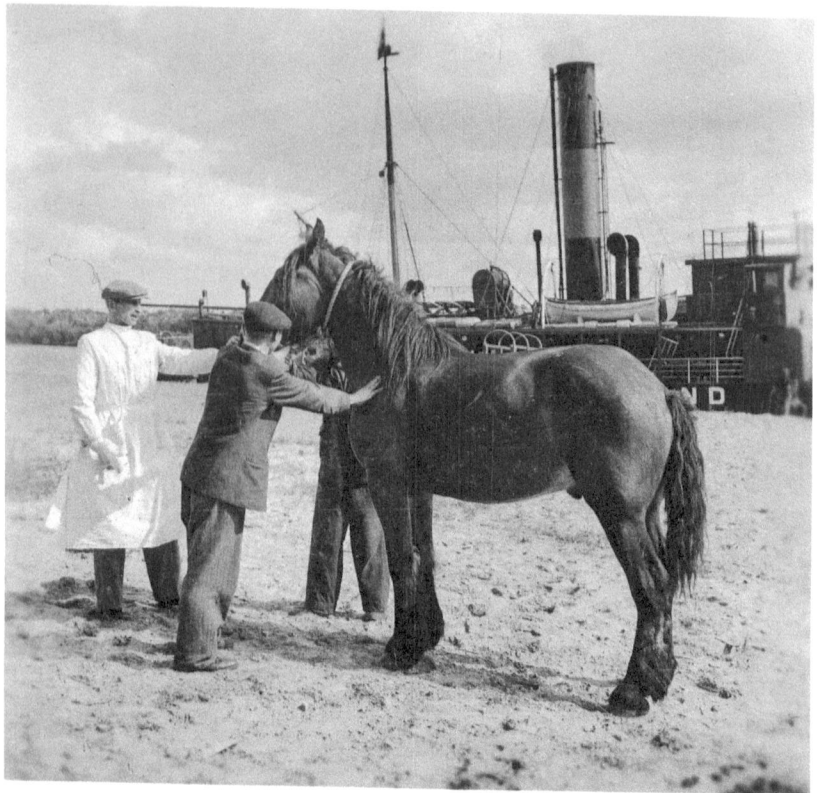

Figure 10. Veterinarian examining UNRRA horses, 1946–48. Reference code 3/3/0/11/441. Collection: Socjalistyczna Agencja Prasowa, Narodowe Archiwum Cyfrowe. https://www.szukajwarchiwach.gov.pl/jednostka/-/jednostka/9743659.

at the clinics more often.[72] Some of the arriving animals were so sick that they died en route to the clinics, even though, in the case of Gdańsk, the distance from the port to the clinic was just several kilometers. Respiratory diseases were the number-one cause of equine death after landing, though horses also died because of fractures or severe wounds that could not be expected to heal properly. At the Gdańsk facility, according to the director of the veterinary clinic in Gdańsk, an average of seven animals, mainly horses, died every day.[73]

The special veterinary clinics were stretched beyond capacity. One early 1946 report from the State Veterinary Institute to the Ministry of Agriculture complained about inadequate staff; there were shortages of veterinarians, pharmacists, veterinary nurses, paramedics, lab technicians, and office admin-

FIGURE 11. Delivery of horses by UNRRA, 1946–48. Reference code 3/3/0/11/441. Collection: Socjalistyczna Agencja Prasowa, Narodowe Archiwum Cyfrowe. https://www.szukajwarchiwach.gov.pl/jednostka/-/jednostka/9743659.

istrators. Even caretakers who provided the animals' daily food and water were in short supply.[74] Though it was built to accommodate 400 to 600 animals at a time, the Gdańsk clinic ended up caring for as many as 1,700 at once.[75] UNRRA provided the clinics with veterinary supplies, including medicine and laboratory equipment, but these contributions were insufficient, and what might have been a treatable condition in other circumstances could prove fatal for animals in crowded conditions with limited resources and too few staff.[76] As it was, a disproportionate amount of time went toward treating the sickest animals, and this sometimes left the only moderately sick animals in a more precarious position than necessary. What this meant, for example, is that sometimes less critical cases were moved outdoors to make room indoors for the sickest animals, but this had the effect of jeopardizing the recovery of the least sick animals, especially during the coldest months of the year.[77]

There were also the considerable financial costs involved in running the clinics (UNRRA donations of veterinary supplies and medicine notwithstanding). For example, the Szczecin veterinary clinic spent over 64,000 złoty on treating 1,287 horses during the three-month period from early September to early December 1946.[78] The especially busy Gdańsk clinic registered expenses of over one million złoty in a single month, August 1946.[79] This money came from Poland's Ministry of Agriculture.[80] Complicating matters further still was the fact that veterinary reference manuals had been lost during the war, and animal care handbooks directed at animal owners and breeders were also gone. The process of republishing these, and then delivering the information to relevant parties, would take some time.[81]

These earliest hours, days, and weeks after the animals arrived in Poland were a delicate time. This period also underscores just how complicated it is to talk about "loss rates" in the postwar live animal aid program. The losses—the deaths—happened at various stages and in several places: from the point of purchase or donation in the United States en route to the ports, during loading, on the ships, during unloading, or in the period right after unloading. UNRRA itself claimed a 3.8 percent loss rate for its livestock shipments overall, as we have seen.[82] On top of this, UNRRA estimated the loss rate for landed animals (animals that had arrived alive, were unloaded, and then died shortly after) to have been low at just 0.22 percent.[83] The reliability of this number is doubtful, however, and is contradicted in UNRRA's own documents: another UNRRA report states that an estimated 2 percent of all horses died "upon arrival" and that 10 percent died within the first few months.[84] Here we come back to the fact that UNRRA's insight into what happened to animals after arrival was ultimately limited because it simply had no jurisdiction in the recipient countries.

On the Road Again

The animals' travels did not of course stop at foreign port areas, just as they did not start at the port of origin; overland journeys were (and remain) a significant part of maritime shipping. Once at the port of delivery, the animals faced in reverse what they had experienced at the beginning. In this next section, we focus on the animals that did what the aid program wanted: they stayed healthy throughout the various stages of becoming relief animals. These healthy animals were typically sent from the ships almost immediately to makeshift stables until the next leg of their trip could be arranged.[85] Some went from the port at Gdańsk to Wiślany Station, where there was room for approximately three thousand animals at a time. Enormous pyramids of pressed hay that had been removed from the UNRRA ships were stored at the station as well, as were donated oats and bags of assorted other types of feed.⁸⁶ Other healthy animals went to the major holding stable that had been established at the hippodrome in Sopot.⁸⁷

Private firms were hired to receive the animals from the ships and to provide food and care while they were in transit to the holding stables or to other designated locations.⁸⁸ Authority during this period, however, rested with the Central Office for Meat (Rolnicza Centrala Mięsna). The Central Office for Meat had been established in October 1945 to regulate Poland's meat supply by balancing breeders' and farmers' needs with consumers' needs.⁸⁹ In this case, it oversaw everything from building fences around designated UNRRA animal holding areas to preparing feed troughs and water stations. Its staff admitted that the conditions that they were able to provide for the animals were not always adequate given the numbers that arrived weekly, but as with so much at this time, expediency trumped quality.⁹⁰

From the temporary stables and holding centers, the healthy animals went on to destinations chosen by the Ministry of Agriculture, which had overall responsibility for incoming livestock. The animals usually traveled by train but sometimes, for closer distances, by truck; for very short distances, and only if the horses had been shod, the animals traveled by foot. Determining the final destinations was a long and highly bureaucratic process that started well before the animals' arrival in Poland and that, in the end, confused just about everyone. It began ostensibly when each Provincial Land Office (Wojewódzki Urząd Ziemski) wrote to the Agriculture Office (Biuro Rolne) of the Department of Agriculture and outlined specific animal needs in its region. The Provincial Land Office based its requests in part on petitions it had received from people and institutions interested in having an UNRRA animal.⁹¹ The Agriculture Office reviewed these provincial assessments of need and determined how many animals and of which type (sometimes including which breed type) ought to be directed to worthy recipients in each province.⁹² These decisions were then communicated to the Provincial Distribution Commission (Wojewódzka Komisja Rozdziału), which was under the control of the Provincial Land Office. The decisions were also conveyed to the District Inventory Distribution Commission (Powiatowa Komisja Rozdziału Inwentarza), which included, among other bodies, representatives of Peasant Self-Help (Samopomoc Chłopska) and the District Agricultural Office (Powiatowe Biuro Rolne). The last layer of bureaucracy between people and their relief animals was the District Inventory Distribution Commission. The district level was the one to inform recipients that their UNRRA animals had arrived in the country and needed to be collected at a specified time and place, either in the port area or at some (more) convenient central location.⁹³

Ultimately, a majority of the UNRRA cattle and horses that Poland received—70 percent—went to small farms. Recipients were chosen based on defined need and on a perceived ability to maximize the animals' potential as laborers, whether on fields or as providers of milk. Farms with no cattle and no horses had priority, and within this group military settlers and repatriates were privileged.⁹⁴ The general calculation was that one horse was required for every fifteen hectares of land (meaning of course that the smallest farms were not eligible to receive a horse). Another 20 percent of the incoming animals went to an agricultural school or center, an experimental farm, or a state farm. The remaining 10 percent went to other state-owned facilities and breeding lots.⁹⁵ Animals that went to breeding lots would be bred and then often moved on again; such animals in effect did double duty.⁹⁶ Though the number of horses sent for breeding was relatively small, a representative from the State Horse Breeding Department met every ship, surveyed incoming stock, and took several horses from some shipments and none from others.⁹⁷

All these decisions and allocations were happening while the government was working on national land reform. As early as September 1944, the Polish Committee of National Liberation had started seizing large estates, including those of ethnic Germans who were fleeing Poland; those estates were subdivided, and the smaller parcels of land were distributed among landless peasants and small farmers. The distributed land parcels varied in size but typically did not exceed five hectares per individual. Though the previous owners of the land were not compensated, the recipients did pay for their new holdings; the costs were low and payments flexible, however. Those entering these arrangements without any previous landholdings at all had the most favorable payment rates.⁹⁸ People on the newest land parcels were especially desperate for animals.

As an invaded country, Poland was not obliged to pay UNRRA directly for the animals or for most of the other relief that it received.⁹⁹ But recipients were generally obliged to pay the Polish government for what they received. There was nothing unusual about this.¹⁰⁰ While urgent food aid from UNRRA was initially distributed on a voucher system and for free, other types of aid, including some maintenance food rations and so-called luxury food items, plus animals, were generally sold by the receiving government to the people at favorable fixed prices that were adjusted as needed.¹⁰¹ The chief advantage of this arrangement for the receiving countries was that it provided a valuable source of income. As a result of these sales, the government secured some of the funds it needed to stabilize and develop different parts of the economy and to thereby fulfill broader rehabilitation goals. Moreover, it was expected that this arrangement would draw out hoarded cash and would thereby combat inflation. And lastly, as some argued, paying for goods would arguably prevent people from feeling like they were living on handouts; it helped normalize life generally. In the end, selling UNRRA goods earned Poland billions of złoty.[102]

The selling costs of animals were set by Poland's Ministry of Agriculture, with specific costs reflecting, as one might expect, the species, the health and physical fitness of the animal, and the animal's suitability for work, either as a milk producer or as draft labor. The prices were fair and attractive, but it was the simple fact that UNRRA made animals available for purchase that was most important; there were no other options for purchasing or otherwise getting animals.

Who received an animal—whether an individual or an institution—did not affect the price, at least formally. Healthy horses sold for between 40,000 and 60,000 złoty, but this price could be higher if an animal was assessed to be especially valuable.[103] The ministry lowered the prices for UNRRA animals in November 1946, as UNRRA entered its final phase, such that healthy horses started to sell for between 25,000 and 50,000 złoty, with the exact price determined at distribution points by supposedly trained sellers acting on behalf of the government. These persons had a fair degree of latitude to determine the animals' overall potential and value. In addition, the guidelines for cost categories overlapped. For example, "lightly sick" horses started at 20,000 złoty but could also fetch as much as 50,000 złoty, making the final price a matter of the appraisers' personal discretion. Horses that needed to go to a veterinary clinic first cost around 9,000 złoty. The base price for cattle was as much as 45,000 złoty initially but dropped to between 18,000 and 38,000 złoty at the end of 1946. Heifers were cheaper at between 13,000 and 25,000 złoty.[104] In comparison, one personal advert placed in the classified section of *The Voice of Pomerania* (*Głos Pomorski*) in 1946 offered a young cow that was milking at twenty liters plus a pregnant heifer for 52,000 and 20,000 złoty respectively. This seller was also willing to contemplate a straight exchange of these two animals for a horse.[105]

In addition to the base cost for the animal, recipients owed for animal feed and animal care, plus there were small administrative and transport costs. These sums ran about 3,000 or 4,000 złoty for a horse and a little less for cattle.[106] Recipients also owed money for the insurance that protected their animals against theft and death as they traveled from the ports en route to their new homes. The insurance was provided through the provincial branches of the General Mutual Insurance Institution (Powszechny Zakład Ubezpieczeń Wzajemnych). The coverage started as soon as the animals started their journeys to their final destinations, and it ended as soon as the animals reached these destinations. That the insurance ended at this point—once the animals were "home"—sometimes came as an unpleasant surprise to farmers (and even to provincial officials), who did not always understand the limits of the coverage that they were buying.[107]

People were generally expected to pay in cash for all the costs associated with the animals, and loans were possible for certain categories of buyers. These included new settlers in the Recovered Territories, repatriates, anyone who had received a plot of land in the recent land reform, agricultural schools, and social welfare agencies and hospitals with agricultural properties. Applicants from the Recovered Territories and from bridgehead areas were given priority over the other categories.[108] Interest-free loans came from the State Agricultural Bank (Państwowy Bank Rolny), but the funds needed to be in place, in full, at the time of pickup. Loan agreements were for a specific amount (40,000 złoty for a horse, for example), meaning that to some extent the quality of the animal that an individual received was determined by the value of the loan that had been negotiated in advance. Loan applicants had to establish need, which was determined by the amount of land owned. Applicants also had to attest to the fact that they did not currently already own a horse or a cow.[109]

The loan money needed to be repaid in three years, with the first installment payable in the first year. Nonpayment was a punishable offense.[110] Some of the payment could be made in rye, with price per bushel established according to rates on the grain market or by the Chamber of Agriculture (Izba Rolnicza) for the given province.[111] In early 1946 one bovine cost between ten and fifteen quintals of rye (ten quintals is 1,000 kilograms or 2,200 pounds), depending on the quality of the animal.[112] The amount was manageable as long as the harvest was good, but the 1947 harvest was suboptimal, and so this made the payments onerous that year.[113] Horses were worth more, from approximately twelve to twenty quintals of rye.[114] Repayment was made to the Land Office (Urząd Ziemski) and was deposited into a special account set up specifically for UNRRA stock. The rye would be used in the region where it was produced. The full debt could also be wiped out if the owner of a cow gave the Chamber of Agriculture a "well raised" ten-month-old heifer or bull.[115]

If an UNRRA animal died within thirty days of receipt, the farmer needed to provide medical proof that nothing he or she had done had caused the animal's death. The farmer also needed to provide evidence of payments already made. The Agricultural Bank could annul debts still owed with proof of death and attestation from a veterinarian that the animal did not die because of careless actions on the part of the new owner.[116] Indeed, many animals died in the month after landing; the rate of insurance claims for animals that died during this period were high (but we must remember that not all animals were even insured during this period).[117] According to one report written in 1948 by Szczecin authorities, the province received a total of over 15,000 horses and almost 2,300 cattle from UNRRA, and of these 291 animals died during the initial thirty-day period after receipt. An additional 460 horses died as a result of accidents during that time.[118]

If stock was still available, farmers whose initial UNRRA animals died (for reasons other than the farmers' negligence) were entitled to a replacement animal at no charge.[119] But in many cases, the cause of an animal's death was unclear, and it was difficult if not impossible for a farmer to prove that there had been something "wrong" with the animal from the start.[120] There was really no documentation that could prove the point. This meant that debts were seldom wiped out; even into the late 1940s and early 1950s, farmers still owed for animals that were long dead.[121]

Horses and Cattle for Poland's New "Wild West"

Though dire conditions in Poland's rural areas were caused both indirectly and directly by the waging of war, the final sweep of the Red Army eastward through Poland back to the Soviet Union after the war had been won took an additional toll on Polish people, agricultural lands, infrastructure, and of course animals.[122] The need for livestock was great all across Poland in the immediate postwar period, but the situation in the so-called Recovered Territories in the west and northeast was especially desperate. It was also there in Poland's new Wild West that the hope for agricultural reconstruction was greatest.[123]

The "Recovered Territories" refer to the lands that Poland received from Germany as part of the postwar settlement in an exchange, of a sort, for having renounced claims to the eastern territories occupied since September 1939 by the Soviet Union. These formerly German lands in the west of the new Polish state had quickly become depopulated in 1945 as ethnic Germans fled the advancing Red Army and later, once the war was over, as the formal expulsion of Germans from Poland (and elsewhere) took place. Ethnic Germans fled only with what they could carry. The few animals that had somehow survived until this late date in the war either were taken along with the fleeing farmers or, if the animals could not travel and were already sick, were left behind to die.

In using the term "recovered" or reclaimed lands (*ziemie odzyskane*), the Polish government conveyed that there was a clear historical basis for Polish control over this region. "We are returning to the Lands of the Piast dynasty," one popular government slogan declared.[124] In addition, the northern- and westernmost parts of the Recovered Territories—the areas along the Baltic coast—were part of what the Polish Communists, during the 1946 Festival of the Sea, were already referring to as "the symbolic return of Poland to the sea."[125] It was both fitting and meaningful that the animals—and all the other forms of humanitarian aid that were meant to help Poland resume normal life after the end of the war—arrived here, at the ports on the Baltic sea.

The Recovered Territories had been savaged by the war, frantically depopulated of their large ethnic German population, then chaotically repopulated, both by ethnic Poles from central Poland and by those who were expelled from the eastern provinces annexed by the Soviet Union. By 1945 almost half of the over two hundred milk kitchens that had been established in Poland to provide emergency food relief were located in the Recovered Territories.[126] The challenge that the Polish government had was to stave off hunger and despair in the short term in this vulnerable spot on Germany's eastern border while also claiming this area for the long term in more than a legal and bureaucratic way.[127]

The Voice of the People (*Głos Ludu*), the official newspaper of the Polish Workers' Party, the Polish Communists, reminded readers that these recovered lands needed to be settled and "put into production" as quickly as possible.[128] For this to happen, for the Recovered Territories to become fully absorbed into postwar Poland, it was not enough just to provide emergency food relief. Agricultural capacity had to be reestablished, and people needed to be given a way to make themselves and the new lands productive; farmers needed to be able to feed themselves and the country.[129] The quick action on land reform in this area reflected this thinking. By the end of 1946, over a million hectares of land in the Recovered Territories had been seized and subdivided, and by the end of the decade almost half a million new farms had been established in the region.[130]

Animals and animal labor were absolutely integral to goals for the region, to the process of western settlement and modernization, and to the affirmation of Poland's new postwar borders. The presence of ethnic Poles and Polish-owned livestock in these territories would confirm Polish rootedness in the region and would buttress the state's claims over it. The goal was to effect what we might call a "moral reconstruction" of the new west, to make it as "home-like" and "normal" as quickly as possible. This required working farms, with animals—and this is where UNRRA came in.[131] This area could be fully absorbed into the new Poland only if the lands were populated by ethnic Poles and if the farmyards were stocked with Polish cows and horses. The horses would supply the labor required to produce the grain and cereal crops that were important to Polish cuisine and that would feed the other livestock animals, including the cows who produced the all-important milk. Alongside their tangible economic value, the animals' presence in the Recovered Territories deepened and completed settlement. The animals offered emotional and symbolic value as well, and this, too, forms an important part of the story of resettling the west in the immediate postwar period.[132]

The numbers reflect the importance of the west to the postwar animal aid program. In total, approximately one hundred thousand UNRRA horses and the majority of UNRRA cattle (about sixteen thousand) were distributed in the Recovered Territories; that amounted to about three-quarters of Poland's total allocation.[133] Twenty percent each went to the provinces of Gdańsk, Western Pomerania, Olsztyn, and Lower Silesia, with 15 percent going to Lubusz and 5 percent to Upper Silesia and Opole.[134] Though these numbers were significant, they of course represented only a small fraction of the number of animals that had been in the area before the war. To cultivate all tillable land in the region, UNRRA estimates said, hundreds of thousands of additional horses (plus many more tractors) were needed.[135]

The settlers were ready and eager to receive whatever animals they could get. Most settlers had traveled in difficult conditions from the eastern and central parts of Poland to the new west with whatever personal belongings they could manage to transport. If they were lucky enough to have an animal at their point of origin, the length of the journey to the Recovered Territories and the conditions they expected to encounter along the way often discouraged traveling with animals. Or sometimes, the animals that had nevertheless been brought along—horses, pigs, and cows (as we might expect, cows were especially prized for providing milk en route and, later, at the destination)—were abandoned or sold to a slaughterhouse somewhere along the way because the journey had indeed become too taxing and because there was scarcely enough food for the humans, let alone enough for animals that were often too old and weak to be of much use at the destination anyway.[136] The settlers therefore reached the Recovered Territories sometimes without any livestock or working animals whatsoever, or with animals that were in extremely poor health.[137]

Indeed, the availability of good agricultural land—the potential to have a farm with animals—was part of the inducement for moving to the Recovered Territories in the first place.[138] In her analysis of memoir literature from the early years of settlement in the Recovered Territories, Małgorzata Praczyk argues that animals formed an important part of people's narratives about leaving one home and establishing roots in a new one. Praczyk shows that the animals provided affective labor and that the inhabitants, in turn, talked about their animals in sentimental and affectionate ways. They mourned

FIGURE 12. Polish farmer from the Recovered Territories with a horse received through UNRRA, 1957. Collection: Fotografia chłopów pomorskich, Bałtycka Biblioteka Cyfrowa. https://biblio tekacyfrowa.eu/publication/30891.

animal deaths too. Józefa Nogat (pseud.), for example, became especially attached to the cow that she had received from UNRRA: "I called her Saba, the Queen," Nogat said, "she was a 'wonder' not a cow." When Józefa had to sell Saba at some point, she says she became changed forever: "My love for livestock has been deadened because I once liked cows so much . . . they used to understand many of my words, and Saba along with me cried when she was being sold . . . with real tears . . . !"[139]

Another western settler, one Stanisław Pawlus in Zielona Góra, was grateful for the UNRRA horse he had received despite the animal's sorry state: the horse was skinny, untrained, and so weak that he fell several times on the walk home from the holding center. For a time the horse was unable to stand in his stall and had to lean against the barn walls; he remained sick with a cold and a cough for some time. But the animal ultimately regained strength, and the farmer was pleased and proud that they had come through the rough early period together, each as new settlers in a new land looking forward to better days. He only regretted that his father was no longer alive to see the success he had achieved by owning a member of this majestic species.[140]

For the animals Poland marked the end of a long and often difficult journey and gave them a chance to settle into new lives as working animals on Polish farms. The animals' presence in postwar Poland was extremely important to individual Poles, to the state, and to the idea of a new postwar Poland that had moved significantly to the west. There were many reasons for everyone to celebrate these UNRRA animals. Yet the animals' arrival in Poland was complicated, and good outcomes were by no means assured. The arriving animals' fates varied because of several factors, as we have seen, and their placement at their final destinations was subject to a great deal of bureaucracy. The next chapter begins by examining how the animals—and UNRRA by extension—were perceived and sometimes weaponized to meet evolving political goals in Poland. As the discussion unfolds, the perspective shifts from viewing animals primarily as functional creatures with defined roles to considering them as carriers of symbolic meaning. This shift supports the broader argument in the book that specific animal species were significant in postwar humanitarian work not just because of their contributions to agricultural recovery but also because of the ideas and values they embodied and conveyed to both donors and recipients.

CHAPTER 8

UNRRA and Animal Politics in Poland

Polish media covered news of the arriving general UNRRA cargo and the UNRRA animals with considerable interest. The frequently used term "Auntie UNRRA" (*Ciocia* or *Cioteczka* UNRRA) reflected gratitude and affection across the political spectrum.[1] There were plenty of reasons for people to shout, "Hip, Hip, U(N)RRA" ("urra" sounds like "hooray" in English or *hura* in Polish).[2] Charles Drury estimated that Auntie UNRRA supplied the urban population with 1,100 of the 1,500 calories that they consumed daily in the immediate postwar period. It was UNRRA dairy cattle that provided Poland with significant volumes of milk, and it was UNRRA horses that facilitated the cultivation of agricultural fields.[3] This was real value under the circumstances.

The Communist-dominated government likewise celebrated the American-dominated UNRRA. It was UNRRA aid, after all, that permitted people's basic needs to be met, and this in turn contributed to a public perception of the new regime as competent, responsive, and engaged. Even *The Republic* (*Rzeczpospolita*), a Communist daily, contributed initially to creating a positive feeling for UNRRA and its American backers when it itemized the enormous volume of aid that flowed into Poland.[4] Very early on in the life of the UNRRA program, in November 1945, the Communist leader Bolesław Bierut delivered an enthusiastic speech praising UNRRA's aid efforts in Poland and affirmed that the aid would "forever remain in the grateful memory of the Polish nation."[5]

When UNRRA Director La Guardia visited Poland less than a year later, in August 1946, he met with Bierut in Warsaw and accepted the Order of Polonia Restituta (Order Odrodzenia Polski).[6] Whether feelings of gratitude and affection were genuine or uncomplicated does not diminish the impact of the aid.

Forward Lower Silesia (*Naprzód Dolnośląski*), the daily of the Polish Socialist Party in southwestern Poland, also celebrated UNRRA's contributions and its concrete positive impact on Polish citizens' lives: "Even a baby in a cradle, sucking milk that comes from an UNRRA can, knows that UNRRA exists in the world. Older children think that UNRRA is a pseudonym of Saint Nicholas, and still others think it's an angel revealed."[7]

Similar messages were delivered by the Polish Military Film Production Agency (Wytwórnia Filmowa Wojska Polskiego). Some of the agency's short films featured the goods and the animals that UNRRA delivered to Poland. In one 1946 film, the narrator praises Auntie UNRRA for her animal gifts: "More than tinned food and powdered eggs," the narrator tells viewers, Auntie UNRRA also sends "real, living—and even very alive—horses." These "noble" four-legged animals are big and fast and healthy-looking, and, we learn, some of them even resemble mustangs, the famed wild horses of the American west. The viewer watches as dozens of such horses gallop away and show off their speed and physical fitness—and, by extension, the prosperity and goodwill of America.[8] The symbolism is unmistakable: UNRRA has ridden to Poland's rescue.

Optimism and gratefulness are further reflected in another state-produced short film, also from 1946. We see peasants working their new fields in the Recovered Territories, the region that received more horses from UNRRA than did any other part of Poland. The voice-over reminds us that the future prosperity of Poland depends on farmers' labor; farmers ensure that every Pole will have bread in the coming year. The camera pans to the farmer husband who is taking a break from his work while he holds his baby; the two share a glass of milk that had just been handed to him by his farmer wife.[9] On Polish farms (and not just Polish ones) it was typically the responsibility of women and girls to care for the family cow(s)—another female of its species—and to ensure that there was enough milk for everyone. Women also used surplus milk to make assorted dairy products that the family would eat or that could be sold for a profit on the open market.[10]

Private market sales of milk and dairy products were especially important during a period of postwar rationing when the agricultural population (estimated to be about eleven million people out of a total population of twenty-four million) did not qualify for ration cards but was instead supposed to provide for itself while also delivering a quota of milk plus grains, meats, and eggs to the state for provision to other (urban) population groups.[11] In the scenario described above, the farmer wife smiles as she watches her husband and baby share the nutritious glass of milk. This moment largely reflects *her* efforts as well as those of her daughter, who moments earlier was shown carrying the milk, food, and the baby to her parents working in the field. In the last scene, we see a foal suckling milk from its mother.[12] Here milk represents maternal nourishment for all species (human and nonhuman), postwar recovery, and stability. There is enough milk, the film tells us, for every living being, and all animals will be nourished by it.

In important ways the film reflects some older patterns in Polish literature that accentuate cows' high status in peasant households and use cows as symbols of hope for a more prosperous future. The film also reflects what scholar Sabina Brzozowska, in an analysis of Władysław Reymont's turn-of-the-century novel *The Peasants* (*Chłopi*), has called an "interspecies parallel" between cows and women.[13] In *The Peasants* it is the presence of a cow that consoles the character Veronka in the immediate aftermath of a violent storm that has destroyed her cottage. As the local priest tells Veronka, the Lord God spared her life and the lives of her children, and he also left her a pregnant cow: "A good milker, no doubt: loins as straight as a beam." Veronka understands that the family's fate rests with the cow as life giver and provider (*żywicielka*) and that it is her job to care for the animal: "We owe our lives to her alone."[14] In another section of *The Peasants*, Hanka, overwhelmed by poverty and by her husband's refusal to work, runs off to the barn to weep. In a display of empathy and affection, Krasula the cow starts to lick Hanka's head and shoulders. The cow's attempts to offer comfort only increase Hanka's lamentations, however. Hanka knows that her husband, Antek, has arranged to sell Krasula for slaughter. "Was it for this, Krasula, that I fed you so well, and cared for all your wants," Hanka asks as the two Jewish buyers are about to begin their negotiations for the animal. Both Krasula and Hanka, two females of their respective species, are powerless to stop fate.[15] The scene in which Reymont describes the Jewish men taking possession of Krasula, recently cleaned and milked by Hanka, reflects the woman's and the animal's resignation. Krasula "made resistance," pulled against the rope that held her, and "burst into long plaintive lowing," but to no avail. For her part, Hanka is "seized with an unbearable pang," and, like her children, she too "burst out crying, unable to do more than watch."[16] Hanka's grief is directed at the animal's destiny no less than the family's: without Krasula, Hanka knows, "there would be nothing for them to eat."[17] And yet even as she is led to the slaughterhouse, Krasula fulfills her role as provider; the money from her sale will keep the family going for at least a short while. And hope remains, too, in the single remaining heifer; with this young female animal on the verge of calving comes the promise of a little milk and thus a better tomorrow.[18] So valued were cattle in peasant households that families even shared with this species the traditional Christmas Eve wafer (*opłatek*). Reymont writes in another scene, "Yagna broke an altar-bread into five pieces, made the sign of the cross over each cow between her horns, and laid the thin bit of wafer upon her broad tongue."[19] Horses were not included in this ritual because they were not present in the manger at the birth of Jesus.[20]

Both the UNRRA livestock program and the Heifer Project understood cows similarly, as the most important life providers, both literally and symbolically. For the purposes of the government's short propaganda films, it did not matter that in reality some of the UNRRA animals were sick, weak, or ill-suited to Polish farmers' immediate requirements. It also did not matter that milk production in Poland continued to lag and could not meet national needs.[21] UNRRA estimated that Poland's urban milk deficit for 1946/47 was still significant at 160 million liters; large numbers of additional dairy cattle were needed to make up the shortfall.[22] Nevertheless, it was in the government's best interest, especially while UNRRA was at the height of its activity, to celebrate both what UNRRA was able to provide (even if it was insufficient) and what Poles were able to accomplish with these infusions of aid in such a short time (like rebuilding the national dairy industry).

Not surprisingly, in its own advertising UNRRA also reflected optimism and positivity about the effects its aid program were having. UNRRA managed the image it projected of itself, both at home and in its target countries, very carefully. Part and parcel of this image-making was constructing a visual narrative that provided evidence of how useful its work was. By featuring recently brutalized people now safe, well fed, productive, and perhaps even happy, UNRRA celebrated the allied nations that were working cooperatively to achieve desired results. The "UNRRA angle," as it was called, showed the successful delivery of aid marked with the letters U-N-R-R-A from a benevolent America to grateful recipients while it also sparked a visceral emotional reaction to suffering and, especially, to suffering relieved.[23]

UNRRA photographer John Vachon was expert in showing the UNRRA angle.[24] Vachon was in Poland, as we have seen, to produce visual documentation of UNRRA's successes, and arguably his best-known work from the UNRRA period shows the three children on the dock in Gdańsk drinking milk from a freshly milked cow.[25] The children's faces are mostly obscured by the large drinking cups, and this is, in a sense, precisely the point: the aid—the solution to the problem of postwar hunger—is the focus here and not the hunger itself. This is the UNRRA angle. This style of messaging was arguably

FIGURE 13. Milking a recently arrived UNRRA cow on a farm near Gdańsk, May 1946. UN photo by John Vachon. UNRRA 4652, from the United Nations Relief and Rehabilitation Administration Collection, United Nations Archives.

more modern and optimistic than showing (or reading about) "the hungry millions," the desperate and the downtrodden, and the daunting task that confronted the United Nations.[26] In a related photograph (see fig. 13), also by Vachon, we see three other young children lined up beside a woman milking a cow outside a barn. One child is drinking her portion of milk while another one holds her mug off to the side, and the third, the youngest, waits. Again, it is the cow and her milk—the solutions to postwar hunger—that animate this photograph, create the UNRRA angle, and bring hopefulness to the scene.

"The Administration of Unfair Distribution of American Goods"

The success of the UNRRA angle was ultimately short-lived, however. In America it was the perception that UNRRA aid was inadvertently benefiting the Soviet Union and the Communists during emerging Cold War tensions that undermined public faith in the organization. In Poland it was frustration with inadequate quantities of aid and a feeling that Poland ought to be given even more considering what it had been through. Not everyone who required a horse or a cow—arguably the most high-profile and coveted "relief items" for rural people—was lucky enough to get one through UNRRA, as need far outstripped supply.[27] Criticisms of UNRRA from Poles themselves also had a lot to do with the Communists' messy and sometimes unfair distribution practices.

Complaints about UNRRA aid distribution came from would-be recipients—the peasants who needed the animals to farm and survive—but also from bureaucrats at various levels. There was a range of criticisms. Some said that distribution methods were quite simply corrupt and that people who had the right connections (but perhaps not the most critical need) were first in line for relief animals. Others said that distribution was just badly organized and that the rules about who qualified for UNRRA aid were unclear and confusing and were too easily misinterpreted as information made its way down to local levels from the Ministry of Agriculture. There were grievances that certain regions hardly received any animals at all, despite evidence that showed need, while others received what looked like more than their fair share. Some regions resented that their special circumstances were not considered seriously. Farmers in Olsztyn, in the eastern Recovered Territories, complained, for example, that because of a cooler climate and a growing season that was a month shorter than in western and central Poland, their work was generally harder. The low horse (and tractor) numbers in this part of the country complicated agricultural production further still. Regional representatives felt Olsztyn ought to have had priority over areas where physical and climatic conditions were more hospitable for growing, and yet these arguments tended to fall on deaf ears.[28]

Others grumbled about broken promises or sloppy accounting. Agreements to send a specific number of UNRRA animals to a particular region, some critics said, had sometimes gone unfulfilled and unexplained. Others pointed to a shortfall in the number of animals delivered. The numbers recorded as having been sent did not always match the numbers received, suggesting either that the counts were wrong to begin with or that animals had been stolen or had died along the way. In any event not everyone who was expecting an animal in fact got one.

Individuals sometimes also felt personally aggrieved about how UNRRA aid distribution was handled. Some believed that their own individual case for an animal was simply stronger than their neighbor's, that they could do more with the resources available, or that they were more deserving. One farmer from Sieradz county in the province of Łódź was incensed that "an ethnic German" had received an UNRRA animal ahead of some local ethnic Poles.[29] The Lemko population in southeast Poland also complained that they were being routinely passed over for UNRRA aid of all kinds, and not just animal aid. The Ministry of Agriculture even had to defend itself to UNRRA directly in late 1946 to dispel these specific accusations, as discrimination on the basis of racial, ethnic, or religious identity in aid distribution contravened UNRRA's rules.[30]

Moreover, poor communication led to misunderstandings and frustration on the part of various parties over who exactly made decisions about animal distribution and how. The Provincial Land Office in Warsaw, for example, was annoyed that farmers were showing up at its offices asking to be given a horse. The bureaucrats needed to explain that decisions about distribution of UNRRA animals were not made at the Provincial Land Office and that anyone interested in getting an animal needed to follow established procedures and had to apply formally through the Ministry of Agriculture. The encounters were both time-consuming and a waste of office resources—as well as farmers' energy, time, and money.[31]

One damning article in *The People's Daily (Dziennik Ludowy)* from August 1946 refers bluntly and ironically to the "secret" rules of horse and cattle distribution that left citizens thoroughly confused about how to get an animal. The author charged that personal relationships with the right people were more important than the completion of the proper forms and a rational assessment of needs. Competition for animals was fierce, and farmers tried all kinds of strategies to make sure their application was successful.[32] Some farmers admitted that it was possible to bribe the right person (including state officials and railway workers) and thereby to bypass the established rules altogether.[33] One settler to Szczecin province named Mieczysław Kaczmarek described being able to buy a horse "for two liters of spiritus."[34] This kind of black-market trading in UNRRA animals had many implications, one of which was that it led to obvious discrepancies between the number of animals promised to a region and the number received. It threw off statistics and made accurate reporting challenging. Arguably, too, it hurt UNRRA's reputation while it also raised questions about the trustworthiness of the Polish government.[35]

Staff at various government offices retorted that they, too, were left in the dark about essential elements of the livestock program. The district or local levels said that the information they received from the provincial authorities about when a livestock-carrying ship was due to arrive was unreliable, meaning that the locals sent to pick up the animals could wait days or even more at the ports for the incoming ships.[36] This was, again, a waste of time, and an expensive one at that. If ships missed their advertised arrival date by quite a bit, the pickup person or crew had to go home empty-handed.[37] This happened despite procedures that were meant to guard against such outcomes. M. E. Hays, the chief of UNRRA's Agricultural Division in Poland, regularly communicated with the chief of the Foreign Section in Poland's Ministry of Agriculture and provided lists of what type and number of animals were due to sail on specific ships and dates. But as we know, there were many factors that could delay departure and arrival times. Whenever necessary UNRRA purportedly updated the Polish Ministry of Agriculture by telegram to revise schedules, but this information was difficult to deliver to all relevant parties in a timely fashion. Moreover, an unpredictable number of animals, as we have also seen, died during the sailings or just after, and many others had to be placed immediately in a veterinary hospital before they could be considered for placement. Animals died at the veterinary clinics too. All of this necessitated constant last-minute revisions to distribution plans.[38]

At other times information about an arriving shipload of animals came at the very last minute, leaving districts with too little time to make the trip to the ports along inadequate transport networks.[39] Given the poor state of the roads and of infrastructure generally, it was no small accomplishment for both human and nonhuman animals to move around the country. Long periods of transport at this end of the journey were stressful for the animals, and, given that the waiting often happened in crowded conditions, the animals' chances of getting sick became greater with each passing day; illnesses spread easily. The waiting meant, too, that births sometimes happened unattended aboard in-country train wagons; the newborns did not often survive, and sometimes the mother died as well.[40] This was yet another factor that led numbers to change at the eleventh hour and that had a cascading effect on distribution plans right down to the local level. Sometimes allocations from one shipment needed to be adjusted to make up for shortfalls in a previous one as well, but this only led to new shortfalls in other places.[41]

One strategy to deal with the unpredictability and chaos was developed at the local level: districts sent out what were called "wild teams" to the piers with nothing more than hope and a vague plan to try to swoop up as many animals as possible when a ship finally arrived, using whatever means possible. Sometimes, too, district officials in the Recovered Territories, tired of feeling "molested by settlers" who had shown up at their offices looking for animals, issued special certificates that bypassed the established application procedures and seemingly allowed individuals to make all the arrangements to buy an animal right there at the ports. When it became clear at the ports that the district authorities had promised farmers too much and that these special certificates would likely not work as hoped, the disappointed would-be buyers returned home full of criticism of UNRRA and various levels of the Polish government.[42] The growing cynicism about the nature of distribution methods was reflected in a manipulation of the initially sympathetic term "Auntie UNRRA." Instead of recalling a kindly older woman that delivered presents to her favorite young nieces and nephews, the letters U-N-R-R-A came to stand for "the Administration of Unfair Distribution of American Goods ("Urząd Niesprawiedliwego Rozdzielania Rzeczy Amerykańskich").[43]

Not surprisingly, the Polish government initially claimed that its handling of UNRRA animals was smooth and that all of the livestock was being dispersed fairly and efficiently, with only minor irregularities that, given the circumstances, had to be expected. Like UNRRA itself when it was faced with criticism, the Polish government argued that certain issues were simply beyond their control and had to do with the inescapable challenge of moving thousands of live animals (and millions of pounds of food, clothing, and other essential items) across an ocean as quickly as possible and then distributing everything just as quickly.[44] Though there were specific cases of mismanagement, both UNRRA and the Polish government agreed that these were isolated instances rather than evidence of systemic problems.[45]

It is quite likely that the Polish government wanted in fact to eliminate unauthorized animal deliveries and rogue decision-making related to humanitarian aid as a way of exercising its own control not just over incoming shipments but, ultimately, over society. There was perhaps also some political advantage that could be wrested from rumors of theft, corruption, bribery, and mismanagement; the rumors, that is, provided an excuse for the authorities to monitor and silence people under the guise of taking decisive action against fraud and incompetence. And that is exactly what the government did.

From the start, a variety of bodies ostensibly protected UNRRA goods that entered Poland. Naval patrols and armed military troops worked in the port areas, and then in March 1946 the Polish government formed the UNRRA Guard (Straż UNRRA).[46] The guard consisted of hundreds of functionaries operating under the direction of the Ministry of Shipping and Foreign Trade (Ministerstwo Żeglugi i Handlu Zagranicznego). Its members were tasked with preventing theft in the port areas and then with ensuring that the incoming goods made it from the ports to their final destinations, wherever those may have been.[47] It is not clear if the guard ever accompanied the animals—who were in the hands of private transport companies as soon as they landed—but livestock-related goods (like feed, hay, and agricultural tools) were part of the general UNRRA shipments that were protected by the guard. At any rate, because of their size, will, and ability to vocalize, animals were obviously more difficult to steal and conceal than, say, the inanimate contents of a crate. But the rewards associated with stealing animals were that much greater too. There were even reports of guards themselves taking the cargo they were employed to protect.[48] The Communist Security Police (Urząd Bezpieczeństwa) was rumored to be stealing UNRRA aid as well, even though it too had a responsibility to protect public property and state interests.[49] Corruption, plus the fact that lines of authority and responsibility overlapped or were unclear, made the overall goal of protection and theft prevention complicated and difficult.[50]

In November 1946, in anticipation of the fully Communist post-UNRRA era, the Polish government created a new body, the Maritime Guard (Straż Morska), to further extend its ability to monitor incoming UNRRA aid, other aid shipments, and, generally, deliveries of other kinds of goods too. Operating until the end of 1947, this new guard was given greater authority to find and fight what it called corruption and theft.[51] The guard was answerable to the Special Commission to Combat Fraud and Harm (Komisja Specjalna do Walki z Nadużyciami i Szkodnictwem). This well-known commission had been created in 1945 to target instances of corruption, fraud, looting, and supposed economic sabotage against the state. In reality the commission, which existed until the 1950s, was part of the repressive Communist security and judicial framework that was being developed in postwar Poland.[52]

The Special Commission prosecuted cases of allegedly illegal UNRRA livestock placements, favoritism, bribery, and other kinds of corruption. It reported finding eighty-five cases of UNRRA aid fraud in 1946 and twenty-nine in 1947 that, in its estimation, justified the most serious penalty of forced labor. These numbers account for approximately 6 percent of the total number of cases that went before the commission in 1946 and in which forced labor was the penalty, and just under 1 percent of the total number of forced-labor sentences handed out by the commission in 1947. The other major offenses with forced-labor sentences fell under the vague categories of "creating economic damage," speculation, and administrative crimes.[53]

The most common UNRRA-related offenses that the commission investigated were related to requests for bribes. According to the commission, horse handlers sometimes expected to be paid under the table before they agreed to distribute the animals that were in their care. In one typical case presented by the commission, Wacław Karczewski took an illegal payment of 4,000 złoty for his "help" in obtaining the best animal for a farmer. Accused persons like Karczewski defended themselves by saying that "everyone" did the same thing and that it was common knowledge that without the extra payments at this last stage in the process taking possession of an animal was extremely difficult. Farmers often calculated that it made sense just to pay the bribes without fuss, get their animals quickly, and be on their way. The Special Commission to Combat Fraud and Harm showed little sympathy for Karczewski, and he was sentenced to two years of forced labor for his actions; his offense was misusing UNRRA goods and therefore harming the state.[54]

In other cases, the commission prosecuted people for giving false testimony on their applications about the amount of land they possessed or for misrepresenting their needs and their potential to contribute to the nation's agricultural economy. Upon investigation, the recipients were found not to have any land at all, or to already have too many horses for the size of farm that they possessed. The commission also found that some farmers promptly sold off their animals shortly after receiving them in an effort to earn a little profit. Alternatively, farmers gave away their UNRRA animal to a family member who already had animals and therefore would have been ineligible for an additional one under the normal rules.[55] Sometimes the men who were in charge of the convoys that brought the animals to their destinations swapped out some of the best animals for sick or weak horses and delivered those instead. They then sold the healthier animals for personal profit.[56] Branding UNRRA animals at the piers had been intended in part to guard against this kind of animal switching, but of course this was no guarantee.[57]

The commission also leveled corruption charges against bureaucrats who they said were at fault for not monitoring UNRRA aid distribution adequately and for allowing all sorts of irregularities to happen. In one case it was an employee at the Inspection Bureau of the Ministry of Agriculture that was held to task for not properly collecting payments for the animals.[58] In another case Anatol Dobrowolski, a Polish Ministry of Agriculture liaison for UNRRA affairs at the ports of Gdańsk, Gdynia, and Szczecin, was condemned for "blanket incompetence" and "a lack of supervision" that resulted in sloppy recordkeeping. Charges of financial mismanagement were useful to the Communists and were employed regularly. Dobrowolski was held accountable for the financial losses that resulted, apparently, from his lack of vigilance and for his inability to regulate distribution better. This, the commission documents state, was ultimately a waste of valuable animal resources, and it meant that regions did not get the animals they had been promised by the ministry (or that they got them much later than anticipated). This jeopardized agricultural renewal, and, ultimately, it slowed down the work of building the new Poland. Even in 1948, many months after UNRRA had quit Poland, some provinces still could not say with certainly how many animals they had received.[59]

The purpose here is not to trace the veracity of each detail in these briefly noted cases pursued by the Special Commission to Combat Fraud and Harm. Instead, the intention is to show that the Polish Communists used rumors and evidence of corruption and fraud to their advantage. Blaming unethical railway workers and livestock handlers as well as incompetent administrators and greedy farmers for chaotic aid distribution preserved the government's rhetorical commitment to protecting principles of fairness and the good of the collective. It also absolved the government of any overall responsibility for mismanaging the aid program to begin with.

Moreover, distribution-related fraud subtly sullied both the aid and its American donors despite broad agreement on the objective value of the aid. UNRRA's gifts were complicated, to say the least, and even if Auntie UNRRA was not the one making choices about who got what and when, her very presence in Poland could be disruptive as well as helpful; the perception of unfairness, inequality, and a rigged system stuck to her. At the extreme, having an UNRRA animal (or being part of the system that determined to whom the animals would be distributed) could ruin lives with political charges and forced labor. For some regular Polish farmers, the only free cheese was indeed in the American trap.

Through the commission's investigations, the Communists effectively flexed their power. This power had grown all the more secure and complete after the January 1947 elections in which the victory of the Communist-left Democratic Bloc (Blok Demokratyczny) had been arranged through corruption and intimidation. UNRRA-related investigations were yet another way for the Communists to neutralize what they perceived to be internal enemies and to signal to the rest of the population that the state was watching all animals (human and nonhuman) and monitoring their every action—albeit for the collective good.

Communist Animal Welfare and the New Humanitarianism

The discourse about UNRRA animal aid, and UNRRA aid generally, evolved along with the emerging political situation in revealing ways. We have seen that in the beginning Poles—the people and the government—celebrated the UNRRA animals. And if and when they remarked on the poor health of some of them, this was not intended to impugn the UNRRA program as a whole or the Americans specifically. Like UNRRA, Poles accepted that animals' poor health reflected long periods of immobilization and crowded conditions on the ships, stale air, and drafts.[60] These were all unavoidable factors. Quite simply, animals bore the physical costs of the world's greatest and fastest humanitarian relief effort that followed on the heels of a disastrous war. This was just the way it was.

As we move closer to 1947, however, by which time the Communists were more confident in their control, attitudes toward the United States were changing, and so was the analysis of the aid that UNRRA sent. Americans were sending Poland their very worst animals, Poles now claimed, and many of them were already sick before they set sail for Poland. In this reading, the UNRRA program was just a way for Americans to get rid of animals that had no value in the United States anyway; it was an insult to the years of suffering Poland's people had endured under Nazi occupation. The chief of the Foreign Section of the Polish Ministry of Agriculture, Ł. Witkowski, was matter-of-fact about the incoming animals' poor quality in a February 1947 letter to T. A. Pato, the chief of the Agricultural Division of UNRRA's Mission to Poland: "The horses sent to us lately from the U.S.A . . . are in very bad condition. Most of these horses are ill. The farmers refuse to accept them."[61] It was left to the Polish government to care for these animals in its veterinary clinics, and this became an additional burden from both a financial and resource perspective while it also complicated distribution plans down to local levels, as we have seen.[62] What value, really, did these animals give Poland?

Or sometimes, the Polish government charged, Americans sent what they knew were the "wrong" kind of animals for Polish agricultural needs. This included horses that were too young (just a few years old) and unsuited in terms of temperament and previous work experience to the conditions of daily labor on farms.[63] Other critics claimed that the wild horses that had been plucked only recently from the vast open ranges of the American west—the once-celebrated mustangs—were useless in the short term because they were not broken and did not know how to work the farms; these animals would not earn their keep, and, again, no farmer would want them.[64] According to this way of thinking, it was absurd to claim that UNRRA was committed to Poland's agricultural renewal; the UNRRA animals' worth was mostly just theoretical.

Criticism of the arriving animals is reflected in a May 1947 short film from the Polish Military Film Production Agency; this was the same unit that had created the earlier positive films about UNRRA aid. The viewer is hit immediately with the news that a recently arrived UNRRA ship has delivered a load of tremendously sick animals to Poland. The sailing itself is described as having been especially hard and unbearably long—three months—and as having resulted in 320 deaths out of the approximately 1,400 horses on board; this was a loss rate of almost 23 percent. The ship is not named in the film, the specific date of its arrival is not indicated, and it is not certain that the statistics provided are accurate or that they even refer to an actual sailing. Over a dozen ships arrived in Poland in the first month or so of 1947 alone. It could be that the example featured in the film refers to SS *Mount Whitney*, which was the only ship capable of carrying 1,400 horses and which had in fact sailed to Poland in early 1947; its posted loss rate, however, was under 7 percent. Or it could have been a reference to SS *Beloit Victory*. This ship, however, carried only 750 horses on its February 1947 sailing to Poland and posted a loss rate of over 35 percent. There were other possible contenders, too, like SS *Lahaina Victory*, which lost 125 (or 22 percent) of its 787 horses. Regardless, what is clear is that difficult winter conditions in early 1947 lengthened and complicated all the ships' sailings, and, indeed, loss rates on these trips were particularly high.[65] The film exploited that for effect. We are told by the film's narrator that upon arrival five hundred horses were sent to the veterinary clinic for urgent care because their conditions were so precarious. The camera lingers on specific individual animals to show viewers just how worn out and sick these American animals were.[66] Auntie UNRRA was giving nothing valuable to Poland; in fact, the film implies, the American-dominated UNRRA was an animal abuser.

Suggesting, even subtly, that the Americans were animal abusers introduced a new and powerful element into the contemporary discourse about UNRRA. This in turn reveals a great deal about changing conceptions of animal welfare, humanitarianism, and civilization in early Communist Poland. Polish animal welfare organizations had formed in the last quarter of the nineteenth century and had remained active until the outbreak of World War II. During the busy years of the Second Republic, organization members popularized a link between high animal welfare standards—which they understood to be part of a broad humanitarianism—and "civilization," a set of ideas, habits, and practices that at the time were associated with western Europe. Interwar Polish animal protectionists argued that Poles would cement their place in (west) European civilization only by transforming their relationships with nonhuman animals and adhering to strict animal protection measures. It was a matter of a relatively poor agricultural nation rising to the level of the west and changing how it treated nonhuman animals.[67] For the middle- and upper-class women and men of interwar animal protection societies, this often meant targeting the urban working poor and rural people, social groups who they assumed had the most cruel interactions with animals; these were the people that needed to be civilized and taught modern standards of animal care.[68]

The reality after the war was very different. Arguments that had worked in the prewar period, and which reflected class-based assumptions about "who" was cruel to animals, no longer made sense in the context of the new workers' utopia of Communist Poland. The party line shifted, as it were, and now it was the "civilized west," with its shipments of sick and suffering animals, that were the animal abusers. The end of the war had laid the groundwork for this reversal. As Tony Judt has written in a more general sense, after the Third Reich the concept of a "civilized west" became a chimera, the "grandest of all illusions."[69] This opened a space for the Polish Communists to imagine a new and different relationship between civilization, humanitarianism, and animal welfare, one in which it was the greedy, unethical, and capitalist Americans that did the most damage to animals.

Ultimately, animal welfare during the Communist period would be rooted less in abstract sentiments about animals' inherent moral value or in arguments about animals' ability to feel pain than in ideas about maximizing animals' social and economic value and not wasting animals' potential; animals were, after all, a national resource. The purpose of animal welfare standards in post–World War II Poland, from official perspectives, was entirely instrumental: it was about maintaining the physical fitness of draft animals so that they could work productively as long as possible, safeguarding public health by providing "meat and milk of high quality," and preventing zoonotic diseases from taking root.[70] This was the new Communist humanitarianism, a humanitarianism focused on ensuring that animals met human needs.

This new approach was partially reflected in the quick action that the government took to regulate horses' working conditions. As early as the fall of 1945, the Main Command of the Citizens' Militia distributed flyers across construction sites warning against "using up" the horses too quickly. There were too few of these valuable animals as it was. People were reminded that the 1928 animal protection legislation still applied in these earliest days of the postwar period and included a provision for protecting work animals: abusing a valuable working animal carried a potential fine of 2,000 złoty and/or three weeks in jail.[71] The prewar animal welfare legislation was used selectively by the Communists when it suited their purposes. It was not invoked because of nostalgia for the Second Republic or because of sentimentality and a desire to save animals from experiencing pain. The goal, rather, was to minimize waste and preserve a productive animal labor force that would facilitate the rebuilding of the country as swiftly as possible.[72] The rhetorical shift was slight but important. Horses were an investment in the collective, and everyone had an obligation to ensure that "their" animal would remain fit for work on behalf of the nation.

Poland's animal welfare activists were quick to sense the changing winds and new emphases. The Society for the Protection of Animals (Towarzystwo

Ochrony Zwierząt), which was Poland's oldest animal welfare organization, was formally reconstituted in 1945 under the leadership of Tadeusz Matecki, a key activist from before the war. Under Matecki's direction the postwar society turned its attention to livestock and working animals rather than to companion animals or pets—the animal type that had received a great deal of attention during the interwar period.[73] It took some time for the society to get up and running, however, and so it was not until 1947 that it resumed its prewar system of animal inspections on building sites and slaughterhouses. In this capacity the society gave out hundreds of tickets every month, especially for overloading horses and hitting them over the head to make them work harder and faster.[74] Treating animals in these ways, the society said, was counterproductive and would result in a waste of precious national resources.[75]

In the new era, animal welfare would need to be justified differently, in ways that echoed the priorities of the Communists. To abuse the nation's animals was to risk national goals, as only fit and well-cared-for animals could be expected to contribute to rebuilding the country's destroyed cities or to producing the high agricultural yields that Poland needed to feed its people. Abused and sick animals also produced inferior or maybe even "bad" milk and meat, and this posed a direct threat to human health.[76] A vocabulary of "rational animal management"—and the attendant collective social good that was presumed to follow from this—thus replaced a broad "animal welfare" agenda that relied on ethical arguments or sentimentality and that invoked the imagined ideals of western civilization.[77] Communist animal protection was about maximizing animals' usefulness.[78]

Ultimately, however, there was little room for even a modified animal welfare in Communist Poland. The Polish Stalinists had come to believe that anything that an independent animal protection society did could be better done by the Veterinary Department of the Ministry of Agriculture. Moreover, by the late 1940s the Communists were shutting down all independent groups, and not surprisingly this included the Society for the Protection of Animals, too. The government manufactured an excuse that made it easy: it accused the society of financial mismanagement and corruption. At issue were four Ford trucks that, the Communists said, the society had purchased with borrowed money that it could not later pay back. For its part the society argued that the trucks had been a donation from none other than UNRRA. Nevertheless, the government's forensic accounting found evidence of financial incompetence and, worse yet, misappropriation of state resources for private purposes. The government ordered the closure of the society in 1951.[79]

Pausing here to consider the short-lived postwar activism of the Society for the Protection of Animals is revealing. It reminds us that "animal welfare" was (and is) a malleable concept with different definitions, histories, and trajectories. In the pre–World War II period, animals' utility and their economic value to the Polish people were not central to animal protectionists' explanations of their activism. After the war, the ethical and sentimental reasons for animal welfare that had predominated in the Second Republic vanished from the society's statements so as to better align with Communist priorities. For everyone, animal welfare in postwar Poland came to be defined in terms of extending animals' value as laborers, whether that involved work on agricultural fields or as milk providers. As we have seen, this was familiar terrain for both UNRRA and the Heifer Project too.

The Society for the Protection of Animals perhaps understood better than most just how complicated the relationship was between animal welfare and humanitarian aid programs. It was not until 1947, just as the last UNRRA livestock ships were arriving in Poland, that Matecki looked into relief animals' transport conditions. He went to the docks—in an unofficial capacity only—and was upset by what he saw.[80] In a letter to the International Humanitarian Bureau, a Geneva-based coordinating and advisory body for animal welfare groups, Matecki described the arriving horses, with their hanging heads and a sad indifference to everything around them, as resembling "concentration camp victims."[81] This is an early example of the comparison made occasionally in subsequent years between the mistreatment of animals, on the one hand, and on the other the exceptionally cruel abuse and murder of human beings under the Nazis. Yet ultimately there was not much that Matecki, the Polish Society for the Protection of Animals, or the International Humanitarian Bureau felt could be done to help these animals. Like UNRRA, the Heifer Project, and the American animal welfare group, they concluded in the end that sailing great distances was simply hard for animals to bear.[82] It was indeed just an inescapable reality.

Chapter 9

Heifer Project Animals in Poland

Though they traveled on the UNRRA ships with the UNRRA cattle and horses, endured the same difficult maritime transport conditions, and were attended to by the same seagoing cowboys, the Heifer Project animals nevertheless had somewhat different experiences once they reached Poland. The Heifer Project animals, as a group, were privileged, both in some tangible ways and in symbolic ones. This was in part because they were all cattle—heifers, mostly, but also a smaller number of cows and bulls. Bovines, in general, had far fewer bad outcomes during the journeys. This meant that they were in better physical condition to begin their new lives in Poland and usually avoided stays in the crowded and underresourced veterinary clinics upon arrival in the country. Life on small Polish farms would be physically grueling, to be sure, but the animals' economic value provided a measure of security too. Cows became celebrated and protected animals precisely because of their milk-giving abilities and because of what this meant in terms of meeting the nutritional and economic needs of families. Moreover, there were fewer Heifer Project animals (several hundred compared to UNRRA's tens of thousands), and this made them far easier to care for as a group as well as to place and track. Significantly, too, as a private donor the Heifer Project Committee had a different relationship with the Polish government, one that gave them a little more insight into the animals' fates after landing. How these animals were placed, and where, was different from how UNRRA animals were settled.

What a Difference an Ear Tag Makes

In the spring of 1945, Greece became the first European country to receive Heifer Project animals. The first Heifer Project animals arrived in Poland at the end of the year, in December 1945. In total, and until February 1947 (toward the very end of the UNRRA period), the Heifer Project delivered 841 heifers to Poland in five transports: 150 on SS *Santiago Iglesias* (which sailed in November 1945 and arrived a few weeks later in Gdańsk, in December), 228 on SS *Woodstock Victory* in the winter of 1946, 95 on SS *Robert W. Hart* (which arrived on August 19, 1946), 328 on SS *William S. Halsted* (which arrived on December 6, 1946), and 40 on SS *Mount Whitney* (which arrived February 8, 1947).[1] This last sailing, uncharacteristically, also included forty-four horses provided by the Methodists and shipped by the Heifer Project; these constituted a "special shipment" to what had recently been East Prussia.[2]

The Heifer Project animals were met at the Baltic ports by a representative from the Brethren's Poland headquarters, which were located in Warsaw on 35 Hoża Street. This was a busy office given that, in addition to the Heifer Project, the Brethren Service Committee ran other aid projects in Poland that delivered food, seed, clothing, and harnesses to people in need. Many of these relief goods were stored at a distribution base in Ostróda, in northeastern Poland a little west of Olsztyn; there were Brethren Service Committee staff at this location too.[3]

From the port and with the assistance of a Brethren representative, the Heifer Project animals were directed to their final destinations. Placing each animal "right" was a priority for the Heifer Project from the start, and to facilitate this the Polish government had agreed to allow the Brethren Service Committee to be involved in the animals' placements. What this meant in concrete terms is that the Brethren Service Committee assessed specific requests for animals and chose animal recipients. Most of the requests were made directly to the Brethren using the Hoża Street address (but, reflecting the chaos and confusion that marked animal distribution in this period generally, some requests were misdirected to local government offices instead.) Requests came from individuals as well as from institutions like orphanages and schools or, in one case, from the Sisters of Virgin Mary Family Home for the Aged in Izabelin, not far from the city of Warsaw. Regardless, applicants invariably invoked the war's destruction, established experiences of hardship, and repeated the ubiquitous claim that the milk that the Heifer Project animals would give was clearly the best possible nourishment for weak and sick children and the elderly in particular. In the Izabelin example, the request, which is dated November 8, 1946, was for one dairy cow to help sustain the "22 old women" who lived at the institution and whose children had died in the war or in the Warsaw Uprising specifically.[4]

What the Brethren did not agree to do was determine placements in advance or deliver specific animals to designated recipients on behalf of the American donors; this, they said, was just too difficult to arrange. At any rate the Brethren felt that decisions about placement needed to be made in-country, after an assessment of the local context, which they rightly understood to be an evolving one. Like UNRRA, the Brethren favored giving animals to farmers and institutions that did not have a cow at all but that desperately needed one or, alternatively, to those who could show a solid reason for needing an additional animal.[5]

But in contrast to UNRRA animals, Brethren Service Committee heifers were distributed as real gifts to individuals and institutions without any cost at all to the recipients.[6] This was a major difference between the aid programs. Not charging for the animals (or for any of the goods they distributed) was extremely important to the Brethren Service Committee.[7] "Cost-free humanitarian aid" was also precisely what Americans might have expected from charity projects, and indeed many other smaller voluntary relief agencies that operated at the time similarly did not expect payment for the aid they gave. As the previous chapters have shown, incoming UNRRA animals (and other types of nonemergency aid from UNRRA) worked differently: UNRRA aid was surrendered to the receiving governments upon arrival, and it was the government, in turn, that handled distribution and sold whatever it wanted to sell at prices it determined.[8]

A document titled "Act of Transferring the Heifer from American Gifts to the Polish Citizens" formed part of the record related to Heifer Project animal placements. The awkward English title suggests that this document was prepared in Polish rather than English and that the Brethren had the Polish original translated; it is this translated and typed-out version that remains available in the Brethren archives. Handwritten and somewhat modified versions of this document also exist, albeit for the post-UNRRA period when the Brethren continued to work in Poland on their own for a short time.[9] (It is likely that the exact content and format of the paperwork related to the animal transfers were left to local government levels to handle as they saw fit.) The name and address of the person or the institution that had received an animal were listed on the "Act of Transferring," and the animal's ear tag number was also indicated. Ear tags were unique identifying numbers that had been attached to every Heifer Project animal when she (or occasionally he) first entered the aid chain in the United States, usually at a collection center. The names and addresses of donors back in America could in turn be matched with the ear tag numbers so that donors and recipients could always find each other if they so wished and if circumstances permitted. In one example of a completed "Act of Transferring the Heifer" dated July 19, 1946, the recipient is listed as having received "heifer No. 4317-H 684962" from Windsor Lloyd of Idaho.[10] While this arrangement created technical and bureaucratic links between givers and receivers, it also arguably brought the parties into much closer emotional contact with one another and confirmed their places in an imagined global community. Even if connections between givers and receivers were not followed up, the very possibility of doing so carried a measure of symbolic importance. This also very much differentiated the Heifer Project animals from those in the UNRRA animal relief program. UNRRA animals did not have traceable links to individuals.

The "Act of Transferring the Heifer" also included two "promises" (this was the word used in the document) made by the recipients to the Brethren. The first was that the recipient would keep the heifer on the farm to which she had been assigned as well as take good care of her and not sell her without the explicit consent of the local Agricultural Chamber, with whom the Brethren cooperated in an administrative capacity to handle the animal placements. The second promise was to summon a veterinarian should the heifer become sick and to "follow his orders exactly."[11]

Recipients of animals were also informed about the standard Heifer Project requirement to give away the first healthy female calf born to the heifer they had received. Male calves were not part of the agreement and could be kept by the owners of the animal or sold off. This new recipient was likewise to be a person in need.[12] The benefits to the secondary recipient of a Heifer Project animal were of course obvious. The appeal of Passing on the Gift to the American donors was that it extended the value of each donated animal and, theoretically at least, widened the donor's reach. This no doubt strengthened donors' identity as givers of charity: each heifer that arrived from the United States could be seen as helping a greater number of families. The benefits of the original gift would multiply as time went on and generations of new animals were spread across a single region.

The Brethren Service Committee also liked that this arrangement allowed aid receivers to become aid givers. This evolution of identities, the Brethren argued, permitted people to "contribute to their own welfare" and to the well-being of their broader communities.[13] Dan West was himself of the view that relief was "degrading" but that giving was "ennobling," and that "blessings" came through giving rather than receiving.[14] Arguably, too, this reinforced a sense (on the American side, at any rate) that solutions to hunger and poverty could be relatively simple as long as they were organized and managed well and as long as everyone participated with a view of the collective good in mind.

Seeing Is Believing

The Brethren's assessment of how their program functioned in Poland was very positive at the time and has remained so in the years since. In Brethren Service Committee records and personal cowboy reminiscences, it is clear that Brethren administrators regarded their relationship with the Polish government as cooperative, collegial, and successful.[15] That this government was increasingly dominated by the Communists was certainly noted and discussed but did not cause a great deal of alarm; the Brethren Service Committee did not dwell on this fact or acknowledge, especially in its public pronouncements, that they were working in what was fast becoming a dangerously repressive context. Instead, the Brethren praised the Polish government for being respectful of the Heifer Project's priorities and preferences in terms of aid distribution. They also openly appreciated the government's help in making sure recipients knew that the gifted animals came from the Heifer Project—from a small group of Christians working together on a good cause and helping other Christians—rather than from the larger (and more impersonal) united governments.[16]

Even though everyone understood that Heifer Project animals had a special status, it could be quite difficult to differentiate them from UNRRA animals on the crowded docks. When "mistakes" happened and Heifer Project animals ended up with the UNRRA animals, it was the Polish government's response that mattered most to the Brethren. In one instance the 228 Brethren heifers that had arrived on SS *Woodstock Victory* "lost their identity as gift animals," as the Brethren said, and were taken for UNRRA animals instead. As such they were sold by the government in the usual way.[17] The Brethren Thurl Metzger protested and contacted the government about the error. At the time, in the fall of 1946, Metzger was a lead representative of the Brethren in Poland whose job it was to oversee animal placements; during his six months in this monitoring role, Metzger did some work for UNRRA too. The Ministry of Agriculture investigated Metzger's complaint, and though they did not find the animals and rehome them (this would have been an onerous task indeed), they did provide what the Brethren regarded as fair financial compensation for each animal that had been misdirected, to a sum total of over four million złoty. The Brethren were convinced that the error had been an honest one, and they considered the government's solution to be fair. The Brethren later used the money to sponsor ten Polish students to travel to the United States to study modern American agricultural methods.[18] For their part the Polish government used these moments as opportunities to burnish its reputation, both inside of Poland and abroad, and to show its integrity as custodians of international aid.[19]

The Brethren continued to define their relationship with the Polish government as satisfactory. They were pleased that the government was consistently cooperative and that it honored its earlier agreement to permit follow-up visits with placed heifers; the Brethren had made these visits a condition of providing the heifers in the first place. (UNRRA could also complete spot checks of placements of UNRRA animals—and it often did so—to ensure that nondiscriminatory distribution practices were being followed.[20]) Sometimes recipient farms were visited just once, but occasionally the Brethren conducted additional follow-up visits so that they could get the most current updates about the donated animals, including when the first calf had been born, to whom that firstborn calf had been given, and how much milk the cow was giving.[21] From the Brethren perspective, these visits ensured that "the spirit of donors" was being carried out and confirmed that the animals were receiving good care and were being used as the program intended.[22] The Brethren regarded this less as surveillance on their part and more as an opportunity to build good relations between donors and receivers, between Americans and Poles. Unlike UNRRA—which typically purchased animals in bulk through intermediaries—the Brethren regarded the donated animals as the beginning point of a real relationship and as a living reminder to suffering people that Christians had not forsaken them. For them, personal relationship-building was itself an important component of international humanitarian aid. Arguably the whole arrangement was also advantageous for the animals, who may have had a better shot at a good placement given the scrutiny that could be expected to follow (but which of course did not happen in every case).

Dillon Throckmorton, a minister with the First Methodist Church in Modesto, California, who sailed to Poland in the summer of 1946, visited many recipient families in Poland. Throckmorton had been asked by the Heifer Project to conduct a survey of the already-placed animals and to provide updates on how they were adjusting. In the end Throckmorton visited almost twenty families, and he reported confidently and enthusiastically that in every case the heifers were right where they were supposed to be, were being treated well, and were delivering the aid they were designed to give.[23] For men like Throckmorton, the personal connection that he was able to establish with recipient families during the visits gave him (and by extension the Heifer Project backers back in America) satisfaction that their program was successful; the pleasure came from seeing that the animal gifts did in fact make a positive difference to people's lives. In an article published in the Brethren's *Gospel Messenger* about his farm visits, Throckmorton led with reassurance and certainly. Titled, "I Saw Your Heifers in Poland," Throckmorton gave his readers concrete evidence of success—healthy animals providing a good volume of milk to their humans when just a short time ago there were no milk-giving animals at all. He also wrote movingly about Poles' great suffering during the war and about wartime killings and separations. Everywhere, he told his readers, people were full of gratitude: "If you could witness this elderly gentleman as he expressed his thanks to God for what the Americans had done for him, you would be tireless in pressing forward in the support of the heifer project."[24]

There were other memorable visits to recipient farms that included Brethren Service Committee administrators and seagoing cowboys too. One group of men was led by Ralph Smeltzer of the Brethren Service Committee; together they visited the village of Suchy Dąb in the Gdańsk region in 1946 to "see some of our heifers." The farm of Bronisław Arcab and his family had previously been owned by an ethnic German family that had just been expelled from Poland, and Arcab's family (which included seven children) was moved onto it in May 1945. The Arcab family's own farm, in the region around Kielce, had been destroyed during the war. Holstein heifer number TB366294, courtesy of the Heifer Project, was intended to give Arcab a good fresh start on his newly acquired farm in a new region that held the promise of a better life. Smeltzer doubted that the heifer was giving the thirty liters of milk a day that Arcab claimed, but he was gratified that the animal looked "good." Smeltzer and his companions took a photograph of the cow and the family and went on to the next farm.[25]

The Smeltzer crew visited another village called Krzywe Koło where the brothers Antoni and Adam Kopania lived with their families. They too had recently relocated to the area from Kielce, where the fields were full of mines (a third brother had died because of a mine in a field). The formerly German property that they now inhabited provided a new start for the Kopania brothers and their families just as it has for Arcab and his family; the land was divided in two, and each branch of the Kopania family got fifteen hectares.[26] The families had been in Krzywe Koło since May 1945, and each had received a Heifer Project cow: Antoni received Jersey heifer number 2910 (which was giving twenty liters of milk a day), and Adam received Holstein heifer number 2878. The Holstein's calf had died, but the Jersey cow was due to calf again in a matter of weeks.[27] The brothers had also bought three horses between them (quite possibly these were UNRRA horses, but there is no evidence of this), which they used to plow their fields.[28]

Another visit happened when foreman Lawrence Shultz—who had been the first chair of the Brethren Service Committee and had played a key role in forming the committee in the first place—traveled with a group of cowboys to visit animals that came from the very first Heifer Project shipment to Poland. These animals had arrived on SS *Santiago Iglesias*. The ship had sailed from Baltimore to Gdańsk with a total of 368 heifers aboard, 150 of which were Brethren heifers (the rest were UNRRA animals and were part of UNRRA's third shipment of animals to Poland).[29] Of the twenty cattle born during the sailing, sixteen survived. The animals were distributed to ten villages within a fifty-mile radius of Gdańsk. Shultz and a crew of almost twenty cowboys—mostly Brethren and Mennonite men but also one Methodist and one Catholic—traveled to visit some of them shortly before Christmas 1945.[30] Shultz wrote about this opportunity in an article published in early 1946 in *Gospel Messenger* and also in a report he filed with the Heifer Project. In both pieces Shultz highlighted the visit to the farm of Josef Truski near Ostrowo (rendered as Ostrovik by Shultz). Shultz called one of the heifers by name; this was Joy, "the Jersey heifer from the farm of Daniel Snyder, New Paris, Indiana," carrying ear tag number 1891. Shultz described her as having "a good home" and as being "much needed by that family of four." The photograph that accompanies the article shows some of the men with the heifers "raised on Brethren farms." As part of their visit, the men also enjoyed lunch at the home of a local farmer.[31]

Shultz was clearly pleased to give readers of *Gospel Messenger* this evidence of a successful placement. He delighted in being able to trace the donation path of a single animal—again, the ear tags were key to this—and he was reassured to see that all the animals "are well cared for in better, warmer barns than they had had in America." The animals were doing what they were supposed to do.[32] When Shultz expressed his delight about this outcome to E. Wiszniewski, a Polish agricultural expert at the Polish Embassy in Washington, Wiszniewski repeated what the Brethren knew already: "Well, no cattle, no children."[33] Without cattle there was no foundation for settled family life or for the type of small-scale agricultural production that dominated in Poland.

Sometimes there were also special banquet suppers where the men's work as cattle attendants was recognized and celebrated by the various parties involved in the humanitarian live aid project: the Brethren Service Committee, UNRRA, Polish state representatives, and local farmers alike.[34] Mennonite cowboy David H. White wrote in his diary about having enjoyed such a banquet in the summer of 1946 as the final part of a farm tour that had been arranged for the men by UNRRA and the Polish Department of Agriculture. White and the other cowboys welcomed the celebration for bringing them into proximity with the people they were helping and for exposing them to the surrounding culture. They left with positive impressions of the humanitarian work that was ongoing in Poland and of the Polish people's determination to rebuild their lives.[35] Art Meyer's cowboy crew also enjoyed what he referred to as an "appreciation dinner" in a hall in Sopot after a tour of some of the farms where UNRRA cattle and horses had been placed. As part of their short tour of the Baltic cities, the men also stopped in at the Oliwa Cathedral and listened to the famed pipe organ.[36]

Sometimes the Brethren Service Committee made arrangements (including the necessary translation services) to facilitate the writing of letters back and forth between donors and heifer recipients.[37] In general Polish letter writers celebrated their cow's good health and provided evidence of this by indicating how many liters of milk she gave daily.[38] From time to time, recipients also included photographs of their well-cared-for cow standing beside the whole family.[39] This—showing the relief animal and the human family in a single frame—has become iconic in humanitarian aid photography and is familiar from modern-day humanitarian agencies' promotional materials, too, including those of Heifer International (the successor to the Heifer Project).[40]

One detailed and touching letter of thanks came not from an aid recipient but from a county animal inspector in Działdowo named Witold Tanski. Tanski wrote to the Brethren on behalf of the eighty-nine local farmers who had received a Heifer Project animal. In his letter Tanski assured the Brethren that he knew the recipient families and the heifers personally and that he could therefore say with certainty that the Brethren gifts were in fact giving people the help that they so desperately needed. Another letter of thanks reached the Brethren from Antoni Lewandowski in Pułtusk. In his letter, Lewandowski remarked how strange he found it that he knew the heifer's ear tag number but not the name of the heifer's donor, and he wrote in part to get this information so that he could thank the donor directly (there is no indication that this happened).[41] Another particularly striking display of gratitude was received by the Heifer Project Committee in late 1946 from children living at the Institute for the Blind in Laski, west of Warsaw. The children, some of whom were orphans, expressed their

FIGURE 14. Children and cow. From Edwin T. Randall, "More Values Than Many Sparrows," *Christian Advocate*, March 6, 1947.

great happiness at receiving cows and heifers because they "like milk very much." The children's letter included musings about how difficult it must have been to transport the cows all the way to Poland "because we heard American cows are very wild and jump even out of a lorry. We would like very much to go to America to the wild prairies to catch wild cows and mustangs."[42]

In one instance Brethren Service Committee cowboys had an opportunity to meet the photographer John Vachon. In February 1946 John Vachon traveled with M. E. Hays, the chief of the Agricultural Rehabilitation Division of UNRRA in Poland, plus a veterinarian, from Warsaw to the port areas and to the Bydgoszcz region. The men inspected a newly arrived aid ship, SS *F. J. Luckenbach*, visited the receiving barns, and watched the reloading of the animals onto what Hays described as well-stocked train cars that would move the animals into the Polish interior. The UNRRA men and a

FIGURE 15. Seagoing cowboys. UN photo by John Vachon. UNRRA 4229, from the United Nations Relief and Rehabilitation Administration Collection, United Nations Archives.

group of twenty-five cowboys then traveled together to visit a state farm that was producing milk for delivery to children as part of a rationing program, and they also toured an agricultural school that had received eight cows and nine horses form UNRRA. Vachon photographed the cowboys outside the school (see fig. 15). It was only at this point, during the field trip, that Vachon seemed to learn about the Brethren Service Committee and the seagoing cowboys program; he wrote about the cowboys in a letter to his wife Penny (Millicent Leeper). Vachon, like the cowboys and UNRRA too, was "favorably impressed" with everything he had seen and with the standards of animal care in Poland. As Hays wrote in his report, the effect of this field trip was also to dispel "rumors which they say are current in the States as to what is happening to UNRRA livestock delivered to Poland."[43]

These examples of encounters between recipients and the Brethren, whether through in-person visits or through letters of gratitude, and whether mediated by UNRRA staff or not, were important and revealing. No doubt some of the recipients had to go to considerable effort and expense to write and send the letters, develop photographs, or host the visitors with food and drink, and this alone is testament to the importance Poles attached to giving gratitude. There was no reason to expect that these small actions would have brought them any additional benefit. The letters and the visits established a meaningful connection between giver and receiver, and when recipients professed their own Christianity and recognized the Christianity of the donors in their letters of thanks, this strengthened the connections further still. Significantly, too, the encounters allowed aid providers to answer honestly that the animals' conditions at their destinations were "good." UNRRA Director General Lehman was pleased that both the letters and the farm visit reports could reassure the American public that the aid program was in fact running smoothly: "Everyone who has had the opportunity to see the care given these animals," Lehman said, "has reported that these conditions are excellent."[44]

Despite satisfactory field trips and repeated reassurances from UNRRA and Brethren administrators that animals ended up where they were supposed to be, there was evidence of problems that even the cowboys—who were generally very eager to believe that everything was running as they hoped—could not ignore. For example, when a group of cowboys visited a widow who had received a Holstein from the Heifer Project, they were shocked to learn that the animal often stayed inside the house, with the widow, so as to prevent "the Russians" from seizing her.[45] Though even here some Brethren argued that keeping cattle in the same building as the family was less about fear of theft than it was a sign of Poles' great appreciation for the animals. Other cowboys reported hearing similar reports from other recipients: the Russians, they were told, took whatever they wanted when they wanted.[46]

It was also no doubt easier for cowboys to treat evidence of corruption as an outlier or oddity and to emphasize successful placements and positive stories instead. It was also much easier to do this in 1946, when the political situation had not yet been definitively settled, than in 1947, by which time the Communists had eliminated their opposition and the new political framework was up and running. As one seagoing cowboy wrote in *Gospel Messenger* in 1946, Brethren communities wanted this assurance that, simply, "the stock we cared for is now helping to provide food for hundreds of people."[47] And even if those people that were being helped were sometimes Communists (or for expediency pretended to be Communists), this did not mean that the animals they received were wasted; the animals were still helping someone to farm and survive.[48] Heifer Project internal documents also reinforce these views; the confidence was not only manufactured for public consumption.

As late as the summer of 1947, in a summary statement written by staff at the Heifer Project about the Brethren Service Committee's work in Poland, we can read that "after many investigations there was not a single instance of Russian confiscation of American cattle in Poland."[49]

That UNRRA Director General Lehman and various UNRRA bureaucrats provided their own reassurances about the integrity of their much larger relief program was interpreted by the Brethren as a positive sign as well. The Russian Mikhail A. Menshikov, who was the leader of the Temporary Mission to Poland in 1945 and who later served as deputy director general at the Bureau of Areas at Washington's UNRRA headquarters, also affirmed in public forums that reports of red tape and misappropriation of both UNRRA and Heifer Project animals (and other donations) were simply unfounded.[50] The Canadian Charles Drury delivered a very similar message to *The New York Times* in 1946, as did Lehman's successor as UNRRA director general, Fiorello La Guardia.[51] All aid organizations were on the same page in this regard and largely just dismissed the view that aid was being stolen or wasted. No doubt this refusal to believe in the real possibilities of corruption and political manipulation contributed to an assessment, at the time and even today, of mid-century aid providers as naïve and as too easily duped by the Communists.[52]

The Heifer Project's Next Phase

As UNRRA started closing its operations in 1947, this left charities like the Heifer Project to pursue relief work on their own, in Poland and of course elsewhere as well. Perhaps this was a mixed blessing for the Brethren. The Brethren generally appreciated that they benefited from UNRRA's considerable resources—most notably its ships but also its in-country contacts and its access to translators, guides, and administrative help. The Brethren administrator Thurl Metzger was of the view that UNRRA did categorically "good" work in Poland, contributed to internal political and social stability, and relieved suffering. Metzger saw this himself during the time he spent in the country from late 1946. Then again, Metzger continued, working with UNRRA came with certain challenges for the Brethren Service Committee too. During a time when so many of the local people were making do with so little, UNRRA staff stood out for their privileges. "There was also the embarrassment," Metzger said, "of being associated with the group that lived in the best hotels, ate at the best restaurants and traveled through the country like high officials in an occupation army." For his part, Metzger walked to work and took every opportunity to socialize with the locals and visit their homes and institutions.[53]

A total of sixteen charitable groups, the Brethren included, were working in Poland in the middle of 1946, and that number doubled by the end of the year as it became clear that UNRRA would soon depart and that there would be both room and a need for additional relief providers.[54] The Danish Red Cross had a presence in Poland, as did Swedish aid groups and CARE (Cooperative for American Remittances to Europe). Many of these groups were small and religious in nature, like the Brethren Service Committee, the Mennonite Central Committee, the Methodist Committee for Overseas Relief, and the Anglo-American Quaker Relief Mission. In 1947 the Friends Service Council (UK) and the American Friends Service Committee were awarded a joint Nobel Peace Prize for their work in postwar aid provision in Poland and elsewhere.[55]

Given that UNRRA aid ships had stopped sailing to Poland by the end of 1947, as UNRRA itself ceased its operations, it became much more expensive and logistically complicated for the Brethren to send large numbers of animals (or any other large volumes of aid) on their own. Yet Poles continued to ask the Brethren for additional animals. Orphanages, for example, continued to write with requests for a "free cow" and underscored in their letters what by this point was obvious: that milk was critically important to children's health. Too often the Brethren had to respond that they did not have enough stock in Poland to distribute to the many Poles that still needed cattle, and that they had no way of bringing cattle from the US to Poland.[56] Moreover, in the post-UNRRA period the $150 that UNRRA had paid each attendant for the trip no longer existed; cattle attendants would need to be paid by the Brethren themselves, or they would have to choose to become real volunteers without receiving any payment whatsoever. Then again, the need for volunteers was not as great after UNRRA closed down; the scale of the Brethren operations by necessity became far more modest. By the spring of 1947, the Brethren Service Committee had 175 interested volunteers lined up, even though estimates were that only 16 would be needed every month.[57]

From late 1946 until March 1949, the Brethren Service Committee's director in Poland was Clara Chaloupka Wood. Chaloupka Wood's husband Bruce ran the Heifer Project for the Brethren Service Committee. Paul A. Getz, a teacher specializing in agriculture, took over for a very short time in 1949. The Brethren maintained their main office in Warsaw and their aid distribution center in Ostróda until August 1949, at which point they packed up and left for good.[58] Until the last days, the Brethren continued to place whatever animals they had with people and institutions that needed them. In addition, the

Brethren in these last months were involved in setting up a home economics program at the Central Agricultural College (Szkoła Główna Gospodarstwa Wiejskiego) in Warsaw. The initiative in expanding agricultural education was an important one, the Brethren said, given how many agricultural leaders had been killed in the war. It was a matter of replacing lost skills.[59]

During this post-UNRRA period, the Brethren also arranged for a shipment of 160 black and red Danish Red cattle—known to be good milk producers—from the port of Naevsted, Denmark, to Poland; the cattle arrived in May 1948.[60] The Danish animals were purchased by the Brethren Service Committee for $40,000 or $250 per animal (with shipping and animal care costs paid in this case by the Polish government). This donation was negotiated directly between the Brethren and Poland's Ministry of Agriculture, and the animals were earmarked specifically to help children, whose milk needs everyone believed had been well established; the animals were directed to households with three or more children or to orphanages. The imperative to "pass on the gift" was part of the new agreement as well, just as it had formed part of the original Heifer Project donations. And recipients were encouraged to share any extra milk that the animals produced with nearby needy families.[61]

The total number of cattle shipped to Poland by the Heifer Project until the end of 1948 (so well past the period when the Brethren worked with UNRRA and ran the seagoing cowboys program) was 1,013.[62] That was a small number compared to UNRRA's many tens of thousands, but it was an earnest number behind which lay a great deal of community-level organizing and genuine desire to affect positive change. The fact was, though, that even at this point the Heifer Project still had hundreds of heifers in holding centers in the United States: 250 at New Windsor and several hundred more across the United States. The care the animals required was burdensome. With no way of getting them to Europe, the Brethren soon sold many of the waiting animals and kept the money in reserve to buy more heifers later, once shipping became possible.[63]

Despite affirmations that Poland deserved much more aid than other countries due to the extent of wartime devastation—and certainly more than it had already received—the Communists had no intention of tolerating representatives of foreign charities in Poland, just as they had no intention of allowing the Americans or the so-called United Nations to stay in the country.[64] All aid coming from outside of the country's borders—and all foreigners who brought that aid—became increasingly suspicious and threatening to the Communists. The Communist authorities came to regard foreign charities in the country as an affront to the country's sovereignty.[65] Unlike in the immediate postwar period when national governments were weak and battered and when there was just a little bit of space for international bodies to shape lives in sovereign countries, by 1947 national boundaries were more rigidly drawn, and there was comparatively less enthusiasm for outside help. Simply being present in the country, by some definitions, constituted unwelcome interference.[66]

As a result, Polish Communist Security Services undertook investigations of the foreign aid groups that operated in Poland.[67] That many of the charities and aid workers active in Poland were Protestants further raised alarm bells for the security apparatus of the Polish state. The Polish security services feared that the aid workers fostered a "German spirit" among the population they worked with, particularly in the north of the country, which had some historical links to German Protestantism. The aid volunteers were sometimes accused of being spies. Of course, those Poles with whom the foreigners worked also came under suspicion.[68] In the summer of 1949, Poland's Ministry of Agriculture formally gave notice to the Brethren Service Committee that they no longer wished to cooperate with them on bringing cattle to Poland.[69] The Brethren Service Committee left Poland in 1949. And this despite the fact that as late as the fall of 1948 the Food and Agriculture Organization insisted that Poland still had the greatest need for milk cattle in all of Europe.[70]

Heifer International

By the end of the 1940s, the Heifer Project Committee that had formed in the midst of World War II as a temporary relief agency designed to address specific postwar needs had been transformed into a significant humanitarian aid organization with a proven track record.[71] The Heifer Project's continuation past the UNRRA phase was by no means certain, however, as going it alone, without UNRRA's resources and with the need to cover cattle attendants' expenses plus freight costs, posed significant logistical and financial challenges. Yet the Brethren believed in the ongoing need for the work they were doing, as agricultural renewal remained key to postwar rebuilding. Moreover, the Brethren Service Committee leaders continued to believe in what they described as "the Christian's opportunity and responsibility" to engage in humanitarian relief work. And besides, the idea and the reality of the Heifer Project had quickly earned an important place in Brethren identity, and no one was prepared to give that up quite yet.[72] "Is it a duty or a privilege to share our material blessings with those who have so little?" one internal Heifer Project document asked. Clearly it was both.[73] The Brethren John D. Metzler, who had been part of the formative phase of the Heifer Project and at one time director of the material aid program at the New

Windsor Brethren complex, offered his opinion at a committee meeting of the Brethren Service Committee in August 1947. Metzler said, simply, "The name of the Heifer project Committee is too well known to be sacrificed."[74] The BSC was proud of its work in Poland and elsewhere, and they saw themselves as making an important contribution to relieving suffering.

The Heifer Project continued its rehabilitation work after the UNRRA period and indeed expanded its engagement into other areas of the world.[75] The first major shipment that the Heifer Project made independently of UNRRA (UNRRA's last shipment of livestock from the US happened in April 1947) was to Japan that same month. Transportation was provided by the US War Department aboard SS *Alfred DuPont*.[76] Heifer Project cattle were also shipped to West Germany from 1949 to 1961. Remarkably, the Heifer Project also shipped cattle to the Soviet Union in 1956. Well-known men from within the organization—Thurl Metzger, Milo Yoder, Mark Schrock, and Paul Miller—accompanied the animals and were guests in the USSR of the Ministry of Agriculture. "You can go anywhere on the back of a heifer," M. R. Zigler said about this unlikely turn of events.[77] And then in 1960 the latest incarnation of the Heifer Project again struck up a relationship with Poland's Ministry of Agriculture to deliver heifers, along with beef cattle, to Poland.[78]

The versatility and utility of cattle—the opportunities they provided—were repeated throughout the life of the Heifer Project; according to the Brethren, it was cattle specifically that had made the Heifer Project such a success: "Heifers are better than howitzers in making steady friends abroad," offered one cowboy.[79] By 1950 the Heifer Project had shipped eleven thousand animals—heifers, mainly, but also bulls and goats—to approximately twenty countries.[80]

In 1951 Thurl Metzger replaced Benjamin Bushong as the executive director of the Heifer Project Committee. As we have seen, Metzger represented the Brethren in Poland and oversaw animal placements. Before that he served in the Civilian Public Service and later worked for the Heifer Project at the Brethren's New Windsor center. Metzger was thus already experienced and had proved his commitment to the Heifer Project.[81] The Heifer Project evolved and expanded under Metzger's leadership, and in 1953 it incorporated as an independent nonprofit organization, Heifer Project Incorporated. This marked a functional and formal separation of the Heifer Project from the Church of the Brethren and the Brethren Service Committee. It also marked the transformation of the organization from a Christian one to one with no formal connections to any faith-based bodies.[82] And of course with the Brethren-UNRRA partnership long over, it was the job of the Heifer Project to recruit men for the sailings (and to pay for the sailings as well).

Peace church men continued to volunteer, as did men from other Christian denominations, and eventually women were eligible to work as volunteer animal handlers as well. The scale of the organization's activities was much smaller and less rushed, not surprisingly, with fewer and less frequent shipments, and trucks and air travel slowly replaced the large, retrofitted ships that defined live transport in the UNRRA days.[83] Today the Heifer Project is called Heifer International and is located in Little Rock, Arkansas. It continues to provide livestock to communities in need around the world, including those in the United States.[84] The current mission statement—"We work to end hunger and poverty in partnership with the communities we serve"—is direct and ambitious. The idea that "ending poverty begins with agriculture" is a core belief of Heifer International, just as it was of the Heifer Project.[85] In this sense the logic that led to the inclusion of animals in humanitarian aid programs at mid-century remains in place in our contemporary period too. Rehabilitation in largely agricultural societies continues to rely on animals.

What is arguably changing, however, is nonhuman animals' place in our ethical, cultural, and social worlds, and this, in turn, is shaping humanitarian aid programs. Today aid providers recognize that for a variety of reasons, including environmental ones, animals should be sourced locally when possible rather than shipped tremendous distances at enormous cost. The environmental impacts of shipping animals across oceans, as well as the environmental impacts of keeping and feeding livestock to begin with, did not register with mid-century actors in the ways that it does today. An understanding of animals' biology and adaptability has evolved with the times too. More recently too, of course, the idea that cows' milk is a nutritious food has been challenged, with many arguing against the consumption of cows' milk entirely. Critics contend that milk's advertised health benefits are overrated or even false and that the dairy industry is built on animal suffering; the demands of modern industrial milk production mean that cows are confined for the duration of their productive lives and subject to unrelenting cycles of forced impregnation.[86] And the very concept of "animal aid" has been the subject of intense scrutiny in the last few decades too. Animal rights advocates argue that, as sentient creatures, nonhuman animals possess basic rights and intrinsic value and are owed moral consideration.[87] This in turn means that they should not be used as means to an end or treated as objects to be bought, sold, donated, or traded to benefit and serve humans. And they should also not be used as diplomatic props or as symbols of international cooperation or goodwill. Instead, and in pursuit of ethical and environmentally sustainable alternatives, plant-based solutions to hunger should replace approaches that rely on the exploitation and abuse of nonhuman animals.[88]

Conclusion
Humanitarian Imaginaries

Live animal maritime transport did not of course begin with UNRRA and the Heifer Project, just as it would not end with them. Animals have been carried aboard ships for as long as maritime vessels have existed. Since ancient times horses and mules have been shipped across waters to meet the military needs of troops fighting wars across the globe. Livestock animals have provided a source of fresh meat (or, depending on the animal type, a source of milk as well) for crews sailing the world for commerce and conquest. Certain animal species—cattle, horses, goats, and sheep—have been part and parcel of transplanting societies and cultures to colonial contexts.[1] As the new global food economy started to take shape at the end of the nineteenth century with the rapid growth of railway networks and the expansion of the steamship industry, some of these same species met growing demand across settler societies for specific kinds of "live meat."[2] Alternatively, pets and animal mascots made for sentimental companions on both merchant and military maritime vessels, with some animals carried aboard simply for good luck. Exotic animals captured in the wild were transported on ships, too, en route to new confinements in menageries and zoos, where they would become living testaments to imperial power. Sometimes particularly rare or seemingly exotic animals formed part of a diplomatic arsenal of lavish gifts offered by one ruler to another.[3]

The transport of live animals across oceans has continued into the twenty-first century. Long-haul "live export ships" are enormous oceangoing vessels that carry thousands of livestock animals from one destination to another. Most of these animals are bound, ultimately, for slaughterhouses, where they are transformed into animal protein for human consumption. The maritime live animal transport industry has quadrupled in the last half century, and this growth mirrors the rapid expansion of intensive animal farming or "factory farming"; Australia, South America, and the European Union dominate the industry.[4]

China is a main target market, but the Middle East, with its lack of space and water but a growing taste for "fresh" meat and dairy as well as a need for halal meat, is the most common destination for sheep in particular. As early as the 1970s, the largest Australian carrier of sheep, the Cormoran, accommodated twenty-eight thousand animals per sailing; that number was surpassed later in the decade with ships that could carry an astounding fifty thousand animals. But the largest-ever animal transport ship, the *Al Qurain*, was purpose-built to accommodate ninety-two thousand sheep; it was sailing as early as in the 1980s. Typically, however, live export ships are smaller; today they generally carry anywhere from a few thousand to over ten thousand animals.[5] Stock people are limited to just a few per sailing as mechanization has ostensibly replaced much of the labor-intensive work that cattlemen—like the Brethren Service Committee's seagoing cowboys—used to do.

The vast majority of livestock ships are better described as "floating feedlots." They are converted car carriers or container ships and sometimes even oil tankers; these are ships that have been retrofitted quickly and cheaply to accommodate as many animals as possible over several tiers or floors. They do not always meet animal welfare standards, which, at any rate, vary by country of origin and are loose, weak, and difficult to enforce. Moreover, because these vessels were not purpose-built, their structure does not account for the unique challenges that "living cargo" creates. What this means, for example, is that if too many animals—particularly those that have been stacked or tiered—choose to move to one side of the ship all at once, then the ship's stability is compromised, and it risks overturning. These can be particularly dangerous ships to sail. Only 20 percent of the current livestock fleet in the world today was designed to carry livestock specifically. Whereas the average age of a commercial container ship is thirteen years, the average age of a ship in the livestock carrier fleet is about three times that at thirty-eight years.[6]

For the animals the conditions on the ships are important, as we have seen, especially given that some transports can take weeks rather than merely days to complete, and if a ship has mechanical problems, then the already tortuously long journeys take even longer. The animals that make these trips are confined in unfamiliar habitats with high noise levels and strange light patterns and intensities. They have no choice but to adjust quickly to their new and hastily established social groups and to their new human handlers, who sometimes have limited experience caring for such large numbers of a specific species. They are packed in to optimize space use and restrict movement; the result is high stocking densities and extreme overcrowding in what are sometimes rough seas in all types of weather and, depending on the route and its length, through changing climate and time zones. Nevertheless, the more animals that can be loaded onto a single ship, the higher the profits for the various stakeholders involved: livestock suppliers, the ship companies, and the meat producers. Some of the most popular and regularly traveled routes are also the longest. The pressure to make trips worthwhile from a financial standpoint is reflected in the large vessel sizes that dominate on the longest routes.[7]

The animals face numerous discomforts on the trips. There is often not enough room for all of them to lie down, and at any rate, lying down carries with it the risk of being stepped on and smothered. As a result, some species, like cattle, become exhausted and weak from standing for the entire journey. The sawdust that is used for bedding is very limited so as to maintain the specially designed nonslip cleating and abrasive surfaces that often make up the vessels' floors. But the rough surfaces mean more discomfort for animals, both when they are standing still and when they have a chance to lie down. Sometimes the animals develop skin abrasions and lesions on their feet because they remain upright for so long. Even small wounds can become infected quickly in the generally unhygienic conditions. The animals spend the voyages covered in excrement and urine, and the smell that this produces announces the ship's entry into its destination harbor long before docking. Moreover, the feces that end up covering animals' coats diminishes their ability to regulate body temperature, and this can quickly lead to heat stress, increased respiration rates, renal dysfunction, and eventually death. The buildup of urine also contributes to the accumulation of high ammonia levels in the cramped quarters (particularly on closed decks where ventilation is restricted or inadequate), and this in turn can cause pulmonary inflammation and mucosal irritation. It also compromises the structural integrity of the ship itself. Manure ferments and releases moisture, ammonia, and carbon dioxide, which interact with the chloride that the animals excrete naturally; the result is a "slurry" that can corrode steel and damage the decks.[8]

CONCLUSION

Animals that are suffering from heat exhaustion or have untreated infections will experience inanition—they stop drinking and eating—which will then precipitate dehydration and starvation; this, of course, will only hasten their deaths. The food on offer is unfamiliar; besides, it takes a while for digestive systems to adjust to dramatic changes in diet. The water and the food troughs are often contaminated with feces anyway, which then become further sources of illness. The fact that the floors are covered in feces makes animals reluctant to lie down, even where there is an opportunity, leading, again, to exhaustion and the attendant risks. Infections can travel easily from one animal to another in the generally crowded conditions aboard the ships; conjunctivitis is a common risk for cattle in particular.

Though it is considered best practice not to ship pregnant animals, it happens that sometimes they find themselves on board and even give birth on the ships. These are very high-risk births that endanger the health of the mother, to say nothing of the newborns, who are not worth the effort they require and are often killed immediately. This can in turn lead to mastitis for the mother. Dead animals (newborns and adults alike) are removed as quickly as possible and when circumstances allow but definitely before the ship reaches port, as the unloading of dead animals in plain sight risks negative publicity for the shipping company as well as for the producer that will eventually sell the animals for their meat potential. Identifying tags often attached to ears are removed from the dead animals' heads before they are thrown overboard so that the carcasses cannot be linked to a specific ship; no company involved in any part of the food production process—because this is overwhelmingly about food—wants the bad publicity that comes with dead animals.[9]

Regulations for live export ships vary greatly by country, but in general the rules are lax and subject to interpretation. Conditions aboard ships can be difficult to monitor, and the resources are often not available to do so properly, even when the will exists. There are also no legal requirements to report mortality rates on live export vessels. Here Australia has been an exception to some extent: Australian laws require reporting on ships with a loss rate that exceeds 1 percent. Loss rates of 1 percent are quite acceptable, generally speaking. On a ship with fifty thousand animals aboard, that means that only deaths in excess of five hundred ought to be reported. This reported mortality rate functions as the main measure of animal welfare in the wider industry.[10]

Sometimes stunningly high losses make the international news, as happened in 2015 when 40 percent of the animals (5,200) that had arrived in Jordan from Romania were dead from dehydration and starvation. In late

2019 an old Romanian ship carrying more than fourteen thousand sheep to Saudi Arabia capsized. The crew of twenty-two persons all survived. Only 180 sheep, or just over 1 percent, lived. Only when a human animal is killed or seriously injured on a live animal transport vessel does the International Maritime Organization require an investigation. Many livestock ships also fly under so-called flags of convenience and have disproportionately high infraction rates, according to the Paris Memorandum of Understanding on Port State Control. This agreement was signed by twenty-seven maritime organizations and covers waters between Europe and North America. Member states have agreed to work together to inspect ships, to ensure that they meet safety and environmental standards, and to monitor compliance with international maritime conventions; the International Maritime Organization completes thousands of inspections in these waters every year.[11]

There are, however, enormous changes coming to the live animal export industry. In April 2023 New Zealand ceased exports of livestock by sea.[12] In May 2024 the Animal Welfare (Livestock Exports) Act became law in Great Britain; the law bans the export of cattle, horses, pigs, goats, and sheep for the purposes of slaughter and fattening (live export for the purposes of breeding remains permitted).[13] In early 2025, Wellard, the leading Australian livestock shipping company, announced that it was selling its last ship and reconsidering the direction of its business.[14] Australia plans to end the export of live sheep by sea by 2028.[15] The subject is a contentious one across the continent and indeed the world. Kristen Stilt, director of Harvard's Animal Law and Policy program, has suggested that the transport of and trade in live animals is approaching its end and will be replaced by the transport of chilled and frozen meat. That may well turn out to be the case. But for the time being, the global live export trade continues to be worth billions of dollars.[16]

Live animal maritime transport in the immediate postwar period was different in important ways. The major differences between then and now stem from the fact that the UNRRA and Heifer Project animals were part of a distinctive project, a mission with a grand purpose. The animals were supposed to arrive at their destinations healthy enough to work and to contribute immediately and for the long term to postwar reconstruction. They were not awaiting almost immediate slaughter, and as such they needed attentive care during the ocean voyages to ensure their physical and psychological well-being upon arrival. As we have seen, this care was provided by the seagoing cowboys, who, at a ratio of twenty-some animals to one cowboy, depending on the specific load and on the species, had ample time to feed the animals, to clean their stalls, and generally to monitor their physical conditions and report problems to the on-board veterinarians. The cowboys were doing a job and were well compensated for it, but, beyond that, the specific subset of men we have focused on in this book saw their work as at least in part an obligation to their communities, their churches, their God, or humanity itself. The success of their mission—the well-being of the cattle and horses—mattered to them personally. It also mattered to the many small American communities from which the men came and that had invested so many material and emotional resources in making this program of postwar aid function smoothly.

Despite this, similarities between live animal maritime transport at midcentury and today remain. Speed and size mattered after the war just as they matter today. In our modern period, commercial enterprises use the fastest ships available to transport the greatest number of animals per sailing; quick deliveries and turnaround times translate into higher profits. For UNRRA the motivation to move the animals quickly stemmed from a desire to stimulate agriculture and self-sufficiency sooner rather than later; it mattered if the animals arrived in time for spring planting in 1946 or not. Besides, UNRRA was always meant to be a temporary organization, and it had only a short window to complete its work.

We have seen throughout this book that the maritime transport of animals, even in the best of circumstances and even when it is conducted with the best of intentions, comes with risks and costs that are borne first and foremost by the animals themselves. Discomforts could be mitigated, but there was nothing that could change the fact of being immobile in a stall on a rocking ship in the ocean for days on end; this has remained a constant feature of maritime animal transport throughout centuries. There are simply significant practical challenges involved in moving animals across oceans. UNRRA was acutely aware of these challenges from the beginning, and indeed its initial reluctance to include living animals in its relief program reflected this understanding. Yet ultimately UNRRA was persuaded that animals were crucially important to the organization's rehabilitation agenda. Like all stakeholders, UNRRA expected and accepted the "losses" that would stack up during the trips; animal deaths, regrettably, were simply part and parcel of improving human lives.

By following the relief animals from point of origin to point of delivery, we have traveled through many different contexts and explored several layered histories. We have visited the international realm, where the idea that the United Nations could and should come together to provide humanitarian aid to the victims of Nazi aggression was born. This was an abstract realm of imaginings, hopes, and wishes, to be sure, but it was also a space of planning and calculation; it was from here that UNRRA and its live animal aid program emerged. In addition, we have spent time in the American context so as to understand the various dimensions—political, social, economic, moral, and religious—that supported humanitarian aid provision in theory and in practice. In this American context, too, we have seen how the perceived need for humanitarian aid mobilized the Brethren in a very creative and unique way. As the Brethren's *Gospel Messenger* reported at the end of 1946, it was through the Heifer Project and through the Brethren Service Committee's management of the seagoing cowboys program that the Brethren "became international"; the Brethren came to understand, even more than they had before, that "we are one world."[17] The seagoing cowboys' labor on the oceangoing ships with horses and dairy cattle was critical in realizing the bold ambitions of postwar humanitarianism. This book brings attention to at least some of those cowboys and to the animals that formed a crucially important component of postwar relief practices and goals but that, despite this importance, have been largely overlooked in the literature on mid-century humanitarianism as well as in the popular imagination.

Our final stop in this book has been the Polish context, one of the many end points for relief animals in both the UNRRA and Heifer Project programs. As we know, of the few hundred thousand living animals shipped by UNRRA to all possible destinations, approximately half went to Poland alone. And though the number of animals the Heifer Project delivered to Poland was less than a thousand, this was still more than any other single country received during the UNRRA period. Poland thus provides a rich landscape for exploring what happened to these animals upon arrival and what these animals meant in both symbolic and practical terms.

In some ways the animal deliveries to Poland form part of a simple success story. Horses used their considerable strength to cultivate ruined and abandoned fields in Poland and to facilitate agricultural rehabilitation faster and better than would have been possible otherwise. As UNRRA analysts calculated at the end of the program, every fifth hectare of land in rural Poland was being farmed with the aid of an UNRRA horse.[18] The horses maximized the value of other types of relief as well. What use were thousands of pounds of seeds, for example, if there was no animal manure to fertilize the fields or draft power to make sowing and harvesting possible?

Dairy cattle labor was likewise essential to agricultural development. All major stakeholders in the postwar period—politicians, nutritionists, UNRRA bureaucrats, the Brethren Service Committee, the seagoing cowboys, and regular people too—believed that the milk that cows produced had unparalleled nutritional value. UNRRA presented a snapshot in mid-1946 of the effects that its cattle shipments were already having on relief and rehabilitation in Poland. It estimated that 40 percent of the heifers distributed in Poland had calves shortly after arriving in the country and that the total milk production that resulted from these animals was 225,750 pounds per day (using an average of 20 to 30 pounds per day); that was enough milk to supply 112,875 persons with one quart of milk per day.[19] By 1947 milk production in Poland was still only at one-fifth of the prewar level, but that was far better than it would have been without the infusion of animals from abroad.[20] All of this shows us that animal labor mattered in the immediate postwar period. It reminds us, too, that the animals functioned—to use the title of a recent book by Benjamin Meiches—as "nonhuman humanitarians." Humanitarianism was (and remains) a heterogenous project that involves the labor of both human and nonhuman actors.[21]

In addition to having practical value, the animals reflected—more powerfully than a crate of tinned food ever could—the bold ambitions of mid-century humanitarianism. Never before in peacetime had so many large living animals been shipped in such a short time to reach so many people.[22] As we have seen, the Brethren reflected frequently in the UNRRA period on cattle's special status and on this species' ability to "do good," to make a difference in people's lives for both the short and the long terms, and to show that collective action on behalf of others was worth taking. What cattle offered did not need translation, the Brethren said, because relief cattle spoke an "international language," one that promised "a more abundant tomorrow." The gift of a cow was a direct gesture of humanitarian aid, and it delivered the same powerful message to all people everywhere: "Someone still cares. Christian goodwill has survived the war.—There is a chance to begin again. There is yet hope for a world of peace."[23]

While the relief animals did not, in the end, achieve world peace or solve global hunger, they did help some people rebuild their lives in this short time between the end of the Second World War and the start of the Cold War. That the animals lived into the period of the People's Republic of Poland—and that their descendants exist even today, in the Third Republic—is important, too. These animals represent a small point of continuity between political regimes and historical periods. And perhaps they continue to exist too as symbols of long-forgotten ideals, of communities imagined, however briefly, on an international scale.

As caretakers of both the Heifer Project and the UNRRA animals, the seagoing cowboys played a unique role in mid-century humanitarianism. They got their hands dirty. They carried hay bales and bags of feed. They shoveled manure and tended to sick and dying animals. They endured seasickness and uncomfortable conditions aboard the ships. They did the unglamorous but indispensable work of the live animal aid program. This was also largely hidden work that happened in crowded animal stalls. It is thanks to the cowboys themselves that we know so much about what it was like aboard the ships. Over the subsequent decades, Brethren and Mennonite cowboys in particular talked often about the time when they "saw the world" from a cattle boat. These men returned to America with photographs to share and stories to tell, and, indeed, telling the story—"recounting witness," as the Brethren like to say—has become an important part of Brethren relief work to this day.[24] Cowboys' willingness to talk about their experiences is what allows us to write this history in the first place. It is, as we have seen, a history full of surprising intersections and unexpected layers.

Perhaps most surprisingly and unexpectedly, a book about one small part of postwar aid programming in Poland turns out to have contemporary relevance for the same general region in Europe. The Russian invasion of Ukraine that started in 2022 has highlighted global food security issues and raised concerns about the impact of food scarcity on political and social stability. Ukraine has long been imagined—by Hitler and the Nazis, by various incarnations of the Russian state, and in different ways by the west, too—as a breadbasket zone, as a land of nearly limitless food resources available for others to use and exploit. Since the start of the war, various international actors and media outlets have expressed concern about how the war threatens the world's grain supply and what, in turn, this means.[25] Animals have a role in these broader discourses too; animals, as we have seen, are integral to discussions about agriculture and food security, whether in times of war or peace.

What has happened with farm animals in Ukraine since the Russian invasion is broadly familiar from the mid-century context. Tens of thousands of cattle were killed in the first months of the war alone, whether by bombs, for food, or from starvation, and numbers decreased further in the subsequent months.[26] Decaying animal carcasses pose a health and environmental risk. In some areas civilians have been killed, displaced, or drafted—meaning that farm work has had to adjust accordingly—and both infrastructure and farm machinery have been damaged. Fields in key areas are littered with mines and unexploded ordinance and thus are too dangerous to be used as pastureland or for planting. Even if some lands are usable and specific herds safe, costs of just about everything associated with agricultural production have risen. Transport and sale networks have also been disrupted, which means that agricultural supplies (including feed for the animals) cannot always

CONCLUSION

reach their destinations, and foodstuffs produced on farms cannot always get to where they are supposed to go either. At any rate where the food products are needed has itself changed as millions of people have left the country since the start of the Russian invasion.

In this context keeping dairy herds alive and maintaining the strength of the dairy industry has taken on symbolic importance and becomes part and parcel of resistance and survival; it has become part of waging war by different means.[27] The Association of Milk Producers, a nongovernmental not-for-profit agency that represents dairy farmers across Ukraine, made the following rhetorically powerful statement on World Milk Day, June 1, 2024: "Milk is a global product, an indispensable element of healthy nutrition and a healthy lifestyle, of happy and healthy childhood, responsible food production and ensuring social stability of households and communities, and food security of countries [sic]."[28] This expression of contemporary enthusiasm for milk brings us back to the mid-1940s and that era's belief in dairy milk's ability to nourish humans both literally and metaphorically. It also reminds us that our relationship with nonhuman animals is always meaningful and always open to interpretation. It is through those relationships that we reflect our identities, aspirations, and anxieties.

Abbreviations

AAN	Archive of Modern Documents (Archiwum Akt Nowych)
AHA	American Humane Association
APW	State Archive in Warsaw (Archiwum Państwowe w Warszawie)
APwSZ	State Archive in Sczecin (Archiwum Państwowe w Szczecinie)
ARA	American Relief Administration
BHLA	Brethren Historical Library and Archives
BSC	Brethren Service Committee
CCWR	Center on Conscience and War Records
CO	Conscientious Objector
CPS	Civilian Public Service
CUP	Centralny Urząd Planowania
DP	Displaced Person
DWP	Dan West Papers
FAO	Food and Agriculture Organization
FINA	National Film Archive (Filmoteka Narodowa—Instytut Audiowizualny)
HP	Heifer Project
JEN	John E. Nunemaker Collection
JMU	James Madison University Special Collections
KSWNSG	Komisja Specjalna do Walki z Nadużyciami i Szkodnictwem Gospodarczym w Warszawie
MCA	Mennonite Church Archives
MCC	Mennonite Central Committee
MGP	Melvin G. Gingerich Papers
MPiOS	Ministerstwo Pracy i Opieki Społecznej w Warszawie
MRiRR	Ministerstwo Rolnictwa i Reform Rolnych
MZO	Ministerstwo Ziem Odzyskanych w Warszawie
NSBRO	National Service Board for Religious Objectors
POW	Poland—Ostróda and Warsaw Offices
SCPC	Swarthmore College Peace Collection

ABBREVIATIONS

TOZ	Society for the Protection of Animals (Towarzystwo Ochrony Zwierząt)
UNA	United Nations Archives
UNC	University of North Carolina
UNICEF	United Nations International Children's Emergency Fund
UNRRA	United Nations Relief and Rehabilitation Administration
USDA	United States Department of Agriculture
UWS	Urząd Wojewódzki Szczeciński
WUZW	Wojewódzki Urząd Ziemski w Warszawie
ZSC	Związek Samopomocy Chłopskiej

Notes

Introduction

1. On animal numbers, see George Woodbridge, *UNRRA: The History of the United Nations Relief and Rehabilitation Administration* (New York: Oxford University Press, 1950), 1:487. The total numbers of smaller animals delivered as part of the UNRRA program, also according to Woodbridge, are as follows: approximately 3,300 sheep, hogs, and goats; 172 rabbits; and 85,000 adult poultry. On animal numbers, see also Robert Lintner, *UNRRA Livestock Program Historical Report*, 1947, UNRRA selected records AG-018-040, accession 2015.245.1, record group RG-67.050, S-1021-0009-03, p. 182, United States Holocaust Memorial Museum (hereafter USHMM). This report, which was "written and compiled" by Lintner, contains over two hundred typed pages and comprises a number of different document categories (e.g., statistical tables and charts, reports and summaries, and blank UNRRA forms.) I treat the Lintner report as a single discrete source. Not all documents in the report are signed or dated, and some are untitled. The report as a whole is not paginated. The page numbers provided here refer to a digital copy of the report available as a PDF through the United States Holocaust Memorial Museum Library and Archives. I take page 1 to be the first page of the digital file. The United Nations Archives holds the original Lintner report. See Robert Lintner, *UNRRA Livestock Program Historical Report*, 1947, UNRRA Livestock Program, UNRRA selected records, S-1021-0009-03, United Nations Archives (hereafter UNA).

2. Lintner, *UNRRA Livestock Program Historical Report*, 182, USHMM.

3. Donald F. Durnbaugh, *Pragmatic Prophet: The Life of Michael Robert Zigler* (Elgin, IL: Brethren Press, 1989), 172–73. On the Brethren Service Committee, see "Cowboy Education Materials," description of the Heifer Project in Polish, 1940s, folder 3, box 2, series 4/1/6, Poland—Ostróda and Warsaw Offices (hereafter POW), Brethren Historical Library and Archives (hereafter BHLA).

4. "Heifer Project Committee," August 6, 1947, folder 44, box 38, series 18, Dan West Papers (hereafter DWP), BHLA; Lintner, *UNRRA Livestock Program Historical Report*, 67–68, USHMM.

5. The number of cowboys who came from the peace churches and from other Christian denominations is discussed in more detail in chapter 3.

6. "Shipping Record of the Heifer Project Committee," Heifer Letters, 1946–55, folder 1, box 3, series 4/1/6, Heifer Project (hereafter HP), BHLA.

7. While the organization has operated publicly as Heifer International since 2003, its legal name remains Heifer Project International. "The Gates Foundation: How Heifer Is Making a Difference," Heifer International, October 3, 2019, https://www.heifer.org/blog/the-gates-foundation-how-heifer-is-making-a

-difference.html. See also "Seagoing Cowboys and the Heifer Project," Civilian Public Service, accessed October 10, 2023, https://civilianpublicservice.org/storycontinues/heiferproject.

8. For a good overview of the Heifer Project and the seagoing cowboys program, see Peggy Reiff Miller, "Seagoing Cowboys and the Heifer Project: The Maryland Story," *Catoctin History*, Fall/Winter 2005, reposted at https://seagoingcowboyswebsite.files.wordpress.com/2015/10/catoctin-history-article-webtext.pdf. See also Peggy Reiff Miller, "Celebrating TWO Anniversaries," *Seagoing Cowboys* (blog), July 12, 2024, https://seagoingcowboysblog.wordpress.com/. Subsequent references to Reiff Miller's blog posts come from this website and can be located by title or by date.

9. "Background Information for the Use of Emergency Livestock Collection Committees," Correspondence 1945–46, folder 9, box 1, series 4/1/6, HP, BHLA.

10. "Herbert H. Lehman to Brethren Service Committee," *Gospel Messenger*, March 20, 1946. See also Amanda Melanie Bundy, "There Was a Man of UNRRA: Internationalism, Humanitarianism, and the Early Cold War in Europe, 1943–1947" (PhD diss., Ohio State University, 2017), 1. Lehman's praise of the cattle tenders is also reflected in "Herbert Lehman to Mr. Zigler," January 31, 1946, Contributed Supplies, Office of Voluntary and International Agency Liaison, Bureau of Service, S-1268-0000-0079-00001, p. 12, UNA. On Lehman, see Duane Tananbaum, *Herbert H. Lehman: A Political Biography* (Albany: SUNY Press, 2016).

11. United Nations Relief and Rehabilitation Administration, *The Story of UNRRA* (Washington, DC: UNRRA, Office of Public Information, 1948), 30. The quotation also appears in Edwin R. Henson, "Livestock for Rebuilding Europe," *Breeder's Gazette*, n.d. A copy of this article is in Clippings and Releases 1, 1940s–1960s, folder 7, box 2, series 4/1/6, HP, BHLA.

12. Woodbridge, *UNRRA*, 2:223.

13. Woodbridge, *UNRRA*, vol. 2. For Czechoslovakia, see p. 196; for Yugoslavia, see p. 158; and for Greece, see p. 117.

14. Historian Jacek Sawicki states that Poland received 135,193 horses and 16,442 cattle. See Jacek Sawicki, *Misja UNRRA w Polsce: Raport zamknięcia (1945–1949)* (Lublin: Wyd. Werset, 2017), 116. Historian Józef Łaptos states that UNRRA delivered "around 140,000" horses to Poland. See Józef Łaptos, *Humanitaryzm i polityka: Pomoc UNRRA dla Polski i polskich uchodźców w latach 1944–1947* (Kraków: Wyd. Naukowe Uniwersytetu Pedagogicznego, 2018), 393. On animal numbers, see also Lintner, *UNRRA Livestock Program Historical Report*, 31–34, 133, USHMM; "Inwentarz żywy z dostaw UNRRA," 1945–47, Ministerstwo Rolnictwa i Reform Rolnych (hereafter MRiRR), 2/162/0/26/3271, p. 2, Archiwum Akt Nowych (hereafter AAN); "Departament Produkcji Rolnej, Wyd. Wychowu Koni, 'Przychód,'" 1946–47, Dostawy koni w ramach UNRRA, MRiRR, 2/162/0/21.5/3377, p. 138, AAN; Division of Operational Analysis UNRRA, "Provisional Report on Agriculture and Food in Poland," 1944–49, UNRRA—Poland Mission, file 1032, S-0527-1068, p. 10, UNA; Charles Drury, "UNRRA in Poland," *The Empire Club of Canada Addresses*, April 24, 1947, 331–44, https://speeches.empireclub.org/details.asp?ID=61185; "Appendix to the Minutes of the 16th Meeting of the Council of Foreign Voluntary Agencies in Poland, Notes from a talk Given by Dr. A.G. Wilder," December 5, 1946, Działalność

rady zagranicznych towarzystw charytatywnych w Polsce, protokóły, Ministerstwo Pracy i Opieki Społecznej w Warszawie (hereafter MPiOS), 2/402/0/6/337, p. 103, AAN; "Thurl Metzger to the Government of the Polish Republic," Correspondence, 1947–49, folder 23, box 1, series 4/1/6, POW, BHLA; Aleksander Juźwik, "Zagraniczna pomoc charytatywna dla dzieci i młodzieży w Polsce w latach 1945–50," *Polska 1944/45–1980: Studia i Materiały* 11 (2013): 114.

15. "Summary of Shipments by Countries," 1945–53 Project Committee Reports, folder 19, box 1, series 4/1/6, HP, BHLA; "Minutes of the Heifer Project Committee," March 29, 1947, Correspondence 1947, folder 10, box 1, series 4/1/6, HP, BHLA. China received 700 Heifer Project cattle, and Czechoslovakia received 500. Greece received just over 200 Heifer Project cattle from 1945 through to 1949. Italy's total number of Heifer Project cattle was very large at 1,576, though half of these came in 1948, after the UNRRA period. Ethiopia and West Germany also received significant numbers of Heifer Project animals, though like with Italy most of these came after the partnership between UNRRA and the Brethren Service Committee had concluded. See also Łaptos, *Humanitaryzm i polityka*, 443.

16. Mikołaj Brenk, "Social Response in Poland in 1944–1948," *Biuletyn Historii Wychowania* 38 (2018): 276.

17. On animals' wartime experiences, see, for example, Ryan Hediger, ed., *Animals and War: Studies of Europe and North America* (Leiden: Brill, 2012); Jacob Darwin Hamblin, "Environmental Dimensions of World War II," in *A Companion to World War Two*, eds. Thomas W. Zeiler and Daniel M. DuBois (Malden, MA: Blackwell, 2013), 698–99.

18. The wording here about transnational spaces is taken from a different context; the original does not refer to relief animals. See Ian Tyrell, *Reforming the World: The Creation of America's Moral Empire* (Princeton, NJ: Princeton University Press, 2010), 6.

19. On bottom-up approaches to internationalism, see Jessica Reinisch and David Brydan, "Introduction: Internationalists in European History," in *Internationalists in European History: Rethinking the Twentieth Century*, eds. Jessica Reinisch and David Brydan (London: Bloomsbury Academic, 2021), 6–8. The Reinisch and Brydan book uses the terms "agents" and "actors" in relation to internationalism, and I adopt both of these in this work too.

20. Donald E. Pienkos, *For Your Freedom Through Ours: Polish American Efforts on Poland's Behalf, 1863–1991* (New York: East European Monographs, 1991), 95. See also Łaptos, *Humanitaryzm i polityka*, 344. Adjusted only for inflation, the $471 million figure was over $6 billion in 2023. See "Inflation Calculator," Federal Reserve Bank of Minneapolis, accessed July 26, 2024, https://www.minneapolisfed.org/about-us/monetary-policy/inflation-calculator. The official history of UNRRA written by George Woodbridge gives the value of the Poland program as both $474 million and $478 million rather than $471 million. $474 million comes from Woodbridge, *UNRRA*, 1:377; and $478 million comes from Woodbridge, *UNRRA*, 2:210. For just one Polish reference to the UNRRA aid program as "471," see the English translation of a *Życie Warszawy* article: "The Problem of UNRRA Supplies," *Życie Warszawy*, May 14, 1946, UNRRA—Poland Mission, 1944–49, file 7, S-0527-1064, UNA.

21. Benon Gaziński and Bogusław Wanot, "Działalność UNRRA i jej pomoc dla rolnictwa w Polsce," *Rocznik Muzeum Narodowego Rolnictwa w Szreniawie* 19 (1993): 18.

22. UNRRA, *Story of UNRRA*, 52.

23. Jessica Reinisch, "'We Shall Rebuild Anew a Powerful Nation': UNRRA, Internationalism and National Reconstruction in Poland," *Journal of Contemporary History* 43, no. 3 (2008): 462.

24. Dan West, "Heifers for Relief: A Challenge," *Gospel Messenger*, July 28, 1945.

25. For an introduction to the large body of literature in human-animal studies (a field that in a broad and general sense informs this work), see Margo Demello, *Animals and Society: An Introduction to Human-Animal Studies* (New York: Columbia University Press, 2021).

1. UNRRA, Food, and Winning the Peace

1. United Nations Relief and Rehabilitation Administration, *The Story of UNRRA* (Washington, DC: UNRRA, Office of Public Information, 1948), 3.

2. William I. Hitchcock, *The Bitter Road to Freedom: A New History of the Liberation of Europe* (New York: Free Press, 2008), 211.

3. Józef Łaptos, "Wpływ wielkich mocarstw na strukturę i kompetencje . . . międzynarodowej organizacji humanitarnej—United Nations Relief and Rehabilitation Administration (UNRRA)," *Rocznik Administracji Publicznej* 2 (2016): 453.

4. UNRRA, *Story of UNRRA*, 6–7.

5. Ruth Jachertz and Alexander Nutzenadel, "Coping with Hunger? Visions of a Global Food System, 1930–1960," *Journal of Global History* 6, no. 1 (2011): 101–2.

6. On the types and volume of UNRRA aid delivered, see Hitchcock, *Bitter Road to Freedom*, 247 and UNRRA, *Story of UNRRA*, 11.

7. The quote comes from "Get a Horse," editorial, *Life*, December 30, 1946. See also Dorothy Stephenson, "Women Get Role in UNRRA Activities," 1940–46, box 77, series A, part 1, Center on Conscience and War Records (hereafter CCWR), DG 025, Swarthmore College Peace Collection (hereafter SCPC).

8. Jessica Reinisch, "'We Shall Rebuild Anew a Powerful Nation': UNRRA, Internationalism and National Reconstruction in Poland," *Journal of Contemporary History* 43, no. 3 (2008): 454. On UNRRA's aid to Belarus and Ukraine, see Andrew Harder, "The Politics of Impartiality: The United Nations Relief and Rehabilitation Administration in the Soviet Union, 1946–7," *Journal of Contemporary History* 47, no. 2 (2012): 347–69.

9. On UNRRA and Polish DPs, see Andrzej M. Brzeziński, "Z polityki rządu RP na uchodźstwie wobec UNRRA," *Przegląd Zachodni* 2 (1998): 89–113; Kamil Kowalski, "Remarks on the Genesis of UNRRA Negotiations Between the Great Powers and Selected Treaty Provisions," *Annales: Ethics in Economic Life* 20, no. 7 (2017): 161–72. See also Paul Betts, *Ruin and Renewal: Civilizing Europe After World War II* (New York: Basic Books, 2020).

10. On UNRRA's finances, see Barry Riley, *The Political History of American Food Aid: An Uneasy Benevolence* (New York: Oxford University Press, 2017), 95–96; Philipp

Weintraub, "An Experiment in International Welfare Planning," *Journal of Politics* 7, no. 1 (1945): 3; Philipp Weintraub, "Reseeding Live-Stock Herds in Liberated Europe," *Baltimore Sun*, June 28, 1945. On the role and evolution of aid programs as part of broader American foreign policy, see Vernon W. Ruttan, *United States Development Assistance Policy: The Domestic Politics of Foreign Economic Aid* (Baltimore: Johns Hopkins University Press, 1996).

11. Harry S. Truman, "United States Participation in UNRRA: President's Message to Congress," US Department of State, November 13, 1945, https://www.cvce.eu/content/publication/2017/4/11/9df14347-dd75-4ae9-9828-a20a095fcf4b/publishable_en.pdf.

12. On American Relief for Poland, see Richard C. Lukas, *Bitter Legacy: Polish-American Relations in the Wake of World War II* (Lexington: University Press of Kentucky, 1982), 96, 104–8; Donald E. Pienkos, *For Your Freedom Through Ours: Polish American Efforts on Poland's Behalf, 1863–1991* (New York: East European Monographs, 1991), 6, 79, 87; Mikołaj Brenk, "Social Response in Poland in 1944–1948," *Biuletyn Historii Wychowania* 38 (2018): 265–81. See also "Council of Foreign Voluntary Agencies in Poland: Reports," 1947–49, Minutes and Reports 1947–49, folder 51, box 1, series 4/1/6, POW, BHLA.

13. Pienkos, *For Your Freedom Through Ours*, 95. On voluntary agencies working abroad, see also *Marine Bull Pen: A Paper Issued in the Interests of Sea-Going Cowboys (CPS Reserve)*, no. 9, July 19, 1946, Marine Bullpens and News Circulars, 1946, folder 10, box 75, Melvin G. Gingerich Papers (hereafter MGP), Hist MSS 1–129, Mennonite Church Archives (hereafter MCA). *Marine Bull Pen* started in the Civilian Public Service and was directed at Conscientious Objectors who would go on to become seagoing cowboys. Copies of *Marine Bull Pen* can also be found in Clippings and Releases 3, 1940s–1960s, folder 9, box 2, series 4/1/6, HP, BHLA.

14. Hitchcock, *Bitter Road to Freedom*, 216.

15. George Woodbridge, *UNRRA: The History of the United Nations Relief and Rehabilitation Administration* (New York: Oxford University Press, 1950), 2:67–78.

16. Tehila Sasson, "From Empire to Humanity: The Russian Famine and the Imperial Origins of International Humanitarianism," *Journal of British Studies* 55, no. 3 (2016): 537.

17. On relief planning in the immediate pre-UNRRA period, see Jessica Reinisch, "Internationalism in Relief: The Birth (and Death) of UNRRA," *Past and Present* 210, suppl. 6 (2011): 261–4.

18. Herbert Lehman, Administrative Order No. 23, "UNRRA Policy Related to (1) Shipping of Relief Goods by Voluntary Agencies and (2) Acceptance and Distribution by UNRRA of Contributed Relief Goods"; UNRRA Standing Technical Committee on Welfare, "Memorandum on the Relation Between UNRRA and Voluntary Relief Organizations," June 1944, 1–8, box 77, series A, part 1, CCWR, DG 025, SCPC. On UNRRA's relations with national governments, see also Woodbridge, *UNRRA*, 2:206–7. The Polish example is featured in this section.

19. Jessica Reinisch, "'Auntie UNRRA' at the Crossroads," *Past and Present* 218, suppl. 8 (2013): 70.

20. Riley, *Political History of American Food Aid*, chap. 6, esp. p. 100. For a discussion of the concept of reconstruction, see Holly Case, "Reconstruction in East-Cen-

tral Europe: Clearing the Rubble of Cold War Politics," *Past and Present* 210, suppl. 6 (2011): 71–102.

21. "UNRRA Plans Are Well Advanced," 1943–45, UNRRA, Rolnictwo, Biuro Zaopatrzenia Kraju, Ministerstwo Przemysłu, Handlu i Żeglugi Rządu RP [emigracyjnego] w Londynie, 2/132/0/7/533, p. 4, AAN.

22. "Get a Horse."

23. Silvia Salvatici, "Sights of Benevolence: UNRRA's Recipients Portrayed," in *Humanitarian Photography: A History*, eds. Heide Fehrenbach and Davide Rodogno (New York: Cambridge University Press, 2015), 216. See also Davide Rodogno, *Night on Earth: A History of International Humanitarianism in the Near East, 1918–1930* (Cambridge: Cambridge University Press, 2021), 36.

24. For a summary of the state of the "history and humanitarianism" field, see Matthew Hilton et al., "History and Humanitarianism: A Conversation," *Past and Present* 241, no. 1 (2018): 1–38.

25. Tom Scott-Smith, *On an Empty Stomach: Two Hundred Years of Disaster Relief* (Ithaca, NY: Cornell University Press, 2020), xiii.

26. Silvia Salvatici, *A History of Humanitarianism, 1755–1989: In the Name of Others*, trans. Philip Sanders (Manchester: Manchester University Press, 2019), 7, 117.

27. Christophe Traïni, *The Animal Rights Struggle: An Essay in Historical Sociology* (Amsterdam: Amsterdam University Press, 2011), 96–97.

28. On evolving definitions of "humanitarian," see Katherine Davies, "Continuity, Change and Contest: Meanings of 'Humanitarian' from the 'Religion of Humanity' to the Kosovo War" (HPG Working Paper, Overseas Development Institute, August 2012), 1–3, https://odi.org/en/publications/continuity-change-and-contest-meanings-of-humanitarian-from-the-religion-of-humanity-to-the-kosovo-war/.

29. Janet M. Davis, *The Gospel of Kindness: Animal Welfare and the Making of Modern America* (New York: Oxford University Press, 2016), 19. On the links between evangelical revivalism and organized animal advocacy, see Davies, "Continuity, Change and Contest," chap. 1.

30. Salvatici, *History of Humanitarianism*, 6.

31. On modern approaches to humanitarianism and hunger, see Davies, "Continuity, Change and Contest," 4, 13, and James Vernon, *Hunger: A Modern History* (Cambridge, MA: Belknap Press of Harvard University, 2007), 2.

32. On DPs see, for example, Mark Wyman, *DPs: Europe's Displaced Persons, 1945–1951* (Ithaca, NY: Cornell University Press, 1989); Jessica Reinisch, "Preparing for a New World Order: UNRRA and the International Management of Refugees," in *Post-War Europe: Refugees, Exile and Resettlement, 1945–1950*, ed. Dan Stone (Gale Digital Collections, 2007); Michael R. Marrus, *The Unwanted: European Refugees in the Twentieth Century* (Philadelphia: Temple University Press, 2001); Gerard Daniel Cohen, *In War's Wake: Europe's Displaced Persons in the Postwar Order* (New York: Oxford University Press, 2011); Matthew Frank and Jessica Reinisch, "Refugees and the Nation-State in Europe, 1919–59," *Journal of Contemporary History* 49, no. 3 (2014): 477–90; David Nasaw, *The Last Million: Europe's Displaced Persons from World War to Cold War* (New York: Penguin Books, 2021). For a recent comparative and transnational approach to European DPs, see the special issue of *Itinerario: Journal of Imperial and Global Interactions* 46, no. 2 (2022).

33. For a selection of key works on UNRRA or the broader humanitarian context of the immediate postwar period, see Hitchcock, *Bitter Road to Freedom*; Ben Shephard, *The Long Road Home: The Aftermath of the Second World War* (New York: Random House, 2010); G. Cohen, *In War's Wake*; Tara Zahra, *The Lost Children: Reconstructing Europe's Families After World War II* (Cambridge, MA: Harvard University Press, 2011); Atina Grossmann, *Jews, Germans, and Allies: Close Encounters in Occupied Germany* (Princeton, NJ: Princeton University Press, 2007); Margarete Myers Feinstein, *Holocaust Survivors in Postwar Germany, 1945–1957* (New York: Cambridge University Press, 2010); Peter Gatrell and Nick Baron, eds., *Warlands: Population Resettlement and State Reconstruction in the Soviet–East European Borderlands, 1945–1950* (London: Palgrave Macmillan, 2009).

34. Jessica Reinisch, "The Reluctant Internationalists: A History of Public Health and International Organisations, Movements and Experts in Twentieth Century Europe," *The Reluctant Internationalists*, September 1, 2018, https://web.archive.org/web/20240422201816/http://www7.bbk.ac.uk/reluctantinternationalists/. Also from Reinisch on internationalism and nationalism, see Jessica Reinisch, "Introduction: Relief in the Aftermath of War," *Journal of Contemporary History* 43, no. 3 (2008): 371–404; Reinisch, "We Shall Rebuild Anew," 451–476; Reinisch, "Internationalism in Relief," 258–89; Reinisch, "'Auntie UNRRA' at the Crossroads," 70–97.

35. For more on the relationship between nationalism and internationalism in UNRRA and the UN more generally, see Mark Mazower, "Reconstruction: The Historiographical Issues," *Past and Present* 210, suppl. 6 (2011): 17–28; Glenda Sluga, *Internationalism in the Age of Nationalism* (Philadelphia: University of Pennsylvania Press, 2013). For a broader discussion of the philosophical and ideological underpinnings of the United Nations, see Mark Mazower, *No Enchanted Palace: The End of Empire and the Ideological Origins of the United Nations* (Princeton, NJ: Princeton University Press, 2009), esp. chap. 2.

36. See, for example, Jessica Reinisch and David Brydan, eds., *Internationalists in European History: Rethinking the Twentieth Century* (London: Bloomsbury Academic, 2021).

37. For an earlier article that reviews the whole of the UNRRA Poland program from an economic perspective specifically, see Bogusław Marks, "Pomoc UNRRA w odbudowie gospodarki Polski (1945–1947)," *Politologia: Acta Universitatis Lodziensis* 19 (1990):163–89.

38. On the Heifer Project, see Józef Łaptos, *Humanitaryzm i polityka: Pomoc UNRRA dla Polski i polskich uchodźców w latach 1944–1947* (Kraków: Wyd. Naukowe Uniwersytetu Pedagogicznego, 2018), 386–89.

39. Jacek Sawicki, *Misja UNRRA w Polsce: Raport zamknięcia (1945–1949)* (Lublin: Wyd. Werset, 2017).

40. On "Auntie UNRRA," see Joanna Papuzińska, "Kochana ciocia UNRA," *Stolica: Warszawski Magazyn Ilustrowany* 1–2 (2010): 31.

41. Jacek Zygmunt Sawicki, ed., *Polska jesień, rosyjska zima: Spotkanie Juliena Bryana z misją UNRRA w Europie Środkowo-Wschodniej 1946–1947—fotografie i zapiski* (Warsaw: IPN, 2022), 63.

42. Ira A. Hirschmann, *The Embers Still Burn* (New York: Simon and Schuster, 1949), 192.

43. Amanda Melanie Bundy, "There Was a Man of UNRRA: Internationalism, Humanitarianism, and the Early Cold War in Europe, 1943–1947" (PhD diss., Ohio State University, 2017), 139.

44. Eastern European Division Loan Department, "Preliminary Paper No. 6 for the Working Party on the Polish Loan Application" (International Bank for Reconstruction and Development, May 26, 1947), https://documents1.worldbank.org/curated/en/558411468095985925/pdf/multi-page.pdf.

45. These figures come from the website accompanying Peggy Reiff Miller's blog. See Reiff Miller, "UNRRA Shipment of Livestock from Western Hemisphere by Destination," Seagoing Cowboys, accessed February 13, 2020, https://seagoingcowboys.com/seagoing-cowboys/the-unrra-years/. This document is organized in chronological order by sailing date and includes the name of the ship, the loading port, and the destination. Reiff Miller relies in turn on the tables found in Robert Lintner, *UNRRA Livestock Program Historical Report*, 1947, UNRRA selected records AG-018-040, accession 2015.245.1, record group RG-67.050, S-1021-0009-03, USHMM. See also UNRRA, *Story of UNRRA*, 52. Note that some UNRRA reports take December 1946 as a tidy end date of the live animal program, meaning that the 1947 shipments are not reflected in the numbers.

46. Eastern European Division Loan Department, "Preliminary Paper No. 6," 8. For a copy of the agreement that UNRRA made with Poland, see Woodbridge, *UNRRA*, 3:318–24.

47. Woodbridge, *UNRRA*, 2:203.

48. Piotr Jachowicz, "Działalność UNRRA w Polsce w latach 1945–1948," *Zeszyty Naukowe* 2, no. 2 (1998): 48.

49. On UNRRA's staff in Poland, see Łaptos, *Humanitaryzm i polityka*, 346–52, 368; Woodbridge, *UNRRA*, 2:205–6. UNRRA's international field staff reached a total of 20,000 in 1946. On UNRRA staffing, see Riley, *Political History of American Food Aid*, 103; Hitchcock, *Bitter Road to Freedom*, 216; Bundy, "There Was a Man of UNRRA," 53; Sharif Gemie, Laure Humbert, and Fiona Reid, *Outcast Europe: Refugees and Relief Workers in an Era of Total War, 1936–48* (London: Continuum, 2012); "Statement of Current Recruitment for UNRRA," box 77, series A, part 1, CCWR, DG 025, SCPC.

50. On this early period in the formation of UNRRA in Poland, see Łaptos, *Humanitaryzm i polityka*, 148; Reinisch, "We Shall Rebuild Anew," 461; Lukas, *Bitter Legacy*, 97; Woodbridge, *UNRRA*, 2:205.

51. Bundy, "There Was a Man of UNRRA," 133. There was some dissatisfaction in the Polish government with the appointment of a Canadian to this role as opposed to some "top-flight" American. See Pierson Underwood, "Memorandum of Conversation, by Mr. Pierson Underwood of the War Areas Economic Division," October 1, 1945, Diplomatic Papers, 1945, vol. 5, Europe, Foreign Relations of the United States, Office of the Historian, US Department of State, https://history.state.gov/historicaldocuments/frus1945v05/d277.

52. Joseph H. Baird, "Polish Envoy Accuses Lehman of 'Injecting Politics into Relief,'" *Evening Star*, April 4, 1945.

53. Susan Armstrong-Reid and David Murray, *Armies of Peace: Canada and the UNRRA Years* (Toronto: University of Toronto Press, 2008), 87–88.

54. For Drury's views on Poland, see Lukas, *Bitter Legacy*, 98; "C.M. Drury to PM Osóbka-Morawski," August 26, 1946, UNRRA-Poland Mission, 1944–49, file 7, S-0527-1064, UNA; Charles Drury, "UNRRA in Poland," *The Empire Club of Canada Addresses*, April 24, 1947, 331–44, https://speeches.empireclub.org/details.asp?ID=61185.

55. United Nations Relief and Rehabilitation Administration, *Economic Recovery in the Countries Assisted by UNRRA* (Washington, DC: UNRRA, 1946), 70.

56. "Draft of the Supply Department's Brief for the PRD's Tour of Poland," 1943–48, PRDG's European Tour, S-1435-0000-0100-00001, p. 62, UNA. The many ways in which the Polish economy was destroyed by the war are summarized in UNRRA, *Economic Recovery*. On coal, see 92.

57. UNRRA, *Economic Recovery*, 91.

58. Herbert W. Robinson, *Operational Analysis Papers No. 45: The Impact of UNRRA on the Polish Economy* (London: Division of Operational Analysis, 1947), 21.

59. Woodbridge, *UNRRA*, 2:200.

60. Łaptos, *Humanitaryzm i polityka*, 381.

61. "Provisional Report on Agriculture and Food in Poland," file 1032, S-0527-1068, p. 9, UNA.

62. Itemized lists of destroyed resources and animal thefts were written up by various Polish authorities. For the province of Warsaw, see, for example, "Straty spowodowane przez przepęd bydła sowieckiego—powiat Grójec," 1945, Wojewódzki Urząd Ziemski w Warszawie (hereafter WUZW), 72/509/0-814, Archiwum Państwowe w Warszawie (hereafter APW); "Protokóły oszacowania strat spowodowanych przepędem bydła do ZSSR—powiat sokołowski," 1945, WUZW, 72/509/0-823, APW.

63. On fertilizers, see Eastern European Division Loan Department, "Preliminary Paper No. 6," 23–28. On seeds, see Amalia Ribi Forclaz, "Seeds of Development: Agriculture, History and Politics," Graduate Institute of Geneva, April 12, 2021, https://www.graduateinstitute.ch/communications/news/seeds-development-agriculture-history-and-politics.

64. Eastern European Division Loan Department, "Preliminary Paper No. 6," 4.

65. "Polish War Losses According to a Statement of the Polish Bureau of War Reparations in Warsaw," Council of Foreign Voluntary Agencies in Poland: Reports, 1947–49, folder 51, box 1, series 4/1/6, POW, BHLA. See also Woodbridge, *UNRRA*, 2:200; Łaptos, *Humanitaryzm i polityka*, 381; "General Situation," July 11, 1946, UNRRA—Poland Mission, 1944–49, file 7, S-0527-1064, UNA.

66. Marcin Zaremba, "The 'War Syndrome': World War II and Polish Society," in *Seeking Peace in the Wake of War: Europe, 1943–1947*, eds. Stean-Ludwig Hoffmann et al. (Amsterdam: Amsterdam University Press, 2015), 29–30; Marcin Zaremba, "Fearing the War After the War," in *Ends of War: Interdisciplinary Perspectives on Past and New Polish Regions After 1944*, eds. Paulina Gulińska-Jurgiel et al. (Düsseldorf: Wallstein, 2019), 275–96.

67. Marcin Zaremba, *Wielka trwoga: Polska 1944–1947* (Kraków: Wyd. Znak, 2012), 550.

68. European Regional Office of UNRRA, *50 Facts About UNRRA* (London: His Majesty's Stationery Office, 1946), fact 20.

69. Reinisch, "'Auntie UNRRA' at the Crossroads," 75.

70. Natasha Wheatley, "Central Europe as Ground Zero of the New International Order," *Slavic Review* 78, no. 4 (2019): 909. See also Patricia Clavin, "The Austrian Hunger Crisis and the Genesis of International Organization After the First World War," *International Affairs* 90, no. 2 (2014): 265–78; Maureen Healy, *Vienna and the Fall of the Habsburg Empire: Total War and Everyday Life in World War I* (Cambridge: Cambridge University Press, 2004).

71. Case, "Reconstruction in East-Central Europe," 85.

72. The cattle were sent to Germany in three shipments on the steamer *West Arrow*. Ethnic Germans from the Russian Empire who had settled in South Dakota were the main supporters of this aid project. The cattle attendants on the ships were sons of the farmers who had donated the cattle. See La Vern J. Rippley, "Gift Cows for Germany," *North Dakota History* 40, no. 3 (1973): 4–15, esp. 13; La Vern J. Rippley, "American Milk Cows for Germany: A Sequel," *North Dakota History* 44, no. 3 (1977): 15–23.

73. Davide Rodogno, Francesca Piana, and Shaloma Gauthier, "Shaping Poland: Relief and Rehabilitation Programmes Undertaken by Foreign Organizations, 1918–1922," in *Shaping the Transnational Sphere: Experts, Networks and Issues from the 1840s to the 1930s*, eds. Davide Rodogno, Bernhard Struck, and Jakob Vogel (New York: Berghahn Books, 2015), 259.

74. For an analysis of the soup-kitchen model of relief provision, see Patrick J. Houlihan, "Renovating Christian Charity: Global Catholicism, the Save the Children Fund, and Humanitarianism During the First World War," *Past and Present* 250, no. 1 (2021): 203–41, esp. p. 210 and p. 227.

75. Mark O. Hatfield, foreword to *Herbert Hoover and Poland: A Documentary History of a Friendship*, ed. George J. Lerski (Stanford, CA: Hoover Institution Press, 1977), xi. See also Salvatici, *History of Humanitarianism*, 106–7. On the European Children's Fund and the ARA, see Rodogno, *Night on Earth*, 37–41. For more on the ARA, Hoover, and the European Children's Fund, see Melissa J. Hibbard, "Children of the Polish Republic: Child Health, Welfare, and the Shaping of Modern Poland, 1915–1939" (PhD diss., University of Illinois at Chicago, 2022), 94–99.

76. Bruno Cabanes, *The Great War and the Origins of Humanitarianism, 1918–1924* (Cambridge: Cambridge University Press, 2014), 213–15. On food as a weapon during the First World War, see Alice Weinreb, *Modern Hungers: Food and Power in Twentieth-Century Germany* (Oxford: Oxford University Press, 2017), chap. 1.

77. Sunil Amrith and Patricia Clavin, "Feeding the World: Connecting Europe and Asia, 1930–1945," *Past and Present* 218, suppl. 8 (2013): 34, 48. On the ARA, see also Nick Cullather, "The Foreign Policy of the Calorie," *American Historical Review* 112, no. 2 (2007): 348–51; Cabanes, *Great War and Humanitarianism*, chap. 4. On relief in the Russian famine of 1921–22, see Sasson, "From Empire to Humanity," 519–37. For Hoover's views on UNRRA, see Duane Tananbaum, *Herbert H. Lehman: A Political Biography* (Albany: SUNY Press, 2016), 226–28.

78. European Regional Office of UNRRA, *50 Facts About UNRRA*, fact 13.

79. Houlihan, "Renovating Christian Charity," 205.

80. Norris E. Dodd, "The Food and Agriculture Organization of the United Nations," *Agricultural History* 23, no. 2 (1949): 83; Frank Trentmann, "Coping with Shortage: The Problem of Food Security and Global Visions of Coordination,

c. 1890s–1950," in *Food and Conflict in Europe in the Age of the Two World Wars*, eds. Frank Trentmann and Flemming Just (London: Palgrave Macmillan, 2006), 35.

81. Cullather, as quoted in Alice Weinreb, "'For the Hungry Have No Past nor Do They Belong to a Political Party': Debates over German Hunger After World War II," *Central European History* 45, no. 1 (2012): 50.

82. Jachertz and Nutzenadel, "Coping with Hunger?," 104.

83. Cullather, "Foreign Policy of the Calorie," 337–38; Atina Grossmann, "Grams, Calories, and Food: Languages of Victimization, Entitlement and Human Rights in Occupied Germany, 1945–49," *Central European History* 44, no. 1 (2011): 121.

84. Scott-Smith, *On an Empty Stomach*, 49, 117. On different national approaches to the calorie, see Jacob Darwin Hamblin, "The Vulnerability of Nations: Food Security in the Aftermath of World War II," *Global Environment* 10 (2012): 46–47.

85. Dodd, "Food and Agriculture Organization," 83.

86. I take the term "hunger studies" from Scott-Smith, *On an Empty Stomach*, chap. 7.

87. Cabanes, *Great War and Humanitarianism*, 225.

88. Scott-Smith, *On an Empty Stomach*, 36, 63, 69. The term "dietary determinism" is used multiple times in the book.

89. Jachertz and Nutzenadel, "Coping with Hunger?," 107.

90. Grossmann, "Grams, Calories, and Food," 119, 145.

91. Lizzie Collingham, *The Taste of War: World War Two and the Battle for Food* (London: Allen Lane, 2011), 298–99, illustration 3.

92. On the contrast between postwar American abundance and European shortages, see Hamblin, "Vulnerability of Nations," 48–59.

93. Weinreb, *Modern Hungers*, 10.

94. Roosevelt, as quoted in Grossmann, "Grams, Calories, and Food," 120.

95. Lucius Clay is quoted in Cullather, "Foreign Policy of the Calorie," 363.

96. Stuart Legg, *Food: Secret of the Peace* (National Film Board of Canada, 1945), https://www.nfb.ca/film/food_secret_of_the_peace/. For analysis of the films produced by Canada's National Film Board for UNRRA, see Suzanne Langlois, "'Neighbors Half the World Away': The National Film Board of Canada at Work for UNRRA (1944–47)," in *Canada and the United Nations: Legacies, Limits, Prospects*, eds. Colin McCullough and Robert Teigrob (Montreal: McGill-Queen's University Press, 2016), 44–81.

97. The term "relief geography" comes from Reinisch, "'Auntie UNRRA' at the Crossroads," 76.

98. "Basis of Requirements for Cows," Raporty misji UNRRA dotyczące rolnictwa i wyżywienia w Polsce, 1945–47, MRiRR, 2/162/0/2.4/506, p. 55, AAN. This is a condensed version of a report, also contained in this file, titled S.G. "The Role of Cattle Breeding in Poland's Agricultural Economy," March 1945.

99. "Introducing Remarks to the Provisional Programme of UNRRA Agricultural Imports for the Last Month of 1945 and the Whole of 1946," UNRRA—Poland Mission, 1944–49, file 7, S-0527-1064, pp. 44–45, UNA. On definitions of hunger, see Vernon, *Hunger*, 158.

100. "Chief Medical Officer to Chief of Mission," June 24, 1946, UNRRA—Poland Mission, 1944–49, file 29, S-0527-1064, UNA.

101. Collingham, *Taste of War*, 481; Grossmann, "Grams, Calories, and Food," 119.

102. Ruth Jachertz, "'To Keep Food out of Politics': The UN Food and Agriculture Organization, 1945–1965," in *International Organizations and Development, 1945–1990*, eds. Marc Frey, Sonke Kunkel, and Corinna Unger (New York: Palgrave Macmillan, 2014), 77. For an influential contemporary British film about food produced for the Ministries of Food and Agriculture and shown at Hot Springs, see Paul Rotha, dir., *World of Plenty* (Paul Rotha Productions, 1943).

103. For a survey of how contemporaries thought about food and food policy, see Theodore W. Schultz, ed., *Food for the World* (Chicago: University of Chicago Press, 1945). For additional context and background, see Patricia Clavin, *Securing the World Economy: The Reinvention of the League of Nations, 1930–1926* (New York: Oxford University Press, 2013), 346.

104. Amy L. S. Staples, "To Win the Peace: The Food and Agriculture Organization, Sir John Boyd Orr, and the World Food Board Proposals," *Peace and Change* 28, no. 4 (2003): 498–99.

105. Adam Puławski, "Revisiting Jan Karski's Final Mission," *Israel Journal of Foreign Affairs* 15, no. 2 (2021): 289, 295.

106. Wojciech Rappak, "Karski's Reports: The Story and the History" (PhD diss., University College London, 2021), 26–27, 266–67.

107. Claude Lanzmann, dir., *Shoah* (New York: New Yorker Films, 1985). See also Interview with Jan Karski, Claude Lanzmann Shoah Collection, USHMM, accessed March 15, 2022, https://collections.ushmm.org/search/catalog/irn1000017. The text of the Lanzmann-Karski interview has been published in *Les Tempes Modernes* (January–March 2010).

108. Puławski, "Revisiting Jan Karski's Final Mission," 295–96.

109. Richard J. Golsan, "'L'Affaire' Karski: Fiction, History, Memory Unreconciled," *L'Esprit Créateur* 50, no. 4 (2010): 81–96. On Karski's meeting with Roosevelt, see also Polish History Museum, curated by Dorota Szkodzińska, "Jan Karski: Humanity's Hero," Google Arts and Culture, accessed October 7, 2024, https://artsandculture.google.com/story/jan-karski-humanity-s-hero-polish-history-museum/EAXRBzXayhMA8A?hl=en.

110. "Introducing Remarks," 44, UNA.

111. "Introducing Remarks," 44, UNA.

112. "Provisional Report," 10, UNA. The same figures are repeated in "Statement Given to UNRA by Stanislaw Mikolajczyk," February 23, 1946, UNRRA—Poland Mission, 1944–49, file 78-B3L4, S-0527-1073, UNA.

113. This general point (not related to Poland specifically) is made by Michael Bresalier, "From Healthy Cows to Healthy Humans: Integrated Approaches to World Hunger, c. 1930–1965," in *Animals and the Shaping of Modern Medicine: One Health and Its Histories*, eds. Abigail Woods et al. (London: Palgrave Macmillan, 2018), 132.

114. "Report on UNRRA Livestock Imported to Poland from September 29, 1945 to July 28, 1946," July 29, 1946, UNRRA Subject Files, file 72, S-0527-1107, UNA.

115. Gladwin Hill, "Bare Polish Farms Face Dark Future," *New York Times*, November 4, 1945.

116. On the situation with cattle in the postwar years, see Joseph H. Short, "Blue-Ribbon Maryland Horses in UNRRA Poland Shipment," *Baltimore Sun*, January 26, 1947; "Introducing Remarks," 44–45, UNA. For replacement projections, see Hill, "Bare Polish Farms."

117. "Provisional Report," 10, UNA. For additional statistics, see also "Statement by Stanislaw Mikolajczyk," UNA.

118. "Statement by Stanislaw Mikolajczyk," UNA.

119. Weintraub, "Reseeding Live-Stock Herds"; Weintraub, "Experiment in International Welfare Planning," 3.

120. For animals' role in colonization, see Nancy Cushing, "'Few Commodities More Hazardous': Australian Live Animal Export, 1788–1880," *Environment and History* 24 (2018): 449–52.

121. "Report on UNRRA Livestock," UNA.

122. David E. Norcross, "The Story of Heifers for Relief," September 1946, Clippings and Releases 1, 1940s–1960s, folder 7, box 2, series 4/1/6, HP, BHLA.

123. On the FAO, see Gove Hambidge, *The Story of FAO* (New York: D. Van Nostrand, 1955); Corinne A. Pernet and Amalia Ribi Forclaz, "Revisiting the Food and Agriculture Organization (FAO): International Histories of Agriculture, Nutrition, and Development," *International History Review* 41, no. 2 (2019): 345–50.

124. Amalia Ribi Forclaz, "From Reconstruction to Development: The Early Years of the Food and Agriculture Organization (FAO) and the Conceptualization of Rural Welfare, 1945–1955," *International History Review* 41, no. 2 (2019): 355.

125. Amy L. S. Staples, *The Birth of Development: How the World Bank, Food and Agriculture Organization, and World Health Organization Changed the World, 1945–1965* (Kent, OH: Kent State University Press, 2006), 76, 91. See also Patricia Clavin, "International Organizations," in *The Cambridge History of the Second World War*, vol. 2, *Politics and Ideology*, eds. Richard Bosworth and Joseph Maiolo (Cambridge: Cambridge University Press, 2015), 153; Pernet and Forclaz, "Revisiting the FAO," 346.

126. Weinreb, *Modern Hungers*, 92–93.

2. The UNRRA–Brethren Service Committee Partnership

1. Margaret Nowak, "Church of the Brethren Send 800 Heifers to Poland," *People's Voice*, November 30, 1946. This article can be found in Clippings and Releases 4, 1940s–1960s, folder 10, box 2, series 4/1/6, HP, BHLA. Additional statistics about the Brethren can also be found in Donald F. Durnbaugh, "Statistics and Addresses," in *Church of the Brethren: Past and Present*, ed. Donald F. Durnbaugh (Elgin, IL: Brethren Press, 1971), 143; Donald F. Durnbaugh, *Pragmatic Prophet: The Life of Michael Robert Zigler* (Elgin, IL: Brethren Press, 1989), 76. On Brethren numbers (divided by congregation), see "M.R. Zigler to Paul French," November 12, 1940, box 19, series A, part 1, CCWR, DG 025, SCPC.

2. Perry Bush, *Two Kingdoms, Two Loyalties: Mennonite Pacifism in Modern America* (Baltimore: Johns Hopkins University Press, 1998), 6–7. See also Steven J. Taylor, *Acts of Conscience: World War II, Mental Institutions, and Religious Objectors* (Syracuse, NY: Syracuse University Press, 2009), 26–27; Mennonite Central Committee, "Relief in Action; Europe," 1941–42, box 21, series A, part 1, CCWR, DG 025, SCPC.

3. Gunnar Jahn, "Award Ceremony Speech," 1947, NobelPrize.org, February 23, 2023, https://www.nobelprize.org/prizes/peace/1947/ceremony-speech.

4. The origins of the Brethren and Mennonites, in the context of pacifism, are discussed in Peter Brock, *Against the Draft: Essays on Conscientious Objection from the Radical Reformation to the Second World War* (Toronto: University of Toronto Press, 2006). On the Brethren specifically, see Donald F. Durnbaugh, "Early History," in Durnbaugh, *Church of the Brethren*, 9–22.

5. Lawrence W. Shultz, *People and Places, 1890–1970: An Autobiography* (Winona Lake, IN: Life and Light, 1971), 182.

6. Bush, *Two Kingdoms, Two Loyalties*, 19–20; M. J. Heisey, *Peace and Persistence: Tracing the Brethren in Christ Through Three Generations* (Kent, OH: Kent State University Press, 2003), 2–3.

7. A. J. R. Groom, Andre Barrinha, and William Olson, *International Relations Then and Now*, 2nd ed. (London: Routledge, 2019), 25.

8. Kenneth I. Morse, *New Windsor Center* (New Windsor, MD: Brethren Service Center, 1979), 19, 20.

9. Durnbaugh, *Pragmatic Prophet*, 189; Morse, *New Windsor Center*, 40.

10. On early Quaker humanitarian relief work, see Tammy M. Proctor, "Repairing the Spirit: The Society of Friends, Total Warm and the Limits of Reconciliation," *Peace and Change: A Journal of Peace Research* 45, no. 2 (2020): 198–224. On the Quakers in Spain, see Daniel Maul, "The Politics of Neutrality: The American Friends Service Committee and the Spanish Civil War, 1936–1939," *European Review of History* 23, no. 1–2 (2016): 82–100.

11. For West's own description of his time in Spain, see Dan West, "Cooperation with the AFSC in Spain," in *To Serve the Present Age: The Brethren Service Story*, ed. Donald F. Durnbaugh (Elgin, IL: Brethren Press, 1975), 107–10. On West's arrival in Spain, see Gabriel Pretus, *Humanitarian Relief in the Spanish Civil War (1936–39)* (Lewiston, New York: Edwin Mellen, 2013), 214.

12. Glee Yoder, *Passing on the Gift: The Story of Dan West* (Elgin, IL: Brethren Press, 1978), chap. 12, esp. 100–101; J. Kenneth Kreider, *A Cup of Cold Water: The Story of Brethren Service* (Elgin, IL: Brethren Press, 2001), 131. On Dan West in Spain, see also Peggy Reiff Miller, "Heifer Project Myths," *Seagoing Cowboys* (blog), July 26, 2024.

13. On humanitarian conversion narratives generally, see Emily Bauman, "The Naïve Republic of Aid: Grassroots Exceptionalism in Humanitarian Memoir," in *Global Humanitarianism and Media Culture*, eds. Michael Lawrence and Rachel Tavernor (Manchester: Manchester University Press, 2019), 83.

14. Edwin T. Randall, "More Values Than Many Sparrows," 1947, Heifer Project 1947, folder 46, box 38, series 18, DWP, BHLA.

15. Peggy Reiff Miller, "Heifer International 75 Years Ago: Dan West's Rationale for the Heifer Project," *Seagoing Cowboys* (blog), February 22, 2019.

16. For references to the almond tree story, see, for example, G. Yoder, *Passing on the Gift*, 11; "Down to Earth Project," *Time Magazine*, July 24, 1944, in *Cowboy Memories*, eds. Bill Beck and Mel West (Little Rock, AR: Heifer Project International, 1994), 15; Peggy Reiff Miller, "Seagoing Cowboys and the Heifer Project: The Maryland Story," *Catoctin History*, Fall/Winter 2005. Reiff Miller has revised her earlier position

on the almond tree story; she now sees it as one of myths surrounding West and the Heifer Project. See "Myth 4" in Peggy Reiff Miller, "Heifer Project Myths, Part II," *Seagoing Cowboys* (blog), August 9, 2024.

17. Reiff Miller, "Heifer Project Myths, Part II"; Peggy Reiff Miller, "Dan West: Mischief Brewing" (speech delivered in Mill Ridge Village, Union, OH, February 22, 2019), 12–18; Peggy Reiff Miller, "The Woman Behind the Man Behind Heifer Project," *Messenger*, July/August 2019.

18. The description of West as a "visionary" appears, for example, in Durnbaugh, *Pragmatic Prophet*, 174.

19. Kermit Eby, "Faith, Hope, and Heifers," *Progressive*, August 1951. This article is part of Clippings and Releases 1, 1940s–1960s, folder 7, box 2, series 4/1/6, HP, BHLA. For more on Eby, see Kermit Eby Papers (1933–63), Hanna Holborn Gray Special Collections Research Center, University of Chicago Library.

20. Reiff Miller, "Dan West," 16–17. On West in Spain, see also Durnbaugh, *Pragmatic Prophet*, 114–17.

21. For context, see John Metzler, "The Relief Goods Program," *Gospel Messenger*, November 10, 1945. For a breakdown of how the Heifer Project developed, see Peggy Reiff Miller, "The Impossible Dream: How the Heifer Project Came to Be," *Messenger*, July/August 2009.

22. "Heifers—Relief on the Hoof," *Weekly Processor*, July 15, 1946.

23. Morse, *New Windsor Center*, 40; G. Yoder, *Passing on the Gift*, 102.

24. George W. Cornell, "Bible-Spurred Cowboys Herding Cattle into Hard-Up Nations," in Beck and West, *Cowboy Memories*, 77. A version of the quote also appears in Eby, "Faith, Hope, and Heifers" and in Kreider, *A Cup of Cold Water*, 131.

25. The phrase "passing on the gift" is used in G. Yoder, *Passing on the Gift*, 103. "Passing on the Gift" is a registered trademark of Heifer International; the practice reflected by this term remains in place to this day. See Erin Snow, "Passing on the Gift: Magic," Heifer International, October 3, 2019, https://www.heifer.org/blog/passing-on-the-gift-magic.html.

26. Robin Patric Clair and Lindsey B. Anderson, "Portrayals of the Poor on the Cusp of Capitalism: Promotional Materials in the Case of Heifer international," *Management Communication Quarterly* 27, no. 4 (2013): 545.

27. For more on these ideas, see Leo R. Ward, "Brethren Heifers for Relief," *Gospel Messenger*, March 22, 1947; Reiff Miller, "Impossible Dream."

28. The subtitle of this section comes from Tim Huber, "High Seas Service," *Mennonite World Review*, September 14, 2015, https://anabaptistworld.org/high-seas-service/.

29. Peggy Reiff Miller, "Heifer Project Myths, Part III," *Seagoing Cowboys* (blog), August 23, 2024; Morse, *New Windsor Center*, 40.

30. Peggy Reiff Miller, private correspondence with author, January 6, 2024, January 23, 2024, and January 30, 2024; Thurl Metzger, "The Heifer Project," in Durnbaugh, *To Serve the Present Age*, 145.

31. Reiff Miller, "Dan West," 17.

32. Ralph E. Smeltzer, "Our Relief Fields," *Gospel Messenger*, November 10, 1945.

33. See various letters to and from Dan West and UNRRA in 1944 and 1945 in Brethren Service Committee, S-1267-0000-0083-00001, UNA.

34. Durnbaugh, *Pragmatic Prophet*, 173.

35. "Heifer Project Committee," August 1947, Correspondence 1947, folder 10, box 1, series 4/1/6, HP, BHLA.

36. Cheryl Brumbaugh-Cayford, with contributions from Peggy Reiff Miller, "'Pass the Baton and Continue On': Puerto Rico Celebrates 75 Years of Heifer," *Messenger*, December 2019; Peggy Reiff Miller, "Celebrating 75 Years of Heifer International: Where It All Began," *World Ark*, Spring 2020. See also "Down to Earth Project," in Beck and West, *Cowboy Memories*, 15.

37. Peggy Reiff Miller, "Heifer Project's Goodwill Mission to Puerto Rico," *Seagoing Cowboys* (blog), May 10, 2019.

38. Roger E. Sappington, *Brethren Social Policy, 1908–1958* (Elgin, IL: Brethren Press, 1961), 112.

39. Reiff Miller, "Impossible Dream"; Bill Beck, "Introduction," in Beck and West, *Cowboy Memories*, 5. See also G. Yoder, *Passing on the Gift*, 105–7; "Report by Ralph M. Delk to Co-workers," December 21, 1946, Correspondence 1945–46, folder 9, box 1, series 4/1/6, HP, BHLA. On Heifer's anniversary date, see Reiff Miller, "Heifer Project Myths, Part III."

40. On this early planning period, see Durnbaugh, *Pragmatic Prophet*, 171–74; J. Kenneth Kreider, "M.R. Zigler, a Crusader for Peace," in *A Dunker Guide to Brethren History*, ed. Walt Wiltschek (Elgin, IL: Brethren Press, 2010), 115–18; Reiff Miller, "Impossible Dream"; "Director General to M.R. Zigler," June 18, 1945, Brethren Service Committee, S-1267-0000-0083-00001, p. 131, UNA.

41. David L. MacFarlane, "The UNRRA Experience in Relation to Developments in Food and Agriculture," *American Journal of Agricultural Economics* 30, no. 1 (1948): 72.

42. F. F. Elliott, "Redirecting World Agricultural Production and Trade Toward Better Nutrition," *Journal of Farm Economics* 26, no. 1 (1944): 13.

43. Robert Lintner, *UNRRA Livestock Program Historical Report*, 1947, UNRRA selected records AG-018-040, accession 2015.245.1, record group RG-67.050, S-1021-0009-03, p. 95, USHMM.

44. "Paul French to M.R. Zigler," March 3, 1944, box 20, series A, CCWR, DG 025, SCPC. The costs of moving animals from point of purchase to the ports is outlined in Lintner, *UNRRA Livestock Program Historical Report*, 95–112, USHMM.

45. George Woodbridge, *UNRRA: The History of the United Nations Relief and Rehabilitation Administration* (New York: Oxford University Press, 1950), 1:478, 1:787.

46. For early planning ideas, see "Director General to M.R. Zigler," June 18, 1945, Brethren Service Committee, S-1267-0000-0083-00001, p. 131, UNA.

47. Lintner, *UNRRA Livestock Program Historical Report*, 4, USHMM.

48. "Information for the Press," December 6, 1945, Brethren Service Committee, S-1267-0000-0083-00001, p. 102, UNA.

49. On the sailing of *Boolongena*, see Reiff Miller, "Seagoing Cowboys and the Heifer Project," as well as Peggy Reiff Miller, "Dr. Martin M. Kaplan: Heifer International's Second Seagoing Cowboy Delivers Bulls to Greece, Part I," *Seagoing Cowboys* (blog), March 22, 2019. Kaplan was a veterinarian on the sailing.

50. "Report from M.E. Hays, Chief, Department of Supply, to Melvin P. McGovern, Mission Historian," May 14, 1947, Office of the Historian, Monographs—Poland—Early History, S-1021-0041-0013-00001, p. 7, UNA; Ministerstwo Przemysłu,

Handlu i Żeglugi Rządu RP [emigracyjnego] w Londynie, 2/132/0/7/533, AAN.

51. Lintner, *UNRRA Livestock Program Historical Report*, 5–15, USHMM. On veterinarians, see Clive J. C. Phillips and Eduardo Santurtun, "The Welfare of Livestock Transported by Ship," *Veterinary Journal* 196, no. 3 (2013): 310. Canadians could also volunteer to work as veterinarians on UNRRA ships. See, for example, "SS No. 9, Clarke," *Canadian Statesman*, April 3, 1947, for a notice about Dr. W. Sherwin of Orono having worked as a vet on a Poland-bound UNRRA ship with 777 horses. See also "Desperate Case of Europe Outlined by Dr. W. Sherwin in Fine Address at Rotary," *Canadian Standard*, July 24, 1947.

52. The various suggestions for where to get livestock attendants are reflected throughout the following file: Brethren Service Committee, S-1267-0000-0083-00001, pp. 112–23, UNA.

53. AMEDD Center of History and Heritage, "Transportation of Animals," August 30, 2022, https://achh.army.mil/history/book-wwii-vetservicewwii-chapter15. On World War I animal transport, see BrookeUSA, "Shipping: Ports of Embarkation," *United States World War One Centennial Commission*, August 30, 2022, https://www.worldwar1centennial.org/index.php/brookeusa-buying-animals/3162-brookeusa-buying-animals-article-2.html#ports-of-embarkation; David McAuslin, "Transport Service (The Innocent Abroad)," *Journal of the American Veterinary Medical Association* VI, no. 4 (1918): 536–47.

54. Lintner, *UNRRA Livestock Program Historical Report*, 8, USHMM.

55. The May agreement between the BSC and UNRRA is available as "Agreement," Brethren Service Committee, S-1267-0000-0006-00001, p. 7, UNA. The document is signed by Benjamin Bushong of the BSC and Phil W. Jordan, Procurement and Property Branch, Administrative Services, UNRRA. The agreement refers to the seagoing cowboys as "cattle tenders." For an earlier draft of the agreement, see "Agreement Between BSC and UNRRA," Correspondence 1945–46, folder 9, box 1, series 4/1/6, HP, BHLA.

56. "UNRRA and the Dunkers," *Gospel Messenger*, September 1, 1945. This is a reprint of "Religion: UNRRA and the Dunkers," *Time*, July 23, 1945. The article was widely reproduced. See also G. Yoder, *Passing on the Gift*, 108.

57. Lintner, *UNRRA Livestock Program Historical Report*, 8, USHMM.

58. Reiff Miller, private correspondence with author, January 6, 2024. Belgium received 335 heifers, and France received 500. See "Summary of Shipments by Countries," 1945–53 Project Committee Reports, folder 19, box 1, series 4/1/6, HP, BHLA.

59. "C.H. Wilson to C.M. Drury," October 7, 1946, UNRRA—Poland Mission, 1944–49, file 29, S-0527-1064, UNA.

60. "M.R. Zigler et al. from A. Stauffer Curry," May 30, 1945, box 85, series A, CCWR, DG 025, SCPC. On these two initial sailings, see Peggy Reiff Miller, "Second UNRRA Livestock Ship Departed the United States 75 Years Ago Today," *Seagoing Cowboys* (blog), June 26, 2020.

61. Even at the time, Friends were quick to point out that providing aid to those that needed it was not distinctly Christian. See Fiona Reid and Sharif Gemie, "The Friends Relief Service and Displaced People in Europe After the Second World War, 1945–48," *Quaker Studies* 17, no. 2 (2013): 223–43.

62. "Text of La Guardia UNRRA Acceptance Speech," *New York Times*, March 30, 1946. La Guardia's term "great army of mercy" was used by the Polish press too. See "UNRRA-Wielka armia miłosierdzia kończy swą pracę," *Głos Wielkopolski*, September 9, 1946. For La Guardia's reference to "practical Christianity," see his letter to the Heifer Project Committee dated November 16, 1946, and reproduced as "UNRRA Expresses Gratitude for Heifer Project," *Gospel Messenger*, January 11, 1947. On Christianity and UNRRA, see also Amanda Melanie Bundy, "There Was a Man of UNRRA: Internationalism, Humanitarianism, and the Early Cold War in Europe, 1943–1947" (PhD diss., Ohio State University, 2017), 196.

63. United Nations Relief and Rehabilitation Administration, *The Story of UNRRA* (Washington, DC: UNRRA, Office of Public Information, 1948), 30.

64. Woodbridge, *UNRRA*, 1:550. Woodbridge's use of this biblical phrasing in his history of UNRRA is also cited in the following: David Mayers, "Destruction Repaired and Destruction Anticipated: United Nations Relief and Rehabilitation (UNRRA), the Atomic Bomb, and US Policy, 1944–1946," *International History Review* 38, no. 5 (2016): 967.

65. Gertrude Samuels, "The Unheard Cry of the World's Children," *New York Times Magazine*, October 12, 1947, reprinted in US Congress, *Proceedings and Debates*, July 26, 1947, to December 19, 1947, 80th Cong., 1st sess., *Congressional Record* 93, part 12, A4619. The reference to "UNRRA" as a holy word also appears in an official UNRRA publication: UNRRA, *Story of UNRRA*, 46.

66. "Get a Horse," editorial, *Life*, December 30, 1946.

67. "Bonnell Supports Truman Food Plea," *New York Times*, February 11, 1946. The Brethren also used the term "Christian statesmanship" to describe the work they were doing in the postwar period. See Thurl Metzger, "Report of Work in Poland, October 15, 1946 to April 16, 1947," 1945–53 Project Committee Reports, folder 19, box 1, series 4/1/6, HP, BHLA.

68. "Churchmen Back Truman on Food," *New York Times*, February 21, 1946. The original documents are at Bureau of Service, Churches—Public Information File, S-1268-0000-0079-00001, UNA.

69. "Plea for Starving Made by Manning," *New York Times*, March 25, 1946.

70. "Bonnell Supports Truman Food Plea."

71. David Miller, dir., *Seeds of Destiny* (United States Department of War, 1946). David Miller and Art Arthur wrote the film script. On the film, see Irene Kahn Atkins, "Seeds of Destiny: A Case History," *Film and History* 11, no. 2 (1981): 25–33.

72. On the ways in which visual images of suffering children remain a part of modern-day humanitarian fundraising campaigns, see Heidi Fehrenbach, "Children and Other Civilians: Photography and the Politics of Humanitarian Image-Making," in *Humanitarian Photography: A History*, ed. Heidi Fehrenbach and Davide Rodogno (New York: Cambridge University Press, 2015), 167; Heide Fehrenbach and Davide Rodogno, "The Morality of Sight: Humanitarian Photography in History," in Fehrenbach and Rodogno, *Humanitarian Photography*, 1; Heide Fehrenbach and Davide Rodogno, "'A Horrific Photo of a Drowned Syrian Child': Humanitarian Photography and NGO Media Strategies in Historical Perspective," *International Review of the Red Cross* 97, no. 900 (2015): 1125–26. For an analysis of earlier uses of the suffering children trope, see Friederike Kind-Kovács, "The Great War, the Child's Body and the

American Red Cross," *European Review of History* 23, no. 1–2 (2016): 33–62. The focus here is on post–World War I Hungary and the work of the American Relief Administration. On the marketing of modern humanitarianism, see Kevin Rozario, "'Delicious Horrors': Mass Culture, the Red Cross, and the Appeal of Modern American Humanitarianism," *American Quarterly* 55, no. 3 (2003): 417–55.

73. Miller, Seeds of Destiny.

74. *Marine Bull Pen*, no. 9, July 19, 1946, Marine Bullpens and News Circulars, 1946, folder 10, box 75, MGP, Hist MSS 1–129, MCA. See also Sappington, *Brethren Social Policy*, 87–88; Roger E. Sappington, "Social Involvement," in Durnbaugh, *Church of the Brethren*, 102; Durnbaugh, *Pragmatic Prophet*, 173; Morse, *New Windsor Center*, 12; Brethren Service, "More Than a Milk Factory," *Gospel Messenger*, June 21, 1947.

75. Philip West, "Dirty Fingernails, Heifers and China: Some Connecting Threads," in Beck and West, *Cowboy Memories*, 112. West delivered this speech in 1993.

76. Kermit Eby as quoted in G. Yoder, *Passing on the Gift*, 114. The reference to bombs here may be picking up on a proposed Heifer Project advertising poster titled "Do You Have a Program for Peace?" which suggested that both atom bombs and heifers offered different types of "security." The front panel features Heifer Project cows on the wharf next to a ship alongside the caption "We need more projects like this" and the words "to prevent" preceding an arrow. The arrow points to a plume of smoke from an atom bomb with the caption "this." See "Do You Have a Program for Peace?," 1945–53 Project Committee Reports, folder 19, box 1, series 4/1/6, HP, BHLA.

77. Michael Barnett, *Empire of Humanity: A History of Humanitarianism* (Ithaca, NY: Cornell University Press, 2011), 2, 17. The argument about the religious elements in interwar humanitarian aid efforts are also made by Davide Rodogno, *Night on Earth: A History of International Humanitarianism in the Near East, 1918–1930* (Cambridge: Cambridge University Press, 2021), 15. See also Sappington, *Brethren Social Policy*, 112.

78. The ideas in this section are inspired by Martin Conway, Michael Barnett, David A. Hollinger, and Mark L. Movsesian in their review of *Christian Human Rights*, by Samuel Moyn, *H-Diplo Roundtable Review* 17, no. 20 (2016): 1–19, http://www.tiny.cc/Roundtable-XVII-20. The Brethren, the Heifer Project, and UNRRA are not discussed in the roundtable. See also Samuel Moyn, *Christian Human Rights* (Philadelphia: University of Pennsylvania Press, 2015), 1–24; Paul Betts, *Ruin and Renewal: Civilizing Europe After World War II* (New York: Basic Books, 2020), 16.

79. Bryan MacDonald, *Food Power: The Rise and Fall of the Postwar American Food System* (New York: Oxford University Press, 2016).

80. Todd H. Hall, *Emotional Diplomacy: Official Emotion on the International Stage* (Ithaca, NY: Cornell University Press, 2015), 3; Yohan Ariffin, "Introduction: How Emotions Can Explain Outcomes in International Relations," in *Emotions in International Politics: Beyond Mainstream International Relations*, eds. Yohan Ariffin, Jean Marc Coicaud, and Vesselin Popovski (New York: Cambridge University Press, 2016), 23–47.

81. Cormac O. Grada, *Famine: A Short History* (Princeton, NJ: Princeton University Press, 2009), 227.

82. Barry Riley, *The Political History of American Food Aid: An Uneasy Benevolence* (New York: Oxford University Press, 2017), 92-96.

83. Kendra Smith-Howard, *Pure and Modern Milk: An Environmental History since 1900* (New York: Oxford University Press, 2013), 77; Ben Shephard, *The Long Road Home: The Aftermath of the Second World War* (New York: Random House, 2010), 255; Riley, *Political History of American Food Aid*, 86–87.

84. Jacob Darwin Hamblin, "The Vulnerability of Nations: Food Security in the Aftermath of World War II," *Global Environment* 10 (2012): 58.

85. Frank Henry, "Through This Port: Life for Europe," *Baltimore Sun*, March 24, 1946.

86. "Steady Stream of Cattle Pours from Newport News," *Suffolk News-Herald*, May 16, 1946.

87. Mark St. John Erickson, "Newport News Became a Springboard for WWI War Horses," AP News, December 4, 2016; BrookeUSA, "Shipping."

88. Lintner, *UNRRA Livestock Program Historical Report*, 165, 167, USHMM. Lintner's report contains a long section devoted specifically to Newport News on pp. 152–67. A list of ships that sailed from Newport News is provided on pp. 168–74.

89. Michael Frome, "Noah's Ark Docks at Newport News," *Washington Post*, May 26, 1946, in Clippings and Releases 4, 1940s–1960s, folder 10, box 2, series 4/1/6, HP, BHLA.

90. Lintner, *UNRRA Livestock Program Historical Report*, 19–25, USHMM.

91. Henry, "Through This Port."

92. Peggy Reiff Miller, "Cattle for Israel," *Seagoing Cowboys* (blog), July 14, 2017. Details in this section about the stockyard also come from "Unique New Stockyard in Operation," *Daily Press*, February 13, 1946. In 1949 the Levinsons started their own cattle delivery program for Israel specifically; there is virtually no research on this subject. According to Peggy Reiff Miller, in 1946 the Heifer Project started working directly with the Russian authorities on a plan to ship animals to Birobidzhan to help Jews living in the Jewish Autonomous Oblast. The plan was apparently never realized. Reiff Miller, private correspondence with author, January 30, 2024.

93.. "Unique New Stockyard in Operation."

94. Philipp Weintraub, "Reseeding Live-Stock Herds in Liberated Europe," *Baltimore Sun*, June 28, 1945, 12; Woodbridge, *UNRRA*, 1:489–91.

95. Benon Gaziński and Bogusław Wanot, "Działalność UNRRA i jej pomoc dla rolnictwa w Polsce," *Rocznik Muzeum Narodowego Rolnictwa w Szreniawie* 19 (1993): 21; Eastern European Division Loan Department, "Preliminary Paper No. 6 for the Working Party on the Polish Loan Application" (International Bank for Reconstruction and Development, May 26, 1947), https://documents1.worldbank.org/curated/en/558411468095985925/pdf/multi-page.pdf, 58. See also "Denmark Gives to UNRRA," *New York Times*, February 17, 1946; A. G. Wilder, "Horses in Poland," *Morgan Horse Magazine*, May 1947; "Przychód," Dostawy koni w ramach UNRRA, 1946–47, MRiRR, 2/162/0/21.5/3377, p. 162, AAN; "Minute Sheet: Denmark," PRDG's European Tour, S-1435-0000-0100-00001, p. 25, UNA.

96. Jarosław Wasielewski, "Jak po wojnie leczono konie z UNRRY w Gdańsku," trojmiasto.pl, February 26, 2019, https://historia.trojmiasto.pl/Jak-w-Gdańsku-po-wojnie-konie-z-UNRRY-leczono-n132173.html#opinions-wrap. See also A. Pępkowski, "Dostawy zwierząt UNRRA dla Polski," *Medycyna Weterynaryjna* 3, no. 6 (1947): 399.

97. Lintner, *UNRRA Livestock Program Historical Report* 19–25, USHMM.
98. Woodbridge, *UNRRA*, 1:488.
99. Baukhage, "UNRRA Test of Sentiment for World Cooperation," *Highland Recorder*, December 7, 1945.
100. I borrow this phrasing from scholar Ilaria Scgalia, who writes about the interwar period. See Ilaria Scgalia, *The Emotions of Internationalism: Feeling International Cooperation in the Alps in the Interwar Period* (New York: Oxford University Press, 2019), 3.
101. On states as emotional actors and on the concept of "emotional diplomacy," see Hall, *Emotional Diplomacy*.
102. Bliss Lane as quoted in Jacek Zygmunt Sawicki, ed., *Polska jesień, rosyjska zima: Spotkanie Juliena Bryana z misją UNRRA w Europie Środkowo-Wschodniej 1946–1947—fotografie i zapiski* (Warsaw: IPN, 2022), 64.
103. For an example see Emma Hutchison, *Affective Communities in World Politics: Collective Emotions After Trauma* (Cambridge: Cambridge University Press, 2016).

3. On Becoming a Seagoing Cowboy

1. On New Windsor in this period, see Carter Brooke Jones, "New Windsor," *Sunday Star*, March 17, 1946; Frank J. Batavick, *Time's Crossroads: The History of New Windsor, MD* (Amazon.com and CreateSpace, 2017), 131; Donald F. Durnbaugh, *Pragmatic Prophet: The Life of Michael Robert Zigler* (Elgin, IL: Brethren Press, 1989), 148; Lorell Weiss, *Ten Years of Brethren Service* (Elgin, IL: Brethren Service Commission, 1952), 52; Peggy Reiff Miller, "Seagoing Cowboys and the Heifer Project: The Maryland Story," *Catoctin History*, Fall/Winter 2005. In the earliest months, the seagoing cowboys program and the Heifer Project were administered from temporary and provisional offices in Nappanee, Indiana; and Lancaster, Pennsylvania. Both the Brethren Service Committee itself and the Church of the Brethren were headquartered in Elgin, Illinois. Peggy Reiff Miller, private correspondence with author, January 23, 2024.
2. "Information and Inspiration . . . ," *Gospel Messenger*, April 6, 1946; L. Weiss, *Ten Years of Brethren Service*, 51; US Congress, *Proceedings and Debates*, February 19, 1946, to March 28, 1946, 79th Cong., 2nd sess., *Congressional Record* 92, part 2: 2388.
3. For more on the work done at New Windsor, see "Methodist Church Sends Clothing to World Service Center," *Suffolk News-Herald*, July 15, 1947. On the donated material that arrived at New Windsor, see *A Scrapbook of Cowboy Memories*, 1994, From the Memories of Roger and Olive Roop, December 1985, folder 14, box 1, John E. Nunemaker Collection (hereafter JEN), Hist. MSS 1893, MCA; R. Jan Thompson and Roma Jo Thompson, *Beyond our Means: How the Brethren Service Center Dared to Embrace the World* (Elgin, IL: Brethren Press, 2009), chap. 9.
4. "World Brotherhood at Work, Notes on BSC Relief Work from Interview with Ben Bushong," Brethren Service Committee, S-1268-0000-0039, p. 65, UNA; Reiff Miller, "Seagoing Cowboys and the Heifer Project."
5. Reiff Miller, "Seagoing Cowboys and the Heifer Project"; Peggy Reiff Miller, "The Brethren Service Center Serves and Is Served by Seagoing Cowboys," *Seagoing Cowboys* (blog), September 12, 2015. The details in Miller's post come from the journal

of J. O. Yoder, who was at New Windsor in the fall of 1945. See J. Olen Yoder, *Crossing to Poland* (self-pub., 1986). Arthur Meyer was one cowboy who stopped at New Windsor before sailing on his assigned livestock ship in 1946. He describes his time at New Windsor in his diary. See Arthur Meyer, "Art Meyer's Cattle Boat Experience: Introduction to Planned Book, Dated January 1991," Seagoing Cowboys, accessed February 13, 2020, https://seagoingcowboyswebsite.files.wordpress.com/2015/10/stories_artmeyer.pdf. Similarly, Wayne Brant also spent time at New Windsor before his sailing. See Wayne Brant, "The Heifer Project," in *Scrapbook of Cowboy Memories*, MCA.

6. For the romance between Kathryn Root and Earl Holderman (who met at the New Windsor Center in 1945 and were married for almost six decades), see Peggy Reiff Miller, "A Seagoing Cowboy Romance," *Seagoing Cowboys* (blog), February 14, 2020.

7. Kenneth I. Morse, *Preaching in a Tavern and 129 Other Surprising Stories from Brethren Life* (Elgin, IL: Brethren Press, 1997), chap. 34; Kenneth I. Morse, *New Windsor Center* (New Windsor, MD: Brethren Service Center, 1979), 37; Jacob deNobel, "Taking a Look at Presidents Who Have Visited Carroll County," *Chicago Tribune*, February 15, 2015; Frank Batavick, "New Windsor History," New Windsor Heritage, accessed March 23, 2023, https://www.newwindsorheritage.org/history. In 2023 the Mission and Ministry Board of the Church of the Brethren decided to close down the Material Resources program at New Windsor. See "Mission and Ministry Board Makes Decision To Close Material Resources Program," Church of the Brethren Newsline, October 23, 2023, https://www.brethren.org/news/2023/board-decides-to-close-material-resources/.

8. Robert Lintner, *UNRRA Livestock Program Historical Report*, 1947, UNRRA selected records AG-018-040, accession 2015.245.1, record group RG-67.050, S-1021-0009-03, pp. 9–10, USHMM.

9. US Department of Commerce, "Income of Nonfarm Families and Individuals: 1946," in *Current Population Reports: Consumer Income*, ser. P-60, no. 1 (January 28, 1948), 1, https://www2.census.gov/prod2/popscan/p60-001.pdf.

10. The salary amounts for the supervisors and veterinarians come from Lintner, *UNRRA Livestock Program Historical Report*, 194, USHMM. See also "Letter to Undisclosed Multiple Recipients from Ralph E. Smeltzer of the BSC," 1945, Correspondence, September 1945 to January 1946, folder 2, box 75, MGP, Hist. MSS 1–129, MCA; "Paul French to Col. Lewis F. Kosch," January 29, 1946, box 85, series A, part 1, CCWR, DG 025, SCPC; "Melvin Gingerich to Verna Gingerich," June 14, 1946, Correspondence June 1946, folder 3, box 75, MGP, Hist. MSS 1–129, MCA.

11. AMEDD Center of History and Heritage, "Transportation of Animals," August 30, 2022, https://achh.army.mil/history/book-wwii-vetservicewwii-chapter15.

12. "Girven H. Culley to Wilmer L. Tjossem," February 18, 1946, box 49, series F, part 1, CCWR, DG 025, SCPC.

13. "Charles C. Kocher Polish Trip Notes and Photos," 1946, folder 1, box 1, Seagoing Cowboys Collection, Hist. MSS 1–973, MCA. See also Peggy Reiff Miller, "Hanging Out in the Port City," *Seagoing Cowboys* (blog), May 22, 2015.

14. L. Weiss, *Ten Years of Brethren Service*, 3–4.

15. There was an exception to the Brethren's control over hiring: Initially, it was UNRRA that permitted African Americans to be cowboys on all-Black crews only. This is discussed later in the chapter.

16. On the Heifer Project's ecumenicalism see Peggy Reiff Miller, "The Impossible Dream: How the Heifer Project Came to Be," *Messenger*, July/August 2009. Advertisements in the Brethren's *Gospel Messenger* encouraged local Heifer Project Committees to recruit seagoing cowboys from their congregations. See, for example, "Information and Inspiration . . . ," *Gospel Messenger*, June 1, 1946.

17. Peggy Reiff Miller, "Mining for Gems in the Heifer Archives," *World Ark*, Spring 2016. For reflections on the number of cowboys that came out of a peace church milieu, I thank Peggy Reiff Miller: Reiff Miller, private correspondence with author, January 7 and 23, 2024. Though some published secondary sources do provide specific numbers of cowboys from the peace churches—for example, that there were about one thousand Mennonite seagoing cowboys in total—Peggy Reiff Miller (who herself made this claim about Mennonite cowboy numbers in her earliest published work)—believes these figures to be unreliable for the reasons described above. See also Peggy Reiff Miller, "Coming of Age on a Cattle Boat," *Mennonite*, January 10, 2006; Dave Janzen, "The Cowboy at Sea," *Mennonite*, April 15, 1947.

18. See, for example, "The Church and World Order," *Gospel Messenger*, November 2, 1946. This article is a reprint of a release from the Federal Council of Churches.

19. For an example of a typical newspaper advertisement, see "Newspaper Advertisement in 1946," in *Cowboy Memories*, eds. Bill Beck and Mel West. Little Rock, AR: Heifer Project International, 1994), 3.

20. *Origins of the Heifer Project* (High Library, Elizabethtown College, 2014), https://archive.org/details/Heifer_Project.

21. Peggy Reiff Miller, "Seagoing Cowboy Program Began 75 Years Ago This Month!," *Seagoing Cowboys* (blog), June 12, 2020.

22. See, for example, "Lowell Zuck Travels for UNRRA," *Etownian*, October 25, 1946. *The Etownian* was published by Elizabethtown College in Elizabethtown, PA. On Brethren projects devoted to German refugees from eastern Europe, see Morse, *New Windsor Center*, 69–70.

23. Harold McNett, interviewed by Gordon Miller, October 18, 2016, SdArch 38. item 38-1, Digital-Materials: SdArch38-SET-001, Harold McNett Seagoing Cowboy Oral History, SdArch 38, James Madison University Libraries Special Collections (hereafter JMU).

24. Melvin Gingerich, "On Becoming a Sea Going Cowboy," 1–2, folder 13, box 75, MGP, HM1–973, Hist. MSS 1–129, MCA. I take the title of chapter 3 from Gingerich's memoir.

25. Thanks to Peggy Reiff Miller for clarifying this point for me.

26. Lintner, *UNRRA Livestock Program Historical Report*, 31–34, 67, USHMM.

27. M. Gingerich, "Sea Going Cowboy," MCA.

28. Dwight Smith, "The Odyssey of a Sea-Going Cowboy," in *Scrapbook of Cowboy Memories*, MCA.

29. Lintner, *UNRRA Livestock Program Historical Report*, 68, USHMM.

30. Don Chatfield, "For Brethren News," March 1, 1946, Brethren Service Committee, S-1268-0000-0039, p. 95, UNA.

31. "Newspaper Advertisement in 1946," in Beck and West, *Cowboy Memories*, 3.

32. "Positions Offered," *Living Church*, October 20, 1946, 22.

33. The information about UNRRA lowering the maximum age for attendants to fifty comes from "Information and Inspiration . . . ," *Gospel Messenger*, December 15, 1945. Peggy Reiff Miller notes that the oldest cowboy she has come across was in his seventies when he sailed in late 1945. Reiff Miller, private correspondence with author, January 23, 2024. Lintner states that the oldest cowboy was seventy-two. See Lintner, *UNRRA Livestock Program Historical Report*, 68, USHMM.

34. Rev. Floyd Bantz is very frank about being motivated by a desire for adventure and "to see the sea." See *Origins of the Heifer Project*.

35. Harvey Cox, *Just as I Am* (Nashville, TN: Abingdon, 1983), 32.

36. "Questionnaire Completed by Albert J. Meyer, Poland Sea-Going Cowboys, 1958–59," Completed Questionnaires, folder 5, box 76, MGP, Hist. MSS 1–129, MCA. For more on men's motivation to become seagoing cowboys, see "With an Attitude of Adventure and Service," *Mennonite*, November 20, 1945.

37. The choice to pursue missionary work versus humanitarian work had been debated by the Brethren even before the war started. See Durnbaugh, *Pragmatic Prophet*, 114–15.

38. Sometimes the Brethren Service Committee included Bibles in its aid packages. See Robert Ebey, "A Trip to Poland with Brethren Service Heifers," box 1, JEN Hist. MSS-1-893, p. 9, MCA. Ebey wrote his memoir in 1947, and then in 1993 he produced a very slightly amended version. I use the 1993 version throughout. See also Lawrence W. Shultz, *People and Places, 1890–1970: An Autobiography* (Winona Lake, IN: Life and Light, 1971), 105; "Seagoing Cowboys Given Bibles to Carry Overseas," *Gospel Messenger*, July 27, 1946.

39. "Positions Offered," 22.

40. M. Gingerich, "Sea Going Cowboy," MCA. For another example, see "Help! Help! Help!," *Arkansas Methodist*, May 9, 1946.

41. "UNRRA," *Baptist Record*, August 29, 1946.

42. M. Gingerich, "Sea Going Cowboy," MCA.

43. On an army veterinarian's perspective on the composition of livestock tender crews during World War I, see David McAuslin, "Transport Service (The Innocent Abroad)," *Journal of the American Veterinary Medical Association* vol. VI, no. 4 (1918), pp. 536–47.

44. Melvin Gingerich, "Recommendations to the BSC and the MCC Related to Sea-Going Cowboys," Correspondence A to G, 1946, folder 4, box 75, MGP, Hist. MSS 1–129, MCA.

45. "Untitled and undated letter," folder 8, box 75, MGP, Hist. MSS 1–129, MCA. See also "Impressions the Crews Made on the Cowboys," in Beck and West, *Cowboy Memories*, 50.

46. "Suggestions for Livestock Attendants," box 1, folder 6, Charles C. Kocher Miscellaneous, 1946–2001, HM1–973, MCA.

47. "Suggestions for Livestock Attendants," MCA.

48. See, for example, "Help Wanted!," *Christian Century*, September 4, 1946.

49. Alison Collis Greene, "Southern Christian Work Camps and a Cold War Campaign for Racial and Economic Justice," in *Working Alternatives: American and Catholic Experiments in Work and Economy*, ed. John C. Seitz and Christine Firer Hinze (New York: Fordham University Press, 2020), 255, 272. The crew members are named

in Peggy Reiff Miller, "Creighton Victory Cowboys Adopt a Polish Boy to Their Crew," *Seagoing Cowboys* (blog), November 12, 2021.

50. Peggy Reiff Miller, "Special Crew #3: Interracial Crew Works and Studies Together—Part II," *Seagoing Cowboys* (blog), July 22, 2016; Collis Greene, "Southern Christian Work Camps," 272.

51. Collis Greene, "Southern Christian Work Camps," 254; Reiff Miller, "Special Crew #3."

52. Mays is quoted in Reiff Miller, "Special Crew #3."

53. A collection of reference letters can be found in General Correspondence, 1946, folder 270, series 1, part 2, Howard Kester Papers, Coll 03834, Wilson Special Collections Library, University of North Carolina (hereafter UNC).

54. Collis Greene, "Southern Christian Work Camps," 273. An account of the sailing was written by William Howard Deihl and is called "Heifers for Europe." It is accessible in folder 276, box 9, Howard Kester Papers, Coll 03834, Wilson Special Collections Library, UNC.

55. "Brethren Fellowship Crew," *Gospel Messenger*, November 2, 1946; Reiff Miller, "Special Crew #3"; Collis Greene, "Southern Christian Work Camps," 255.

56. Elmer S. Yoder, "Seagoing Cowboys from Stark County," *Heritage*, October 2002.

57. For a full list of medical conditions that disqualified a man from serving as a cattle attendant, see "Suggested Medical Standards to Be Applied by UNRRA," box 85, series A, part 1, CCWR, DG 025, SCPC.

58. "Ruth Steenburgh (FOR) to Dan West (BSC)," May 13, 1947, box 13, series E, John Nevin Sayre Papers (hereafter JNS), DG 117, SCPC.

59. Peggy Reiff Miller, "Seagoing Cowgirls?," *Seagoing Cowboys* (blog), April 28, 2017. Reiff Miller guesses that the first "seagoing cowgirl" was Julia Byrd in 1950; Byrd was a journalist and accompanied her husband on a ship bound for Germany. This was well past the UNRRA period. For cowgirl reminiscences from later periods, see Bill Beck, "Cowboys of the Future," in Beck and West, *Cowboy Memories*, esp. the entry by Arlene Roehner, 131–33.

60. Lintner, *UNRRA Livestock Program Historical Report*, 10, USHMM.

61. E. Yoder, "Seagoing Cowboys from Stark County"; "Memorandum to Paul French from Girven H. Culley," February 8, 1946, box 85, series A, part 1, CCWR, DG 025, SCPC.

62. G. Yoder, *Passing on the Gift*, 107. See also Durnbaugh, *Pragmatic Prophet*, 174.

63. The Heifer Project's first executive director, from 1943 to 1944, was Marvin Senger. See Peggy Reiff Miller, "The Three Executives Who Helped Shape the Heifer Project, Part I," *Seagoing Cowboys* (blog), September 13, 2024. On Bushong, see also Peggy Reiff Miller, "Benjamin Bushong: Chief Engineer of the Seagoing Cowboy Program," *Seagoing Cowboys* (blog), May 26, 2023; "Edwin R. Henson to M.E. Hays," January 20, 1947, file 721.2, S-0518-0864, UNA.

64. Morse, *New Windsor Center*, 34. A thank-you card dated July 3, 1946, and signed by Bushong is part of the Ernest L. Boyer Center Archives at Messiah College; see "Notecard," July 3, 1946, catalog no. 1000 0001 8752, https://messiah.pastperfectonline.com/archive/6E49F89F-C755-4417-8D9F-364458938209.

65. Reiff Miller, "Impossible Dream"; Reiff Miller, private correspondence with author, January 24, 2024. On Carol Stine, see *Marine Bull Pen*, no. 6, June 7, 1946,

Marine Bullpens and News Circulars, 1946, folder 10, box 75, MGP, Hist. MSS 1–129, MCA.

66. "Letter by Ben Bushong," in Beck and West, *Cowboy Memories*, 25.

67. Brant, "Heifer Project," in *Scrapbook of Cowboy Memories*, MCA.

68. "Military Conscription," *Gospel Messenger*, June 23, 1945.

69. Robert S. Zigler, interview by W. Haven North, November 5, 1998, Association for Diplomatic Studies and Training Foreign Affairs Oral History Collection Foreign Assistance Series, https://adst.org/OH%20TOCs/Zigler-Robert-S.pdf.

70. Byron P. Royer, "Diary of Seagoing Cowboys," in Beck and West, *Cowboy Memories*, 29. On the swearing of oaths, see also Vernard Eller, "Beliefs," in *Church of the Brethren: Past and Present*, ed. Donald F. Durnbaugh (Elgin, IL: Brethren Press, 1971), 49.

71. On the seagoing cowboys program and CPS see Peggy Reiff Miller, "Civilian Public Service Unit for Seagoing Cowboys," *Seagoing Cowboys* (blog), May 13, 2016.

72. On the peace churches' efforts to influence government conscription policy, see Donald F. Durnbaugh, "The Fight Against War of the Historic Peace Churches, 1919–1941," in *Challenge to Mars: Essays on Pacifism from 1918 to 1945*, eds. Peter Brock and Thomas P. Socknat (Toronto: University of Toronto Press, 1999), 218–39, esp. 232.

73. J. Howard Kauffman, "Dilemmas of Christian Pacifism Within a Historic Peace Church," *Sociological Analysis* 49, no. 4 (1989): 369. On Mennonite pacifism see Steven J. Taylor, *Acts of Conscience: World War II, Mental Institutions, and Religious Objectors* (Syracuse, NY: Syracuse University Press, 2009), chap. 1 and 2. On the prewar debates within American Mennonite communities about the meaning of pacifism, see Melvin Gingerich, *Service for Peace: A History of Mennonite Civilian Public Service* (Akron, PA: Mennonite Central Committee, 1949), chap. 2. For an exploration of related ideas, see Melvin Gingerich, *Youth and Christian Citizenship* (Scottsdale, PA: Herald, 1949).

74. Perry Bush, *Two Kingdoms, Two Loyalties: Mennonite Pacifism in Modern America* (Baltimore: Johns Hopkins University Press, 1998), 6–7; J. Kenneth Kreider, *A Cup of Cold Water: The Story of Brethren Service* (Elgin, IL: Brethren Press, 2001), 1–4; Durnbaugh, *Pragmatic Prophet*, 38–40; Cynthia Eller, *Conscientious Objectors and the Second World War: Moral and Religious Arguments in Support of Pacifism* (New York: Praeger, 1991), 22–23.

75. "Relief Work with the American Friends Service Committee," November 2, 1944, box 77, series A, part 1, CCWR, DG 025, SCPC; Hertha Kraus, *International Relief in Action, 1914–1943* (Philadelphia: Research Center, 1943), 227.

76. "Correspondence of Albert M. Gaeddert," box 24, series A, part 1, CCWR, DG 025, SCPC. Gaeddert was the director of Mennonite Central Committee camps during the war. On the subject of the Friends and relief work, see J. William Frost, "'Our Deeds Carry Our Message': The Early History of the American Friends Service Committee," *Quaker Studies* 81, no. 1 (1992): 1–51.

77. NSBRO was first called the National Council for Religious Objectors; the group took the NSBRO name in November 1940. It later became the National Interreligious Service Board for Conscientious Objectors, and today it is known as the

Center for Conscience and War. See Taylor, *Acts of Conscience*, 16–19; Durnbaugh, *Pragmatic Prophet*, 127–30. The correspondence between Paul Comly French and M. R. Zigler about NSBRO and the formation of an alternative service program is extensive. See box 19, series A, part 1, CCWR, DG 025, SCPC.

78. L. Weiss, *Ten Years of Brethren Service*, 29; Cynthia Eller, "Oral History as Moral Discourse: Conscientious Objectors and the Second World War," *Oral History Review* 18, no. 1 (1990): 51–53. For an overview of Selective Service in World War II, see Eller, *Conscientious Objectors*, chap. 2, esp. p. 27.

79. "Lewis Hershey to Herbert Lehman," January 30, 1946, box 85, series A, part 1, CCWR, DG 025, SCPC. See also Bush, *Two Kingdoms, Two Loyalties*, 18, 72–73; Taylor, *Acts of Conscience*, chap. 3. On Roosevelt, see Paul Kennedy, *The Parliament of Man: The Past, Present and Future of the United Nations* (New York: Random House, 2006), 25.

80. The UN Charter is reprinted in Thomas G. Weiss and Sam Daws, *The Oxford Handbook on the United Nations* (New York: Oxford University Press, 2007), 736–55. The quote here is from the preamble on p. 736.

81. Taylor, *Acts of Conscience*, 22, 34. For examples of Draft Board decisions regarding CO status, see box 19, series A, part 1, CCWR, DG 025, SCPC.

82. Morse, *New Windsor Center*, 37; M. Gingerich, *Service for Peace*, chap. XXI; "M.R. Zigler to Paul French," March 22, 1944, M. R. Zigler Correspondence, 1944, box 20, series A, part 1, CCWR, DG 025, SCPC.

83. These figures are a little different in various secondary sources. See Eller, *Conscientious Objectors*, 28–30, 49–50; L. Weiss, *Ten Years of Brethren Service*, 14; M. Gingerich, *Service for Peace*, 1, 90, 452; Morse, *New Windsor Center*, 23–24; Taylor, *Acts of Conscience*, 35; Bush, *Two Kingdoms, Two Loyalties*, esp. chap. 3. For additional context see Joseph Kip Kosek, *Acts of Conscience: Christian Nonviolence and Modern American Democracy* (New York: Columbia University Press, 2009), chap. 5.

84. Durnbaugh, "Fight Against War," 235; Mitchell L. Robinson, "Conscience and Conscription in a Free Society: U.S. Civilian Public Service," in Brock and Socknat, *Challenge to Mars*, 316–17; Taylor, *Acts of Conscience*, 49–50; Bush, *Two Kingdoms, Two Loyalties*, 75–76; M. Gingerich, *Service for Peace*, chap. XXI. Camp costs are also discussed in E. Leroy Dakin, memo dated December 29, 1943, Correspondence of Albert Gaeddert, box 24, series A, part 1, CCWR, DG 025, SCPC; "Paul French to M.R. Zigler," November 10, 1943, M. R. Zigler Correspondence, July–December 1943, box 20, series A, part 1, CCWR, DG 025, SCPC. On Mennonite costs specifically, see Mennonite Central Committee, "Relief in Action: Europe," box 21, series A, part 1, CCWR, DG 025, SCPC. In the same archival collection, see *A Year of Civilian Public Service* (Akron, PA: MCC, 1942).

85. Bush, *Two Kingdoms, Two Loyalties*, 72–74.

86. M. R. Zigler, "Our Testimony of 1942–43," February 10, 1943, M. R. Zigler Correspondence, December 1942–June 1943, box 19, series A, part 1, CCWR, DG 025, SCPC.

87. Taylor, *Acts of Conscience*, 43–44.

88. M. Gingerich, *Service for Peace*, 276.

89. "The Rural Life School," *Gospel Messenger*, n.d., box 39, series C1, part 1, CCWR, DG 025, SCPC.

90. M. R. Zigler, "Memorandum to Men in Brethren CPS Camps," January 29, 1943, M. R. Zigler Correspondence, December 1942–June 1943, box 19, series A, part 1, CCWR, DG 025, SCPC.

91. Robinson, "Conscience and Conscription," 316; Durnbaugh, *Pragmatic Prophet*, 136; L. Weiss, *Ten Years of Brethren Service*, 16–17, 21–24, 27; Eller, *Conscientious Objectors*, 31. For samples of documents related to CPS and the seagoing cowboys see Reiff Miller, "Civilian Public Service Unit."

92. "Paul French to Col. Lewis F. Kosch," SCPC. CPS camp directors had to approve men's applications to become cattle handlers with the BSC. Applications can be found in "UNRRA: Selection of Cattle Men (Questions)," box 85, series A, part 1, CCWR, DG 025, SCPC. For a personal description of the application process, see Gerhard Friesen, "Observations on My Trip to Poland," *Mennonite*, March 5, 1946.

93. "Hershey to Lehman," January 30, 1946, box 85, series A, part 1, CCWR, DG 025, SCPC. The change of date to October 1944 is confirmed in "Lewis H. Beckford to Charles Brasharen," May 1, 1946, CPS no. 24 Washington County, MD: Director, box 39, series C1, part 1, CCWR, DG 025, SCPC. See also M. Gingerich, *Service for Peace*, 187–89. Gingerich refers to a June 1944 cutoff date rather than an October cutoff date.

94. "Albert M. Gaeddert (MCC) to Paul French," January 19, 1946, UNRRA: Cattle Reserves, box 85, series A, part 1, CCWR, DG 025, SCPC.

95. "Edwin R. Henson to Col. Lewis Kosch," April 5, 1946, UNRRA: Employment of COs as Cattleboat Attendants, box 106, series B (formerly series G), part 1, CCWR, DG 025, SCPC. See also Mitchell L. Robinson, "'Healing the Bitterness of War and Destruction': CPS and Foreign Service," *Quaker History* 85, no. 2 (1996): 41.

96. E. Yoder, "Seagoing Cowboys from Stark County"; Robinson, "Conscience and Conscription," 312. See also "Cattleboat Attendants Approved by Selective Service (as of June 10, 1946)," 1–6, UNRRA: Cattle Reserves, box 85, series A, part 1, CCWR, DG 025, SCPC.

97. "CPS Unit Number 152-01," Civilian Public Service, https://civilianpublicservice.org/camps/152/1. On the religious background of COs see also Durnbaugh, *Pragmatic Prophet*, 144–45; Reiff Miller, "Civilian Public Service Unit"; M. Gingerich, *Service for Peace*, 188.

98. Anne M. Yoder, "Seagoing Cowboys," SCPC, December 12, 2012, http://www.swarthmore.edu/library/peace/conscientiousobjection/CPSResources/SeagoingCowboys.html.

99. Taylor, *Acts of Conscience*, 108; M. Gingerich, *Service for Peace*, 384–86; Durnbaugh, *Pragmatic Prophet*, 133; Robinson, "Conscience and Conscription," 324, 326; Eller, *Conscientious Objectors*, 72. For an outline of discharge procedures for CPS men, see "J.N. Weaver to Benjamin Bushong," March 28, 1946, UNRRA: Cattle Handlers, box 85, series A, part 1, CCWR, DG 025, SCPC.

100. Henry A. Fast, "Present MCC Evaluation of CPS," April 24, 1943, General Correspondence, August 31, 1941–January 22, 1945, box 21, series A, part 1, CCWR, DG 025, SCPC.

101. Wilbur Nachtigall, "Directors' Conference," *Pike View Peace News*, September–October 1945, from Mennonite Library and Archives, Bethel College, North

Newton, KS. This was the internal newspaper of the CPS Camp #5 in Colorado Springs, Colorado.

102. *Heifer Moos*, August 27, 1946, Heifer Letters, 1946–55, folder 1, box 3, series 4/1/6, HP, BHLA. Though the experiment started with thirty-six men, it ended with thirty-two.

103. Ancel Keys et al., *The Biology of Human Starvation* (Minneapolis: University of Minnesota Press, 1950), 14–15.

104. Leah M. Kalm and Richard D. Semba, "They Starved So That Others Be Better Fed: Remembering Ancel Keys and the Minnesota Experiment," *Journal of Nutrition* 135, no. 6 (2005): 1352.

105. *Heifer Moos*, BHLA. According to the note in *Heifer Moos*, Lutz's article first appeared in a Methodist Youth Fellowship paper called CONCERN (the upper case is used in the original reference).

106. Keys et al., *Biology of Human Starvation*; Harold Steere Guetzkow and Paul Hoover Bowman, *Men and Hunger: A Psychological Manual for Relief Workers* (Elgin, IL: Brethren Publishing House, 1946). See also Kreider, *Cup of Cold Water*, 18.

107. M. R. Zigler, "From the Sponsors," in Guetzkow and Bowman, *Men and Hunger*, 9.

108. Guetzkow and Bowman, *Men and Hunger*, 9.

109. Guetzkow and Bowman, *Men and Hunger*, 12.

110. Keys et al., *Biology of Human Starvation*, 13.

111. "Irwin Abrams to Julia Branson et al.," January 16, 1945, Relief and Rehabilitation, box 77, series A, part 1, CCWR, DG 025, SCPC. On the Friends' withdrawal from the administration of CPS, see Eller, *Conscientious Objectors*, 68.

112. American Friends Service Committee, "Foreign Service Policy," January 1945, Relief and Rehabilitation, box 77, series A, part 1, CCWR, DG 025, SCPC. On the Friends' position, see also "Paul J. Furnas to 'All Men in Friends' CPS,'" January 24, 1946, section 1, box 49, series F, part 1, CCWR, DG 025, SCPC.

113. Melvin Gingerich, "'Two Weeks at Sea' (Draft)," Speeches and Manuscripts, folder 13, box 75, MGP, HM1-973, Hist. MSS 1-129, MCA.

114. For biographical details about Melvin, see Owen Gingerich, "The Return of the Seagoing Cowboy: Horses Afloat and Books Astray," *American Scholar* 68, no. 4 (1999): 71–81. The questionnaires that the seagoing cowboys completed are available in the Melvin G. Gingerich collection at the Mennonite Church Archives in Elkhart, Indiana. See Completed Questionnaires, folder 5, box 76, MGP, Hist. MSS 1-129, MCA. The questionnaires number in the hundreds.

115. O. Gingerich, "Return of the Seagoing Cowboy," 72.

116. "J.N. Byler to Melvin Gingerich," letters from September 25, 1945, and December 5, 1945, Correspondence, folder 2, box 75, MGP, Hist. MSS 1-129, MCA.

117. "Final Directions for Gingerich-Oswald Crew," folder 2, box 75, MGP, Hist. MSS 1-129, MCA; Melvin Gingerich, "Cowboys Going to Sea," *Mennonite Weekly Review*, June 18, 1946, Speeches and Manuscripts, folder 13, box 75, MGP, HM1-973, MSS 1-129, MCA. The Gingerich and Oswald crews were combined for logistical reasons, according to Reiff Miller, private correspondence with author, January 23, 2024.

118. "Miscellaneous Items," *Gospel Messenger*, May 25, 1946.

119. "Brethren Fellowship Crew." This article is mainly about the interracial cowboy crew that sailed to Poland in 1946, but the reflections in it on the place of Christianity in the livestock program are broader.

120. M. Gingerich, "'Two Weeks at Sea' (Draft)," MCA.

121. "Melvin Gingerich to 'Dear Fellows' from," May 21, 1946, Correspondence September 1945 to January 1946, folder 2, box 75, MGP, Hist. MSS 1–129, MCA.

122. Nelle Morton, general secretary, Fellowship of Christian Churchmen, "to the fellowship cattle boat crew," June 8, 1946, General Correspondence, 1946, series 1, part 2, folder 273, Scan 7, Howard Kester Papers, Coll 03834, Wilson Special Collections Library, UNC.

123. "Final Directions," folder 2, box 75, MGP, Hist. MSS 1–129, MCA.

124. "Paul Erb to Melvin Gingerich," April 29,1946, Correspondence A to G, 1946, folder 4, box 75, MGP, Hist. MSS 1–129, MCA.

125. Peggy Reiff Miller relayed to me that an administrator at the New Windsor Center heard one of the first outbound groups of men refer to themselves as "cowboys." Reiff Miller, private correspondence with author, January 23, 2024. A Polish journalist has speculated that the term "seagoing cowboy" was simply more attractive, from a recruiting perspective, than the appellation "cattleman." See Andrzej Fedorowicz, "Morscy kowboje przybywają do Gdańska," *Polityka*, March 1–7, 2017, 57.

126. Katie Nodjimbadem, "The Lesser-Known History of African-American Cowboys," *Smithsonian Magazine*, February 13, 2017, https://www.smithsonianmag.com/history/lesser-known-history-african-american-cowboys-180962144/. On American cowboys, see also Jacqueline M. Moore, *Cow Boys and Cattle Men: Class and Masculinities on the Texas Frontier, 1865–1900* (New York: NYU Press, 2009). In 2005 the United States Senate decreed the fourth Saturday of July "National Day of the American Cowboy."

127. Nodjimbadem, "Lesser-Known History."

128. "Cowboy Education (Pre-Sailing Study)," Publicity, 1940s, folder 3, box 2, series 4/1/6, POW, BHLA.

129. For more on Protestant masculinities (and on the feminization of Christianity), see Yvonne Maria Werner, ed., *Christian Masculinity: Men and Religion in Northern Europe in the 19th and 20th Centuries* (Leuven, Belgium: Leuven University Press, 2011).

130. "Herbert H. Lehman to Brethren Service Committee," *Gospel Messenger*, March 20, 1946. See also Amanda Melanie Bundy, "There Was a Man of UNRRA: Internationalism, Humanitarianism, and the Early Cold War in Europe, 1943–1947" (PhD diss., Ohio State University, 2017), 1.

4. Working Animals as Humanitarian Aid

1. Hannah Velten, *Cow* (London: Reaktion Books, 2007), 10.
2. Velten, *Cow*, 17.
3. Cynthia Clark Northrup, ed., *Encyclopedia of World Trade: From Ancient Times to the Present* (New York: Routledge, 2015), 2:588.
4. Ann Norton Greene, *Horses at Work: Harnessing Power in Industrial America* (Cambridge, MA: Harvard University Press, 2008), 28.

5. Velten, *Cow*, 7, 69.

6. Tom Scott-Smith, *On an Empty Stomach: Two Hundred Years of Disaster Relief* (Ithaca, NY: Cornell University Press, 2020), 131. See also Maggie Black, *Children First: The Story of UNICEF, Past and Present* (New York: Oxford University Press, 1996), 64.

7. I am indebted to Yelena Abdullayeva for drawing my attention to the myth's relevance to this story.

8. "National Sides," European Central Bank, accessed August 12, 2024, https://www.ecb.europa.eu/euro/coins/2euro/html/index.en.html.

9. Ian Manners, "Global Europa: Mythology of the European Union in World Politics," *Journal of Common Market Studies* 48, no. 1 (2010): 68–70. See also Sarah Dejaegher, "Europa and the Bull: The Significance of the Myth in Modern Europe," *New Federalist*, June 14, 2011, https://www.thenewfederalist.eu/Europa-and-the-bull-The-significance-of-the-myth-in-modern-Europe,4280?lang=fr. On the myth and contemporary Poland, see Beata Klocek Di Biasio and Bohdan Michalski, "The Myth of Europe in Art and European Identities," *Politeja* 5, no. 44 (2016): 1–31.

10. Leo R. Ward, "Brethren Heifers for Relief," *Gospel Messenger*, March 22, 1947.

11. Frank Trentmann, "Coping with Shortage: The Problem of Food Security and Global Visions of Coordination, c. 1890s–1950," in *Food and Conflict in Europe in the Age of the Two World Wars*, eds. Frank Trentmann and Flemming Just (London: Palgrave Macmillan, 2006), 34.

12. The expression "is fun to think with" normally appears in reference to animals or to food; I adapt it to refer to milk specifically. See Deborah Valenze, *Milk: A Local and Global History* (New Haven, CT: Yale University Press, 2011), ix. The phrase "gospel of milk" in the subtitle comes from Valenze, *Milk*, 249.

13. Hannah Velten, *Milk: A Global History* (New York: Reaktion Books, 2010), 10, 13.

14. Valenze, *Milk*, chap. 7.

15. Valenze, *Milk*, 148.

16. Valenze, *Milk*, 148. For a feminist criticism of the term "dairy cattle," see Carol J. Adams, "Feminized Protein: Meaning, Representations, and Implications," in *Making Milk: The Past, Present, and Future of Our Primary Food*, eds. Mathilde Cohen and Yoriko Otomo (London: Bloomsbury, 2017), 26.

17. Valenze, Milk, 235.

18. Kendra Smith-Howard, *Pure and Modern Milk: An Environmental History since 1900* (New York: Oxford University Press, 2013), 5.

19. Mathilde Cohen, "Regulating Milk: Women and Cows in France and the United States," *American Journal of Comparative Law* 65, no. 3 (2017): 475.

20. This section is adapted from Velten, *Milk*, 66, 71, 88, 91; Smith-Howard, *Pure and Modern Milk*, 157.

21. M. Cohen, "Regulating Milk," 475–76. The association of milk with the word "purity" is made in many ways and contexts. On this, see Smith-Howard, *Pure and Modern Milk*, 8.

22. The terms come from Velten, *Milk*, 7.

23. Smith-Howard, *Pure and Modern Milk*, 34.

24. Matthew Lloyd Adams, "Herbert Hoover and the Organization of the American Relief Effort in Poland (1919–1923)," *European Journal of American Studies* 4, no. 2 (2009): 9. For the place of milk in British Quakers' relief efforts after World War I, see

Nerissa Kalee Aksamit, "Training Friends and Overseas Relief: The Friends Ambulance Unit and the Friends Relief Service, 1939 to 1948" (PhD diss., West Virginia University, 2019), 114–15.

25. League of Nations, *Final Report of the Mixed Committee of the League of Nations on the Relation of Nutrition to Health, Agriculture and Economic Policy* (Geneva: League of Nations, 1937), 87. The italics appear in the original report. On the League, see Patricia Clavin, *Securing the World Economy: The Reinvention of the League of Nations, 1930–1926* (New York: Oxford University Press, 2013); Peter Becker and Natasha Wheatley, eds., *Remaking Central Europe: The League of Nations and the Former Habsburg Lands* (New York: Oxford University Press, 2020).

26. Abigail Woods, "Breeding Cows, Maximizing Milk: British Veterinarians and the Livestock Economy, 1930–50," in *Healing the Herds: Essays on Livestock Economies and the Globalization of Veterinary Medicine*, eds. Karen Brown and Daniel Gilfoyle (Athens: Ohio University Press, 2010), 60.

27. Velten, *Cow*, 160–61. For a description of dairy cows' lives in the context of the modern dairy industry, see Greta Gaard, "Critical Ecofeminism," in Cohen and Otomo, *Making Milk*, 217.

28. Nick Cullather, "The Foreign Policy of the Calorie," *American Historical Review* 112, no. 2 (2007): 354. For an overview of early nutritional science, see James Vernon, *Hunger: A Modern History* (Cambridge, MA: Belknap Press of Harvard University, 2007), chap. 4.

29. Michael Bresalier, "From Healthy Cows to Healthy Humans: Integrated Approaches to World Hunger, c. 1930–1965," in *Animals and the Shaping of Modern Medicine: One Health and Its Histories*, ed. Abigail Woods et al. (London: Palgrave Macmillan, 2018), 123; Scott-Smith, *On an Empty Stomach*, chap. 5; Vernon, *Hunger*, 90.

30. Valenze, *Milk*, 251. See also 253, 289.

31. Amy L. S. Staples, "To Win the Peace: The Food and Agriculture Organization, Sir John Boyd Orr, and the World Food Board Proposals," *Peace and Change* 28, no. 4 (2003): 497.

32. Peter J. Atkins, "Fattening Children or Fattening Farmers? School Milk in Britain, 1921–1941," *Economic History Review* 58, no. 1 (2005): 64.

33. Thomas Webb et al., "'We Cows Are in a Very Serious Predicament': Constructions of Land Girls and Cattle in Britain in the Second World War," *Gender and History* 34, no. 1 (2022): 181–82. On the provision of milk to schoolchildren, see Atkins, "Fattening Children or Fattening Farmers," 57–78. See also Chris Otter, "Milk in Motion: Logistical Geographies in Twentieth-Century Britain," *Global Food History* 9, no. 1 (2023): 48.

34. Dan West, "Hope for the World," *Gospel Messenger*, September 11, 1948. This article makes reference to a meeting between West and Orr in the fall of 1946, in the middle of the Heifer Project's work with UNRRA. Thanks to Peggy Reiff Miller for drawing my attention to this article. The description of Orr as a "crusading nutritionist" comes from Staples, "To Win the Peace," 500.

35. Valenze, *Milk*, 254. See also *So Bold an Aim: Ten Years of International Co-Operation Toward Freedom from Want* (Rome: Food and Agriculture Organization of the United Nations, 1955), 35.

36. Valenze, *Milk*, 254. For a postwar celebration of milk, see Frank G. Boudreau, "Nutrition in War and Peace" (1947), repr., *Milbank Quarterly* 83, no. 4 (2005): 609–23.

This paper was presented at the Conference of State and Provincial Health Authorities of North America in Quebec City, May 21, 1947.

37. Patrick J. Houlihan, "Renovating Christian Charity: Global Catholicism, the Save the Children Fund, and Humanitarianism During the First World War," *Past and Present* 250, no. 1 (2021): 205; Bruno Cabanes, *The Great War and the Origins of Humanitarianism, 1918–1924* (Cambridge: Cambridge University Press, 2014), 298.

38. Herbert Hoover, "Can Europe's Children Be Saved?" (address, National Committee on Food for the Small Democracies, New York, October 19, 1941), 1.

39. United Nations Relief and Rehabilitation Administration, *Out of Chaos* (Washington, DC: UNRRA, 1945). On postwar concern about children's health, see also Jacob Darwin Hamblin, "The Vulnerability of Nations: Food Security in the Aftermath of World War II," *Global Environment* 10 (2012): 47.

40. "Report by Dr. Henry Holle to Brig. Charles Drury, 'Field Visit to Provinces of Cracow and Katowice,'" November 15, 1945, Health Country Mission Reports: Poland, S-1448-0000-0030-00001, p. 8, UNA. See also Józef Łaptos, *Humanitaryzm i polityka: Pomoc UNRRA dla Polski i polskich uchodźców w latach 1944–1947* (Kraków: Wyd. Naukowe Uniwersytetu Pedagogicznego, 2018), 372–73.

41. John Vachon, "Poland—Gdańsk, Fresh Milk on the Dock," S-0800-0009-0005-00005, UNRRA 4459, UNA.

42. Dan West, "Heifers for Relief: A Challenge," *Gospel Messenger*, July 28, 1945.

43. "Answering Your Questions Regarding Heifers for Relief," on or after January 1948, Relief Work (FOR): Brethren Service Committee and Heifer Project, 1945–48, box 13, series E, JNS, DG 117, SCPC.

44. Heifer Project Committee, *Heifers for Relief: A Primer* (Nappanee, IN: Heifer Project Committee, n.d. but the book refers to the war as ongoing), box 85, series A, part 1, CCWR, DG 025, SCPC. The average costs of a heifer come from "Greenbelt Youngsters Buy Heifer for Needy Children," *Evening Star*, July 15, 1946. A copy of *Heifers for Relief* is also in Clippings and Releases 3, 1940s–1960s, folder 9, box 2, series 4/1/6, HP, BHLA. See also "World Brotherhood at Work, Notes on BSC Relief Work from Interview with Ben Bushong," Brethren Service Committee, S-1268-0000-0039, p. 65, UNA.

45. "Basis of Requirements for Cows," MRiRR, 2/162/0/2.4/506, p. 56, AAN.

46. On cattle breeds, see "Answering Your Questions," SCPC.

47. Philipp Weintraub, "Reseeding Live-Stock Herds in Liberated Europe," *Baltimore Sun*, June 28, 1945, 12. A Polish short film celebrating tractor donations appears as Polska Kronika Filmowa, *Dostawy UNRRA—Wyładunek w porcie* (Wytwórnia Filmowa Wojska Polskiego, 1945), accessed March 23, 2023, Filmoteka Narodowa—Instytut Audiowizualny (hereafter FINA), http://repozytorium.fn.org.pl/?q=en/node/4545.

48. A. Pępkowski, "Dostawy zwierząt UNRRA dla Polski," *Medycyna Weterynaryjna* 3, no. 6 (1947): 399. See also Marek Żak, "Sytuacja aprowizacyjna Legnicy w latach 1945–1945," *Szkice Legnickie* 36 (2015): 160, 166–68.

49. George Woodbridge, *UNRRA: The History of the United Nations Relief and Rehabilitation Administration* (New York: Oxford University Press, 1950), 1:488. On cattle breeds, see "M.R. Zigler to 'to Whom It May Concern' at UNRRA," 1945, Brethren Service Committee, S-1267-0000-0083-00001, pp. 151–52, UNA; "A.G.

Wilder to T.A. Pato," October 31, 1946, file 945, S-0527-1105, UNA; Otter, "Milk in Motion," 49.

50. Zigler, interviewed by North, Association for Diplomatic Studies and Training Foreign Affairs Oral History Collection Foreign Assistance Series.

51. Robert Lintner, *UNRRA Livestock Program Historical Report*, 1947, UNRRA selected records AG-018-040, accession 2015.245.1, record group RG-67.050, S-1021-0009-03, p. 78, USHMM.

52. "M.R. Zigler to 'to Whom It May Concern,'" 151–52, UNA.

53. Lintner, *UNRRA Livestock Program Historical Report*, 114, USHMM.

54. Bresalier, "From Healthy Cows to Healthy Humans," 132.

55. See Gertrude Samuels, "The Unheard Cry of the World's Children," *New York Times Magazine*, October 12, 1947, repr. in US Congress, *Proceedings and Debates*, July 26, 1947, to December 19, 1947, 80th Cong., 1st sess., *Congressional Record* 93, part 12: A4620.

56. Piotr Woltanowski, Andrzej Wincewicz, and Stanisław Sulkowski, "Protection of Children's Human Rights and Health: A Legacy of Julian Kramsztyk, Janusz Korczak, and Ludwik Rajchman," *Global Pediatric Health* 5 (2018): 5; Davide Rodogno, *Night on Earth: A History of International Humanitarianism in the Near East, 1918–1930* (Cambridge: Cambridge University Press, 2021), 41–42.

57. UNICEF first used the general UN logo before adopting the cup-of-milk logo; the logo changed again in the 1960s. See Martina Tomassini and Ruthia Yi, "UNICEF: History of a Logo," UNICEF, accessed April 28, 2022, https://www.unicef.org/about-unicef/unicef-logo-history. On the impetus behind the creation of UNICEF, see UNICEF, *Today's Children—Tomorrow's Citizens* (Lake Success, NY: UNESCO, 1948). See also Angela Villani, "Children in the Development Debate: The Role of UNICEF from 1946 to the First UN Development Decade," *Journal of World History* 32, no. 3 (2021): 410.

58. Not all recipients agreed to drink powdered milk, however. See Maggie Black, *Children and the Nations: The Story of UNICEF* (Port Sydney, Australia: UNICEF, 1986), 44, http://www.cf-hst.net/unicef-temp/Child-Nation/Child-Nation-contents.htm.

59. UNICEF, *Today's Children*, 3. See also Darel McConkey, *Food and People: A UNESCO Project* (New York: Manhattan Publishing, 1951), 8; Black, *Children and the Nations*, 47.

60. See Scott-Smith, *On an Empty Stomach*, 131.

61. "Basis of Requirements for Cows," MRiRR, 2/162/0/2.4/506, p. 55, AAN.

62. Departament Ekonomiczny, Wyd. Obrotu Zewnętrznego, "UNRRA w Polsce," Dostawy UNRRA, MRiRR, 2/162/0/2.4/511, p. 20, AAN.

63. On the history of horses in pre–World War II Poland, see Joanna Gellner, "Zauważone!—Zmiana stosunku do koni w Krakowie na przełomie XIX i XX wieku," in *Miasta/Zwierzęta*, ed. Anna Jaroszuk, Igor Piotrowski, and Karolina Wróbel-Bardzik, vol. 8 of *Almanach antropologiczny: Communicare* (Warsaw: Wydawnictwa Uniwersytetu Warszawskiego, 2021), 90–101.

64. On horse physiology, see Greene, *Horses at Work*, 16–22.

65. Greene, *Horses at Work*, 5.

66. "Provisional Report on Agriculture and Food in Poland," file 1032, S-0527-1068, p. 10, UNA; "Hodowla koni w Polsce," *Dziennik Bałtycki* 156 (1946): 3.

67. "A.G. Wilder to T.A. Pato," October 31, 1946, UNA.

NOTES TO PAGES 88-91   241

68. "J.W. Kent, Regional Delegate, to E. Wróblewski, Chief Distribution Division," July 2, 1946, Monthly Reports, 1946, S-1400-0000-0029, p. 21, UNA.
69. On horse numbers, see "Provisional Report," 10, UNA; "Statement Given to UNRA by Stanisław Mikołajczyk," file 78-B3L4, S-0527-1073, UNA; "UNRRA Mission to Poland," February 1, 1947, Raporty misji UNRRA, MRiRR, 2/162/0/2.4/506, p. 119, AAN; "The Impact of UNRRA on the Polish Economy," September 1946, Raporty misji UNRRA dotyczące wpływu dostaw UNRRA na godspodarkę Polski, MRiRR, 2/162/0/2.4/509, AAN.
70. "Provisional Report," 9, UNA. The same statistics are presented in Eastern European Division Loan Department, "Preliminary Paper No. 6 for the Working Party on the Polish Loan Application" (International Bank for Reconstruction and Development, May 26, 1947), https://documents1.worldbank.org/curated/en/558411468095985925/pdf/multi-page.pdf, 5.
71. Charles Drury, "UNRRA in Poland," *The Empire Club of Canada Addresses*, April 24, 1947, 331–44, https://speeches.empireclub.org/details.asp?ID=61185; Łaptos, *Humanitaryzm i polityka*, 398.
72. Woodbridge, *UNRRA*, 2:221. Woodbridge also discusses tractors in *UNRRA*, 1:480–87.
73. At UNRRA's request early in 1947, the Mennonite Central Committee formed a tractor unit; it was formally called the Unit for Tractor Operator Training in Poland. The job of the unit was to train people how to use the tractors that UNRRA had already sent. See Zygmunt Dulczewski and Andrzej Kwilecki, eds., *Pamiętniki osadników Ziem Odzyskanych*, 2nd ed. (Poznań: Wyd. Poznańskie, 1970), 296; Art Jost, "Tractor Unit to Poland," *Civilian Public Service Bulletin* 6, no. 5 (1947), 2. This bulletin was a weekly publication of the Mennonite Civilian Public Service.
74. Irving Swerdlow, "UNRRA and Poland," November 24, 1945, Bureau of Areas, Poland, S-1242-0000-0124-00003, p. 29, UNA.
75. "Reports—Field Trips Dr. Wilder, A.G. Wilder to M.E. Hays," September 3, 1946, UNRRA Subject Files, file 72, S-0527-1107, UNA.
76. For a history of horse breeds in Poland, see Ministerstwo Obrony Narodowej, *Koń i dogląd nad nim* (Warsaw: Wojskowy Instytut Naukowo-Wydawniczy, 1946). On horses in medieval Poland, see Marcin Henryk Gapski, *Koń w kulturze Polskiego średniowiecza* (Poznań: Wyd. Nauka i Innowacje, 2014). On horses today, see Magdalena Anita Gajewska, "Polskie narracje o dobrostanie koni," in *Dobrostan zwierząt: Różne perspektywy*, ed. Hanna Mamzer (Gdańsk: Katedra, 2018), 321–44.
77. "Reports—Field Trips Dr. Wilder," UNA. On UNRRA's support for artificial breeding programs, see Eastern European Division Loan Department, "Preliminary Paper No. 6." On cattle breeding programs in Poland see Marian Kuczaj, "Przeszłość, teraźniejszość i przyszłość na Dolnym Śląsku," *Przegląd Hodowlany* 10 (2011): 18–22.
78. "Report on Field Trip, 24 January," January 31, 1946, UNRRA—Poland Mission, 1944–49, Requirements Branch, file 7, S-0527-1064, UNA.
79. "Reports—Field Trips Dr. Wilder," UNA.
80. "Report on Field Trip, 24 January," UNA. On Vachon's photography mission, see also the letter from John Vachon to Penny, January 24, 1946, in *Poland, 1946: The Photographs and Letters of John Vachon*, ed. Ann Vachon, with an introduction by Brian Moore (Washington, DC: Smithsonian Institution Press, 1995), 20.
81. "Report on Field Trip, 24 January," UNA.

82. Weintraub, "Reseeding Live-Stock Herds," 12; Departament Ekonomiczny, Wyd. Obrotu Zewnętrznego, "Uwagi o planie importu rolniczego," Dostawy UNRRA, MRiRR, 2/162/0/2.4/511, p. 125, AAN.
83. Lintner, *UNRRA Livestock Program Historical Report*, 77, USHMM.
84. "Report on Field Trip, 24 January," UNA.
85. Lintner, *UNRRA Livestock Program Historical Report*, 77, 113, USHMM. Lintner writes that 65 percent of the horses were mares, but another UNRRA document puts that number at 80 percent. See "The Impact of UNRRA on the Polish Economy," MRiRR, 2/162/0/2.4/509, p. 14, AAN.
86. Woodbridge, *UNRRA*, 1:488–89. On horse breeds sent by UNRRA, see also A. Pępkowski, "Dostawy zwierząt UNRRA dla Polski," *Medycyna Weterynaryjna* 3, no. 5 (1947): 305.
87. Lintner, *UNRRA Livestock Program Historical Report*, 137, USHMM.
88. "Reports—Field Trips Dr. Wilder," UNA.

5. The Making of "Relief Animals"

1. Lizzie Collingham, *The Taste of War: World War Two and the Battle for Food* (London: Allen Lane, 2011), 78, 87–88.
2. Kendra Smith-Howard, *Pure and Modern Milk: An Environmental History since 1900* (New York: Oxford University Press, 2013), 6.
3. Robert Lintner, *UNRRA Livestock Program Historical Report*, 1947, UNRRA selected records AG-018-040, accession 2015.245.1, record group RG-67.050, S-1021-0009-03, p. 16, USHMM.
4. Lintner, *UNRRA Livestock Program Historical Report*, 97, USHMM. One of the consequences of a surplus horse population was a rise in horse meat production. UNRRA sent Canadian and American horse meat as part of its aid packages, including to Poland. See "Alta. and Sask. Get Horse Meat Packing Plants," *Coleman Journal*, August 23, 1945; "6 Plants Pack Horse Meat," *New York Sun*, August 29, 1946; Charles Grutzner, "Flesh Being Canned Here," *New York Times*, September 26, 1946; Morley Murray, "Horse Meat for the Hungry," *Maclean's Magazine*, February 1, 1947.
5. The purchasing procedure is outlined in Lintner, *UNRRA Livestock Program Historical Report*, 76–80, USHMM.
6. E. Wiszniewski, "Notatka," Inwentarz żywy z dostaw UNRRA, MRiRR, 2/162/0/2.4/517, pp. 3–4, AAN. Wiszniewski's claims are repeated in the following article: Benon Gaziński and Bogusław Wanot, "Działalność UNRRA i jej pomoc dla rolnictwa w Polsce," *Rocznik Muzeum Narodowego Rolnictwa w Szreniawie* 19 (1993): 20.
7. Lintner, *UNRRA Livestock Program Historical Report*, 83–84, 136, USHMM.
8. "Ticks Tie Up UNRRA," *New York Times*, February 17, 1946.
9. On the inland movement of animals, see Lintner, *UNRRA Livestock Program Historical Report*, 19–21, 80–82, 86, 91–94, USHMM.
10. USDA, "Regulations Governing the Inspection, Humane Treatment, and Safe Transport of Animals for Export," 1944, Brethren Service Committee, S-1267-0000-0083-00001, UNA. This legislation also governed space and ventilation requirements for animals aboard ships and general care standards (including the need for animal attendants, though the specific ratio of men to animals was not provided; section

91.17 on p. 6 says that the number should be "sufficient"). On inspections, see also United States Bureau of Animal Industry, *Report of the Chief of the Bureau of Animal Industry, Agricultural Research Administration* (1945), 75.

11. On inspecting procedures, see Lintner, *UNRRA Livestock Program Historical Report*, 82–87, USHMM.

12. Letter from Ralph M. Delk, "Heifer News," May 14, 1947, Heifer Letters, 1946–55, folder 1, box 3, series 4/1/6, HP, BHLA.

13. Lintner, *UNRRA Livestock Program Historical Report*, 86, 135, USHMM.

14. Lintner, *UNRRA Livestock Program Historical Report*, 82–87, 133–35, USHMM.

15. Lintner, *UNRRA Livestock Program Historical Report*, 136, USHMM.

16. *A Scrapbook of Cowboy Memories*, 1994, From the Memories of Roger and Olive Roop, December 1985, folder 14, box 1, JEN, Hist. MSS 1893, MCA.

17. Lintner, *UNRRA Livestock Program Historical Report*, 22–25, USHMM.

18. For a description of sick animals arriving at the port of Newport News, see Lintner, *UNRRA Livestock Program Historical Report*, 154–56, USHMM.

19. Lintner, *UNRRA Livestock Program Historical Report*, 88, USHMM.

20. George Woodbridge, *UNRRA: The History of the United Nations Relief and Rehabilitation Administration* (New York: Oxford University Press, 1950), 2:219.

21. Lintner, *UNRRA Livestock Program Historical Report*, 80, USHMM.

22. "Horses in War," *National Humane Review*, December 1939.

23. The American Red Star gave assistance to England's Royal Society for the Protection of Animals, for example. See Janet M. Davis, *The Gospel of Kindness: Animal Welfare and the Making of Modern America* (New York: Oxford University Press, 2016), 209–11; "Foreign War Animal Relief," *National Humane Review*, July 1940; "Aid to Britain," *National Humane Review*, December 1941; "The History of American Humane's Rescue Team," American Humane, July 8, 2022, https://www.americanhumane.org/fact-sheet/the-history-of-american-humanes-red-star-rescue-team/. Red Star also intervened in animal care during rail strikes in the US in May 1946. See "American Red Star Animal Relief Saves Livestock," *National Humane Review*, August 1946.

24. US Congress, Senate, Committee on Armed Services, *Hearing Before a Subcommittee of the Committee on Armed Services United States Senate*, 80th Cong., 1st sess., 1947, 108.

25. "Mr. Norgord's Findings," *National Humane Review*, April 1946; *Hearing Before a Subcommittee*, 111.

26. James M. Ross, "Kindness and Comfort Paramount in Shipping Horses and Dairy Cattle Overseas to Replace Losses in Farm Animals," *National Humane Review*, April 1946. On veterinary care and military-related animal shipments during World War II, see AMEDD Center of History and Heritage, "Transportation of Animals," August 30, 2022, https://achh.army.mil/history/book-wwii-vetservicewwii-chapter15.

27. Ross, "Kindness and Comfort Paramount."

28. On Christian elements in American animal welfare, see Davis, *Gospel of Kindness*, 21, 219.

29. John C. MacFarlane, "Heifers for Hope," *Our Dumb Animals*, April 1968; John C. MacFarlane, "Livestock Conservation—Part I," *Our Dumb Animals*, June 1966. This paper was published jointly by the Massachusetts Society for the Prevention of Cruelty to Animals and the American Humane Education Society.

30. "Massachusetts S.P.C.A. Sponsors Step Ramp," *Our Dumb Animals*, September 1966.

31. James M. Ross, "Horses Under UNRRA for Overseas," *Our Dumb Animals*, November 1946.

32. Ross, "Horses Under UNRRA for Overseas."

33. "Federal Laws Urged for Livestock Safety," *National Humane Review*, January 1948. The rules governing export animal transport appear here: USDA, "Regulations Governing the Inspection," UNA.

34. C. P. Norgord, "American Humane Association, Local SPCAs, Act to Protect Animals Shipped Overseas," *National Humane Review*, August 1946.

35. "UNRRA Shipments," *Our Dumb Animals*, December 1946.

36. The Contributed Supplies Branch was established in June 1944 and headed for a time (at least until the spring of 1945) by one Dan Albert West; this Dan West was born in 1894 in Lansing, Michigan, and was no relation to the Brethren Dan West. On the Contributed Supplies Branch, see Carson W. Clements, "The Development and Failure of American Policy Toward Czechoslovakia, 1938–1948" (PhD diss., Miami University, 2001). For more on UNRRA's relationship to donors and its policies on donated goods, see Administrative Order No. 23, June 12, 1945, Committee on Contributed Supplies, S-1263-0000-0029-00001, UNA. The same information appears in "Rec. Administrative Order No. 23," June 12, 1945, Brethren Service Committee, S-1267-0000-0083-00001, p. 2402, UNA. On animal acquisitions, see also Lintner, *UNRRA Livestock Program Historical Report*, 16, USHMM.

37. On the Rebuilders of Poland, see "2,300 koni w darze od Polonii Amerykańskiej," *Zagoń Ojczysty*, February 1947, Wnioski o odznaczenia dla obywateli amerykańskich, 1947, MRiRR, 162/0/24/5068, p. 16, AAN. On horses donated by American Polonia, see "Departament Ekonomiczny, Wyd. Obrotu Wewnętrznego," Rozliczenia za towary z dostaw UNRRA, 1947–49, MRiRR, 2/162/0/2.5/564, AAN; "Inwentarz żywy z dostaw UNRRA," 1947, MRiRR, 2/162/0/26/3271, p. 2, AAN. Occasionally, the animals purchased by organizations other than UNRRA (and the Heifer Project) but traveling on UNRRA ships were counted as "UNRRA animals" and therefore appear in UNRRA's statistics related to the number of animals it delivered.

38. Lintner, *UNRRA Livestock Program Historical Report*, 149, USHMM.

39. "Polish Supply and Reconstruction Mission in North America to the Ministry of Agriculture in Warsaw," September 30, 1946, MRiRR, 2/162/0/2.4/519, p. 49, AAN.

40. "Brethren Overseas Relief: How It Is Distributed," *Gospel Messenger*, November 24, 1945.

41. Donald F. Durnbaugh, *Pragmatic Prophet: The Life of Michael Robert Zigler* (Elgin, IL: Brethren Press, 1989), 173; Duane Tananbaum, *Herbert H. Lehman: A Political Biography* (Albany: SUNY Press, 2016), 245–46.

42. "M.R. Zigler to 'To Whom It May Concern' at UNRRA," 1945, Brethren Service Committee, S-1267-0000-0083-00001, pp. 151–52, UNA.

43. "Report by Ralph M. Delk to Co-Workers," folder 9, box 1, series 4/1/6, HP, BHLA.

44. Philip West, "Dirty Fingernails, Heifers and China: Some Connecting Threads," in *Cowboy Memories*, eds. Bill Beck and Mel West (Little Rock, AR: Heifer Project International, 1994), 112.

45. William I. Hitchcock, *The Bitter Road to Freedom: A New History of the Liberation of Europe* (New York: Free Press, 2008), 243–44.

46. Woodbridge, *UNRRA*, 1:488. See also M. P. Coppock, "I Wanted to See if I Would Get Seasick," in Beck and West, *Cowboy Memories*, 39.

47. Clara Wood and Bruce Wood, "Nie Mam Nic," *Gospel Messenger*, August 16, 1947; Clarence H. Rosenberger, "A 'Cowboy' Evaluates the Trip to Europe with Relief Cattle," *Gospel Messenger*, September 22, 1945.

48. Peggy Reiff Miller, private correspondence with author, January 23, 2024.

49. Glee Yoder, *Passing on the Gift: The Story of Dan West* (Elgin, IL: Brethren Press, 1978), 103–4.

50. Peggy Reiff Miller, "The Impossible Dream: How the Heifer Project Came to Be," *Messenger*, July/August 2009.

51. Peggy Reiff Miller, "'Hope' the Heifer: A Christmas Story," *Seagoing Cowboys* (blog), December 23, 2016. That many heifers were called "Hope" comes from Reiff Miller, private correspondence with author, January 23, 2024. On the orphanage in Konstancin, see Adam Zyszczyk, "Domy Dziecka w gminie Konstancin-Jeziorna 1919–2015," OkoliceKonstancina.pl, June 1, 2019, https://okolicekonstancina.pl/2019/06/01/domy-dziecka-w-gminie-konstancin-jeziorna-1919-2015/.

52. "Poland Has Hope," Clippings and Releases 2, 1940s–1960s, folder 8, box 2, series 4/1/6, HP, BHLA.

53. Brethren Service, "More Than a Milk Factory," *Gospel Messenger*, June 21, 1947.

54. "Report by Ralph M. Delk" (emphasis in original).

55. *Marine Bull Pen*, no. 6, June 7, 1946, Marine Bullpens and News Circulars, 1946, folder 10, box 75, MGP, Hist. MSS 1-129, MCA.

56. "Six Heifers and a Bull Bound for Europe," *Baltimore Sun*, August 25, 1945.

57. The donation was made through the American Baptist Convention. See "Weston Children's Gift to Europe's Hungry," *Boston Globe*, June 22, 1947. For another example, see "Church Gives $737 to Buy Heifers for Overseas Aid," *Sunday Star*, June 9, 1946.

58. "Sea-Going Cowboys Sought to Escort 200,000 Heifers," *Boston Globe*, March 27, 1946.

59. "Ralph M. Delk (BSC) to His Co-Workers," November 6, 1946, Relief Work (FOR): Brethren Service Committee and Heifer Project, 1945–48, box 13, series E, JNS, DG 117, SCPC.

60. Leo R. Ward, "Brethren Heifers for Relief," *Gospel Messenger*, March 22, 1947.

61. Ward, "Brethren Heifers for Relief."

62. "Bon Voyage Party Given Europe-Bound Heifer," *Hollywood Citizen News*, July 31, 1946, Clippings and Releases 4, 1940s–1960s, folder 10, box 2, series 4/1/6, HP, BHLA.

63. Annex #1, "Feeding of 150 Heifers en Route," 1945, and Annex #2, "Bedding for 150 Heifers en Route," 1945, Brethren Service Committee, S-1267-0000-0083-00001, pp. 171, 172, UNA. This file contains detailed costs for many other parts of the animals' trip to a receiving country and for their earliest days at their destinations.

64. Dan West, "Heifers for Relief," September 20, 1945, Heifer Project before November 8, 1946, 1938–46, folder 48, box 38, series 18, DWP, BHLA. On the loca-

tions of specific collection farms, see Loren Walters, "Material and Projects: Commission on World Service," March 8, 1946, Heifer Project before November 8, 1946, 1938–46, folder 48, box 38, series 18, DWP, BHLA.

65. "Ralph M. Delk to Co-Workers," November 21, 1946, 1945–53 Project Committee Reports, folder 19, box 1, series 4/1/6, HP, BHLA.

66. Peggy Reiff Miller, "The Roger Roop Heifer Project Collection Farm," *The Seagoing Cowboys* (blog), September 25, 2015.

67. West, "Dirty Fingernails, Heifers and China," 112.

68. Letter from Ralph M. Delk, "Heifer News," May 14, 1947, Heifer Letters, HP, BHLA.

69. For details about the Roop farm, see Peggy Reiff Miller, "Activities of Heifer Project, Part II," *Seagoing Cowboys* (blog), October 23, 2015; Peggy Reiff Miller, "Seagoing Cowboys and the Heifer Project: The Maryland Story," *Catoctin History*, Fall/Winter 2005.

70. Peggy Reiff Miller, "Activities of Heifer Project, Part I," *Seagoing Cowboys* (blog), October 9, 2015.

71. Reiff Miller, "Seagoing Cowboys and the Heifer Project." Details also come from E. W. Wixson, "The Roop Holding Center," in Beck and West, *Cowboy Memories*, 21; Pat Roop Bubel, "A Place for Heifers," *Messenger*, May 1976.

72. Letter from Ralph M. Delk, "Heifer News," May 14, 1947, Heifer Letters, HP, BHLA. For more about the activities on the Roop farm, see Reiff Miller, "Activities of Heifer Project, Part II."

73. "Minutes of the Heifer Project Committee," March 29, 1947, Correspondence 1947, folder 10, box 1, series 4/1/6, HP, BHLA.

74. The dedication comes from Reiff Miller, "Seagoing Cowboys and the Heifer Project." On dedications, see also Robert Tate Allen, "350 Heifers for France Dedicated at Union Bridge," *Washington Post*, April 7, 1946, Brethren Service Committee, S-1268-0000-0039, p. 40, UNA.

75. Wixson, "Roop Holding Center," in Beck and West, *Cowboy Memories*, 21.

76. Reiff Miller, "Seagoing Cowboys and the Heifer Project."

77. Ross, "Kindness and Comfort Paramount."

78. Jacob C. Wine, "Diary of My Trip to Europe on a Cattle Boat," 1946, Seagoing Cowboy Diary, part 2, Manchester University Archives and Brethren Historical Collection, accessed August 19, 2022, https://www.manchester.edu/oaa/library/archives/DigitalCollections/seagoingcowboydiary.htm. Thank you to Peggy Reiff Miller for clarifying details about Wine's route.

79. Woodbridge, *UNRRA*, 1:489–90.

80. W. R. Strieber, "UNRRA Veterinarian's Duties," *Iowa State University Veterinarian* 9, no. 3 (1947): 152.

81. Lintner, *UNRRA Livestock Program Historical Report*, 24, USHMM.

82. Lintner, *UNRRA Livestock Program Historical Report*, 22–26, 135–36, USHMM. The quoted term comes from p. 23.

6. Cowboys and Animals at Sea

1. On the lack of source material generally, see Nancy Cushing, "Hazardous Commodities: Australian Live Animal Export from the Long Nineteenth Century to

Today," *whitehorsepress*, February 19, 2018, https://whitehorsepress.blog/2018/02/19/hazardous-commodities-australian-live-animal-export-from-the-long-nineteenth-century-to-today/.

2. There are rare accounts of animal transport during World War I, such as this one from the perspective of an army veterinarian: David McAuslin, "Transport Service (The Innocent Abroad)," *Journal of the American Veterinary Medical Association* VI, no. 4 (1918): 536–47.

3. Peggy Reiff Miller estimates that she has had some degree of contact with four hundred former seagoing cowboys. Reiff Miller, private correspondence with author, July 22, 2024. See also Peggy Reiff Miller, "In Memoriam," *Seagoing Cowboys* (blog), May 31, 2024. On seagoing cowboy reunions, see Peggy Reiff Miller, "Seagoing Cowboy Crew Reunions," *Seagoing Cowboys* (blog), October 14, 2016; and Dick Wanner, "Seagoing Cowboys Hold a Roundup, Talk About Old Times," *Lancaster Farming*, last updated December 7, 2022, https://www.lancasterfarming.com/farming-news/news/seagoing-cowboys-hold-a-roundup-talk-about-old-times/article_9f358722-4957-5864-b394-24daea6132bf.html.

4. George Woodbridge, *UNRRA: The History of the United Nations Relief and Rehabilitation Administration* (New York: Oxford University Press, 1950), 1:516.

5. Dan Regan, "UNRRA: World Shipper," *Army Transportation Journal* 2, no. 7 (1946): 5.

6. On the ship conversion process, see Robert Lintner, *UNRRA Livestock Program Historical Report*, 1947, UNRRA selected records AG-018-040, accession 2015.245.1, record group RG-67.050, S-1021-0009-03, pp. 26–30, USHMM.

7. The number of ships and ships' capacities are not consistent throughout various sources. In the official history of UNRRA, Woodbridge says there were seventy-one livestock carriers. See Woodbridge, *UNRRA*, 1:516. In his history of UNRRA in Poland, Łaptos states that the UNRRA fleet consisted of seventy-three ships, which is also the number that Robert Lintner provides. See Józef Łaptos, *Humanitaryzm i polityka: Pomoc UNRRA dla Polski i polskich uchodźców w latach 1944–1947* (Kraków: Wyd. Naukowe Uniwersytetu Pedagogicznego, 2018), 389; Lintner, *UNRRA Livestock Program Historical Report*, 90, USHMM. See also "Youths Sail World with UNRRA Herds," *New York Times*, July 1, 1946; United Nations Relief and Rehabilitation Administration, *The Story of UNRRA* (Washington, DC: UNRRA, Office of Public Information, 1948), 30.

8. Woodbridge, *UNRRA*, 1:479.

9. Woodbridge, *UNRRA*, 1:487. See also Elmer S. Yoder, "Seagoing Cowboys from Stark County," *Heritage*, October 2002.

10. On Liberty production, see M. D. Harris et al., "Revisiting (Some of) the Lasting Impacts of the Liberty Ships via a Metallurgical Analysis of Rivets from the SS 'John W. Brown,'" *Journal of the Minerals, Metals and Materials Society* 67 (2015): 2965–66.

11. Kathryn C. Hulme, *Undiscovered Country: A Spiritual Adventure* (Boston: Little, Brown, 1966), 176–77, 184.

12. Lintner, *UNRRA Livestock Program Historical Report*, 7–8, 90, USHMM. See also Peggy Reiff Miller, "WWII Ships Re-Purposed as Livestock Carriers," *Seagoing Cowboys* (blog), August 28, 2015; "Youths Sail World with UNRRA Herds."

13. Lintner, *UNRRA Livestock Program Historical Report*, 90, USHMM. On Victory ship, see also "Victory Ships Take Cattle to Europe," *Baltimore Sun*, January 7, 1946.

14. Lintner, *UNRRA Livestock Program Historical Report*, 7, 90, USHMM.
15. Lintner, *UNRRA Livestock Program Historical Report*, 17, USHMM. See also Regan, "UNRRA: World Shipper," 4.
16. E. Yoder, "Seagoing Cowboys from Stark County."
17. E. Yoder, "Seagoing Cowboys from Stark County."
18. "Ice-Coated Freighter Docks Here with Pulp After Stormy Passage," *Boston Globe*, January 24, 1947.
19. I discuss modern-day live animal maritime shipping in the conclusion.
20. This description of the loading process refers to Newport News and is taken from Lintner, *UNRRA Livestock Program Historical Report*, 158, USHMM. See also Peggy Reiff Miller, "Seagoing Cowboy Myths," *Seagoing Cowboys* (blog), January 10, 2025. For other descriptions of loading, see James M. Ross, "Kindness and Comfort Paramount in Shipping Horses and Dairy Cattle Overseas to Replace Losses in Farm Animals," *National Humane Review*, April 1946; "Greece Cattle Sails Today," *Baltimore Sun*, June 25, 1945; McNett, interviewed by Miller, Harold McNett Seagoing Cowboy Oral History, JMU.
21. J. Olen Yoder, *Crossing to Poland* (self-pub., 1986), 30. Thanks to Peggy Reiff Miller for sharing this resource with me.
22. This phrasing comes from Jonathan Peyton and is quoted in Nancy Cushing, "Animal Mobilities and the Founding of New South Wales," in "Visions of Australia: Environments in History," eds. Christof Mauch, Ruth Morgan, and Emily O'Gorman, special issue, *RCC Perspectives: Transformations in Environment and Society* 2 (2017): 19, https://doi.org/10.5282/rcc/7905.
23. Dave Janzen, "The Cowboy at Sea," *Mennonite*, April 15, 1947.
24. Smith, "The Odyssey of a Sea-Going Cowboy," in *A Scrapbook of Cowboy Memories*, 1994, From the Memories of Roger and Olive Roop, December 1985, folder 14, box 1, JEN, Hist. MSS 1893, MCA. This anecdote is also repeated in Peggy Reiff Miller, "The Odyssey of a Seagoing Cowboy by Dwight Smith—Part II," *Seagoing Cowboys* (blog), February 14, 2025.
25. On the optimal sanitary-spatial conditions for cattle, see Chris Otter, "Milk in Motion: Logistical Geographies in Twentieth-Century Britain," *Global Food History* 9, no. 1 (2023): 50.
26. E. Yoder, "Seagoing Cowboys from Stark County."
27. Luke Bomberger, "Man Overboard?," in *Scrapbook of Cowboy Memories*, MCA.
28. "Reed Ramsey's Trip to Poland," Josephine's Journal, accessed February 13, 2020, http://www.josephinesjournal.com/reed.htm. Ramsey traveled to Poland in 1946 when he was seventeen years old.
29. M. P. Coppock, "I Wanted to See if I Would Get Seasick," in *Cowboy Memories*, eds. Bill Beck and Mel West (Little Rock, AR: Heifer Project International, 1994), 39.
30. US Congress, Senate, Committee on Armed Services, *Hearing Before a Subcommittee of the Committee on Armed Services United States Senate*, 80th Cong., 1st sess., 1947, 108, see "Question of Ownership of Captured Horses."
31. Woodbridge, *UNRRA*, 1:490.
32. Reuel B. Pritchett with Dale Aukerman, *On the Ground Floor of Heaven* (Elgin, IL: Brethren Press, 1980), 105.
33. Byron P. Royer, "Diary of Seagoing Cowboys," in Beck and West, *Cowboy Memories*, 32. The full diary can be found at the Brethren Historical Library and

Archives: "'A Seagoing Cowboy in Italy,' by Byron P. Royer," 1947, series 18, Byron P. Royer Papers, BHLA. This passage appears on p. 42.

34. J. Yoder, *Crossing to Poland*, 33.

35. J. Yoder, *Crossing to Poland*, 33, 35.

36. W. R. Strieber, "UNRRA Veterinarian's Duties," *Iowa State University Veterinarian* 9, no. 3 (1947): 153.

37. Owen Gingerich, "The Return of the Seagoing Cowboy: Horses Afloat and Books Astray," *American Scholar* 68, no. 4 (1999): 73.

38. "Announcement," *Gospel Messenger*, November 16, 1946. The accident is also described in "Delk to His Co-Workers," box 13, series E, JNS, DG 117, SCPC.

39. Peggy Reiff Miller, "Coming of Age on a Cattle Boat," *Mennonite*, January 10, 2006.

40. Janzen, "Cowboy at Sea."

41. O. Gingerich, "Return of the Seagoing Cowboy," 75.

42. E. Yoder, "Seagoing Cowboys from Stark County"; Melvin Gingerich, "We Reach Poland," *Mennonite Weekly Review*, August 22, 1946, Travel, Poland Sea-Going Cowboys, Speeches and Manuscripts, folder 13, box 75, MGP, HM1–973, Hist. MSS 1–129, MCA.

43. E. Yoder, "Seagoing Cowboys from Stark County."

44. "Greece Cattle Sails Today."

45. Maynard Miller, "Nunemaker's Voyage," *Mennonite Historical Bulletin*, October 1991.

46. Lintner, *UNRRA Livestock Program Historical Report*, 9, USHMM.

47. Robert Ebey, "A Trip to Poland with Brethren Service Heifers," box 1, JEN, Hist. MSS-1-893, p. 25, MCA.

48. *Marine Bull Pen*, no. 4, May 10, 1946, Marine Bullpens and News Circulars, folder 10, box 75, MGP, Hist. MSS 1–129, MCA. For more on what ships' captains thought about cowboys, see Don Chatfield, "For Brethren News," March 1, 1946, Brethren Service Committee, S-1268-0000-0039, p. 93, UNA.

49. Lintner, *UNRRA Livestock Program Historical Report*, 6, USHMM; Peggy Reiff Miller, "UNRRA Livestock Trips from the Eyes of a Veterinarian," *Seagoing Cowboys* (blog), March 12, 2021.

50. Strieber, "UNRRA Veterinarian's Duties," 152.

51. McNett, interviewed by Miller, Harold McNett Seagoing Cowboy Oral History, JMU.

52. O. Gingerich, "Return of the Seagoing Cowboy," 73. Rev. Floyd Bantz also called the veterinarian on his ship to Greece in the summer of 1945 incompetent. See *Origins of the Heifer Project* (High Library, Elizabethtown College, 2014), https://archive.org/details/Heifer_Project.

53. Strieber, "UNRRA Veterinarian's Duties," 153. See also Lintner, *UNRRA Livestock Program Historical Report*, 10–11, USHMM. The veterinarians documented illnesses on a form called "Veterinarian's Report on Voyage" (Form S-148). A copy of this form, dated May 9, 1946, is included in Lintner's report on p. 63.

54. AMEDD Center of History and Heritage, "Transportation of Animals," August 30, 2022, https://achh.army.mil/history/book-wwii-vetservicewwii-chapter15.

55. E. Yoder, "Seagoing Cowboys from Stark County."

56. Lintner, *UNRRA Livestock Program Historical Report*, 187–93, esp. 188, USHMM.

57. Strieber, "UNRRA Veterinarian's Duties," 153.

58. E. Yoder, "Seagoing Cowboys from Stark County."

59. Arthur Meyer, "Art Meyer's Cattle Boat Experience: Introduction to Planned Book, Dated January 1991," Seagoing Cowboys, accessed February 13, 2020, https://seagoingcowboyswebsite.files.wordpress.com/2015/10/stories_art meyer.pdf. Arthur Meyer also completed one of Melvin Gingerich's questionnaires about the seagoing cowboy experience. See Completed Questionnaires, folder 5, box 76, MGP, Hist. MSS 1–129, MCA.

60. Cushing, "Animal Mobilities," 19.

61. Frank Henry, "Through This Port: Life for Europe," *Baltimore Sun*, March 24, 1946.

62. "Horse Foaling," Texas A&M University Veterinary Medicine and Biomedical Sciences News, March 10, 2011, https://vetmed.tamu.edu/news/pet-talk/horse-foaling/.

63. Lintner, *UNRRA Livestock Program Historical Report*, 87, USHMM.

64. Ira M. Wine, "Untitled" in *Scrapbook of Cowboy Memories*, MCA. For a reminiscence about a colt's birth—and death, along with the mare—on board a ship to Poland, see Kenneth M. Heatwole, "Cattleboat Trip of Kenneth Heatwole, 1946," Seagoing Cowboys, accessed February 13, 2020, https://seagoingcowboyswebsite.files.wordpress.com/2015/11/stories_kenheatwole.pdf. Paul Libby, who was twenty-four when he went to Poland in 1946, also talks about the many calves that were born and died on board his sailing. Libby had been a Methodist Conscientious Objector during the war. See A. Kern, *Better Days Films—Day 12* (Seattle Community Media, 2013), https://archive.org/details/scm-316182-betterdaysfilms-day12-. This short film includes many terrific photographs from Libby's personal collection. On-board births are also described in the biography of author William Styron; Styron worked as a cowboy aboard a sailing of SS *Cedar Rapids Victory* to Trieste in 1946. See James L. W. West III, *William Styron, a Life* (New York: Random House, 1998), 131. For a story of a calf born en route from Union Bridge to the port in Baltimore, see Thurl Metzger, "A Calf Is Born in Baltimore," 1945–53, folder 1, box 1, series 4/1/6, HP, BHLA.

65. Melvin Gingerich, "Cowboys Going to Sea," *Mennonite Weekly Review*, June 18, 1946, Speeches and Manuscripts, folder 13, box 75, MGP, HM1–973, Hist. MSS 1–129, MCA.

66. Ebey, "Trip to Poland," 11, MCA.

67. E. Yoder, "Seagoing Cowboys from Stark County."

68. *Scrapbook of Cowboy Memories*, MCA.

69. Elmer Summy, "Care of the Livestock," in Beck and West, *Cowboy Memories*, 25.

70. Richard Rush, "My Cattle-Boat Experience, December 29, 1945–March 3, 1946," folder 14, box 1, Seagoing Cowboys Collection, HM 1–973, MCA.

71. E. Yoder, "Seagoing Cowboys from Stark County"; entry for July 8, 1946, in Meyer, "Art Meyer's Cattle Boat Experience." The work routine is also outlined in Leslie Eisan, *Pathways of Peace: A History of the Civilian Public Service Program Administered by the Brethren Service Committee* (Elgin, IL: Brethren Publishing House, 1948), 327–30.

72. "George Weber, to Greece by Cattleship," Completed Questionnaires, folder 5, box 76, MGP, Hist. MSS 1–129, MCA.

73. "Greece Cattle Sails Today."
74. See entry for July 18, 1946, in Heatwole, "Cattleboat Trip of Kenneth Heatwole."
75. E. Yoder, "Seagoing Cowboys from Stark County."
76. Heatwole, "Cattleboat Trip of Kenneth Heatwole."
77. Russell Helstern and Ed Grater, "Information for Livestock Attendants," February 28, 1946, Travel, Poland Sea-Going Cowboys, folder 8, box 75, MGP, Hist. MSS 1–129, MCA.
78. Deborah Valenze, *Milk: A Local and Global History* (New Haven, CT: Yale University Press, 2011), 1.
79. Miller, "Nunemaker's Voyage."
80. "John Nunemaker," in *Scrapbook of Cowboy Memories*, MCA. In Peggy Reiff Miller's picture book, *The Seagoing Cowboy*, the characters are composites, but Nunemaker is one of the main models for the titular cowboy, and Nunemaker's horse Queen is represented as Queenie in the book. See Peggy Reiff Miller, *The Seagoing Cowboy*, illustrated by Claire Ewart (Elgin, IL: Brethren Press, 2016). For more on this horse and Nunemaker, see Peggy Reiff Miller, "The Real Cowboy John," *Seagoing Cowboys* (blog), May 27, 2016.
81. Martine Hausberger et al., "A Review of the Human-Horse Relationship," *Applied Animal Behaviour Science* 109, no. 1 (2008): 1–24.
82. For human-nonhuman emotional communities in another context, see Thomas Webb et al., "More-Than-Human Emotional Communities: British Soldiers and Mules in Second World War Burma," *Cultural and Social History* 17, no. 2 (2020): 246.
83. Perry D. Avery, Ralph B. Diller and Andrew Avery Jr., "Trip to Poland, Summer 1946," in Beck and West, *Cowboy Memories*, 49.
84. Elaine Walker, *Horse* (London: Reaktion Books, 2008), 34, 140.
85. E. Yoder, "Seagoing Cowboys from Stark County."
86. M. Gingerich, "Cowboys Going to Sea," MCA.
87. E. Yoder, "Seagoing Cowboys from Stark County."
88. Helstern and Grater, "Information for Livestock Attendants."
89. Janzen, "Cowboy at Sea."
90. See entry for June 28, 1946, in Meyer, "Art Meyer's Cattle Boat Experience."
91. *Marine Bull Pen*, no. 3, April 26, 1946, Marine Bullpens and News Circulars, folder 10, box 75, MGP, Hist. MSS 1–129, MCA.
92. E. Yoder, "Seagoing Cowboys from Stark County."
93. Peggy Reiff Miller, "Luke Bomberger," *Seagoing Cowboys* (blog), August 26, 2016. See also Reiff Miller, "Coming of Age."
94. Gerald Liepert, "Jerry Liepert's Cattleboat Trip to Europe: 1946–47," ed. Jamie Liepert Langston, *Keepers* (blog), April 3, 2008, http://keepersthe.blogspot.com/2008/04/jerry-lieperts-cattleboat-trip-to.html. On horses, see also Harvey Cox, *Just as I Am* (Nashville, TN: Abingdon, 1983), 36.
95. "'Seagoing Cowboy in Italy,' by Byron P. Royer," BHLA.
96. *Scrapbook of Cowboy Memories*, MCA.
97. Ebey, "Trip to Poland," 10, MCA.
98. On the subject of bad weather, see Ebey, "Trip to Poland," MCA; Peggy Reiff Miller, "Seagoing Cowboy Meets German Relatives, December 1946," *Seago-

ing Cowboys (blog), December 8, 2017. A particularly bad storm is also described by Jerry Liepert; the storm threw seventy horses overboard. See Liepert, "Jerry Liepert's Cattleboat Trip."

99. *Hearing Before a Subcommittee*, 108, see "Question of Ownership of Captured Horses."

100. *Hearing Before a Subcommittee*, 109.

101. "Letters to Lillian," March 31–May 1, 1946, 20, Foreign Travel, Involvement and Contacts, series D, part 1, George and Lillian Willoughby Papers, DG 236, SCPC.

102. Royer, "Diary of Seagoing Cowboys," in Beck and West, *Cowboy Memories*, 32.

103. E. Yoder, "Seagoing Cowboys from Stark County." Cowboy James Martin (who had been in the CPS) also remarked in his memoir that the captain ordered the regular removal of manure. See James Martin, "Seagoing Cowboy, March 6, 2007," Seagoing Cowboys, accessed July 26, 2024, https://seagoingcowboyswebsite.files.wordpress.com/2016/02/stories_jamesmartin.pdf.

104. Warren Sawyer, interview by Shaun Illingworth, July 18, 2008, https://oralhistory.rutgers.edu/interviewees/64-text-html/1513-sawyer-warren.

105. J. Yoder, *Crossing to Poland*, 33.

106. On horse deaths, see Edgar H. Grater, "Sea Horses," *Gospel Messenger*, September 20, 1947.

107. J. Yoder, *Crossing to Poland*, 29.

108. On animals that died aboard the ships, see J. Yoder, *Crossing to Poland*, 40; entry for July 2, 1946, in Meyer, "Art Meyer's Cattle Boat Experience"; E. Yoder, "Seagoing Cowboys from Stark County."

109. J. Yoder, *Crossing to Poland*, 31.

110. E. Yoder, "Seagoing Cowboys from Stark County." See also Cox, *Just as I Am*, 35.

111. See entry for July 8, 1946, in Meyer, "Art Meyer's Cattle Boat Experience."

112. "Dead labor" is adapted from Jonathan Peyton, "'A Strange Enough Way': An Embodied Natural History of Experience, Animals and Food on the Teslin Trail," *Geoforum* 58 (2015): 19.

113. J. Yoder, *Crossing to Poland*, 40.

114. See entries for July 9 and July 13, 1946, in Meyer, "Art Meyer's Cattle Boat Experience."

115. John E. Gingerich, "Cattle Boat Memoir," in *Scrapbook of Cowboy Memories*, MCA.

116. J. Yoder, *Crossing to Poland*, 29.

117. "Telegram from Warsaw to Washington," December 17, 1945, Brethren Service Committee—Poland, S-1267-0000-0093-00001, p. 12, UNA.

118. "Report on SS Mount Whitney," UNRRA Subject Files, S-0527-1107, UNA.

119. For a detailed description of some of the common ailments that affected horses, see Lintner, *UNRRA Livestock Program Historical Report*, 154–57, USHMM.

120. "5,000 Horses Wait for Ships to Europe," *New York Times*, September 27, 1946.

121. "Copy and Translation of the Minutes of the Conference Held on 10.3.47 at the Offices of the Representative for UNRRA and Import Affairs of the Ministry of Agriculture at Sopot, Rokossowskiego," Minutes of Meetings, file 54, S-0527-1107, UNA. A Polish report summarizes the health risks for horses aboard the UNRRA

ships. See E. Wiszniewski, "Notatka," Inwentarz żywy z dostaw UNRRA, MRiRR, 2/162/0/2.4/517, pp. 8–11, AAN.

122. Strieber, "UNRRA Veterinarian's Duties," 153.
123. "UNRRA in Operation—by Countries," *Monthly Review*, August 1945.
124. Lintner, *UNRRA Livestock Program Historical Report*, 24, USHMM. See also Jacek Sawicki, *Misja UNRRA w Polsce: Raport zamknięcia (1945–1949)* (Lublin: Wyd. Werset, 2017), 124.
125. Woodbridge, *UNRRA*, 1:491. A loss rate of approximately 4 percent is confirmed in *Hearing Before a Subcommittee*, 109, see "Question of Ownership of Captured Horses."
126. Loss rates are different in different documents because the various reports sometimes feature only specific ports, or they organize the animal species differently, or they deal with slightly different periods. The figures here are taken from data included in Lintner, *UNRRA Livestock Program Historical Report*, 40–41, USHMM. See esp. table 3 in "Number of animals shipped and lost by ports" and "Shipment of livestock from western hemisphere with losses by ships."
127. "Heifer Project Committee," August 6, 1947, Heifer Project Committee, c. 1947–48, folder 44, box 38, series 18, DWP, BHLA.
128. Peggy Reiff Miller, "UNRRA Livestock Shipments with Losses by Ship," Seagoing Cowboys, accessed August 16, 2024, https://seagoingcowboys.com/seagoing-cowboys/the-unrra-years/.
129. "Report on UNRRA Livestock Imported to Poland from September 29, 1945 to July 28, 1946," July 29, 1946, UNRRA Subject Files, file 72, S-0527-1107, UNA.
130. "Henson to Kosch," April 5, 1946, box 106, series B (formerly series G), part 1: NSBRO Files, CCWR, DG 025, SCPC.
131. "Reports—Field Trips Dr. Wilder, A.G. Wilder to M.E. Hays," September 3, 1946, UNRRA Subject Files, file 72, S-0527-1107, UNA.
132. The first horse shipments to Szczecin came in September 1946. See "Woj. Komisja Rozdziału Inwentarzy to Woj. Pełnomocnika Akcji Siewnej Szczecin," November 11, 1946, UNRRA—Przydziały koni, Urząd Wojewódzki Szczeciński (hereafter UWS), 65/317/0/19.1/5129, p. 133, Wojewódzkie Archiwum Państwowe w Szczecinie (hereafter APwSz). On the state of Poland's ports immediately after the war, see "Transport Rehabilitation in Poland" (London: Division of Operational Analysis, April 1947), chap. 5, S-1297-0000-0426-00001, UNA. For a brief history of the Gdańsk port in the immediate postwar period and beyond, see Bronisław Poźniak, "70 Lat Urzędu Celnego w Gdańsku," *Strefa Historii*, June 15, 2015, http://strefahistorii.pl/article/1147-70-lat-urzedu-celnego-w-Gda%C5%84sku.
133. "Report on UNRRA Livestock," UNA.
134. "Letters to Lillian," 7, 11, SCPC.
135. On the response from the American Humane Association to losses, see "UNRRA Horse Ships Caught in Hurricane and Ice at Sea," *National Humane Review*, November 1947.
136. "Report on UNRRA Livestock," UNA.
137. See, for example, "Dispatch by Leith White," January 9, 1945, UNRRA—Poland Mission, 1944–49, file 1222, S-0527-1073, UNA. On the fate of other goods delivered to Poland, see "Co się dzieje z towarami UNRRA," *Kurier Szczeciński*, November 4, 1945.

138. Jacob Darwin Hamblin, "The Vulnerability of Nations: Food Security in the Aftermath of World War II," *Global Environment* 10 (2012): 49–51, 58–59.

139. Rev. Peter H. Bury, "Poland," *Brethren Missionary*, January 25, 1947.

140. "Final Directions for Gingerich-Oswald Crew," folder 2, box 75, MGP, Hist. MSS 1–129, MCA.

141. E. S. Rowland, "Poland Found in Ruins," *Gospel Messenger*, May 25, 1946.

142. Ebey, "Trip to Poland," 27, MCA.

143. O. Gingerich, "Return of the Seagoing Cowboy," 75.

144. Peggy Reiff Miller, "Seagoing Cowboys Mingle with Returning WWII Soldiers," *Seagoing Cowboys* (blog), March 2015. See also Eisan, *Pathways of Peace*, 330.

145. Alpheus Rohrer, "Diary of a Saltwater Cowboy to Poland in January and February of 1946," in *Scrapbook of Cowboy Memories*, MCA.

146. Daniel Hertzler, "With Heifers to Poland and Greece," *Mennonite*, June 20, 2016, https://anabaptistworld.org/heifers-poland-greece/. Cowboy Hertzler was a former editor of *Gospel Herald*, which was predecessor to *The Mennonite*.

147. Janzen, "Cowboy at Sea."

148. J. Yoder, *Crossing to Poland*, 13.

149. Helstern and Grater, "Information for Livestock Attendants."

150. Melvin Gingerich, "We Return to Newport News," folder 13, box 75, MGP, HM1–973, Hist. MSS 1–129, MCA.

151. Lintner, *UNRRA Livestock Program Historical Report*, 193, USHMM.

152. For views of the regular crew, see Completed Questionnaires, folder 5, box 76, MGP, Hist. MSS 1–129, MCA.

153. O. Gingerich, "Return of the Seagoing Cowboy," 76.

154. O. Gingerich, "Return of the Seagoing Cowboy," 76.

155. "Erb to Gingerich," folder 4, box 75, MGP, Hist. MSS 1–129, MCA.

156. Ebey, "Trip to Poland," 9, MCA.

157. Edwin T. Randall, "A Privilege for a Preacher," *Gospel Messenger*, November 9, 1946.

7. Bovines, Equines, and Humans in Poland

1. On Constanza, see Jacek Sawicki, *Misja UNRRA w Polsce: Raport zamknięcia (1945–1949)* (Lublin: Wyd. Werset, 2017), chap. 1; Józef Łaptos, *Humanitaryzm i polityka: Pomoc UNRRA dla Polski i polskich uchodźców w latach 1944–1947* (Kraków: Wyd. Naukowe Uniwersytetu Pedagogicznego, 2018), 337–39.

2. Duane Tananbaum, *Herbert H. Lehman: A Political Biography* (Albany: SUNY Press, 2016), 223.

3. George Woodbridge, *UNRRA: The History of the United Nations Relief and Rehabilitation Administration* (New York: Oxford University Press, 1950), 1:350. See also "Draft of the Supply Department's Brief for the PRD's Tour of Poland," PRDG's European Tour, S-1435-0000-0100-00001, p. 60, UNA.

4. Łaptos, *Humanitaryzm i polityka*, 338; Benon Gaziński and Bogusław Wanot, "Działalność UNRRA i jej pomoc dla rolnictwa w Polsce," *Rocznik Muzeum Narodowego Rolnictwa w Szreniawie* 19 (1993): 18.

5. "UNRRA Activities in Poland," UNRRA—Poland Mission, 1944–49, file 74, S-0527-1068, UNA; Woodbridge, *UNRRA*, 2:212. See also Sawicki, *Misja UNRRA w Polsce*, 100.

6. "Report on UNRRA Livestock Imported to Poland from September 29, 1945 to July 28, 1946," July 29, 1946, UNRRA Subject Files, file 72, S-0527-1107, UNA.

7. Łaptos, *Humanitaryzm i polityka*, 338; Gaziński and Wanot, "Działalność UNRRA i jej pomoc," 18. For a brief contemporary overview of the three Polish ports of Gdynia, Gdańsk, and Szczecin, see *Porty Gdynia, Gdańsk, Szczecin* (Gdynia: Główny Urząd Morski, 1946).

8. Sawicki, *Misja UNRRA w Polsce*, 108.

9. Herbert W. Robinson, *Operational Analysis Papers No. 45: The Impact of UNRRA on the Polish Economy* (London: Division of Operational Analysis, 1947), 4, 7.

10. Bruno Kamiński, "Fear Management: Foreign Threats in the Postwar Polish Propaganda—the Influence and the Reception of the Communist Media (1944–1956)" (PhD diss., European University Institute, 2016), 234–35.

11. "Provisional Report on Agriculture and Food in Poland," file 1032, S-0527-1068, p. 10, UNA.

12. Robert S. Zigler, interview by W. Haven North, November 5, 1998, Association for Diplomatic Studies and Training Foreign Affairs Oral History Collection Foreign Assistance Series, https://adst.org/OH%20TOCs/Zigler-Robert-S.pdf.

13. See, for example, Ralph E. Smeltzer, "From a Relief Worker's Diary," *Gospel Messenger*, December 28, 1946; L. W. Shultz, "'Poland Devastated' Is Visitor's Report," *Gospel Messenger*, June 15, 1946.

14. Glenn N. Rohrer, "My Sea-Going Cowboy Experience," in *A Scrapbook of Cowboy Memories*, 1994, From the Memories of Roger and Olive Roop, December 1985, folder 14, box 1, JEN, Hist. MSS 1893, MCA.

15. "Lowell Zuck Travels for UNRRA," *Etownian*, October 25, 1946.

16. See entry for July 16, 1946, in Arthur Meyer, "Art Meyer's Cattle Boat Experience: Introduction to Planned Book, Dated January 1991," Seagoing Cowboys, accessed February 13, 2020, https://seagoingcowboyswebsite.files.wordpress.com/2015/10/stories_artmeyer.pdf.

17. Gerhard Friesen, "Observations on My Trip to Poland," *Mennonite*, March 5, 1946. In their memoirs cowboys frequently used the prewar German name for Gdańsk: Danzig. I use Gdańsk because the city was within Polish borders after the war and this was its official name.

18. Friesen, "Observations on My Trip."

19. Dwight Smith, "The Odyssey of a Sea-Going Cowboy," in *Scrapbook of Cowboy Memories*, MCA.

20. Smith, "Odyssey of a Sea-Going Cowboy," in *Scrapbook of Cowboy Memories*, MCA.

21. Owen Gingerich, "The Return of the Seagoing Cowboy: Horses Afloat and Books Astray," *American Scholar* 68, no. 4 (1999): 76.

22. "Questionnaire Completed by Leroy L. Peachey (Who Had Been in the CPS) About His 1946 Trip to Poland," Completed Questionnaires, folder 5, box 76, MGP, Hist. MSS 1-129, MCA.

23. Harvey Cox, *Just as I Am* (Nashville, TN: Abingdon, 1983), 37.

24. J. Olen Yoder, *Crossing to Poland* (self-pub., 1986), 49–50.

25. On Stutthof, see Peggy Reiff Miller, "Stories from the S.S. Mount Whitney—We Must Never Forget," *Seagoing Cowboys* (blog), April 28, 2023; and "More on the Stutthof Concentration Camp #1," *Seagoing Cowboys* (blog), June 9, 2023.

26. "Outgoing Cablegram from R. Lintner to Warsaw," November 26, 1946, Brethren Service Committee—Personnel, S-1267-0000-0091-00001, p. 4, UNA.

27. See entry for July 25, 1946, in Kenneth M. Heatwole, "Cattleboat Trip of Kenneth Heatwole, 1946," Seagoing Cowboys, accessed February 13, 2020, https://seagoingcowboyswebsite.files.wordpress.com/2015/11/stories_kenheatwole.pdf.

28. Warren D. Sawyer, "I Took One Trip to Danzig . . . ," in *Scrapbook of Cowboy Memories*, MCA.

29. Alpheus Rohrer, "Diary of a Saltwater Cowboy to Poland in January and February of 1946," in *Scrapbook of Cowboy Memories*, 4, MCA; Richard Rush, "My Cattle-Boat Experience, December 29, 1945–March 3, 1946," folder 14, box 1, Seagoing Cowboys Collection, HM 1–973, MCA.

30. Peggy Reiff Miller, "Cowboys at Christmas," *World Ark*, Holiday 2014.

31. J. Yoder, *Crossing to Poland*, 49. On labor shortages on the docks, see also McNett, interviewed by Miller, Harold McNett Seagoing Cowboy Oral History, JMU.

32. Cox, *Just as I Am*, 37, 39.

33. See entry for July 26, 1946, in Heatwole, "Cattleboat Trip of Kenneth Heatwole."

34. "Suggestions for Livestock Attendants," folder 8, box 75, MGP, Hist. MSS. 1–129, MCA.

35. Melvin Gingerich, "Recommendations to the BSC and the MCC Related to Sea-Going Cowboys," Correspondence A to G, 1946, folder 4, box 75, MGP, Hist. MSS 1–129, MCA. The BSC's opposition to smoking suited UNRRA very well, as the fire hazard on ships packed with hay was great. See Melvin Gingerich, "We Reach Poland," *Mennonite Weekly Review*, August 22, 1946, Travel, Poland Sea-Going Cowboys, Speeches and Manuscripts, folder 13, box 75, MGP, HM1–973, Hist. MSS 1–129, MCA. For the BSC's views on the black market, see also "Cowboy Education (Pre-Sailing Study)," folder 3, box 2, series 4/1/6, POW, BHLA. On the search for souvenirs, see Friesen, "Observations on My Trip." On the long history of Mennonites in what became northern Poland in the postwar period, see Edmund Kizik, "Mennonici," in *Pod wspólnym niebem*, eds. M. Kopczyński and W. Tygielski (Warsaw: Muzeum Historii Polski, 2010), 215–34.

36. Russell Helstern and Ed Grater, "Information for Livestock Attendants," February 28, 1946, Travel, Poland Sea-Going Cowboys, folder 8, box 75, MGP, Hist. MSS 1–129, MCA.

37. Friesen, "Observations on My Trip."

38. "Protokół," May 6, 1946, Biuro Odbioru Transportów Morskich w Gdańsku, 2/319/0/2/21, AAN. Specific firms were hired for unloading; these included Bałtyk, Pantarei, and Wiator. See "Notatka w sprawie wyładunku inwentarza żywego z UNRRA," Dostawy koni i bydła z UNRRA, 1946–48, Związek Samopomocy Chłopskiej (hereafter ZSC), 2/160/0/3/1104, p. 3, AAN. See also "Protokół," June 26, 1946, Biuro Odbioru Transportów Morskich w Gdańsku, 2/319/0/2/21, AAN. On dock workers' employment conditions, including the chronic shortage of skilled men for the job, see various articles in *Gazeta Morska—Pismo Marynarki Wojennej* from 1946.

39. Woodbridge, *UNRRA*, 2:212.

40. "Departament Kontroli, Samopomoc Chłopska to Pełnomocnik do Spraw Akcji Siewnej," February 14, 1946, Kontrola przeprowadzona przez główny inspektorat..., 1946, MRiRR, 2/162/0/4/682, pp. 11–12, AAN.
41. Shultz, "Poland Devastated." See also "Proposed Church of the Brethren Relief Party," December 1946, Brethren Service Committee, S-1267-0000-0093-00001, p. 3, UNA.
42. "Departament Kontroli, Samopomoc Chłopska," p. 11, AAN.
43. "Copy and Translation of the Minutes of the Conference Held on 10.3.47 at the Offices of the Representative for UNRRA and Import Affairs of the Ministry of Agriculture at Sopot, Rokossowskiego," Minutes of Meetings, file 54, S-0527-1107, UNA.
44. "J.B. Oliver to UNRRA," January 24, 1947, file 2000, S-0527-1105, UNA.
45. M. M., "Przychodzą statki z końmi," *Dziennik Bałtycki* 199 (1946): 3.
46. Joel, "Farmboy Seminarian on a Cattleboat to Poland, 1946," Far Outliers, December 26, 2009, https://faroutliers.com/2009/12/26/farmboy-seminarian-on-a-cattleboat-to-poland-1946/.
47. Peggy Reiff Miller, "The Real Cowboy John," *Seagoing Cowboys* (blog), May 27, 2016.
48. "Sea-Going Cowboys Research," "UNRRA Livestock Summary" (copied from *UNRRA Weekly Bulletin*), June 29, 1946, folder 2, box 76, Melvin C. Gingerich Collection, Hist. MSS 1–129, MCA; Gingerich, "We Reach Poland."
49. "Letters to Lillian," March 31–May 1, 1946, Foreign Travel, Involvement and Contacts, series D, part 1, George and Lillian Willoughby Papers, DG 236, SCPC. George wrote pages and pages to Lillian about everything he saw and experienced on all parts of his trip to Poland in April 1946 aboard SS *Clarksville Victory* with a crew composed mostly of men from the Civilian Public Service (George himself had been in the CPS).
50. Woodbridge, *UNRRA*, 2:223.
51. "Questionnaire of Leroy D. Reitz of Pennsylvania Who Made Two Trips to Poland, Both in 1946," Completed Questionnaires, folder 5, box 76, MGP, HIST. MSS. 1–129, MCA.
52. "Livestock: Rough on General Story," Clippings and Releases 2, 1940s–1960s, folder 8, box 2, series 4/1/6, HP, BHLA.
53. "Farm Folk Grateful for Animals from American Farms," Clippings and Releases 1, folder 7, box 2, series 4/1/6, HP, BHLA.
54. Peggy Reiff Miller, "The SS Park Victory: Livestock Trip #2, Poland, December 1945—Part IV," *Seagoing Cowboys* (blog), March 23, 2018.
55. For other examples, see L. W. Shultz, "Mission to Poland," *Gospel Messenger*, February 23, 1946; and Mark Ebersole, "The Story of the Cattle Sent to Italy," *Gospel Messenger*, April 5, 1947.
56. Dan Shenk, "Aftermath," *Truth*, August 25, 1996.
57. Marek Żak, "Sytuacja aprowizacyjna Legnicy w latach 1945–1945," *Szkice Legnickie* 36 (2015): 160.
58. See entry for July 18, 1946, in Meyer, "Art Meyer's Cattle Boat Experience."
59. William Reams, "Colby's Cowboys," 2005, folder 9, box 1, Seagoing Cowboy Collection, HM 1–973, p. 4, MCA.
60. "Copy and Translation of the Minutes," UNA.

61. The large ministries involved in receiving UNRRA (and other aid) shipments included the Ministry of Food Supply and Trade (Ministerstwo Aprowizacji i Handlu) and the Ministry of Shipping and Foreign Trade (Ministerstwo Żeglugi i Handlu Zagranicznego). See Aleksander Juźwik, "Zagraniczna pomoc charytatywna dla dzieci i młodzieży w Polsce w latach 1945–50," *Polska 1944/45–1980: Studia i Materiały* 11 (2013): 96; Łaptos, *Humanitaryzm i polityka*, 352; Woodbridge, *UNRRA*, 2:39.

62. United Nations Relief and Rehabilitation Administration, *The Story of UNRRA* (Washington, DC: UNRRA, Office of Public Information, 1948), 14–15.

63. "Report on Field Trip to Baltic Port Area and Bydgoszcz," February 12, 1946, UNRRA—Poland Mission, 1944–49, Food and Agricultural Rehabilitation Division, Warsaw, file 7, S-0527-1064, UNA. See also Piotr Jachowicz, "Działalność UNRRA w Polsce w latach 1945–1948," *Zeszyty Naukowe* 2, no. 2 (1998): 47.

64. Woodbridge, *UNRRA*, 2:48.

65. Rohrer, "Diary of a Saltwater Cowboy," in *Scrapbook of Cowboy Memories*, MCA; Woodbridge, *UNRRA*, 1:489.

66. Departament produkcji rolnej, MRiRR, 2/162/0/21.5/3378, AAN.

67. "Państwowa lecznica wet. UNRRA to naczelnik wojewódzki, wydział wet.," September 29, 1946, UWS, 65/317/0/25/5518, p. 7, APwSz.

68. "Report on UNRRA Livestock," UNA. See also Departament Produkcji Rolnej, Wyd. Chowu Koni, MRiRR, 2/162/0/21.5/3378, p. 56, AAN.

69. "Instrukcja w sprawie przydziału koni chorych z dostaw UNRRA," October 25, 1946, Ministerstwo Ziem Odzyskanych w Warszawie (hereafter MZO), 2/196/0/06/1031, p. 1, AAN.

70. A. Pępkowski, "Dostawy zwierząt UNRRA dla Polski," *Medycyna Weterynaryjna* 3, no. 4 (1947): 233. On Polish veterinarians, see "Monthly Report," c. May 1946, in "Reports—Field Trips Dr. Wilder, A.G. Wilder to M.E. Hays," September 3, 1946, UNRRA Subject Files, file 72, S-0527-1107, UNA.

71. Jarosław Wasielewski, "Jak po wojnie leczono konie z UNRRY w Gdańsku," trojmiasto.pl, February 26, 2019, https://historia.trojmiasto.pl/Jak-w-Gdańsku-po-wojnie-konie-z-UNRRY-leczono-n132173.html#opinions-wrap.

72. "Report on UNRRA Livestock," UNA. A report on the clinic itself is in the same UN file folder: A. G. Wilder, "Report on field trip," July 1946.

73. A. Pępkowski, "Dostawy zwierząt UNRRA dla Polski," *Medycyna Weterynaryjna* 3, no. 4 (1947): 233.

74. "Dr. B. Nowicki, Państwowy Instytut Weterynaryjny to MRiRR (February 18, 1946)," MRiRR, 2/162/0/4/682, p. 10, AAN. See also A. Pępkowski, "Dostawy zwierząt UNRRA dla Polski," *Medycyna Weterynaryjna* 3, no. 6 (1947): 400. On postwar rebuilding of the veterinary field, see *Sprawozdanie z działalności spółdzielni lekarzy weterynaryjnych R.P. z.o.u. "Składnica weterynaryjna" za rok 1946* (Warsaw: Nakładem Składnicy Weterynaryjnej Spółdzielni Lekarzy Weterynaryjnych R.P., 1947), 7.

75. Wasielewski, "Jak po wojnie leczono konie."

76. Witold Stefański, "Materiały w sprawie produkcji antygenu," *Medycyna Weterynaryjna* 3, no. 10 (1947): 656. See also the February 1947 issue of *Medycyna Weterynaryjna*.

77. "Protokół, November 28, 1946 w biurze przedstawiciela MRiRR do Spraw UNRRA," MRiRR, 2/162/0/26/3259, pp. 42, 45, AAN.

NOTES TO PAGES 150-152   259

78. "Rachunek," January 15, 1947, UWS, 65/317/0/25/5518, p. 1, APwSZ. See also "Instrukcja w sprawie rozdziału artykułów rolniczych z dostaw UNRAA," 13; Sprawa przydziału inwentarza żywego z dostaw UNRA—korespondencja z powiatami, 1946, WUZW, 72/509/0-542, p. 13, APW.

79. "Rolnicza Centrala Mięsna, oddz. w Warszawie, to MRiRR," September 19, 1946, Dostawy koni i bydła z UNRRA, 1946–48, ZSC, 2/160/0/3/1104, AAN.

80. "Protokół w sprawie państwowej lecznicy zwierząt z dostaw UNRRA," September 12, 1946, 9; Ministry of Agriculture to Wydział Wet. Woj. Urz. Ziem. W Szczecinie, 77, Dział Weterynaryjny, Lecznice UNRRA, UWS, 65/317/0/25/5518, ApwSZ.

81. Veterinary manuals included the following: Władysław Jastrzębiec, ed., *Poradnik weterynaryjny dla rolników i hodowców* (Warsaw: Wyd. Księgarnia Rolnicza, 1945); Ministerstwo Obrony Narodowej, *Instrukcja weterynaryjna: Zapobieganie i zwalczanie chorób zaraźliwych u koni* (Łódź: Wojskowy Instytut Naukowo-Wydawniczy, 1946); Jan K. Chodowiecki, *Gospodarska hodowla koni*, 3rd ed. (Kraków: Polskie Towarzystwo Zootechnicze, 1946); A. Sztremer, *Opieka nad źrebną klaczą i źrebnięciem* (Olsztyn: Druk Państwowa, 1947).

82. Woodbridge, *UNRRA*, 1:491.

83. "Report on UNRRA Livestock," UNA.

84. Departament Ekonomiczny, Wyd. Obrotu Zewnętrznego, "UNRRA Mission to Poland," February 1, 1947, MRiRR, 2/162/0/2.4/506, p. 112, AAN.

85. Rohrer, "Diary of a Saltwater Cowboy," in *Scrapbook of Cowboy Memories*, MCA.

86. M. M., "Przychodzą statki z końmi," *Dziennik Bałtycki* 199 (1946): 3.

87. Łaptos, *Humanitaryzm i polityka*, 391.

88. Sprawa przydziału inwentarza, WUZW, 72/509/0-542, APW. On the role of private companies in transporting animals, see also Thurl Metzger, "Report of Work in Poland, October 15, 1946 to April 16, 1947," 1945–53 Project Committee Reports, folder 19, box 1, series 4/1/6, HP, BHLA.

89. The Central Office for Meat was also translated as the Agricultural Meat Corporation. On this body's work, see "The Agricultural Meat Corporation Ltd. in Warsaw," in *Katalog oficjalny pierwszych Międzynarodowych Targów Gdańskich, 2.VIII-10.VIII, 1947* (Gdańsk: Wydawcy Międzynarodowe Targi Gdańskie, 1947), 116; "Rolnicza centrala mięsna to MRiRR," November 9, 1945, ZSC, 2/160/0/3/1104, AAN; "Leo Gerstenzang to C.M. Drury," February 18, 1946, Monthly Reports: December–January, S-1400-0000-0025-00001, p. 55, UNA. Gerstenzang was the chief officer of Regional Delegates of the UNRRA Mission to Poland.

90. "Uwagi do konferencji," September 28, 1946, ZSC, 2/160/0/3/1104, AAN.

91. See assorted letters throughout the following files: Dotyczy: podziału koni otrzymanych z Ameryki przez UNRRA, 1945–46, WUZW, 72/509/0-828, APW; Sprawa przydziału inwentarza, WUZW, 72/509/0-542, APW.

92. "Report on UNRRA Livestock," UNA; "Urząd Ziemski to Biuro Kontroli, Szczecin," August 31, 1946, UWS, 5/317/0/19.1/5129, pp. 29–30, APwSZ; Sprawa przydziału inwentarza, WUZW, 72/509/0-542, APW.

93. "Naczelnik Wyd. Rolnego to Woj. Inspektorat Pożarnictwa w Pruszkowie," May 7, 1946, Sprawa przydziału inwentarza, WUZW, 72/509/0-542, APW; "Konie z UNRRA," *Zagoń Ojczysty*, August 1946.

94. "Powiatowa Komisja Rozdziału, Szczecin to Urząd Ziemski Zachodnio Pomorski," October 5, 1946, UWS, 65/317/0/19.1/5129, p. 85, APwSZ.

95. "Report on UNRRA Livestock," UNA; Łaptos, *Humanitaryzm i polityka*, 393.

96. M. E. Hays, "Field Trip," September 10, 1945, UNRRA—Poland Mission, 1944–49, file 7, S-0527-1064, UNA. See also Łaptos, *Humanitaryzm i polityka*, 393.

97. "Report on UNRRA Livestock," UNA. See also "Dr. Wilder Describes Polish Trip," *Morgan Horse Magazine*, May 1946.

98. The process of expropriating large holdings and distributing plots of land to individual peasants or, alternatively, creating state farms, is described in Marta Błąd, "Land Reform in People's Poland (1944–89)," *Rural History* 32 (2021): 149–65, esp. 152. For additional context, see also Anna Wylegała, "Beyond the Victimhood Narrative: A Case Study of Unexpectedly Successful Collectivization in Communist Poland," *Journal of Social History* 56, no. 4 (2023): 805–27.

99. For payments in kind that Poland made for some of the goods it received, see Andrzej Jezierski and Cecylia Leszczyńska, *Historia Gospodarcza Polski* (Warsaw: Wyd. Key Text, 1997), 397.

100. Woodbridge, *UNRRA*, 2:40–41. For a contemporary analysis in the US media of the need to pay for UNRRA aid, see Douglas Larsen, "Critics Charge Breakdown of UNRRA Financing Means Hunger for Millions," *Wilmington Morning Star*, November 25, 1945. For a discussion of payment arrangements related to Hoover's ARA, see Davide Rodogno, *Night on Earth: A History of International Humanitarianism in the Near East, 1918–1930* (Cambridge: Cambridge University Press, 2021), 33–35.

101. Sawicki, *Misja UNRRA w Polsce*, 15–16, 112. On postwar rationing in Poland, see Mateusz Pazgan, "Zagadnienia aprowizacji ludności województwa wrocławskiego z perspektywy starostwa kamiennogórskiego w latach 1945–1947," *Annales Universitatis Mariae-Curie-Skłodowska* 69, no. 1–2 (2014): 75, 77–78; Woodbridge, *UNRRA*, 2:221. On Communist food policies more generally, see Katarzyna Stańczyk-Wiślicz, "Eating Healthy, Eating Modern: The 'Urbanization' of Food Tastes in Communist Poland (1945–1989)," *Ethnologia Polona* 41 (2020): 141–62.

102. Jessica Reinisch, "'We Shall Rebuild Anew a Powerful Nation': UNRRA, Internationalism and National Reconstruction in Poland," *Journal of Contemporary History* 43, no. 3 (2008): 461–62. See also "Impact of UNRRA on Poland: Highlights—April 1947," Council of Foreign Voluntary Agencies in Poland: Reports, 1947–49, folder 51, box 1, series 4/1/6, POW, BHLA.

103. Different documents give approximate costs for horses, and these can vary quite a bit. See, for example, Ministerstwo Ziem Odzyskanych w Warszawie, 2/196/0/7/1442, p. 301, AAN.

104. "Wg rozdzielnika," November 27, 1946, MZO, 2/196/0/06/1031, p. 23, AAN.

105. "KROWA," *Głos Pomorski*, July 27–28, 1946.

106. "Wojewódzki Urząd Ziemski Szczeciński to Kierownik Pow. Biura Rolnego," November 21, 1946, UWS, 65/317/0/19.1/5129, p. 143, APwSZ. See also "Wojewódzki Urząd Ziemski w Lublinie to Powiatowy Urząd Ziemski w Puławach," October 5, 1946, Powiatowy Urząd Ziemski w Puławach, 35/733/0/-/108, p. 19, Archiwum Państwowe w Lublinie.

107. For complaints about the insurance rules, see Departament Kontroli, starting on 58, Kontrole przeprowadzone w działach Rolnictwa i Reform Rolnych Urzędów..., 1946–49, MRiRR, 2/162/0/4/797, AAN.

108. Ministerstwo Rolnictwa i Reform Rolnych, "Wg rozdzielnika," November 27, 1946, MZO, 2/196/0/06/1031, p. 23, AAN.

109. Korespondencja, umowy, sprawozdania związane z rozdziałem, 1946–47, MZO, 2/196/0/11/1971, p. 201, AAN.

110. "Zarząd Powiatowy Zw. Samopomocy Chłopskiej w Wałczu to Narodowy Bank Polski w Szczecinie," September 3, 1949, UWS, 65/317/0/19.1/5130, p. 68, APwSZ.

111. "Regulamin administrowania przez Państwowy Bank Rolny," June 26, 1946, UWS, 65/317/0/19.1/5128, p. 3, APwSZ. See also Łaptos, *Humanitaryzm i polityka*, 395.

112. "23,000 koni oraz 60,00 sztuk bydła," 1946. This is a newspaper clipping that comes from Wycinki Prasowe, 1945–46, Centralny Urząd Planowania (hereafter CUP), 2/192/0/3.22/1183,p. 26, AAN. See also Sawicki, *Misja UNRRA w Polsce*, 117.

113. "Henryk Bartold to BSC," January 29, 1948, Thank-You Letters 1948, folder 31, box 1, series 4/1/6, POW, BHLA.

114. "Konie z UNRRA w drodze," 1946. This newspaper clipping comes from Wycinki Prasowe, 1945–46, CUP, 2/192/0/3.22/1183, p. 26, AAN.

115. "Instrukcja," 1946, Komisja "A"- Ustalenia priorytetów przywozowych. Odbudowa Rolnictwa, 1946, CUP, 2/192/0/8.18/3804A, p. 5, AAN.

116. "Powiatowa Komisja Rozdziału, Szczecin to Urząd Ziemski Zachodnio Pomorski," October 1, 1946, UWS, 65/317/0/19.1/5129, pp. 87–89, APwSZ.

117. Departament Kontroli, "Sprawozdanie from Dr. Stefan Trzeciak, Inspektor, Biuro Kontroli MRiRR to Minister MRiRR," December 22, 1947, MRiRR, 2/162/0/4/797, AAN.

118. "Woj. Szczeciński, Dział Reform Rolnych, to Ministerstwo Rolnictwa i Reform Rolnych," February 1948, Wykazy Sprowadzonych Koni, UWS, 65/317/0/19.1/5130, p. 25, APwSZ.

119. Pazgan, "Zagadnienia aprowizacji ludności," 80–81; Sawicki, *Misja UNRRA w Polsce*, 116.

120. On how horses adjusted to their new environments, see "Konie z UNRRA," *Zagoń Ojczysty*, August 1946; P. J., "Jak należy obchodzić się z koniem z dostaw UNRRA," *Głos Pomorski*, October 4, 1946; A. Pępkowski, "Dostawy zwierząt UNRRA dla Polski," *Medycyna Weterynaryjna* 3, no. 5 (1947): 305.

121. Gaziński and Wanot, "Działalność UNRRA i jej pomoc," 21–22.

122. "Notatka w sprawie wyładunku," ZSC, 2/160/0/3/1104, p. 7, AAN.

123. The term "Wild West" was used by postwar contemporaries and is the title of Beata Halicka's book: *The Polish Wild West: Forced Migration and Cultural Appropriation in the Polish-German Borderlands, 1945–1948*, trans. Paul McNamara (London: Routledge, 2020). On the origins of the term, see Kinga Siewor, "Regained Landscapes: The Transfer of Power and Tradition in Polish Discourse of the Regained Territories," in *East Central Europe Between the Colonial and the Postcolonial in the Twentieth Century*, eds. Siegfried Huigen and Dorota Kołodziejczyk (Cham, Switzerland: Palgrave Macmillan, 2023), 190–91. The script from the 1967 movie

NOTES TO PAGES 156-158

Our Folks (*Sami swoi*) (dir. Sylwester Chęciński) also makes this link between the "wild" region and "wild" horses. A character says, "He he! UNRRA knows that it's the Wild West here and so sends wild horses." See "Scenariusz filmu 'Sami Swoi' Sylwestra Chęcińskiego," Film Sami Swoi, accessed August 23, 2022, https://filmsamiswoi.wixsite.com/strona/scenariusz1. On the subject of the film, see Agata Zborowska, *Życie Rzeczy w Powojennej Polsce* (Warsaw: Wydawnictwa Uniwersytetu Warszawskiego, 2018), 220–21.

124. Halicka, *Polish Wild West*, 2.

125. "Na nowym szlaku," *Gazeta Informacyjna*, July 27, 1946.

126. Urszula Kozłowska and Tomasz Sikowski, "The Implementation of the Soviet Healthcare Model in 'People's Democracy' Countries—the Case of Post-War Poland (1944–1953)," *Social History of Medicine* 34, no. 4 (2020): 1204.

127. Małgorzata Praczyk, "Śmierć zwierząt w narracjach autobiograficznych osadników na 'Ziemiach Odzyskanych': Uwagi o obecności," *Autobiografia* 1, no. 12 (2019): 50–51. See also Kamiński, "Fear Management," 234.

128. Z. Tomaszewski, "Obejmujemy folwarki poniemieckie," *Głos Ludu*, March 21, 1946.

129. "Report from the Regional Delegate for the Districts of Łódź and Kielce to Edward Z. Wróblewski, Chief of Distribution Division," July 23, 1946, Monthly Reports, 1946, S-1400-0000-0029, p. 33, UNA.

130. Błąd, "Land Reform in People's Poland," 153–54.

131. The term "moral reconstruction" was used slightly differently by Russell W. Yohn of North Manchester, Indiana, when he called for more aid to be given to a specific ethnic German family in the region. See "Yohn to 'Ostroda', Warsaw," February 14, 1948, General 1946–48, folder 1, box 1, series 4/1/6, POW, BHLA. On reconstructing the west, see Praczyk, "Śmierć zwierząt," 50–51. See also Kamiński, "Fear Management," 234.

132. Praczyk, "Śmierć zwierząt," 41–55, esp. 46–47, 50–51.

133. Małgorzata Praczyk, *Pamięć środowiskowa we wspomnieniach osadników na "Ziemiach Odzyskanych"* (Poznań: Wydawnictwo Instytutu Historii UAM, 2018), 191; Łaptos, *Humanitaryzm i polityka*, 393. See also Emilia Kledzik, Maciej Michalski, and Małgorzata Praczyk, eds., *"Ziemie Odzyskane": W poszukiwaniu nowych narracji* (Poznań: Instytut Historii UAM, 2018).

134. "Rozdzielnik Geograficzny," Sprawa przydziału inwentarza, WUZW, 72/509/0-542, APW.

135. Eastern European Division Loan Department, "Preliminary Paper No. 6 for the Working Party on the Polish Loan Application" (International Bank for Reconstruction and Development, May 26, 1947), https://documents1.worldbank.org/curated/en/558411468095985925/pdf/multi-page.pdf, 17.

136. Praczyk, *Pamięć środowiskowa*, 210–16.

137. Holly Case, "Reconstruction in East-Central Europe: Clearing the Rubble of Cold War Politics," *Past and Present* 210, suppl. 6 (2011): 88.

138. Metzger, "Report of Work in Poland," BHLA.

139. Praczyk, *Pamięć środowiskowa*, 297.

140. Zygmunt Dulczewskis and Andrzej Kwilecki, eds., *Pamiętniki osadników Ziem Odzyskanych*, 2nd ed. (Poznań: Wyd. Poznańskie, 1970), 349. For additional references

to UNRRA in peasant memoirs, see Józef Skrzypski, "Opis mojej wsi," 1949–51, Towarzystwo Pamiętnikarstwa Polskiego, 2/2617/0/11068, AAN.

8. UNRRA and Animal Politics in Poland

1. For Polish uses of "Auntie UNRRA," see, for example, Mateusz Pazgan, "Zagadnienia aprowizacji ludności województwa wrocławskiego z perspektywy starostwa kamiennogórskiego w latach 1945–1947," *Annales Universitatis Mariae-Curie-Skłodowska* 69, no. 1–2 (2014): 79; "Zaraz po wojnie przyjechała do Polski 'Cioteczka Unra,'" Polskie Radio, November 9, 2020, https://www.polskieradio.pl/39/156/Artykul/2616894,Zaraz-po-wojnie-przyjechala-do-Polski-cioteczka-Unra. On the general Polish reception of UNRRA donations, see Józef Łaptos, *Humanitaryzm i polityka: Pomoc UNRRA dla Polski i polskich uchodźców w latach 1944–1947* (Kraków: Wyd. Naukowe Uniwersytetu Pedagogicznego, 2018), 448.

2. This phrase comes from a drawing by Jerzy Zaruba published in the satirical magazine *Pins* (*Szpilki*). See *Szpilki*, September 25, 1945.

3. Łaptos, *Humanitaryzm i polityka*, 395.

4. That the aid contributed to creating a positive view of the government is discussed in Bruno Kamiński, "Fear Management: Foreign Threats in the Postwar Polish Propaganda—the Influence and the Reception of the Communist Media (1944–1956)" (PhD diss., European University Institute, 2016), 236–39, esp. 238.

5. "Pomoc UNRRA zachowa Polska we wdzięcznej pamięci," *Kurier Szczeciński*, November 14, 1945.

6. "Przekrój tygodnia," *Przekrój*, September 8–14, 1946. See also the three-minute film *Generalny dyrektor UNRRA La Guardia z wizytą w Polsce* (Wytwórnia Filmowa Wojska Polskiego, 1946), accessed January 27, 2022, FINA, http://repozytorium.fn.org.pl/?q=pl/node/4444.

7. W. B., "W Sezamie UNRRA," *Naprzód Dolnośląski*, August 30, 1946. On Silesia, see John J. Kulczycki, *Belonging to the Nation: Inclusion and Exclusion in the Polish-German Borderlands, 1939–1951* (Cambridge, MA: Harvard University Press, 2016).

8. *Przybycie i wyładunek transportu koni z darów UNRRA* (Wytwórnia Filmowa Wojska Polskiego, 1946), accessed July 26, 2024, FINA, http://www.repozytorium.fn.org.pl/?q=pl/node/4368. The film is also discussed in Agata Zborowska, *Życie rzeczy w powojennej Polsce* (Warsaw: Wydawnictwa Uniwersytetu Warszawskiego, 2018), 220.

9. *Orka wiosenna* (Wytwórnia Filmowa Wojska Polskiego, 1946), accessed July 26, 2024, FINA, http://www.repozytorium.fn.org.pl/?q=pl/node/4316.

10. On dairying as "women's work," see Richie Nimmo, "The Mechanical Calf," in *Making Milk: The Past, Present, and Future of Our Primary Food*, eds. Mathilde Cohen and Yoriko Otomo (London: Bloomsbury, 2017), 84.

11. Eastern European Division Loan Department, "Preliminary Paper No. 6 for the Working Party on the Polish Loan Application" (International Bank for Reconstruction and Development, May 26, 1947), https://documents1.worldbank.org/curated/en/558411468095985925/pdf/multi-page.pdf, 78–81. See also UNRRA, *Economic Recovery in the Countries Assisted by UNRRA* (Washington, DC: UNRRA, 1946), 76; Richard C. Lukas, *Bitter Legacy: Polish-American Relations in the Wake of*

World War II (Lexington: University Press of Kentucky, 1982), 101; Łaptos, *Humanitaryzm i polityka*, 352. On milk rations, see "Translated Letter from Lublin District Office, Supply and Trade Division to Melvin P. McGovern," June 28, 1946, Monthly Reports, 1946, S-1400-0000-0029, p. 25, UNA; George Woodbridge, *UNRRA: The History of the United Nations Relief and Rehabilitation Administration* (New York: Oxford University Press, 1950), 2:221; Łaptos, *Humanitaryzm i polityka*, 372–73.

12. *Orka wiosenna*.

13. Sabina Brzozowska, "Człowiek—zwierzę—rzecz w *Chłopach* Władysława Reymonta," *Porównania* 2, no. 29 (2021): 99–103. The term "interspecies parallel" appears on p. 100.

14. Ladislas Reymont, *The Peasants: Spring*, trans. Michael H. Dziewicki (New York: Alfred A. Knopf, 1928), 92, https://archive.org/details/bwb_P8-CSD-500/page/n3/mode/2up?q=. The English phrase "we owe our lives to her alone" appears in the Polish version as "*moja żywicielka jedyna*," "my only breadwinner" or "life giver." See Władysław Reymont, *Chłopi, Część trzecia—Wiosna*, wolnelektury.pl, para. 1055, accessed July 28, 2024, https://wolnelektury.pl/katalog/lektura/chlopi-czesc-trzecia-wiosna.html#f1055. Thanks to Rafał Stolarz for drawing my attention to Reymont's depiction of cows as *żywicielki*.

15. Ladislas Reymont, *The Peasants: Winter*, trans. Michael H. Dziewicki (New York: Alfred A. Knopf, 1925), 19, https://archive.org/details/peasantswinter0000ladi/mode/2up.

16. L. Reymont, *Peasants: Winter*, 18, 20.

17. L. Reymont, *Peasants: Winter*, 15.

18. L. Reymont, *Peasants: Winter*, 16.

19. L. Reymont, *Peasants: Winter*, 83.

20. See also Brzozowska, "Człowiek—zwierzę," 101.

21. L. W. Shultz, "Notes Concerning the Livestock Situation in Poland," 1945–53, folder 1, box 1, series 4/1/9, Heifer Project, BHLA.

22. This figure was achieved through a calculation that assumed that only kids under twelve plus pregnant women and nursing mothers would consume milk; it did not account for other demographic groups, such as the elderly. "UNRRA Mission to Poland," February 1, 1947, MRiRR, 2/162/0/2.4/506, p. 140, AAN; UNRRA, *Economic Recovery*, 76.

23. On the UNRRA angle, see Silvia Salvatici, "Sights of Benevolence: UNRRA's Recipients Portrayed," in *Humanitarian Photography: A History*, eds. Heide Fehrenbach and Davide Rodogno (New York: Cambridge University Press, 2015), 202, 216–17. On visual imagery, see also Heide Fehrenbach and Davide Rodogno, "The Morality of Sight: Humanitarian Photography in History," in *Humanitarian Photography: A History*, ed. Heide Fehrenbach and Davide Rodogno (New York: Cambridge University Press, 2015), 1; Paul Betts, "The Polemics of Pity: British Photographs of Berlin, 1945–47," in *Humanitarianism and Media, 1900 to the Present*, ed. Johannes Paulmann (New York: Berghahn, 2019), 128–29.

24. Vachon uses the term "UNRRA angle" in a letter to his wife Penny, April 6, 7, or so, 1946, in *Poland, 1946: The Photographs and Letters of John Vachon*, ed. Ann Vachon, with an introduction by Brian Moore (Washington, DC: Smithsonian Institution Press, 1995), 53.

25. See fig. 1 in chap. 4.

26. Merle Curti, *American Philanthropy Abroad: A History* (New Brunswick, NJ: Rutgers University Press, 1963), 484. See also Robin Patric Clair and Lindsey B. Anderson, "Portrayals of the Poor on the Cusp of Capitalism: Promotional Materials in the Case of Heifer international," *Management Communication Quarterly* 27, no. 4 (2013): 548.

27. Eastern European Division Loan Department, "Preliminary Paper No. 6."

28. "Wojewoda Olsztyński to Wicepremier W. Gomulka, Minister Ziem Odzyskanych," July 17, 1947, MZO, 2/196/07/1428, pp. 30–32, AAN.

29. Departament Kontroli, K.L., "Dzielą się zgodnie z ludzką krzywdą," *Dziennik Ludowy*, August 18, 1946, MRiRR, 2/162/0/4/948, p. 3, AAN.

30. Pomoc UNRRA dla Polski. Sprawozdanie, MPiOS, 2/402/0/6/328, pp. 107–21, AAN.

31. "The Provincial Land Office to the Zw. Samopomocy Chłopskiej," February 11, 1946, WUZW, 72/509/0-828, p. 22, APW.

32. O. S., "Tajemnica rozdziału koni i krów dla osadników," *Dziennik Ludowy*, August 13, 1946. The article is reprinted on p. 27 in Wydz. Rolniczy, UNRRA—Przydziały Koni, UWS, 65/317/0/19.1/5129, APwSz.

33. See "Visitation Notes Related to the Family of Eryka Bienkowska," June 19, 1948, Visitations, 1948, folder 32, box 1, series 4/1/6, POW, BHLA; Kontrola rozdzielnictwa UNRRA (inwentarza żywego), 1947–48, MZO, 2/196/0/06/1031, AAN. Cases related to fraud tactics are on pp. 63–74.

34. Zygmunt Dulczewski and Andrzej Kwilecki, eds., *Pamiętniki osadników Ziem Odzyskanych*, 2nd ed. (Poznań: Wyd. Poznańskie, 1970), 354.

35. "Woj. Urząd Ziemski w Warszawie to MRiRR," April 16, 1946, Sprawa przydziału inwentarza, WUZW, 72/509/0-542, APW. On bribery and corruption, see also Pobierania łapówek za przydział koni z darów UNRRA, Komisja Specjalna do Walki z Nadużyciami i Szkodnictwem Gospodarczym w Warszawie (hereafter KSWNSG), 2/170/0/3.22/1000, AAN. See also "Niesprawiedliwy rozdział koni z UNRRA," in *Jedność Narodowa*, which appears in this archival file on p. 20.

36. "Urząd Ziemski to Biuro Kontroli, Szczecin," August 31, 1946, Wydz. Rolniczy, UNRRA—Przydziały Koni, UWS, 65/317/0/19.1/5129, pp. 29–30, APwSz.

37. "Raport," February 12, 1946, Dotyczy: podziału koni otrzymanych z Ameryki przez UNRRA, 1945–46, WUZW, 72/509/0-828, p. 23, APW.

38. "M.E. Hays to Ł. Witkowski," August 1, 1946, MRiRR, 2/162/0/21.5/3012, pp. 79, 81, AAN.

39. On the Polish transportation system, see "Transport Rehabilitation in Poland" (London: Division of Operational Analysis, April 1947), S-1297-0000-0426-00001, UNA.

40. "Rozdzielnictwo inwentarza żywego," June 30, 1947, Kontrola rozdzielnictwa UNRRA, MZO, 2/196/0/06/1031, pp. 54–57, AAN.

41. "Rozdzielnik Geograficzny," Sprawa przydziału inwentarza, WUZW, 72/509/0-542, APW.

42. "Urząd Ziemski to Biuro Kontroli, Szczecin," August 31, 1946, UWS, 65/317/0/19.1/5129, pp. 29–30, APwSz.

43. The contemporary popularity of the phrase is highlighted in Aleksandra Sułwa, "Skarby z UNRRA i zrzuty od innych ciotek: W paczkach przysyłano do Polski też wolność," *Dziennik Polski*, June 23, 2017, https://dziennikpolski24.pl/skarby

-z-unrra-i-zrzuty-od-innych-ciotek-w-paczkach-przysylano-do-polski-tez-wolnosc /ar/12203627. Another play on the acronym (in English) is "You Never Really Relieved Anybody." See Łaptos, *Humanitaryzm i polityka*, 276–77.

44. "Sprawozdanie," July 24, 1947, Kontrola rozdzielnictwa UNRRA, MZO, 2/196/0/06/1031, p. 41, AAN.

45. See, for example, "Napad rabusiów na transport UNRRA," 1946. This is a newspaper clipping and comes from Wycinki Prasowe, 1945–46, CUP, 2/192/0/3.22/1183, p. 22, AAN.

46. Aleksander Juźwik, "Zagraniczna pomoc charytatywna dla dzieci i młodzieży w Polsce w latach 1945–50," *Polska 1944/45–1980: Studia i Materiały* 11 (2013): 96.

47. On the Guard, see Ochrona transportów towarów UNNRA: Organizacja i działalność Straży Wartowniczo-Konwojowej UNRRA, 1946–47, Ministerstwo Żeglugi i Handlu Zagranicznego w Warszawie, 2/286/0/24/417, AAN. On the problem of theft, see also "Protokół konferencji Polskich władz portowych," July 16, 1946, Protokoły, sprawozdania, raporty, zestawienia dostaw, 1946–48, ZSC, 2/160/0/3/1104, AAN.

48. "Dr. George Tells Trip Experience," *Union County Journal*, July 1, 1946.

49. Juźwik, "Zagraniczna pomoc charytatywna," 96. For a scathing contemporary account of the Communist corruption that plagued UNRRA efforts in Poland, see Edward S. Kerstein, *Red Star over Poland: A Report from Behind the Iron Curtain* (Appleton, WI: C. C. Nelson, 1947). Kerstein was a Polish-speaking American dispatched by *The Milwaukee Journal* in the fall of 1945 to Poland to report on the evolving situation there.

50. Benon Gaziński and Bogusław Wanot, "Działalność UNRRA i jej pomoc dla rolnictwa w Polsce," *Rocznik Muzeum Narodowego Rolnictwa w Szreniawie* 19 (1993): 18.

51. Jerzy Kukliński, "Straż wartowniczo-konwojowa UNRRA i straż morska," Gedanopedia, December 15, 2015, https://gdansk.gedanopedia.pl/gdansk/?title=STRA%C5%BB_WARTOWNICZO-KONWOJOWA_UNRRA_I_STRA%C5%BB_MORSKA.

52. For the relevant legislation, see "Dziennik Ustaw—rok 1945 nr 53 poz. 302," Infor, accessed June 6, 2022, https://www.infor.pl/akt-prawny/DZU.1945.053.000 0302,metryka,dekret-o-utworzeniu-i-zakresie-dzialania-komisji-specjalnej-do-walki -z-naduzyciami-i-szkodnictwem-gospodarczym.html. See also "Wysiedlanie złodziei towarów UNRRA," *Gazeta Morska*, August 6, 1946.

53. Piotr Majer, "Komisja Specjalna do Walk z Nadużyciami i Szkodnictwem Gospodarczym (1945–1954): Uwagi o genezie, działalności i ewolucji," *Studia Prawnoustrojowe* 6 (2006): 186–87. For a detailed analysis of the commission and for a few brief references to cases that involved UNRRA animals and/or goods, see Piotr Fiedorczyk, *Komisja specjalna do walki z nadużyciami i szkodnictwem gospodarczym 1945–1954* (Białystok: Temida 2, 2002).

54. "Delegatura w Gdańsku to Komisja Specjalna w Warszawie," August 30, 1946, KSWNSG, 2/170/0/4/1937, pp. 2–3, AAN. Additional cases of corruption can be found in UNRRA—w latach 1947, 1948, 1949: Wnioski, postanowienia, orzeczenia, 1946–1949, KSWNSG, 2/170/0/4/1939, AAN. A particularly well-documented case is in Sfałszowanie rachunku oraz nabycie konia po cenie niższej od obowiązującej, 1946, KSWNSG, 2/170/0/3.22/1011, AAN. This case pertains to one Józef Kiercz, a

member of the local distribution commission in Września, who was sentenced to a year of forced labor for obtaining an UNRRA horse without paying for it.

55. Kontrola rozdzielnictwa UNRRA (inwentarza żywego), 1947–48, MZO, 2/196/0/06/1031, pp. 63–74, AAN.

56. For an example, see "Delegatura w Gdańsku to Komisja Specjalna w Warszawie," September 30, 1947, KSWNSG, 2/170/0/4/1939, pp. 2–3, AAN.

57. Thurl Metzger, "Report of Work in Poland, October 15, 1946 to April 16, 1947," 1945–53 Project Committee Reports, folder 19, box 1, series 4/1/6, HP, BHLA.

58. "Inspektor MRiRR J. Konarzewski to Biuro Kontroli," November 5, 1948, MRiRR, 2/162/0/4/797, pp. 1–2, AAN.

59. "Report by Stefan Radwański," October 30, 1948, MRiRR, 2/162/0/4/797, pp. 17–20, AAN. Radwański was an inspector with the Inspection Department of the Ministry of Agriculture. Depositions from witnesses critical of distribution methods can be found in Kontrole przeprowadzone w Działach Rolnictwa i Reform Rolnych Urzędów . . . , 1946–49, MRiRR, 2/162/0/4/797, AAN, starting on p. 21.

60. "Report on UNRRA Livestock Imported to Poland from September 29, 1945 to July 28, 1946," July 29, 1946, UNRRA Subject Files, file 72, S-0527-1107, UNA; "Report on Field Trip to Baltic Port Area and Bydgoszcz," February 12, 1946, UNRRA—Poland Mission, 1944–49, Food and Agricultural Rehabilitation Division, Warsaw, file 7, S-0527-1064, UNA.

61. "Ł. Witkowski to T.A. Pato," February 17, 1947, S-0527-1107, UNA.

62. "Protokóły z konferencji i narad," MRiRR, 162/0/26/3259, AAN.

63. "Sprawozdanie Urzędu woj. Szczecińskiego do dnia 30. XI.46 r.," UWS, 65/317/0/25/5518, pp. 66, 68, APwSz.

64. Dulczewski and Kwilecki, *Pamiętniki osadników*, 292–93.

65. Peggy Reiff Miller, "UNRRA Livestock Shipments with Losses by Ship," Seagoing Cowboys, accessed August 16, 2024, https://seagoingcowboys.com/seagoing-cowboys/the-unrra-years/; Łaptos, *Humanitaryzm i polityka*, 391.

66. Konie z pomocy UNRRA dla Polski (Przedsiębiorstwo Państwowe "Film Polski," 1947), accessed July 26, 2024, FINA, http://www.repozytorium.fn.org.pl/?q=pl/node/9350.

67. For an overview of interwar Polish animal welfare, see Eva Plach, "The Animal Welfare Movement in Interwar Poland," *Polish Review* 57, no. 2 (2012): 21–43.

68. Protokóły z zebrań, 1946–51, Towarzystwo Ochrony Zwierząt w Polsce (hereafter TOZ), 2/152/0/2/7, AAN; Sprawozdania z działalności Oddziałów TOZ, 1946–51, TOZ, 2/152/0/2/18, AAN.

69. Tony Judt as quoted in Paul Betts, *Ruin and Renewal: Civilizing Europe After World War II* (New York: Basic Books, 2020), 2–3.

70. "Higiena Zwierząt," c. 1950, MRiRR, AAN.

71. "Okólnik Nr. 34 Komendanta Głównego Milicji Obywatelskiej z dn. 27 list. 1945," Zjednoczenie Towarzystwa Opieki nad Zwierzętami RP, 2/554, p. 82, AAN. On the 1928 legislation, see Plach, "Animal Welfare Movement," 21–43.

72. "Likwidacja niehumanitarnego uboju," *Kurier Codzienny*, March 11, 1948; "List otwarty do Pana Prezesa TOZ," *Dziennik Ludowy*, March 21, 1948; "Nie dręczyć zwierząt," *Express Wieczorny*, September 4, 1946, Wycinki prasowe, 1947–51, TOZ, 2/152/0/2/59, pp. 9, 11, 17, AAN. On horses, see also Gabriela Czapiewska,

"Historyczne uwarunkowania rozwoju rolnictwa uspołecznionego na Pomorzu Środkowym," *Słupskie Prace Geograficzne* 1 (2003): 55.

73. Sprawozdania z działalności: Zarządu Głównego od kwietnia 1939, TOZ, 2/152/0/2/15, AAN.

74. "Tadeusz Matecki to Bureau International Humanitaire Zoophile," December 29, 1947, TOZ, 2/152/0/5/57, pp. 52–53, AAN.

75. "Apel do społeczeństwa," Współpraca z instytucjami zagranicznymi: Korespondencja, informacje, TOZ, 2/152/0/5/57, p. 111, AAN. On horse inspections, see also "Sprawozdanie z kontroli działalności Zarządu Głównego Tow-a Och. Zw. w Polsce," December 23, 1950, TOZ, 2/152/0/2/16, p. 4, AAN.

76. "Sprawozdanie z działalności Zarządu Głównego Zjednoczenia TOZ," TOZ, 2/152/0/2/15, AAN.

77. A focus on the "rational" care of horses (including UNRRA horses) is reflected in A. Sztremer, *Opieka nad źrebną klaczą i źrebnięciem* (Olsztyn: Druk Państwowa, 1947).

78. "Sprawozdanie z kontroli działalności," 4, AAN.

79. "Sprawozdanie z kontroli działalności," 1, AAN; "Pełnomocnik, TOZ w Likwidacji," December 19, 1951, TOZ- ZG, 2/62, p. 24, AAN.

80. "Tadeusz Matecki to Margrethe Astrup," December 31, 1947, TOZ, 2/152/0/5/57, p. 82, AAN; "Co przywozimy i wywozimy przez porty Polskie," *Dziennik Bałtycki* 123 (1946): 4.

81. "TOZ/Matecki to Bureau International Humanitaire Zoophile," after February 12, 1947, TOZ, 2/152/0/5/57, p. 56, AAN. For another description of the arriving animals, see "Tadeusz Matecki to the Bureau International Humanitaire Zoophile," September 22, 1947, TOZ, 2/152/0/5/57, p. 45, AAN. The bureau was under the leadership of a Swedish British woman called Lizzy Lind-Af-Hageby and was supported by some British royals. See "Bureau International Humanitaire Zoophile to Tadeusz Matecki," September 3, 1947, February 18, 1947, TOZ, 2/152/0/5/57, pp. 42, 60, AAN.

82. "Tadeusz Matecki to Bureau International Humanitaire Zoophile," December 29, 1947, TOZ, 2/152/0/5/57, pp. 50–51, AAN.

9. Heifer Project Animals in Poland

1. On Heifer Project shipments to Poland, see "Letter from Ralph M. Delk," January 14, 1947, Heifer Letters, HP, BHLA; Departament Ekonomiczny, Wyd. Obrotu Zewnętrznego, "Assorted Lists," MRiRR, 2/162/0/2.4/528, pp. 2–12, AAN; "Rozchód 5.X.1945 do 31.XI. 1947," MRiRR, 2/262/0/26/3271, p. 2, AAN; "Pomoc Zagraniczna," 1945–46, MPiOS, 2/402/0/260, p. 76, AAN; Relief Work (FOR): Brethren Service Committee and Heifer Project, 1945–48, box 13, series E, JNS, DG 117, SCPC; "Report by Ralph M. Delk to Co-Workers," folder 9, box 1, series 4/1/6, HP, BHLA; "Heifer Project Committee," August 1947, Correspondence 1947, folder 10, box 1, series 4/1/6, HP, BHLA.

2. "Shipments Made by Heifer Project Committee as of January 1, 1949," in 1945–53 Project Committee Reports, folder 19, box 1, series 4/1/6, HP, BHLA; Thurl Metzger, "Report of Work in Poland, October 15, 1946 to April 16, 1947," 1945–53 Project Committee Reports, folder 19, box 1, series 4/1/6, HP, BHLA. The fact that

horses were included in this shipment does not appear in all references to the *Mount Whitney* sailing of early 1947.

3. John Bowman, "Relief Workers in Europe," *Gospel Messenger*, September 13, 1946; "Shipped: One Harness Maker with Supplies," *Gospel Messenger*, November 29, 1947; J. Kenneth Kreider, *A Cup of Cold Water: The Story of Brethren Service* (Elgin, IL: Brethren Press, 2001), chap. 9.

4. Many examples of requests for animals (including from the Izabelin Home for the Aged) can be found in Applications Granted, 1946–47, folder 27, box 1, series 4/1/6, POW, BHLA. This file contains English translations of requests sent to the Brethren but also some original Polish-language requests.

5. Letter from Ralph M. Delk, "Heifer News," May 14, 1947, Heifer Letters, HP, BHLA.

6. Peggy Reiff Miller, "Special Post: SS Woodstock Victory Carries Heifer Project Cattle to Poland 70 Years Ago Today," *Seagoing Cowboys* (blog), March 3, 2016.

7. UNRRA Standing Technical Committee on Welfare, "Memorandum on the Relation Between UNRRA and Voluntary Relief Organizations," June 1944, 7, box 77, series A, part 1, CCWR, DG 025, SCPC.

8. On the financial aspects of aid distribution, see Ben Shephard, "'Becoming Planning Minded': The Theory and Practice of Relief, 1940–1945," *Journal of Contemporary History* 43, no. 3 (2008): 410; Mathew Lloyd Adams, "Herbert Hoover and the Organization of the American Relief Effort in Poland (1919–1923)," *European Journal of American Studies* 4, no. 2 (2009): 1–19.

9. "Oświadczenie Odbioru," Applications Granted, 1946–47, folder 27, box 1, series 4/1/6, POW, BHLA.

10. "Act of Transferring the Heifer from American Gifts to the Polish Citizens," Heifer Project before November 8, 1946, folder 48, box 38, series 18, DWP, BHLA. Another example of a completed animal transfer document appears as "Act of Transferring the Heifer," July 19, 1946, 1945–53 Project Committee Reports, folder 19, box 1, series 4/1/6, HP, BHLA.

11. "Act of Transferring the Heifer from American Gifts," DWP, BHLA. See also Departament Ekonomiczny, Wyd. Obrotu Zewnętrznego, "Assorted Lists," MRiRR, 2/162/0/2.4/528, pp. 2–12, AAN; "Rozchód 5.X.1945 do 31. XI. 1947," MRiRR, 2/262/0/26/3271, p. 2, AAN.

12. Richard Rush, "My Cattle-Boat Experience, December 29, 1945–March 3, 1946," folder 14, box 1, Seagoing Cowboys Collection, HM 1–973, MCA.

13. Mr. and Mrs. Joe Thomasson, "Madera County Aids World Peace Through Project," in *Cowboy Memories*, eds. Bill Beck and Mel West (Little Rock, AR: Heifer Project International, 1994), 89.

14. Glee Yoder, *Passing on the Gift: The Story of Dan West* (Elgin, IL: Brethren Press, 1978), 103.

15. "Delk to His Co-Workers," box 13, series E, JNS, DG 117, SCPC.

16. Metzger, "Report of Work in Poland," BHLA.

17. Metzger, "Report of Work in Poland," BHLA.

18. "K. Załuski, Ministry of Shipping and Foreign Trade, to Donald R. Sabin, Acting Chief of Mission to Poland, UNRRA," March 13, 1947, Brethren Service Committee, Poland Mission, Department of Finance and Administration, S-1397-0000-0006-00001, p. 4, UNA; "UNRRA 1947–49," Correspondence 1947–49, folder 21, box 1, series 4/1/6,

POW, BHLA; Thurl Metzger, *The Road to Development* (Little Rock, AR: Heifer Project International, 1981), 21; Thurl Metzger, "The Polish Student Project," *Gospel Messenger*, May 8, 1948; Peggy Reiff Miller, "Was There Confiscation of UNRRA and Heifer Project Livestock?," *Seagoing Cowboys* (blog), June 23, 2017.

19. Józef Łaptos, *Humanitaryzm i polityka: Pomoc UNRRA dla Polski i polskich uchodźców w latach 1944–1947* (Kraków: Wyd. Naukowe Uniwersytetu Pedagogicznego, 2018), 443.

20. "Report of the Council of Foreign Voluntary Relief Agencies in Poland," June 1949, Zagraniczna dobrowolna pomoc dla Polski, Sprawozdanie za okres 1945–49, MPiOS, 2/402/0/6/351, p. 9, AAN.

21. Visitations, 1948, folder 32, box 1, series 4/1/6, POW, BHLA.

22. Metzger, "Report of Work in Poland," BHLA.

23. Dillon W. Throckmorton, "I Saw Your Heifers in Poland," *Gospel Messenger*, November 30, 1946; *Marine Bull Pen*, no. 10, August 29, 1946, Marine Bullpens and News Circulars, folder 10, box 75, MGP, Hist. MSS 1–129, MCA. On Throckmorton's mission to check up on animal placements, see also "Benjamin Bushong to 'To Whom It May Concern,'" June 8, 1946, Poland Mission, Department of Finance and Administration, Brethren Service Committee, S-1397-0000-0006-0001, p. 13, UNA.

24. Throckmorton, "I Saw Your Heifers."

25. Ralph E. Smeltzer, "From a Relief Worker's Diary," *Gospel Messenger*, December 28, 1946.

26. Smeltzer, "From a Relief Worker's Diary." The village of Krzywe Koło is rendered as Krzyive Kele in Smeltzer's account.

27. A cow in the early 2000s might be expected to produce a peak yield of thirty-five liters each day. Milk yields have increased significantly with factory farming, and this has had the effect of shortening cows' productive working lives to just a few years. Hannah Velten compares the effect of this intensive work to a person jogging for six hours each day of the week. See Hannah Velten, *Cow* (London: Reaktion Books, 2007), 160.

28. Smeltzer, "From a Relief Worker's Diary."

29. Peggy Reiff Miller, "Meeting Heifer Recipients in Poland, Part I," *Seagoing Cowboys* (blog), March 11, 2016.

30. L. W. Shultz, "Mission to Poland," *Gospel Messenger*, February 23, 1946; L. Shultz, "Report to Heifer Committee," January 19, 1946, 1945–53, folder 1, box 1, series 4/1/6, HP, BHLA. The cowboys are named in this report. See also Reiff Miller, "Meeting Heifer Recipients."

31. Shultz, "Mission to Poland." Shultz also recounts seeing Joy in Lawrence W. Shultz, *People and Places, 1890–1970: An Autobiography* (Winona Lake, IN: Life and Light, 1971), 105. See also "Bringing Joy to Poland," *Poland Today*, January 1947. *Poland Today* was the paper of the Polish Embassy in the United States.

32. "Report on Field Trip to Baltic Port Area and Bydgoszcz," February 12, 1946, UNRRA—Poland Mission, 1944–49, Food and Agricultural Rehabilitation Division, Warsaw, file 7, S-0527-1064, UNA. See also "Brethren Overseas Relief: How It Is Distributed," *Gospel Messenger*, November 24, 1945. George Willoughby wrote about his field trip in letters to his wife Lillian. See "Letters to Lillian," March 31–May 1, 1946, Foreign Travel, Involvement and Contacts, series D, part 1, George and Lillian Willoughby Papers, 48–50, DG 236, SCPC.

NOTES TO PAGES 184-188   271

33. Shultz, "Mission to Poland"; Shultz, *People and Places*, 105; Kreider, *Cup of Cold Water*, 135.

34. Peggy Reiff Miller, "Okanogan County Sea-Going Cowboys and Their Errands of Mercy," *Okanogan County Heritage*, Winter 2014, reposted in https://seagoingcowboys.com/wp-content/uploads/2022/02/okanagan-seagoing-cowboy-article_2014.pdf.

35. See entry from July 20, 1946, in David. H. White, "My Trip to Poland in 1946 Working on a UNRRA Ship," Seagoing Cowboys, accessed July 26, 2024, https://seagoingcowboyswebsite.files.wordpress.com/2015/10/stories_davidwhite.pdf.

36. See entry for July 18, 1946, in Arthur Meyer, "Art Meyer's Cattle Boat Experience: Introduction to Planned Book, Dated January 1991," Seagoing Cowboys, accessed February 13, 2020, https://seagoingcowboyswebsite.files.wordpress.com/2015/10/stories_artmeyer.pdf.

37. Shultz, "Mission to Poland."

38. Many letters of thanks are found in Thank-You Letters 1948, folder 31, box 1, series 4/1/6, POW, BHLA.

39. Heifer Letters, 1946–55, folder 1, box 3, series 4/1/6, HP, BHLA. Additional letters of thanks, with photographs, are in Brethren Service Committee, S-1268-0000-0039, pp. 17–34, UNA.

40. Robin Patric Clair and Lindsey B. Anderson, "Portrayals of the Poor on the Cusp of Capitalism: Promotional Materials in the Case of Heifer international," *Management Communication Quarterly* 27, no. 4 (2013): 543–44. The article includes examples of Heifer International's modern-day promotional materials.

41. "Witold Tanski to Thurl Metzger," January 15, 1948, and "Antoni Lewandowski to the BSC," April 22, 1948, Thank-You Letters 1948, POW, BHLA.

42. "Letter from 'The Small Blind Children from Laski' to Thurl Metzger," December 15, 1946, Relief Work (FOR): Brethren Service Committee and Heifer Project, 1945–48, box 13, series E, JNS, DG 117, SCPC. The institute also received two horses from UNRRA. See "Woj. Urząd Ziemski w Warszawie to Powiatowy Urząd Ziemski w Warszawie," May 24, 1946, Sprawa przydziału inwentarza, WUZW, 72/509/0-542, APW.

43. "Report on Field Trip," UNA; letters from John Vachon to Penny, February 12, 1946?, in *Poland, 1946: The Photographs and Letters of John Vachon*, ed. Ann Vachon, with an introduction by Brian Moore (Washington, DC: Smithsonian Institution Press, 1995), 31–33. In the letter to his wife Vachon does not get the details about the Brethren Service Committee or the Heifer Project quite right.

44. "Assurance of Good Treatment Given by Director General Lehman," *National Humane Review*, April 1946.

45. "Questionnaire of Wilbert Kropf of Oregon," Completed Questionnaires, folder 5, box 76, MGP, Hist. MSS 1–129, MCA.

46. Metzger, "Report of Work in Poland," BHLA.

47. Clarence H. Rosenberger, "A 'Cowboy' Evaluates the Trip to Europe with Relief Cattle," *Gospel Messenger*, September 22, 1945. See also "Russians Are Not Stealing Polish Livestock," *Gospel Messenger*, November 30, 1946.

48. Norman E. Thomas, ed., *Horses for Humanity: A Report on a Mission to Poland by Eleven Ministers* (St. Johnsville, NY: Enterprise and News, 1949), 17. The chapter

titled "The Government" is all about the difficult political situation in Poland and how it affected aid delivery.

49. Allen L. Eagles (FOR), "National Heifer Project Committee Meeting," March 29, 1947, Relief Work (FOR): Brethren Service Committee and Heifer Project, 1945–48, box 13, series E, JNS, DG 117, SCPC.

50. "Menshikov to M.R. Zigler," September 1, 1945, file 34, S-0527-1080, UNA. See also Robert Ebey, "A Trip to Poland with Brethren Service Heifers," box 1, JEN, Hist. MSS-1-893, p. 2, MCA.

51. "UNRRA Aide Denies Obstacles in Poland," *New York Times*, January 9, 1946; Amanda Melanie Bundy, "There Was a Man of UNRRA: Internationalism, Humanitarianism, and the Early Cold War in Europe, 1943–1947" (PhD diss., Ohio State University, 2017), 40. For general distribution problems and irregularities, see George Woodbridge, *UNRRA: The History of the United Nations Relief and Rehabilitation Administration* (New York: Oxford University Press, 1950), 2:212–14.

52. Jessica Reinisch, "'We Shall Rebuild Anew a Powerful Nation': UNRRA, Internationalism and National Reconstruction in Poland," *Journal of Contemporary History* 43, no. 3 (2008): 453.

53. Metzger, "Report of Work in Poland," BHLA.

54. "Report of the Council of Foreign Voluntary Relief Agencies," MPiOS, 2/402/0/6/351, pp. 3–17, AAN.

55. On the Quakers, see Lyndon S. Back, "The Quaker Mission in Poland: Relief, Reconstruction, and Religion," *Quaker History* 101, no. 2 (2012): 1; David S. Richie, "American Friends Service Committee in Poland: Color and Background Material No. 11," 1–27, box 38, series B, JNS, DG 117, SCPC. On CARE, see Susan Levine, "CARE Packages and the Business of Food Aid," *Food, Fatness and Fitness: Critical Perspectives* (blog), September 22, 2015, http://foodfatnessfitness.com/2015/09/22/care-packages/. On charities in Poland generally, see Łaptos, *Humanitaryzm i polityka*, 442; Dariusz Jarosz, "Zapomniani przyjaciele: Zagraniczna pomoc charytatywna w Polsce Ludowej (1945–1949)," in *Społeczeństwo, państwo, modernizacja*, ed. Włodzimierz Mędrzecki (Warsaw: Neriton, 2002), 163–75; Aleksander Juźwik, "Zagraniczna pomoc charytatywna dla dzieci i młodzieży w Polsce w latach 1945–50," *Polska 1944/45–1980: Studia i Materiały* 11 (2013): 97.

56. Examples of letters requesting aid can be found in "Applications 1948," folder 26, box 1, series 4/1/6, POW, BHLA.

57. "Robert Zigler to E.M. Hersch," May 21, 1947, Correspondence 1947, folder 10, box 1, series 4/1/6, HP, BHLA. A blank application form for potential cattle attendants is contained in this file as well. The application asks some interesting questions about whether the applicant believes in racial equality, considers himself a pacifist, participates in world peace efforts, and believes enemy nations should also be given relief supplies.

58. "Report of the Council of Foreign Voluntary Relief Agencies," MPiOS, 2/402/0/6/351, p. 31, AAN; Roger E. Sappington, "Social Involvement," in *Church of the Brethren: Past and Present*, ed. Donald F. Durnbaugh (Elgin, IL: Brethren Press, 1971), 102.

59. Opal D. Stech, "Brethren Service in Poland," in *To Serve the Present Age: The Brethren Service Story*, ed. Donald F. Durnbaugh (Elgin, IL: Brethren Press, 1975), chap. 12; Ralph M. Delk, "Heifer News," July 30, 1947, 1945–53 Project Committee Reports, 1945–53, folder 19, box 1, series 4/1/6, HP, BHLA.

60. Martin F. Strate, "H.P.C. News," May 25, 1948, Relief Work (FOR): Brethren Service Committee and Heifer Project, 1945–48, box 13, series E, JNS, DG 117, SCPC.

61. "Heifer Project Committee in Warsaw to the Ministry of Agriculture in Poland," February 16, 1948, Dary bractw kościelnych, 1946–48, MRiRR, 2/162/0/2.4/528, p. 13, AAN.

62. "Summary of Shipments by Countries 1944 to 1953 Inclusive" and "Shipments Made by Heifer Project Committee as of January 1, 1949," in 1945–53 Project Committee Reports, folder 19, box 1, series 4/1/6, HP, BHLA.

63. Ralph M. Delk, "Heifer News," July 30, 1947, 1945–53 Project Committee Reports, HP, BHLA.

64. Bierut himself articulated this position about the inadequacy of UNRRA aid. See "Prezydent Bierut i prezydent Truman o zwiększeniu pomocy UNRRA dla Polski," Głos Ludu, March 21, 1946. See also "W imię sprawiedliwości," Gazeta Lubelska, March 30, 1946; "Pomoc otrzymywana od UNRRA nie jest dostarczająca," Gazeta Lubelska, March 31, 1946.

65. Piotr Jachowicz, "Działalność UNRRA w Polsce w latach 1945–1948," Zeszyty Naukowe 2, no. 2 (1998): 49; Marek Żak, "Sytuacja Aprowizacyjna Legnicy w latach 1945–1945," Szkice Legnickie 36 (2015): 158.

66. Natasha Wheatley, "Central Europe as Ground Zero of the New International Order," Slavic Review 78, no. 4 (2019): 900–11.

67. Grzegorz Jasiński, "Akcje władz bezpieczeństwa przeciwko środowisku luterańskiemu na Mazurach i Warmii w latach 1947–1956," Gdański Rocznik Ewangelicki 5 (2011): 179–81.

68. Jasiński, "Akcje władz bezpieczeństwa," 182, 184.

69. "Warsaw Branch of the Brethren Service Committee to Benjamin Bushong," July 26, 1949, Poland 1948–49, folder 4, box 2, series 4/1/6, HP, BHLA.

70. "John Metzler, Jr. to Ben Bushong," September 17, 1948, Poland 1948–49, folder 4, box 2, series 4/1/6, HP, BHLA.

71. John Metzler, "For Inclusion in Minutes," August 6, 1947, Relief Work (FOR): Brethren Service Committee and Heifer Project, 1945–48, box 13, series E, JNS, DG 117, SCPC. This file contains many documents relevant to the post-UNRRA period of the Heifer Project.

72. Assorted post-UNRRA paths are discussed here: Ben Bushong, "Resume of Heifer Project," 1951, 1945–53 Project Committee Reports, HP, BHLA.

73. Strate, "H.P.C. News," SCPC.

74. Metzler, "For Inclusion in Minutes," SCPC. See also Kenneth I. Morse, New Windsor Center (New Windsor, MD: Brethren Service Center, 1979), 12, 46.

75. "Heifer Project Committee Meeting Minutes, Chicago," August 6, 1947, Relief Work (FOR): Brethren Service Committee and Heifer Project, 1945–48, box 13, series E, JNS, DG 117, SCPC.

76. On the Heifer Project's 1947 trip to Japan, see Peggy Reiff Miller, "70th Anniversary of the Ceremony of the Bulls," Seagoing Cowboys (blog), May 12, 2017.

77. Zigler is quoted in G. Yoder, Passing on the Gift, 110.

78. "Ministry of Health and Public Welfare to Heifer Project Inc.," August 11, 1960, Clippings and Releases 2, 1940s–1960s, folder 8, box 2, series 4/1/6, HP, BHLA.

79. George W. Cornell, "Bible-Spurred Cowboys Herding Cattle into Hard-Up Nations," in *Cowboy Memories*, eds. Bill Beck and Mel West (Little Rock, AR: Heifer Project International, 1994), 77.

80. "Report of the Heifer Project Committee," March 17, 1950, 1945–53 Project Committee Reports, HP, BHLA.

81. Jake Blouch, Walt Wiltschek, and Cheryl Brumbaugh-Cayford, "Thurl Metzger: Former Executive Director of Heifer International," *Messenger*, October 2006, https://www.brethren.org/messenger/wp-content/uploads/sites/3/2021/02/Messenger-2006-10.pdf; Peggy Reiff Miller, "The Three Executives Who Helped Shape the Heifer Project, Part II," *Seagoing Cowboys* (blog), September 27, 2024.

82. Peggy Reiff Miller, "Histories Intertwined," interview by Jason Woods, *World Ark*, Summer 2019. See also Metzger, *Road to Development*.

83. Bill Beck, "Introduction," in Beck and West, *Cowboy Memories*, 5; Bill Beck, "Cowboys of the Future," in Beck and West, *Cowboy Memories*, 179.

84. Morse, *New Windsor Center*, 36. See also Peggy Reiff Miller, "Touring Heifer Ranch with the Heifer Foundation Trustees," *Seagoing Cowboys* (blog), June 8, 2018. On the archival holding at the Heifer Project headquarters in Arkansas, see Peggy Reiff Miller, "Mining for Gems in the Heifer Archives," *World Ark*, Spring 2016.

85. "Heifer's Mission," Heifer International, accessed July 19, 2024, https://www.heifer.org/about-us/index.html.

86. For a snapshot of milk consumption in the United States in the early 2020s, see Kim Severson, "Got Milk? Not This Generation," *New York Times*, April 4, 2023, https://www.nytimes.com/2023/04/04/dining/milk-dairy-industry-gen-z.html. For a criticism and a defense of the American dairy industry, see Andrew Jacobs, "Is Dairy Farming Cruel to Cows?," *New York Times*, December 29, 2020. https://www.nytimes.com/2020/12/29/science/dairy-farming-cows-milk.html.

87. For an introduction to the animal rights position and to animal ethics, see Martha C. Nussbaum, *Justice for Animals: Our Collective Responsibility* (New York: Simon and Schuster, 2023).

88. There are a number of charities that argue against animal gifting in food aid programs entirely. See, for example, "A Well-Fed World," A Well-Fed World: Plant-Based Hunger Solutions, accessed July 19, 2024, https://awellfedworld.org/.

Conclusion

1. Nancy Cushing, "Live Export Is a Centuries-Old Australian Industry, but the Cameras Are New," ABC News, April 10, 2018, https://www.abc.net.au/news/2018-04-11/australias-history-of-animal-exports/9640502.

2. On the development of the global food economy and on meat's place in this development, see Lizzie Collingham, *The Taste of War: World War Two and the Battle for Food* (London: Allen Lane, 2011), 18–19.

3. Liza Verity, *Animals at Sea* (London: National Maritime Museum, 2004), 9–10.

4. Naomi Larsson and Tom Levitt, "'Floating Feedlots': Animals Spending Weeks at Sea on Ships Not Fit for Purpose," *Guardian*, January 26, 2020, https://www.theguardian.com/environment/2020/jan/26/floating-feedlots-animals-spending-weeks-at-sea-on-ships-not-fit-for-purpose.

5. Gonzalo Villanueva, "'Pain for Animals, Profit for People': The Campaign Against Live Sheep Exports, 1974–1986," in *Animals Count: How Population Size Matters in Animal-Human Relations*, ed. Nancy Cushing and Jodi Frawley (New York: Routledge, 2018), 100. For the importance of the Middle East to the live export trade, see Tom Levitt, "Animals Farmed: Live Exports Risk of Disease, China Goes Big on Pork, and EU Meat Tax," *Guardian*, February 4, 2020, https://www.theguardian.com/animals-farmed/2020/feb/04/animals-farmed-live-exports-risk-of-disease-china-goes-big-on-pork-and-eu-meat-tax. On live animal export statistics for Australia, see Susan F. Foster and Karen L. Overall, "The Welfare of Australian Livestock Transported by Sea," *Veterinary Journal* 200, no. 2 (2014): 205.

6. Larsson and Levitt, "Floating Feedlots." See also Sophie Kevany, "Exclusive: Livestock Ships Twice as Likely to Be Lost as Cargo Vessels," *Guardian*, October 28, 2020, https://www.theguardian.com/environment/2020/oct/28/exclusive-livestock-ships-twice-as-likely-to-be-lost-as-cargo-vessels.

7. Jo-Anne McArthur, "'We Could Smell the Boat Approaching': The Grim Truth About Animal Exports," *Guardian*, December 11, 2018, https://www.theguardian.com/environment/2018/dec/11/we-could-smell-the-boat-approaching-grim-truth-animal-exports-israel-haifa. This article is reprinted in a slightly modified version as Jo-Anne McArthur, "The Grim Truth About Animal Exports," We Animals, December 11, 2018, https://weanimalsmedia.org/2018/12/11/the-grim-truth-about-animal-exports/. See also Clive J. C. Phillips and Eduardo Santurtun, "The Welfare of Livestock Transported by Ship," *Veterinary Journal* 196, no. 3 (2013): 309.

8. Kevany, "Exclusive"; Phillips and Santurtun, "Welfare of Livestock," 309, 312.

9. The description in this paragraph and in the preceding three paragraphs of the on-board conditions experienced by the animals is based on "What's It Really Like on Board a Live Export Ship?," Animals Australia, December 3, 2018, updated May 22, 2024, https://animalsaustralia.org/latest-news/whats-it-like-on-a-live-export-ship/. On conditions, see also McArthur, "We Could Smell the Boat."

10. Phillips and Santurtun, "Welfare of Livestock," 309.

11. Larsson and Levitt, "Floating Feedlots."

12. Lucy Craymer, "New Zealand Ships Last Livestock as Ban Takes Effect," Reuters, April 21, 2023, https://www.reuters.com/world/asia-pacific/new-zealand-ships-its-last-livestock-ban-takes-effect-2023-04-21/. For an earlier perspective on the ban, see Calla Wahlquist, "New Zealand to Stop Exporting Livestock by Sea," *Guardian*, April 13, 2021, https://www.theguardian.com/world/2021/apr/14/new-zealand-to-stop-exporting-livestock-by-sea

13. Department for Environment, Food and Rural Affairs, "Export of Live Animals Banned," news release, May 20, 2024, https://www.gov.uk/government/news/export-of-live-animals-banned#:~:text=A%20new%20ban%20on%20exporting,leader%20in%20animal%20welfare%20standards. See also Sophie Kevany, "England and Wales to Ban Live Animal Exports in European First," *Guardian*, December 3, 2020, https://www.theguardian.com/environment/2020/dec/03/uk-to-become-first-country-in-europe-to-ban-live-animal-exports.

14. Daniel Fitzgerald, "Livestock Shipping Company Wellard to Sell Only Remaining Vessel, Considers Delisting from ASX," Australian Broadcasting Corporation, January 14, 2025, https://www.abc.net.au/news/rural/2025-01-14/wellard-to-sell-mv-ocean-drover-and-consider-winding-up-business/104814504.

15. Katherine Sivert and Christine Parker, "Our Beef With 'Big Meat': The Power Perpetuating Australia's Live Export Trade is At Play Elsewhere," *The Conversation*, July 29, 2024, https://theconversation.com/our-beef-with-big-meat-the-power-perpetuating-australias-live-export-trade-is-at-play-elsewhere-235655.

16. Kevany, "Exclusive."

17. D. W. B., "The Brethren Become International," *Gospel Messenger*, November 2, 1946.

18. József Łaptos, *Humanitaryzm i polityka: Pomoc UNRRA dla Polski i polskich uchodźców w latach 1944–1947* (Kraków: Wyd. Naukowe Uniwersytetu Pedagogicznego, 2018), 395.

19. "Report on UNRRA Livestock Imported to Poland from September 29, 1945 to July 28, 1946," July 29, 1946, UNRRA Subject Files, file 72, S-0527-1107, UNA.

20. "Thurl Metzger to Ralph Delk," May 20, 1947, Correspondence 1947, folder 10, box 1, series 4/1/6, HP, BHLA.

21. Benjamin Meiches, *Nonhuman Humanitarians: Animal Interventions in Global Politics* (Minneapolis: University of Minnesota Press, 2023), esp. 10.

22. "Heifer Project Committee," August 1947, Correspondence 1947, HP, BHLA.

23. Heifer Project Committee poster titled, "She Talks in Any Language!," Clippings and Releases 1, folder 7, box 2, series 4/1/6, HP, BLHA.

24. Bill Beck, "Introduction," in *Cowboy Memories*, eds. Bill Beck and Mel West (Little Rock, AR: Heifer Project International, 1994), 5. See the advertisement in *The Boston Globe* for a talk titled "I Saw the World on a Cattle Boat," May 3, 1947.

25. See, for example, "Reviving Ukraine's Breadbasket," Food and Agriculture Organization of the United Nations, accessed July 16, 2024, https://www.fao.org/support-to-investment/news/reviving-the-breadbasket/en/; "Cautious Optimism for the Recovery of Cattle Herds," Association of Milk Producers, accessed July 16, 2024, https://avm-ua.org/en/post/cautious-optimism-for-the-recovery-of-cattle-herds. See also Asia Bazdyrieva, "No Milk, No Love," *e-flux Journal*, May 2022, https://www.e-flux.com/journal/127/465214/no-milk-no-love/. On the "resourcification" of Ukraine, see Victoria Donovan, "Against Academic 'Resourcification': Collaboration as Delinking from Extractivist 'Area Studies' Programs," *Canadian Slavonic Papers* 65, no. 2 (2023): 163–73.

26. Maximilian Luz Reinhardt and Tetiana Shyrochenko, "The Impact of the Russian War of Aggression on Ukrainian Livestock Production," Friedrich Naumann Foundation for Freedom, accessed June 20, 2024, https://www.freiheit.org/germany/impact-russian-war-aggression-ukrainian-livestock-production. On cattle numbers, see also Tetiana Shyrochenko, "Ukraine's Dairy Industry During the War," Ministerie van Landbouw, Visserij, Voedselzekerheid en Natuur, accessed July 16, 2024, https://www.agroberichtenbuitenland.nl/actueel/nieuws/2024/03/28/ukrainian-dairy-industry.

27. Andrew Hunt, "Living Amid Conflict: The True Stories of Ukrainian Dairy Farmers During War," *Bullvine*, June 1, 2024, https://www.thebullvine.com/the-bullvine/living-amid-conflict-the-true-stories-of-ukrainian-dairy-farmers-during-war/.

28. World Milk Day was proclaimed on June 1, 2001, by the Food and Agriculture Organization. "The Update of the Ukraine Dairy Map-2024 Infographic Dedicated to the World Milk Day," Association of Milk Producers, accessed June 20, 2024, https://avm-ua.org/en/post/the-update-of-the-ukraine-dairy-map-2024-infographic-dedicated-to-the-world-milk-day.

Bibliography

Archives and Libraries

Archive of Modern Documents (Archiwum Akt Nowych), Warsaw
    Biuro Odbioru Transportów Morskich w Gdańsku
    Centralny Urząd Planowania
    Komisja Specjalna do Walki z Nadużyciami i Szkodnictwem Gospodarczym w Warszawie
    Ministerstwo Pracy i Opieki Społecznej w Warszawie
    Ministerstwo Przemysłu, Handlu i Żeglugi Rządu RP [emigracyjnego] w Londynie
    Ministerstwo Rolnictwa i Reform Rolnych
    Ministerstwo Żeglugi i Handlu Zagranicznego w Warszawie
    Ministerstwo Ziem Odzyskanych w Warszawie
    Towarzystwo Ochrony Zwierząt
    Towarzystwo Pamiętnikarstwa Polskiego
    Związek Samopomocy Chłopskiej. Zarząd Główny w Warszawie
Association for Diplomatic Studies and Training
    Association for Diplomatic Studies and Training Foreign Affairs Oral History Collection (https://adst.org/oral-history/)
Baltic Digital Library (Bałtycka Biblioteka Cyfrowa)
    Fotografia chłopów pomorskich
Brethren Historical Library and Archives, Elgin, IL
    Byron P. Royer Papers
    Dan West Papers
    Heifer Project
    Poland—Ostróda and Warsaw Offices
Hanna Holborn Gray Special Collections Research Center, University of Chicago Library
    Kermit Eby Papers (1933–63)
James Madison University Libraries Special Collections, Harrisonburg, VA
    Harold McNett Seagoing Cowboy Oral History
Manchester University Archives and Brethren Historical Collection
    Seagoing Cowboy Diary (https://www.manchester.edu/oaa/library/archives/DigitalCollections/seagoingcowboydiary.htm)
Mennonite Central Committee
    Civilian Public Service (https://civilianpublicservice.org)
Mennonite Church Archives, Elkhart, IN
    Charles C. Kocher Miscellaneous
    John E Nunemaker Collection

Melvin G. Gingerich Papers
Seagoing Cowboys Collection
National Digital Archives (Narodowe Archiwum Cyfrowe)
Socjalistyczna Agencja Prasowa (https://www.szukajwarchiwach.gov.pl
/jednostka/-/jednostka/9743659)
National Film Archive (Filmoteka Narodowa—Instytut Audiowizualny)
Dostawy UNRRA—Wyładunek w porcie. Wytwórnia Filmowa Wojska
Polskiego, 1945.
Generalny dyrektor UNRRA La Guardia z wizytą w Polsce. Wytwórnia Filmowa
Wojska Polskiego, 1946.
Konie z pomocy UNRRA dla Polski. Przedsiębiorstwo Państwowe "Film Polski,"
1947.
Przybycie i wyładunek transportu koni z darów UNRRA. Wytwórnia Filmowa
Wojska Polskiego, 1946.
Orka wiosenna. Wytwórnia Filmowa Wojska Polskiego, 1946.
Rutgers School of Arts and Sciences
Rutgers Oral History Archives (https://oralhistory.rutgers.edu)
State Archive in Szczecin (Archiwum Państwowe w Szczecinie), Szczecin
Urząd Wojewódzki Szczeciński
State Archive in Warsaw (Archiwum Państwowe w Warszawie), Warsaw
Towarzystwo Ochrony Zwierząt
Wojewódzki Urząd Ziemski w Warszawie
Swarthmore College Peace Collection, Swarthmore, PA
Center on Conscience and War Records
Daniel J. Peacock Collection
George and Lillian Willoughby Papers
John Nevin Sayre Papers
United Nations Archives
United Nations Relief and Rehabilitation Administration (UNRRA)
(1943–49)
United States Holocaust Memorial Museum
Claude Lanzmann Shoah Collection
UNRRA selected records AG-018-040: Office of the Historian
Wilson Special Collections Library, University of North Carolina, Chapel Hill, NC
Howard Kester Papers

Historical Periodicals

Arkansas Methodist (1946)
Baltimore Sun (1945–47)
The Baptist Record (1946)
Boston Globe (1946–47)
Brethren Missionary (1947)
The Canadian Standard (1947)
The Canadian Statesman (1947)
The Christian Century (1946)
The Coleman Journal (1945)
Daily Press (1946)

BIBLIOGRAPHY

Dziennik Bałtycki (1946)
Dziennik Ludowy (1946–48)
The Etownian (1946)
Evening Star (1945–1946)
Express Wieczorny (1946)
Gazeta Informacyjna (1946)
Gazeta Lubelska (1946)
Gazeta Morska—Pismo Marynarki Wojennej (1946)
Głos Ludu (1946)
Głos Pomorski (1946)
Głos Wielkopolski (1946)
Gospel Messenger (1945–48)
Highland Recorder (1945)
Kurier Codzienny (1948)
Kurier Szczeciński (1945)
Life (1946)
The Living Church (1945–46)
Maclean's Magazine (1947)
Marine Bull Pen (1946)
Medycyna Weterynaryjna (1947)
The Mennonite (1946–47)
Mennonite Weekly Review (1946)
Monthly Review (1945)
The Morgan Horse Magazine (1946–47)
Naprzód Dolnośląski (1946)
The National Humane Review (1939–48)
The New York Sun (1946)
New York Times (1945–46)
New York Times Magazine (1947)
Our Dumb Animals (1946, 1966–68)
People's Voice (1946)
Pike View Peace News (1945)
Poland Today (1947)
The Progressive (1951)
Przekrój (1946)
The Suffolk News-Herald (1946)
The Sunday Star (1946)
Szpilki (1945)
Time (1944–45)
The Union County Journal (1946)
The Weekly Processor (1946)
Wilmington Morning Star (1945)
Zagoń Ojczysty (1946–47)

Primary Sources

Beck, Bill, and Mel West, eds. *Cowboy Memories.* Little Rock, AR: Heifer Project International, 1994.

BIBLIOGRAPHY

Chęciński, Sylwester, dir. *Sami swoi*. 1967.
Chodowiecki, Jan K. *Gospodarska hodowla koni*. Kraków: Polskie Towarzystwo Zootechnicze, 1946.
Cox, Harvey. *Just as I Am*. Nashville, TN: Abingdon, 1983.
Dodd, Norris E. "The Food and Agriculture Organization of the United Nations." *Agricultural History* 23, no. 2 (1949): 81–86.
Drury, Charles. "UNRRA in Poland." *The Empire Club of Canada Addresses*, April 24, 1947, 331–44. https://speeches.empireclub.org/details.asp?ID=61185.
Dulczewski, Zygmunt, and Andrzej Kwilecki, eds. *Pamiętniki osadników Ziem Odzyskanych*. 2nd ed. Poznań: Wyd. Poznańskie, 1970.
"Dziennik Ustaw—rok 1945 nr 53 poz. 302." Infor. Accessed June 6, 2022. https://www.infor.pl/akt-prawny/DZU.1945.053.0000302,metryka,dekret-o-utworzeniu-i-zakresie-dzialania-komisji-specjalnej-do-walki-z-naduzyciami-i-szkodnictwem-gospodarczym.html.
Eastern European Division Loan Department. "Preliminary Paper No. 6 for the Working Party on the Polish Loan Application." International Bank for Reconstruction and Development, May 26, 1947. https://documents1.worldbank.org/curated/en/558411468095985925/pdf/multi-page.pdf.
Elliott, F. F. "Redirecting World Agricultural Production and Trade Toward Better Nutrition." *Journal of Farm Economics* 26, no. 1 (1944): 10–30.
European Regional Office of UNRRA. *50 Facts About UNRRA*. London: His Majesty's Stationery Office, 1946.
Guetzkow, Harold Steere, and Paul Hoover Bowman. *Men and Hunger: A Psychological Manual for Relief Workers*. Elgin, IL: Brethren Publishing House, 1946.
Gunnar, Jahn. "Award Ceremony Speech." 1947. NobelPrize.org. Accessed February 23, 2023. https://www.nobelprize.org/prizes/peace/1947/ceremony-speech.
Heatwole, Kenneth M. "Cattleboat Trip of Kenneth Heatwole, 1946." Seagoing Cowboys. Accessed February 13, 2020. https://seagoingcowboyswebsite.files.wordpress.com/2015/11/stories_kenheatwole.pdf.
Hendrickson, Roy F. "The Coming Winter in Europe: Food Situation in Devastated Countries." June 26, 1945. Ibiblio. Accessed February 12, 2021. http://www.ibiblio.org/pha/policy/1945/1945-06-26d.html.
Hirschmann, Ira A. *The Embers Still Burn*. New York: Simon and Schuster, 1949.
Hoover, Herbert. "Can Europe's Children Be Saved?" Address presented to the National Committee on Food for the Small Democracies, New York, October 19, 1941.
Hulme, Kathryn C. *Undiscovered Country: A Spiritual Adventure*. Boston: Little, Brown, 1966.
Jastrzębiec, Władysław. *Poradnik weterynaryjny dla rolników i hodowców*. Warsaw: Wyd. Księgarnia Rolnicza, 1945.
Jost, Art. "Tractor Unit to Poland." *Civilian Public Service Bulletin* 6, no. 5 (1947): 2.
Katalog oficjalny pierwszych Międzynarodowych Targów Gdańskich, 2.VIII-10.VIII, 1947. Gdańsk: Wydawcy Międzynarodowe Targi Gdańskie, 1947.
Kerstein, Edward S. *Red Star over Poland: A Report from Behind the Iron Curtain*. Appleton, WI: C. C. Nelson, 1947.

BIBLIOGRAPHY 281

Keys, Ancel, Josef Brozek, Austin Henschel, Olaf Mickelsen, and Henry Longstreet Taylor. *The Biology of Human Starvation*. Minneapolis: University of Minnesota Press, 1950.

Kraus, Hertha. *International Relief in Action, 1914–1943*. Philadelphia: Research Center, 1943.

Lanzmann, Claude, dir. *Shoah*. New York: New Yorker Films, 1985.

League of Nations. *Final Report of the Mixed Committee of the League of Nations on the Relation of Nutrition to Health, Agriculture and Economic Policy*. Geneva: League of Nations, 1937.

Legg, Stuart. *Food: Secret of the Peace*. National Film Board of Canada, 1945. https://www.nfb.ca/film/food_secret_of_the_peace/.

Liepert, Gerald. "Jerry Liepert's Cattleboat Trip to Europe: 1946–47." Edited by Jamie Liepert Langston. *Keepers* (blog). April 3, 2008. http://keepersthe.blogspot.com/2008/04/jerry-lieperts-cattleboat-trip-to.html.

MacFarlane, David. "The UNRRA Experience in Relation to Developments in Food and Agriculture." *American Journal of Agricultural Economics* 30, no. 1 (1948): 69–77.

Martin, James. "Seagoing Cowboy, March 6, 2007." Seagoing Cowboys. Accessed July 26, 2024. https://seagoingcowboyswebsite.files.wordpress.com/2016/02/stories_jamesmartin.pdf.

McAuslin, David. "Transport Service (The Innocent Abroad)." *Journal of the American Veterinary Medical Association* VI, no. 4 (1918): 536–47.

McConkey, Darel. *Food and People: A UNESCO Project*. New York: Manhattan Publishing, 1951.

Meyer, Arthur. "Art Meyer's Cattle Boat Experience: Introduction to Planned Book, Dated January 1991." Seagoing Cowboys. Accessed February 13, 2020. https://seagoingcowboyswebsite.files.wordpress.com/2015/10/stories_artmeyer.pdf.

Miller, David, dir. *Seeds of Destiny*. United States Department of War, 1946.

Ministerstwo Obrony Narodowej. *Instrukcja weterynaryjna: Zapobieganie i zwalczanie chorób zaraźliwych u koni*. Łódź: Wojskowy Instytut Naukowo-Wydawniczy, 1946.

Ministerstwo Obrony Narodowej. *Koń i dogląd nad nim*. Warsaw: Wojskowy Instytut Naukowo-Wydawniczy, 1946.

Nachtigall, Wilbur. "Directors' Conference." *Pike View Peace News*, September–October 1945, 3–5.

Norgord, C. P. "American Humane Association, Local SPCAs, Act to Protect Animals Shipped Overseas." *National Humane Review*, August 1946, 18–23.

Porty Gdynia, Gdańsk, Szczecin. Gdynia: Główny Urząd Morski, 1946.

Regan, Dan. "UNRRA: World Shipper." *Army Transportation Journal* 2, no. 7 (1946): 2–5.

Reymont, Ladislas. *The Peasants: Spring*. Translated by Michael H. Dziewicki. New York: Alfred A. Knopf, 1928. https://archive.org/details/bwb_P8-CSD-500/mode/2up?q=.

Reymont, Ladislas. *The Peasants: Winter*. Translated by Michael H. Dziewicki. New York: Alfred A. Knopf, 1925. https://archive.org/details/peasantswinter0000ladi/mode/2up.

Reymont, Władysław. *Chłopi, Część trzecia—Wiosna*. wolnelektury.pl. Accessed July 28, 2024. https://wolnelektury.pl/katalog/lektura/chlopi-czesc-trzecia-wiosna/.

Robinson, Herbert W. *Operational Analysis Papers No. 45: The Impact of UNRRA on the Polish Economy*. London: Division of Operational Analysis, 1947.

Ross, James M. "Kindness and Comfort Paramount in Shipping Horses and Dairy Cattle Overseas to Replace Losses in Farm Animals." *National Humane Review*, April 1946, 8.

Rotha, Paul, dir. *World of Plenty*. Paul Rotha Productions, United Kingdom, 1943.

Schultz, Theodore W., ed. *Food for the World*. Chicago: University of Chicago Press, 1945.

Shultz, Lawrence W. *People and Places, 1890–1970: An Autobiography*. Winona Lake, IN: Life and Light, 1971.

So Bold an Aim: Ten Years of International Co-Operation Toward Freedom from Want. Rome: Food and Agriculture Organization of the United Nations, 1955.

Sprawozdanie z działalności spółdzielni lekarzy weterynaryjnych R.P. z.o.u. "Składnica weterynaryjna" za rok 1946. Warsaw: Nakładem Składnicy Weterynaryjnej Spółdzielni Lekarzy Weterynaryjnych R.P., 1947.

Strieber, W. R. "UNRRA Veterinarian's Duties." *Iowa State University Veterinarian* 9, no. 3 (1947): 152–53.

Sztremer, A. *Opieka nad źrebną klaczą i źrebnięciem*. Olsztyn: Druk Państwowa, 1947.

Thomas, Norman E., ed. *Horses for Humanity: A Report on a Mission to Poland by Eleven Ministers*. St. Johnsville, NY: Enterprise and News, 1949.

Truman, Harry S. "United States Participation in UNRRA: President's Message to Congress." US Department of State, November 13, 1945. https://www.cvce.eu/content/publication/2017/4/11/9df14347-dd75-4ae9-9828-a20a095fcf4b/publishable_en.pdf.

Underwood, Pierson. "Memorandum of Conversation, by Mr. Pierson Underwood of the War Areas Economic Division." October 1, 1945. Diplomatic Papers, 1945, vol. 5, Europe, Foreign Relations of the United States, Office of the Historian, US Department of State. https://history.state.gov/historicaldocuments/frus1945v05/d277.

UNICEF. *Today's Children—Tomorrow's Citizens*. Lake Success, NY: UNESCO, 1948.

United Nations Relief and Rehabilitation Administration. *Economic Recovery in the Countries Assisted by UNRRA*. Washington, DC: UNRRA, 1946.

United Nations Relief and Rehabilitation Administration. *Out of Chaos*. Washington, DC: UNRRA, 1945.

United Nations Relief and Rehabilitation Administration. *The Story of UNRRA*. Washington, DC: UNRRA, Office of Public Information, 1948.

United States Bureau of Animal Industry. *Report of the Chief of the Bureau of Animal Industry, Agricultural Research Administration*. 1945.

US Congress. *Proceedings and Debates*. December 5, 1945. 79th Cong., 1st sess. *Congressional Record* 91, part 9: 11514.

US Congress. *Proceedings and Debates*. February 19, 1946, to March 28, 1946. 79th Cong., 2nd sess. *Congressional Record* 92, part 2: 2388.

US Congress. *Proceedings and Debates*. July 26, 1947, to December 19, 1947. 80th Cong., 1st sess. *Congressional Record* 93, part 12: A4620.

US Congress. Senate. Committee on Armed Services. *Hearing Before a Subcommittee of the Committee on Armed Services United States Senate*. 80th Cong., 1st sess., 1947.

US Department of Commerce. "Income of Nonfarm Families and Individuals: 1946." In *Current Population Reports: Consumer Income*, ser P-60, no. 1 (January 28, 1948). https://www2.census.gov/prod2/popscan/p60-001.pdf.

Vachon, Ann, ed. *Poland, 1946: The Photographs and Letters of John Vachon*. With an introduction by Brian Moore. Washington, DC: Smithsonian Institution Press, 1995.

White, David H. "My Trip to Poland in 1946 Working on a UNRRA Ship." Seagoing Cowboys. Accessed July 26, 2024. https://seagoingcowboyswebsite.files.wordpress.com/2015/10/stories_davidwhite.pdf.

Woodbridge, George. *UNRRA: The History of the United Nations Relief and Rehabilitation Administration*. New York: Oxford University Press, 1950.

Yoder, Elmer S. "Seagoing Cowboys from Stark County." *Heritage*, October 2002.

Yoder, J. Olen. *Crossing to Poland*. Self-published, 1986.

Secondary Sources

Adams, Carol. "Feminized Protein: Meaning, Representations, and Implications." In Cohen and Otomo, *Making Milk*, 19–40.

Adams, Matthew Lloyd. "Herbert Hoover and the Organization of the American Relief Effort in Poland (1919–1923)." *European Journal of American Studies* 4, no. 2 (2009): 1–19.

Aksamit, Nerissa Kalee. "Training Friends and Overseas Relief: The Friends Ambulance Unit and the Friends Relief Service, 1939 to 1948." PhD diss., West Virginia University, 2019.

AMEDD Center of History and Heritage. "Transportation of Animals." Accessed August 30, 2022. https://achh.army.mil/history/book-wwii-vetservicewwii-chapter15.

Amrith, Sunil, and Patricia Clavin. "Feeding the World: Connecting Europe and Asia, 1930–1945." *Past and Present* 218, suppl. 8 (2013): 29–50.

Ariffin, Yohan, Jean Marc Coicaud, and Vesselin Popovski, eds. *Emotions in International Politics: Beyond Mainstream International Relations*. New York: Cambridge University Press, 2016.

Armstrong-Reid, Susan, and David Murray. *Armies of Peace: Canada and the UNRRA Years*. Toronto: University of Toronto Press, 2008.

Atkins, Peter J. "Fattening Children or Fattening Farmers? School Milk in Britain, 1921–1941." *Economic History Review* 58, no. 1 (2005): 57–78.

Back, Lyndon S. "The Quaker Mission in Poland: Relief, Reconstruction, and Religion." *Quaker History* 101, no. 2 (2012): 1–23.

Barnett, Michael. *Empire of Humanity: A History of Humanitarianism*. Ithaca, NY: Cornell University Press, 2011.

Batavick, Frank. "New Windsor History." New Windsor Heritage. Accessed March 23, 2023. https://www.newwindsorheritage.org/history.

Batavick, Frank J. *Time's Crossroads: The History of New Windsor, MD.* Amazon.com and CreateSpace, 2017.

Bauman, Emily. "The Naïve Republic of Aid: Grassroots Exceptionalism in Humanitarian Memoir." In *Global Humanitarianism and Media Culture*, edited by Michael Lawrence and Rachel Tavernor, 83–102. Manchester, UK: Manchester University Press, 2019.

Bazdyrieva, Asia. "No Milk, No Love." *e-flux Journal*, May 2022. https://www.e-flux.com/journal/127/465214/no-milk-no-love/.

Becker, Peter, and Natasha Wheatley, eds. *Remaking Central Europe: The League of Nations and the Former Habsburg Lands.* New York: Oxford University Press, 2020.

Betts, Paul. "The Polemics of Pity: British Photographs of Berlin, 1945–47." In *Humanitarianism and Media, 1900 to the Present*, edited by Johannes Paulmann, 126–50. New York: Berghahn, 2019.

Betts, Paul. *Ruin and Renewal: Civilizing Europe After World War II.* New York: Basic Books, 2020.

Black, Maggie. *Children and the Nations: The Story of UNICEF.* Port Sydney, Australia: UNICEF, 1986. http://www.cf-hst.net/unicef-temp/Child-Nation/Child-Nation-contents.htm.

Black, Maggie. *Children First: The Story of UNICEF, Past and Present.* New York: Oxford University Press, 1996.

Błąd, Marta. "Land Reform in People's Poland (1944–89)." *Rural History* 32 (2021): 149–65.

Blouch, Jake, Walt Wiltschek, and Cheryl Brumbaugh-Cayford. "Thurl Metzger: Former Executive Director of Heifer International." *Messenger*, October 2006. https://www.brethren.org/messenger/wp-content/uploads/sites/3/2021/02/Messenger-2006-10.pdf.

Boudreau, Frank G. "Nutrition in War and Peace." *Milbank Quarterly* 83, no. 4 (2005): 609–23.

Brenk, Mikołaj. "Social Response in Poland in 1944–1948." *Biuletyn Historii Wychowania* 38 (2018): 265–80.

Bresalier, Michael. "From Healthy Cows to Healthy Humans: Integrated Approaches to World Hunger, c. 1930–1965." In *Animals and the Shaping of Modern Medicine: One Health and Its Histories*, edited by Abigail Woods, Michael Bresalier, Angela Cassidy, and Rachel Mason Dentinger, 119–60. London: Palgrave Macmillan, 2018.

Brock, Peter. *Against the Draft: Essays on Conscientious Objection from the Radical Reformation to the Second World War.* Toronto: University of Toronto Press, 2006.

BrookeUSA. "Shipping: Ports of Embarkation." *United States World War One Centennial Commission* (blog), August 30, 2022. https://www.worldwar1centennial.org/index.php/brookeusa-buying-animals/3162-brookeusa-buying-animals-article-2.html#ports-of-embarkation.

Brumbaugh-Cayford, Cheryl, with contributions from Peggy Reiff Miller. "'Pass the Baton and Continue On': Puerto Rico Celebrates 75 Years of Heifer." *Messenger*, December 2019.

Bryant, Sheila J. "Pay It Forward: The Heifer International Story." *Journal of Agricultural and Food Information* 5, no. 4 (2003): 5–9.
Brzeziński, Andrzej M. "Z polityki rządu RP na uchodźstwie wobec UNRRA." *Przegląd Zachodni* 2 (1998): 89–113.
Brzozowska, Sabina. "Człowiek—zwierzę—rzecz w *Chłopach* Władysława Reymonta." *Porównania* 2, no. 29 (2021): 97–116.
Bundy, Amanda Melanie. "There Was a Man of UNRRA: Internationalism, Humanitarianism, and the Early Cold War in Europe, 1943–1947." PhD diss., Ohio State University, 2017.
Bush, Perry. *Two Kingdoms, Two Loyalties: Mennonite Pacifism in Modern America*. Baltimore: Johns Hopkins University Press, 1998.
Cabanes, Bruno. *The Great War and the Origins of Humanitarianism, 1918–1924*. Cambridge: Cambridge University Press, 2014.
Case, Holly. "Reconstruction in East-Central Europe: Clearing the Rubble of Cold War Politics." *Past and Present* 210, suppl. 6 (2011): 71–102.
"Cautious Optimism for the Recovery of Cattle Herds." Association of Milk Producers. Accessed July 16, 2024. https://avm-ua.org/en/post/cautious-optimism-for-the-recovery-of-cattle-herds.
Clair, Robin Patric, and Lindsey B. Anderson. "Portrayals of the Poor on the Cusp of Capitalism: Promotional Materials in the Case of Heifer International." *Management Communication Quarterly* 27, no. 4 (2013): 537–67.
Clavin, Patricia. "The Austrian Hunger Crisis and the Genesis of International Organization After the First World War." *International Affairs* 90, no. 2 (2014): 265–78.
Clavin, Patricia. "International Organizations." In *The Cambridge History of the Second World War*, vol. 2, *Politics and Ideology*, edited by Richard Bosworth and Joseph Maiolo, 139–61. Cambridge: Cambridge University Press, 2015.
Clavin, Patricia. *Securing the World Economy: The Reinvention of the League of Nations, 1930–1926*. New York: Oxford University Press, 2013.
Claycomb, Holly. "Bound for Adventure—Church of the Brethren, UN Relief Mission Share History of the 'Seagoing Cowboys.'" *Altoona Mirror*. May 28, 2023. https://www.altoonamirror.com/life/area-life/2021/05/bound-for-adventure-church-of-the-brethren-un-relief-mission-share-history-of-the-seagoing-cowboys/.
Clements, Carson W. "The Development and Failure of American Policy Toward Czechoslovakia, 1938–1948." PhD diss., Miami University, 2001.
Cohen, Gerard D. *In War's Wake: Europe's Displaced Persons in the Postwar Order*. Oxford: Oxford University Press, 2011.
Cohen, Mathilde. "Regulating Milk: Women and Cows in France and the United States." *American Journal of Comparative Law* 65, no. 3 (2017): 469–526.
Cohen, Mathilde, and Yoriko Otomo, eds. *Making Milk: The Past, Present, and Future of Our Primary Food*. London: Bloomsbury, 2017.
Collingham, Lizzie. *The Taste of War: World War Two and the Battle for Food*. London: Allen Lane, 2011.
Collis Greene, Alison. "Southern Christian Work Camps and a Cold War Campaign for Racial and Economic Justice." In *Working Alternatives: American and Catho-*

lic Experiments in Work and Economy, edited by John C. Seitz and Christine Firer Hinze, 253–79. New York: Fordham University Press, 2020.

Conway, Martin, Michael Barnett, David A. Hollinger, and Mark L. Movsesian. Review of *Christian Human Rights*, by Samuel Moyn, H-Diplo Roundtable Review 17, no. 20 (2016): 1–19. http://www.tiny.cc/Roundtable-XVII-20.

Craymer, Lucy. "New Zealand Ships Last Livestock as Ban Takes Effect." Reuters, April 21, 2023. https://www.reuters.com/world/asia-pacific/new-zealand-ships-its-last-livestock-ban-takes-effect-2023-04-21/.

Cullather, Nick. "The Foreign Policy of the Calorie." *American Historical Review* 112, no. 2 (2007): 337–64.

Curti, Merle. *American Philanthropy Abroad: A History*. New Brunswick, NJ: Rutgers University Press, 1963.

Cushing, Nancy. "Animal Mobilities and the Founding of New South Wales." In "Visions of Australia: Environments in History," edited by Christof Mauch, Ruth Morgan, and Emily O'Gorman. Special issue, *RCC Perspectives: Transformations in Environment and Society* 2 (2017): 19–25. https://doi.org/10.5282/rcc/7905.

Cushing, Nancy. "'Few Commodities More Hazardous': Australian Live Animal Export, 1788–1880." *Environment and History* 24 (2018): 449–52.

Cushing, Nancy. "Hazardous Commodities: Australian Live Animal Export from the Long Nineteenth Century to Today." *Whitehorsepress*. February 19, 2018. https://whitehorsepress.blog/2018/02/19/hazardous-commodities-australian-live-animal-export-from-the-long-nineteenth-century-to-today/.

Cushing, Nancy. "Live Export Is a Centuries-Old Australian Industry, but the Cameras Are New." ABC News, April 10, 2018. https://www.abc.net.au/news/2018-04-11/australias-history-of-animal-exports/9640502.

Czapiewska, Gabriela. "Historyczne uwarunkowania rozwoju rolnictwa uspołecznionego na Pomorzu Środkowym." *Słupskie Prace Geograficzne* 1 (2003): 51–67.

Davies, Katherine. "Continuity, Change and Contest: Meanings of 'Humanitarian' from the 'Religion of Humanity' to the Kosovo War." HPG Working Paper, Overseas Development Institute, August 2012. https://odi.org/en/publications/continuity-change-and-contest-meanings-of-humanitarian-from-the-religion-of-humanity-to-the-kosovo-war/.

Davis, Janet M. *The Gospel of Kindness: Animal Welfare and the Making of Modern America*. New York: Oxford University Press, 2016.

Dejaegher, Sarah. "Europa and the Bull: The Significance of the Myth in Modern Europe." *New Federalist*, June 14, 2011. https://www.thenewfederalist.eu/Europa-and-the-bull-The-significance-of-the-myth-in-modern-Europe,4280?lang=fr.

Demello, Margo. *Animals and Society: An Introduction to Human-Animal Studies*. 2nd ed. New York: Columbia University Press, 2021.

deNobel, Jacob. "Taking a Look at Presidents Who Have Visited Carroll County." *Chicago Tribune*, February 15, 2015. https://www.chicagotribune.com/ph-cc-presidents-day-20150215-story.html.

Department for Environment, Food and Rural Affairs. "Export of Live Animals Banned." News release. May 20, 2024. https://www.gov.uk/government/news/export-of-live-animals-banned#:~:text=A%20new%20ban%20on%20exporting,leader%20in%20animal%20welfare%20standards.

De Vries, James. "Passing on the Gift as an Approach to Sustainable Development Programmes." *Development in Practice* 22, no. 3 (2012): 373–84.

Donovan, Victoria. "Against Academic 'Resourcification': Collaboration as Delinking from Extractivist 'Area Studies' Programs." *Canadian Slavonic Papers* 65, no. 2 (2023): 163–73.

Durnbaugh, Donald F., ed. *Church of the Brethren: Past and Present*. Elgin, IL: Brethren Press, 1971.

Durnbaugh, Donald F. "The Fight Against War of the Historic Peace Churches, 1919–1941." In *Challenge to Mars: Essays on Pacifism from 1918 to 1945*, edited by Peter Brock and Thomas P. Socknat, 18–40. Toronto: University of Toronto Press, 1999.

Durnbaugh, Donald F. *Pragmatic Prophet: The Life of Michael Robert Zigler*. Elgin, IL: Brethren Press, 1989.

Durnbaugh, Donald F., ed. *To Serve the Present Age: The Brethren Service Story*. Elgin, IL: Brethren Press, 1975.

Eisan, Leslie. *Pathways of Peace: A History of the Civilian Public Service Program Administered by the Brethren Service Committee*. Elgin, IL: Brethren Publishing House, 1948.

Eller, Cynthia. *Conscientious Objectors and the Second World War: Moral and Religious Arguments in Support of Pacifism*. New York: Praeger, 1991.

Eller, Cynthia. "Oral History as Moral Discourse: Conscientious Objectors and the Second World War." *Oral History Review* 18, no. 1 (1990): 45–75.

Erickson, Mark St. John. "Newport News Became a Springboard for WWI War Horses." AP News. December 4, 2016.

Fedorowicz, Andrzej. "Morscy kowboje przybywają do Gdańska." *Polityka*, March 1–7, 2017, 56–58.

Fehrenbach, Heidi. "Children and Other Civilians: Photography and the Politics of Humanitarian Image-Making." In Fehrenbach and Rodogno, *Humanitarian Photography*, 165–99.

Fehrenbach, Heide, and Davide Rodogno. "'A Horrific Photo of a Drowned Syrian Child': Humanitarian Photography and NGO Media Strategies in Historical Perspective." *International Review of the Red Cross* 97, no. 900 (2015): 1121–55.

Fehrenbach, Heide, and Davide Rodogno, eds. *Humanitarian Photography: A History*. New York: Cambridge University Press, 2015.

Feinstein, Margarete Myers. *Holocaust Survivors in Postwar Germany, 1945–1957*. New York: Cambridge University Press, 2010.

Fiedorczyk, Piotr. *Komisja specjalna do walki z nadużyciami i szkodnictwem gospodarczym 1945–1954*. Białystok: Temida 2, 2002.

Fitzgerald, Daniel. "Livestock Shipping Company Wellard to Sell Only Remaining Vessel, Considers Delisting from ASX." Australian Broadcasting Corporation, January 14, 2025. https://www.abc.net.au/news/rural/2025-01-14/wellard-to-sell-mv-ocean-drover-and-consider-winding-up-business/104814504.

Food and Agriculture Organization of the United Nations. "Reviving Ukraine's Breadbasket." Accessed July 16, 2024. https://www.fao.org/support-to-investment/news/reviving-the-breadbasket/en/.

Forclaz, Amalia R. "From Reconstruction to Development: The Early Years of the Food and Agriculture Organization (FAO) and the Conceptualization of Rural Welfare, 1945–1955." *The International History Review* 41, no. 2 (2019): 351–71.

Forclaz, Amalia Ribi. "Seeds of Development: Agriculture, History and Politics." Graduate Institute of Geneva. April 12, 2021. https://www.graduate institute.ch/communications/news/seeds-development-agriculture-history-and-politics.

Foster, Susan F., and Karen L. Overall. "The Welfare of Australian Livestock Transported by Sea." *Veterinary Journal* 200, no. 2 (2014): 205–9.

Frank, Matthew, and Jessica Reinisch. "Refugees and the Nation-State in Europe, 1919–59." *Journal of Contemporary History* 49, no. 3 (2014): 477–90.

Frost, J. William. "'Our Deeds Carry Our Message': The Early History of the American Friends Service Committee." *Quaker Studies* 81, no. 1 (1992): 1–51.

Gaard, Greta. "Critical Ecofeminism." In Cohen and Otomo, *Making Milk*, 213–34.

Gajewska, Magdalena Anita. "Polskie narracje o dobrostanie koni." In *Dobrostan zwierząt: Różne perspektywy*, edited by Hanna Mamzer, 321–44. Gdańsk: Katedra, 2018.

Gapski, Marcin Henryk. *Koń w kulturze polskiego średniowiecza*. Poznań: Wyd. Nauka i Innowacje, 2014.

Gatrell, Peter, and Nick Baron, eds. *Warlands: Population Resettlement and State Reconstruction in the Soviet–East European Borderlands, 1945–1950*. London: Palgrave Macmillan, 2009.

Gaziński, Benon, and Bogusław Wanot. "Działalność UNRRA i jej pomoc dla rolnictwa w Polsce." *Rocznik Muzeum Narodowego Rolnictwa w Szreniawie* 19 (1993): 5–30.

Gellner, Joanna. "Zauważone!—Zmiana stosunku do koni w krakowie na przełomie XIX i XX wieku." In *Miasta/Zwierzęta*, edited by Anna Jaroszuk, Igor Piotrowski, and Karolina Wróbel-Bardzik, 90–101. Vol. 8 of *Almanach antropologiczny: Communicare*. Warsaw: Wydawnictwa Uniwersytetu Warszawskiego, 2021.

Gemie, Sharif, Laure Humbert, and Fiona Reid. *Outcast Europe: Refugees and Relief Workers in an Era of Total War, 1936–48*. London: Continuum, 2012.

Gingerich, Melvin. *Service for Peace: A History of Mennonite Civilian Public Service*. Akron, PA: Mennonite Central Committee, 1949.

Gingerich, Melvin. *Youth and Christian Citizenship*. Scottsdale, PA: Herald, 1949.

Gingerich, Owen. "The Return of the Seagoing Cowboy: Horses Afloat and Books Astray." *American Scholar* 68, no. 4 (1999): 71–81.

Golsan, Richard J. "'L'Affaire' Karski: Fiction, History, Memory Unreconciled." *L'Esprit Créateur* 50, no. 4 (2010): 81–96.

Grada, Cormac O. *Famine: A Short History*. Princeton, NJ: Princeton University Press, 2009.

Greene, Ann Norton. *Horses at Work: Harnessing Power in Industrial America*. Cambridge, MA: Harvard University Press, 2008.

Groom, A. J. R., Andre Barrinha, and William Olson. *International Relations Then and Now*. 2nd ed. London: Routledge, 2019.

Grossmann, Atina. "Grams, Calories, and Food: Languages of Victimization, Entitlement and Human Rights in Occupied Germany, 1945–49." *Central European History* 44, no. 1 (2011): 118–48.

Grossmann, Atina. *Jews, Germans, and Allies: Close Encounters in Occupied Germany*. Princeton, NJ: Princeton University Press, 2007.

Halicka, Beata. *The Polish Wild West: Forced Migration and Cultural Appropriation in the Polish-German Borderlands, 1945–1948*. Translated by Paul McNamara. London: Routledge, 2020.

Hall, Todd H. *Emotional Diplomacy: Official Emotion on the International Stage*. Ithaca, NY: Cornell University Press, 2015.

Hambidge, Gove. *The Story of FAO*. New York: Van Nostrand, 1955.

Hamblin, Jacob Darwin. "Environmental Dimensions of World War II." In *A Companion to World War Two*, edited by Thomas W. Zeiler and Daniel M. DuBois, 698–716. Malden, MA: Blackwell, 2013.

Hamblin, Jacob Darwin. "The Vulnerability of Nations: Food Security in the Aftermath of World War II." *Global Environment* 10 (2012): 42–65.

Harder, Andrew. "The Politics of Impartiality: The United Nations Relief and Rehabilitation Administration in the Soviet Union, 1946–7." *Journal of Contemporary History* 47, no. 2 (2012): 347–69.

Harris, M. D., W. J. Grogg, A. Akoma, B. J. Hayes, R. F. Reidy, E. F. Imhoff, and P. C. Collins. "Revisiting (Some of) the Lasting Impacts of the Liberty Ships via a Metallurgical Analysis of Rivets from the SS 'John W. Brown.'" *Journal of the Minerals, Metals and Materials Society* 67 (2015): 2965–75.

Hatfield, Mark O. Foreword to *Herbert Hoover and Poland: A Documentary History of a Friendship*, edited by George J. Lerski, xi–xii. Stanford, CA: Hoover Institution Press, 1977.

Hausberger, Martine, et al. "A Review of the Human-Horse Relationship." *Applied Animal Behaviour Science* 109, no. 1 (2008): 1–24.

Healy, Maureen. *Vienna and the Fall of the Habsburg Empire: Total War and Everyday Life in World War I*. Cambridge: Cambridge University Press, 2004.

Hediger, Ryan. *Animals and War: Studies of Europe and North America*. Leiden: Brill, 2012.

Heifer International. "The Gates Foundation: How Heifer Is Making a Difference." October 3, 2019. https://www.heifer.org/blog/the-gates-foundation-how-heifer-is-making-a-difference.html.

Heifer International. "Heifer's Mission." Accessed July 19, 2024. https://www.heifer.org/about-us/index.html.

Heisey, M. J. *Peace and Persistence: Tracing the Brethren in Christ Through Three Generations*. Kent, OH: Kent State University Press, 2003.

Hertzler, Daniel. "With Heifers to Poland and Greece." *Mennonite*. June 20, 2016. https://anabaptistworld.org/heifers-poland-greece/.

Hibbard, Melissa J. "Children of the Polish Republic: Child Health, Welfare, and the Shaping of Modern Poland, 1915–1939." PhD diss., University of Illinois at Chicago, 2022.

BIBLIOGRAPHY

Hilton, Matthew, Emily Baughan, Eleanor Davey, Bronwen Everill, Kevin O'Sullivan, and Tehila Sasson. "History and Humanitarianism: A Conversation." *Past and Present* 241, no. 1 (2018): 1–38.

"The History of American Humane's Rescue Team." American Humane. July 8, 2022. https://www.americanhumane.org/fact-sheet/the-history-of-american-humanes-red-star-rescue-team/.

Hitchcock, William I. *The Bitter Road to Freedom: A New History of the Liberation of Europe.* New York: Free Press, 2008.

"Horse Foaling." Texas A&M University Veterinary Medicine and Biomedical Sciences News. March 10, 2011. https://vetmed.tamu.edu/news/pet-talk/horse-foaling/.

Houlihan, Patrick J. "Renovating Christian Charity: Global Catholicism, the Save the Children Fund, and Humanitarianism During the First World War." *Past and Present* 250, no. 1 (2021): 203–41.

Huber, Tim. "High Seas Service." *Mennonite World Review*, September 14, 2015. https://anabaptistworld.org/high-seas-service/.

Hunt, Andrew. "Living Amid Conflict: The True Stories of Ukrainian Dairy Farmers During War." *Bullvine*, June 1, 2024. https://www.thebullvine.com/the-bullvine/living-amid-conflict-the-true-stories-of-ukrainian-dairy-farmers-during-war/.

Hutchison, Emma. *Affective Communities in World Politics: Collective Emotions After Trauma.* Cambridge, UK: Cambridge University Press, 2016.

"Inflation Calculator." Federal Reserve Bank of Minneapolis. Accessed July 26, 2024. https://www.minneapolisfed.org/about-us/monetary-policy/inflation-calculator.

Itinerario: Journal of Imperial and Global Interactions 46, no. 2 (2022).

Jachertz, Ruth. "'To Keep Food out of Politics:' The UN Food and Agriculture Organization, 1945–1965." In *International Organizations and Development, 1945–1990*, edited by Marc Frey, Sonke Kunkel, and Corinna Unger, 75–100. New York: Palgrave Macmillan, 2014.

Jachertz, Ruth, and Alexander Nutzenadel. "Coping with Hunger? Visions of a Global Food System, 1930–1960." *Journal of Global History* 6, no. 1 (2011): 99–119.

Jachowicz, Piotr. "Działalność UNRRA w Polsce w latach 1945–1948." *Zeszyty Naukowe* 2, no. 2 (1998): 41–55.

Jacobs, Andrew. "Is Dairy Farming Cruel to Cows?" *New York Times*, December 29, 2020. https://www.nytimes.com/2020/12/29/science/dairy-farming-cows-milk.html.

Jarosz, Dariusz. "Zapomniani przyjaciele: Zagraniczna pomoc charytatywna w Polsce Ludowej (1945–1949)." In *Społeczeństwo, państwo, modernizacja*, edited by Włodzimierz Mędrzecki, 163–75. Warsaw: Neriton, 2002.

Jasiński, Grzegorz. "Akcje władz bezpieczeństwa przeciwko środowisku luterańskiemu na Mazurach i Warmii w latach 1947–1956." *Gdański Rocznik Ewangelicki* 5 (2011): 179–99.

Jezierski, Andrzej, and Cecylia Leszczyńska. *Historia gospodarcza Polski.* Warsaw: Wyd. Key Text, 1997.

Joel. "Farmboy Seminarian on a Cattleboat to Poland, 1946." *Far Outliers*. December 26, 2009. https://faroutliers.com/2009/12/26/farmboy-seminarian-on-a-cattleboat-to-poland-1946/.

Juźwik, Aleksander. "Zagraniczna pomoc charytatywna dla dzieci i młodzieży w Polsce w latach 1945–1950." *Polska 1944/45–1980: Studia i Materiały* 11 (2013): 93–118.

Kahn Atkins, Irene. "Seeds of Destiny: A Case History." *Film and History* 11, no. 2 (1981): 25–33.

Kalm, Leah M., and Richard D. Semba. "They Starved So That Others Be Better Fed: Remembering Ancel Keys and the Minnesota Experiment." *Journal of Nutrition* 135, no. 6 (2005): 1347–52.

Kamiński, Bruno. "Fear Management: Foreign Threats in the Postwar Polish Propaganda—the Influence and the Reception of the Communist Media (1944–1956)." PhD diss., European University Institute, 2016.

Kauffman, J. Howard. "Dilemmas of Christian Pacifism Within a Historic Peace Church." *Sociological Analysis* 49, no. 4 (1989): 368–85.

Kennedy, Paul. *The Parliament of Man: The Past, Present and Future of the United Nations*. New York: Random House, 2006.

Kern, A. *Better Days Films—Day 12*. Seattle Community Media, 2013. https://archive.org/details/scm-316182-betterdaysfilms-day12-.

Kersten, Krystyna. "Ludzie na drogach: O przesiedleniach ludności w Polsce 1939–1948." *Res Publica* 4 (1987): 54–64.

Kevany, Sophie. "England and Wales to Ban Live Animal Exports in European First." *Guardian*, December 3, 2020. https://www.theguardian.com/environment/2020/dec/03/uk-to-become-first-country-in-europe-to-ban-live-animal-exports.

Kevany, Sophie. "Exclusive: Livestock Ships Twice as Likely to Be Lost as Cargo Vessels." *Guardian*, October 28, 2020. https://www.theguardian.com/environment/2020/oct/28/exclusive-livestock-ships-twice-as-likely-to-be-lost-as-cargo-vessels.

Kind-Kovács, Friederike. "The Great War, the Child's Body and the American Red Cross." *European Review of History* 23, no. 1–2 (2016): 33–62.

Kizik, Edmund. "Mennonici." In *Pod wspólnym niebem*, edited by M. Kopczyński and W. Tygielski, 215–34. Warsaw: Muzeum Historii Polski, 2010.

Kledzik, Emilia, Maciej Michalski, and Małgorzata Praczyk, eds. *"Ziemie Odzyskane": W poszukiwaniu nowych narracji*. Poznań: Instytut Historii UAM, 2018.

Klocek Di Biasio, Beata, and Bohdan Michalski. "The Myth of Europe in Art and European Identities." *Politeja* 5, no. 44 (2016): 1–31.

Kosek, Joseph Kip. *Acts of Conscience: Christian Nonviolence and Modern American Democracy*. New York: Columbia University Press, 2009.

Kowalski, Kamil. "Remarks on the Genesis of UNRRA Negotiations Between the Great Powers and Selected Treaty Provisions." *Annales: Ethics in Economic Life* 20, no. 7 (2017): 161–72.

Kozłowska, Urszula, and Tomasz Sikowski. "The Implementation of the Soviet Healthcare Model in 'People's Democracy' Countries—the Case of Post-War Poland (1944–1953)." *Social History of Medicine* 34, no. 4 (2020): 1185–211.

Kreider, J. Kenneth. *A Cup of Cold Water: The Story of Brethren Service*. Elgin, IL: Brethren Press, 2001.

Kreider, J. Kenneth. "M.R. Zigler, a Crusader for Peace." In *A Dunker Guide to Brethren History*, edited by Walt Wiltschek, 115–18. Elgin, IL: Brethren Press, 2010.

Kuczaj, Marian. "Przeszłość, teraźniejszość i przyszłość na Dolnym Śląsku." *Przegląd Hodowlany* 10 (2011): 18–22.

Kukliński, Jerzy. "Straż wartowniczo-konwojowa UNRRA i straż morska." Gedanopedia. December 15, 2015. https://gdansk.gedanopedia.pl/gdansk/?title=STRA%C5%BB_WARTOWNICZO-KONWOJOWA_UNRRA_I_STRA%C5%BB_MORSKA.

Kulczycki, John J. *Belonging to the Nation: Inclusion and Exclusion in the Polish-German Borderlands, 1939–1951*. Cambridge, MA: Harvard University Press, 2016.

Langlois, Suzanne. "'Neighbours Half the World Away': The National Film Board of Canada at Work for UNRRA (1944–47)." In *Canada and the United Nations: Legacies, Limits, Prospects*, edited by Colin McCullough and Robert Teigrob, 44–81. Montreal: McGill-Queen's University Press, 2016.

Larsson, Naomi, and Tom Levitt. "'Floating Feedlots': Animals Spending Weeks at Sea on Ships Not Fit for Purpose." *Guardian*, January 26, 2020. https://www.theguardian.com/environment/2020/jan/26/floating-feedlots-animals-spending-weeks-at-sea-on-ships-not-fit-for-purpose.

Levine, Susan. "CARE Packages and the Business of Food Aid." *Food, Fatness and Fitness: Critical Perspectives* (blog), September 22, 2015. http://foodfatnessfitness.com/2015/09/22/care-packages/.

Levitt, Tom. "Animals Farmed: Live Exports Risk of Disease, China Goes Big on Pork, and EU Meat Tax." *Guardian*. February 4, 2020. https://www.theguardian.com/animals-farmed/2020/feb/04/animals-farmed-live-exports-risk-of-disease-china-goes-big-on-pork-and-eu-meat-tax.

"Looking Back at the Reluctant Internationalists Project, After Four Years of Collaboration with Exceptional Researchers from Across the World." Reluctant Internationalists. November 6, 2018. https://www.bbk.ac.uk/news/the-reluctant-internationalists.

Lukas, Richard C. *Bitter Legacy: Polish-American Relations in the Wake of World War II*. Lexington: University Press of Kentucky, 1982.

Łaptos, Józef. *Humanitaryzm i polityka: Pomoc UNRRA dla Polski i polskich uchodźców w latach 1944–1947*. Kraków: Wyd. Naukowe Uniwersytetu Pedagogicznego, 2018.

Łaptos, Józef. "Wpływ wielkich mocarstw na strukturę i kompetencje . . . międzynarodowej organizacji humanitarnej—United Nations Relief and Rehabilitation Administration (UNRRA)." *Rocznik Administracji Publicznej* 2 (2016): 452–70.

MacDonald, Bryan. *Food Power: The Rise and Fall of the Postwar American Food System*. New York: Oxford University Press, 2016.

Majer, Piotr. "Komisja Specjalna do Walk z Nadużyciami i Szkodnictwem Gospodarczym (1945–1954): Uwagi o genezie, działalności i ewolucji." *Studia Prawnoustrojowe* 6 (2006): 179–91.

Manners, Ian. "Global Europa: Mythology of the European Union in World Politics." *Journal of Common Market Studies* 48, no. 1 (2010): 67–87.

Marks, Bogusław. "Pomoc UNRRA w odbudowie gospodarki Polski (1945–1947)." *Politologia: Acta Universitatis Lodziensis* 19 (1990): 163–89.
Marrus, Michael R. *The Unwanted: European Refugees in the Twentieth Century*. Philadelphia: Temple University Press, 2001.
Maul, Daniel. "The Politics of Neutrality: The American Friends Service Committee and the Spanish Civil War, 1936–1939." *European Review of History* 23, no. 1–2 (2016): 82–100.
Mayers, David. "Destruction Repaired and Destruction Anticipated: United Nations Relief and Rehabilitation (UNRRA), the Atomic Bomb, and US Policy, 1944–1946." *International History Review* 38, no. 5 (2016): 961–83.
Mazower, Mark. *No Enchanted Palace: The End of Empire and the Ideological Origins of the United Nations*. Princeton, NJ: Princeton University Press, 2009.
Mazower, Mark. "Reconstruction: The Historiographical Issues." *Past and Present* 210, suppl. 6 (2011): 17–28.
McArthur, Jo-Anne. "'We Could Smell the Boat Approaching': The Grim Truth About Animal Exports." *Guardian*. December 11, 2018. https://www.theguardian.com/environment/2018/dec/11/we-could-smell-the-boat-approaching-grim-truth-animal-exports-israel-haifa.
McArthur, Jo-Anne. "'The Grim Truth About Animal Exports,'" We Animals, December 11, 2018. https://weanimalsmedia.org/2018/12/11/the-grim-truth-about-animal-exports/.
Meiches, Benjamin. *Nonhuman Humanitarians: Animal Interventions in Global Politics*. Minneapolis: University of Minnesota Press, 2023.
Metzger, Thurl. "The Heifer Project." In Durnbaugh, *To Serve the Present Age*, 144–47.
Metzger, Thurl. *The Road to Development*. Little Rock, AR: Heifer Project International, 1981.
Miller, Maynard. "Nunemaker's Voyage." *Mennonite Historical Bulletin*, October 1991.
"Mission and Ministry Board Makes Decision to Close Material Resources Program." Church of the Brethren Newsline. October 23, 2023. https://www.brethren.org/news/2023/board-decides-to-close-material-resources/.
Moore, Jacqueline M. *Cow Boys and Cattle Men: Class and Masculinities on the Texas Frontier, 1865–1900*. New York: NYU Press, 2009.
Morse, Kenneth I. *New Windsor Center*. New Windsor, MD: Brethren Service Center, 1979.
Morse, Kenneth I. *Preaching in a Tavern and 129 Other Surprising Stories from Brethren Life*. Elgin, IL: Brethren Press, 1997.
Moyn, Samuel. *Christian Human Rights*. Philadelphia: University of Pennsylvania Press, 2015.
Nasaw, David. *The Last Million: Europe's Displaced Persons from World War to Cold War*. New York: Penguin Books, 2021.
"National Sides." European Central Bank. Accessed August 12, 2024. https://www.ecb.europa.eu/euro/coins/2euro/html/index.en.html.
Nimmo, Richie. "The Mechanical Calf." In Cohen and Otomo, *Making Milk*, 81–98.

Nodjimbadem, Katie. "The Lesser-Known History of African-American Cowboys." *Smithsonian Magazine*, February 13, 2017. https://www.smithsonianmag.com/history/lesser-known-history-african-american-cowboys-180962144/.

Northrup, Cynthia Clark, ed. *Encyclopedia of World Trade: From Ancient Times to the Present.* Vol. 2. New York: Routledge, 2015.

Nussbaum, Martha, C. *Justice for Animals: Our Collective Responsibility.* New York: Simon and Schuster, 2023.

Origins of the Heifer Project. High Library, Elizabethtown College, 2014. https://archive.org/details/Heifer_Project.

Otter, Chris. "Milk in Motion: Logistical Geographies in Twentieth-Century Britain." *Global Food History* 9, no. 1 (2023): 47–71.

Papuzińska, Joanna. "Kochana ciocia UNRA." *Stolica: Warszawski Magazyn Ilustrowany* 1–2 (2010): 31.

Pazgan, Mateusz. "Zagadnienia aprowizacji ludności województwa wrocławskiego z perspektywy starostwa kamiennogórskiego w latach 1945–1947." *Annales Universitatis Mariae-Curie-Skłodowska* 69, no. 1–2 (2014): 75–88.

Pernet, Corinne A., and Amilia Ribi Forclaz. "Revisiting the Food and Agriculture Organization (FAO): International Histories of Agriculture, Nutrition, and Development." *International History Review* 41, no. 2 (2019): 345–50.

Peyton, Jonathan. "'A Strange Enough Way': An Embodied Natural History of Experience, Animals and Food on the Teslin Trail." *Geoforum* 58 (2015): 14–22.

Phillips, Clive J. C., and Eduardo Santurtun. "The Welfare of Livestock Transported by Ship." *Veterinary Journal* 196, no. 3 (2013): 309–14.

Pienkos, Donald E. *For Your Freedom Through Ours: Polish American Efforts on Poland's Behalf, 1863–1991.* New York: East European Monographs, 1991.

Plach, Eva. "The Animal Welfare Movement in Interwar Poland." *Polish Review* 57, no. 2 (2012): 21–43.

Polish History Museum. Curated by Dorota Szkodzińska. "Jan Karski: Humanity's Hero." Google Arts and Culture. https://artsandculture.google.com/story/jan-karski-humanity-s-hero-polish-history-museum/EAXRBzXayhMA8A?hl=en, accessed October 7, 2024.

Poźniak, Bronisław. "70 lat Urzędu Celnego w Gdańsku." *Strefa Historii.* June 15, 2015. http://strefahistorii.pl/article/1147-70-lat-urzedu-celnego-w-Gda%C5%84sku.

Praczyk, Małgorzata. *Pamięć środowiskowa we wspomnieniach osadników na "Ziemiach Odzyskanych."* Poznań: Wydawnictwo Instytutu Historii UAM, 2018.

Praczyk, Małgorzata. "Śmierć zwierząt w narracjach autobiograficznych osadników na 'Ziemiach Odzyskanych': Uwagi o obecności." *Autobiografia* 1, no. 12 (2019): 41–55.

Pretus, Gabriel. *Humanitarian Relief in the Spanish Civil War (1936–39).* Lewiston, NY: Edwin Mellen, 2013.

Pritchett, Reuel B., and Dale Aukerman. *On the Ground Floor of Heaven.* Elgin, IL: Brethren Press, 1980.

Proctor, Tammy M. "Repairing the Spirit: The Society of Friends, Total Warm and the Limits of Reconciliation." *Peace and Change: A Journal of Peace Research* 45, no. 2 (2020): 198–224.

Puławski, Adam. "Revisiting Jan Karski's Final Mission." *Israel Journal of Foreign Affairs* 15, no. 2 (2021): 289–97.
Rappak, Wojciech. "Karski's Reports: The Story and the History." PhD diss., University College London, 2021.
"Reed Ramsey's Trip to Poland." Josephine's Journal. Accessed February 13, 2020. http://www.josephinesjournal.com/reed.htm.
Reid, Fiona, and Sharif Gemie. "The Friends Relief Service and Displaced People in Europe After the Second World War, 1945–48." *Quaker Studies* 17, no. 2 (2013): 223–43.
Reiff Miller, Peggy. "Celebrating 75 Years of Heifer International: Where It All Began." *World Ark*, Spring 2020.
Reiff Miller, Peggy. "Coming of Age on a Cattle Boat." *Mennonite*, January 10, 2006.
Reiff Miller, Peggy. "Cowboys at Christmas." *World Ark*, Holiday 2014.
Reiff Miller, Peggy. "Dan West: Mischief Brewing." Speech delivered in Mill Ridge Village, Union, OH, February 22, 2019.
Reiff Miller, Peggy. "Histories Intertwined." Interview by Jason Woods. *World Ark*, Summer 2019.
Reiff Miller, Peggy. "The Impossible Dream: How the Heifer Project Came to Be." *Messenger*, July/August 2009.
Reiff Miller, Peggy. "Mining for Gems in the Heifer Archives." *World Ark*, Spring 2016.
Reiff Miller, Peggy. "Okanogan County Sea-Going Cowboys and Their Errands of Mercy." *Okanogan County Heritage*, Winter 2014.
Reiff Miller, Peggy. "Ride 'Em, Seagoing Cowboy! A 1940s Brethren/UNRRA Partnership Touched Countless Lives." *Messenger*, May 2005.
Reiff Miller, Peggy. *The Seagoing Cowboy*. Illustrated by Claire Ewart. Elgin, IL: Brethren Press, 2016.
Reiff Miller, Peggy. The Seagoing Cowboys. https://seagoingcowboys.com.
Reiff Miller, Peggy. *The Seagoing Cowboys* (blog). https://seagoingcowboysblog.wordpress.com/.
Reiff Miller, Peggy. "Seagoing Cowboys and the Heifer Project: The Maryland Story." *Catoctin History*, Fall/Winter 2005.
Reiff Miller, Peggy. "Seagoing Cowboys: Delivering Animals to Post-WWII Europe." *Pennsylvania Magazine*, October 2006.
Reiff Miller, Peggy. "The Woman Behind the Man Behind Heifer Project." *Messenger*, July/August 2019.
Reinhardt, Maximilian Luz, and Tetiana Shyrochenko. "The Impact of the Russian War of Aggression on Ukrainian Livestock Production." Friedrich Naumann Foundation for Freedom. Accessed June 20, 2024. https://www.freiheit.org/germany/impact-russian-war-aggression-ukrainian-livestock-production.
Reinisch, Jessica. "'Auntie UNRRA' at the Crossroads." *Past and Present* 218, suppl. 8 (2013): 70–97.
Reinisch, Jessica. "Internationalism in Relief: The Birth (and Death) of UNRRA." *Past and Present* 210, suppl. 6 (2011): 258–89.
Reinisch, Jessica. "Introduction: Relief in the Aftermath of War." *Journal of Contemporary History* 43, no. 3 (2008): 371–404.

Reinisch, Jessica. "Preparing for a New World Order: UNRRA and the International Management of Refugees." In *Post-War Europe: Refugees, Exile and Resettlement, 1945–1950*, edited by Dan Stone. Gale Digital Collections, 2007.

Reinisch, Jessica. "The Reluctant Internationalists: A History of Public Health and International Organisations, Movements and Experts in Twentieth Century Europe." *The Reluctant Internationalists*, September 1, 2018. https://web.archive.org/web/20240422201816/http://www7.bbk.ac.uk/reluctantinternationalists/.

Reinisch, Jessica. "'We Shall Rebuild Anew a Powerful Nation': UNRRA, Internationalism and National Reconstruction in Poland." *Journal of Contemporary History* 43, no. 3 (2008): 451–76.

Reinisch, Jessica, and David Brydan, eds. *Internationalists in European History: Rethinking the Twentieth Century*. London: Bloomsbury Academic, 2021.

Riley, Barry. *The Political History of American Food Aid: An Uneasy Benevolence*. New York: Oxford University Press, 2017.

Rippley, La Vern J. "American Milk Cows for Germany: A Sequel." *North Dakota History* 44, no. 3 (1977): 15–23.

Rippley, La Vern J. "Gift Cows for Germany." *North Dakota History* 40, no. 3 (1973): 4–15.

Robinson, Mitchell L. "Conscience and Conscription in a Free Society: U.S. Civilian Public Service." In *Challenge to Mars: Essays on Pacifism from 1918 to 1945*, edited by Peter Brock and Thomas P. Socknat, 312–30. Toronto: University of Toronto Press, 1999.

Robinson, Mitchell L. "'Healing the Bitterness of War and Destruction': CPS and Foreign Service." *Quaker History* 85, no. 2 (1996): 24–48.

Rodogno, Davide. *Night on Earth: A History of International Humanitarianism in the Near East, 1918–1930*. Cambridge: Cambridge University Press, 2021.

Rodogno, Davide, Francesca Piana, and Shaloma Gauthier. "Shaping Poland: Relief and Rehabilitation Programmes Undertaken by Foreign Organizations, 1918–1922." In *Shaping the Transnational Sphere: Experts, Networks and Issues from the 1840s to the 1930s*, edited by Davide Rodogno, Bernhard Struck, and Jakob Vogel, 259–78. New York: Berghahn Books, 2015.

Rozario, Kevin. "'Delicious Horrors': Mass Culture, the Red Cross, and the Appeal of Modern American Humanitarianism." *American Quarterly* 55, no. 3 (2003): 417–55.

Ruttan, Vernon W. *United States Development Assistance Policy: The Domestic Politics of Foreign Economic Aid*. Baltimore: Johns Hopkins University Press, 1996.

Salvatici, Silvia. *A History of Humanitarianism, 1755–1989: In the Name of Others*. Translated by Philip Sanders. Manchester: Manchester University Press, 2019.

Salvatici, Silvia. "Sights of Benevolence: UNRRA's Recipients Portrayed." In *Humanitarian Photography: A History*, edited by Heide Fehrenbach and Davide Rodogno, 200–222. New York: Cambridge University Press, 2015.

Sappington, Roger E. *Brethren Social Policy, 1908–1958*. Elgin, IL: Brethren Press, 1961.

Sasson, Tehila. "From Empire to Humanity: The Russian Famine and the Imperial Origins of International Humanitarianism." *Journal of British Studies* 55, no. 3 (2016): 519–37.

Sawicki, Jacek. *Misja UNRRA w Polsce: Raport zamknięcia (1945–1949)*. Lublin: Wyd. Werset, 2017.
Sawicki, Jacek Zygmunt, ed. *Polska jesień, rosyjska zima. Spotkanie Juliena Bryana z misją UNRRA w Europie Środkowo-Wschodniej 1946–1947—fotografie i zapiski*. Warsaw: IPN, 2022.
Scgalia, Ilaria. *The Emotions of Internationalism: Feeling International Cooperation in the Alps in the Interwar Period*. New York: Oxford University Press, 2019.
Scott-Smith, Tom. *On an Empty Stomach: Two Hundred Years of Disaster Relief*. Ithaca, NY: Cornell University Press, 2020.
Severson, Kim. "Got Milk? Not This Generation." *New York Times*. April 4, 2023. https://www.nytimes.com/2023/04/04/dining/milk-dairy-industry-gen-z.html.
Shenk, Dan. "Aftermath." *Truth*, August 25, 1996.
Shephard, Ben. "'Becoming Planning Minded': The Theory and Practice of Relief, 1940–1945." *Journal of Contemporary History* 43, no. 3 (2008): 405–19.
Shephard, Ben. *The Long Road Home: The Aftermath of the Second World War*. New York: Random House, 2010.
Shyrochenko, Tetiana. "Ukraine's Dairy Industry During the War." Ministerie van Landbouw, Visserij, Voedselzekerheid en Natuur. Accessed July 16, 2024. https://www.agroberichtenbuitenland.nl/actueel/nieuws/2024/03/28/ukrainian-dairy-industry.
Siewor, Kinga. "Regained Landscapes: The Transfer of Power and Tradition in Polish Discourse of the Regained Territories." In *East Central Europe Between the Colonial and the Postcolonial in the Twentieth Century*, edited by Siegfried Huigen and Dorota Kołodziejczyk, 183–208. Cham, Switzerland: Palgrave Macmillan, 2003.
Sivert, Katherine and Christine Parker. "Our Beef With 'Big Meat': The Power Perpetuating Australia's Live Export Trade Is at Play Elsewhere." *The Conversation*. July 29, 2024, https://theconversation.com/our-beef-with-big-meat-the-power-perpetuating-australias-live-export-trade-is-at-play-elsewhere-235655.
Sluga, Glenda. *Internationalism in the Age of Nationalism*. Philadelphia: University of Pennsylvania Press, 2013.
Smith-Howard, Kendra. *Pure and Modern Milk: An Environmental History since 1900*. New York: Oxford University Press, 2013.
Snow, Erin. "Passing on the Gift: Magic." Heifer International. October 3, 2019. https://www.heifer.org/blog/passing-on-the-gift-magic.html.
Stańczyk-Wiślicz, Katarzyna. "Eating Healthy, Eating Modern: The 'Urbanization' of Food Tastes in Communist Poland (1945–1989)." *Ethnologia Polona* 41 (2020): 141–62.
Staples, Amy L. S. *The Birth of Development: How the World Bank, Food and Agriculture Organization, and World Health Organization Changed the World, 1945–1965*. Kent, OH: Kent State University Press, 2006.
Staples, Amy L. S. "To Win the Peace: The Food and Agriculture Organization, Sir John Boyd Orr, and the World Food Board Proposals." *Peace and Change* 28, no. 4 (2003): 498–523.
Sułwa, Aleksandra. "Skarby z UNRRA i zrzuty od innych ciotek: W paczkach przysyłano do Polski też wolność." *Dziennik Polski*, June 23, 2017.

https://dziennikpolski24.pl/skarby-z-unrra-i-zrzuty-od-innych-ciotek-w-paczkach-przysylano-do-polski-tez-wolnosc/ar/12203627.

Tananbaum, Duane. *Herbert H. Lehman: A Political Biography*. Albany: SUNY Press, 2016.

Taylor, Steven J. *Acts of Conscience: World War II, Mental Institutions, and Religious Objectors*. Syracuse, NY: Syracuse University Press, 2009.

Thompson, R. Jan, and Roma Jo Thompson. *Beyond Our Means: How the Brethren Service Center Dared to Embrace the World*. Elgin, IL: Brethren Press, 2009.

Tomassini, Martina and Ruthia Yi. "UNICEF: History of a Logo." UNICEF. Accessed April 28, 2022. https://www.unicef.org/about-unicef/unicef-logo-history.

Traini, Christophe. *The Animal Rights Struggle: An Essay in Historical Sociology*. Amsterdam: Amsterdam University Press, 2011.

Trentmann, Frank. "Coping with Shortage: The Problem of Food Security and Global Visions of Coordination, c. 1890s–1950." In *Food and Conflict in Europe in the Age of the Two World Wars*, edited by Frank Trentmann and Flemming Just, 12–48. London: Palgrave Macmillan, 2006.

Tyrell, Ian. *Reforming the World: The Creation of America's Moral Empire*. Princeton, NJ: Princeton University Press, 2010.

"The Update of the Ukraine Dairy Map-2024 Infographic Dedicated to the World Milk Day." Association of Milk Producers. Accessed June 20, 2024. https://avm-ua.org/en/post/the-update-of-the-ukraine-dairy-map-2024-infographic-dedicated-to-the-world-milk-day.

Valenze, Deborah. *Milk: A Local and Global History*. New Haven, CT: Yale University Press, 2011.

Velten, Hannah. *Cow*. London: Reaktion Books, 2007.

Velten, Hannah. *Milk: A Global History*. New York: Reaktion Books, 2010.

Verity, Liza. *Animals at Sea*. London: National Maritime Museum, 2004.

Vernon, James. *Hunger: A Modern History*. Cambridge, MA: Belknap Press of Harvard University, 2007.

Villani, Angela. "Children in the Development Debate: The Role of UNICEF from 1946 to the First UN Development Decade." *Journal of World History* 32, no. 3 (2021): 405–38.

Villanueva, Gonzalo. "'Pain for Animals, Profit for People': The Campaign Against Live Sheep Exports, 1974–1986." In *Animals Count: How Population Size Matters in Animal-Human Relations*, edited by Nancy Cushing and Jodi Frawley, 99–109. New York: Routledge, 2018.

Wahlquist, Calla. "New Zealand to Stop Exporting Livestock by Sea." *Guardian*. April 13, 2021. https://www.theguardian.com/world/2021/apr/14/new-zealand-to-stop-exporting-livestock-by-sea.

Walker, Elaine. *Horse*. London: Reaktion Books, 2008.

Wanner, Dick. "Seagoing Cowboys Hold a Roundup, Talk About Old Times." *Lancaster Farming*. Last updated December 7, 2022. https://www.lancasterfarming.com/farming-news/news/seagoing-cowboys-hold-a-roundup-talk-about-old-times/article_9f358722-4957-5864-b394-24daea6132bf.html.

Wasielewski, Jarosław. "Jak po wojnie leczono konie z UNRRY w Gdańsku." trojmiasto.pl. February 26, 2019. https://historia.trojmiasto.pl/Jak-w-Gdansku-po-wojnie-konie-z-UNRRY-leczono-n132173.html#opinions-wrap.
Webb, Thomas, Chris Pearson, Penny Summerfield, and Mark Riley. "More-Than-Human Emotional Communities: British Soldiers and Mules in Second World War Burma." *Cultural and Social History* 17, no. 2 (2020): 245–62.
Webb, Thomas, Penny Summerfield, Mark Riley, and Chris Pearson. "'We Cows Are in a Very Serious Predicament': Constructions of Land Girls and Cattle in Britain in the Second World War." *Gender and History* 34, no. 1 (2022): 179–200.
Weinreb, Alice. "'For the Hungry Have No Past nor Do They Belong to a Political Party': Debates over German Hunger After World War II." *Central European History* 45, no. 1 (2012): 50–78.
Weinreb, Alice. *Modern Hungers: Food and Power in Twentieth-Century Germany.* Oxford: Oxford University Press, 2017.
Weintraub, Philipp. "An Experiment in International Welfare Planning." *Journal of Politics* 7, no. 1 (1945): 1–24.
Weiss, Lorell. *Ten Years of Brethren Service.* Elgin, IL: Brethren Service Commission, 1952.
Weiss, Thomas G., and Sam Daws. *The Oxford Handbook on the United Nations.* New York: Oxford University Press, 2007.
"A Well-Fed World." A Well-Fed World: Plant-Based Hunger Solutions. Accessed July 19, 2024. https://awellfedworld.org.
Werner, Yvonne Maria, ed. *Christian Masculinity: Men and Religion in Northern Europe in the 19th and 20th Centuries.* Leuven, Belgium: Leuven University Press, 2011.
West, Dan. "Cooperation with the AFSC in Spain." In Durnbaugh, *To Serve the Present Age,* 107–10.
West, James L. W. *William Styron, a Life.* New York: Random House, 1998.
"What's It Really Like on Board a Live Export Ship?" Animals Australia, December 3, 2018 (updated May 22, 2024). https://animalsaustralia.org/latest-news/whats-it-like-on-a-live-export-ship/.
Wheatley, Natasha. "Central Europe as Ground Zero of the New International Order." *Slavic Review* 78, no. 4 (2019): 900–911.
Woltanowski, Piotr, Andrzej Wincewicz, and Stanisław Sulkowski. "Protection of Children's Human Rights and Health: A Legacy of Julian Kramsztyk, Janusz Korczak, and Ludwik Rajchman." *Global Pediatric Health* 5 (2018): 1–7.
Woods, Abigail. "Breeding Cows, Maximizing Milk: British Veterinarians and the Livestock Economy, 1930–50." In *Healing the Herds: Essays on Livestock Economies and the Globalization of Veterinary Medicine,* edited by Karen Brown and Daniel Gilfoyle, 59–75. Athens: Ohio University Press, 2010.
Wylegała, Anna. "Beyond the Victimhood Narrative: A Case Study of Unexpectedly Successful Collectivization in Communist Poland." *Journal of Social History* 56, no. 4 (2023): 805–27.
Wyman, Mark. *DPs: Europe's Displaced Persons, 1945–1951.* Ithaca, NY: Cornell University Press, 1989.

Yoder, Glee. *Passing on the Gift: The Story of Dan West*. Elgin, IL: Brethren Press, 1978.

Zahra, Tara. *The Lost Children: Reconstructing Europe's Families After World War II*. Cambridge, MA: Harvard University Press, 2011.

Żak, Marek. "Sytuacja aprowizacyjna w Legnicy w latach 1945–1946." *Szkice Legnickie* 36 (2015): 123–82.

"Zaraz po wojnie przyjechała do Polski 'Cioteczka Unra.'" Polskie Radio. November 9, 2020. https://www.polskieradio.pl/39/156/Artykul/2616894,Zaraz-po-wojnie-przyjechala-do-Polski-cioteczka-Unra.

Zaremba, Marcin. "Fearing the War After the War." In *Ends of War: Interdisciplinary Perspectives on Past and New Polish Regions After 1944*, edited by Paulina Gulinska-Jurgiel, Yvonne Kleinmann, Milos Reznik, and Dorothea Warneck, 275–96. Düsseldorf: Wallstein, 2019.

Zaremba, Marcin. "The 'War Syndrome': World War II and Polish Society." In *Seeking Peace in the Wake of War: Europe, 1943–1947*, edited by Stefan-Ludwig Hoffmann, Oliver Wieviorka, Sandrine Kott, and Peter Romijn, 27–62. Amsterdam: Amsterdam University Press, 2015.

Zaremba, Marcin. *Wielka trwoga: Polska 1944–1947*. Kraków: Wyd. Znak, 2012.

Zborowska, Agata. *Życie rzeczy w powojennej Polsce*. Warsaw: Wydawnictwa Uniwersytetu Warszawskiego, 2018.

Zyszczyk, Adam. "Domy Dziecka w gminie Konstancin-Jeziorna 1919–2015." OkoliceKonstancina.pl. June 1, 2019.https://okolicekonstancina.pl/2019/06/01/domy-dziecka-w-gminie-konstancin-jeziorna-1919-2015/.

INDEX

Page numbers followed by letter "f" refer to figures.

African Americans: cowboys, 74; on seagoing cowboy crews, 60, 229n15
agriculture: American, wartime boom in, 49; rehabilitation of, animals' essential role in, 5, 7, 8, 28, 30, 31–32, 42–43
agriculture, Polish: postwar condition of, 23–24, 88–89, 137; prewar, 29; Roosevelt's concern about, 30, 89; UNRRA reports on crisis of, 31
Albania, UNRRA aid to, 1
American Dairy Cattle Company, 25
American Friends Service Committee, 64; Nobel Peace prize for, 190; and post–World War I aid, 25; and relief work during Spanish Civil War, 36. *See also* Quakers
American Humane Association (AHA), 96–97, 99; on animal losses during overseas travel, 131; inspections of UNRRA animal holding centers and ports, 97–98, 106, 112
American Red Cross, 25
American Red Star Animal Relief program, 97, 243n23
American Relief Administration (ARA), 25–26, 80
Anglo-American Atlantic Charter, 27–28, 82
Animal Rescue League of Boston, 106
animals: and "cycle of empowerment," 39; and humanitarian aid programming, 5, 7, 10, 194, 202; killed during Russian invasion of Ukraine, 203; killed during World War II, 1; maritime transport of, history of, 195–96; modern-day transport on live export ships, 196–98; and postwar rehabilitation, 5, 7, 8, 28, 30, 31–32, 42–43, 194; as symbols, 10, 88, 159. *See also* cattle; horses
animals, Heifer Project's, in Poland, 10, 87, 102, 177, 201; follow-up visits with, 182–88; placement of, 178–80

animals, UNRRA: black-market trading in Poland, 166; branding at ports in Poland, 142, 170; conditions on ships, 114–17, 115f; distribution upon arrival in Poland, 151–53, 157–59, 158f; distribution practices in Poland, complaints about, 165–71; feeding on ships, 117, 119–21, 120f; loading onto ships, 112–13; overland journeys in Poland, 150–51, 186; poor health of, Polish responses to, 171–73; sale by recipient (Polish) government, 152–54; theft in Poland, 169; unhealthy, fate upon arrival in Poland, 145–50; unloading at ports in Poland, 141–42, 143f, 146f, 147f; used as breeding stock, 2, 152; vaccination of, 95, 107; winter sailing and hardships for, 126, 129, 173
animal welfare: Christian ethics and, 98; class-based assumptions regarding, 173–74; in Communist Poland, 174–76; Heifer Program and, 106; and humanitarianism, 17, 173, 176; in prewar Poland, 173, 175, 176; UNRRA and, 96–99
Arcab, Bronisław, 183
Australia, and animal exports, 196, 198, 199
Austria, UNRRA aid to, 14, 23

Baltic Sea: ports in, and UNRRA deliveries, 136; unexploded mines in, 117–18, 135
Baltimore (Maryland), port of, 45, 50, 104, 106, 117, 128
Bantz, Floyd, 230n34, 249n52
Baptists, and Heifer Project, 39, 103
Belgium, Heifer Project aid to, 44–45, 223n58
Bierut, Bolesław, 160, 161, 273n64
births, animal: during maritime animal transport, 198; during overland transportation in Poland, 167; on UNRRA ships, 122, 184, 250n64
Black Sea shipments, 135–36

301

INDEX

Bolshevism, spread of, ARA food aid program aiming to stop, 26, 28
Bomberger, Luke R., 125
Bonnell, John Sutherland, 47
Bowman, Paul Hoover, 71
Brant, Wayne, 62, 228n5
Brethren: beliefs of, 34–35; and conscientious objection, 65, 66; donations to Heifer Project, 101, 103; food aid during Spanish Civil War, 3, 36; international outlook of, 201; relief advertising by, 83–85; relief work by, 35–36, 64; seagoing cowboys, 2, 68; service ethic of, 35, 37
Brethren Service Committee (BSC): Christian inflections in recruiting approach of, 57, 58–59; commitment to relief and charity-giving, 35, 192–93; establishment of, 64; headquarters of, 227n1; and Heifer Project, 2–3, 38, 39, 52, 64–65, 192; Material Goods program of, 52, 228n7; New Windsor (Maryland) center of, 52–53; partnership with UNRRA, 3–4, 6, 7, 8, 9, 41, 43–45, 189, 223n55; Polish operations of, 178, 179, 190–91, 192; and recruitment of seagoing cowboys, 2, 3, 6, 43–44, 52, 55–62; relief programs of, 40; volunteers for, 52–53, 190
Bushong, Benjamin G., 61, 62, 72, 193, 231n64
Byler, Delmar, 72
Byler, Joe, 72
Byrd, Julia, 231n59

Canada: relief animals sent from, 43, 50, 92; support for UNRRA, 14, 22
Catholics: and Heifer Project, 39, 103; and NSBRO, 65; and relief work, 15
cattle, 76–77; on board of UNRRA ships, 115, 120f, 177; bred before shipping overseas, 38, 121; breeds chosen for aid programs, 85, 86; cost of, 42; dual-purpose approach to, 85–86; in Heifer Project, 76; "international language" of, 202; as key to agricultural production, 5; killed during Russian invasion of Ukraine, 203; killed during World War II, 1; lactating, on ships, 122; losses during UNRRA operation, 130–31, 150; Poland's need for, 192; Polish prewar population of, 24, 31; and postwar rehabilitation of agricultural societies, 7, 28; real and symbolic value of, 8, 78; shipping as humanitarian aid, idea for, 3; in UNRRA livestock program, 76; UNRRA shipments to Poland, impact of, 201–2; use as draft animals, in postwar Poland, 89. *See also* cow(s)
Chaloupka Wood, Clara, 190
children: American, as potential givers of aid, 84–85; donated animals earmarked for, 191; images of, in humanitarian fundraising campaigns, 47, 224n72; letters of gratitude to American donors, 185–86; milk as essential to development of, 82, 83–84, 87, 191; Polish, photographed with cows/drinking milk, 83, 83f, 163–64, 164f, 186f; as victims of World War II, 82
China: Heifer Project and, 4, 209n15; live animal exports to, 196; post–World War I relief work in, 35; UNRRA aid to, 1, 7, 14
Christianity/Christian ethics: and animal welfare activism in postwar period, 98; and Heifer Project, 47–48; and mid-century humanitarianism, 7, 9, 45–48, 134; and seagoing cowboys, 57, 58–59, 60, 62, 72–73, 74, 75; and statesmanship, 46, 224n67; and UNRRA, 7, 45–47, 73
Churchill, Winston, 12, 81
Civilian Public Service (CPS), 63, 66; applications for, 65–66; Brethren-managed camp, 53; peace churches and, 66–67, 69, 101; Puerto Rico camp, 40; seagoing cowboys coming from, 67–68, 69, 234n92; and University of Minnesota Starvation Experiment, 69–70, 235n102
Clay, Lucius, 28
Coast Guard, and seagoing cowboys, 61, 62
Cohnstadt, Martin, 73
colleges, recruitment of seagoing cowboys at, 55–56, 72
concentration camp(s): images of starving bodies at, and commitment to food as global human right, 32–33; seagoing cowboys' visit to, 139; victims of, horses arriving in Poland compared to, 176
Conscientious Objectors: number of, 66; peace churches and, 55, 62–63, 64, 65; as seagoing cowboys, 8, 55, 63, 67–68, 211n13. *See also* Civilian Public Service
Constanza (Romania), and UNRRA deliveries destined for Poland, 135–36
corruption: in distribution of UNRRA aid/animals, 165, 166, 169–71; in

INDEX   303

procurement of UNRRA animals, 93–94; among veterinarians, 133
cow(s): and civilization, 77; as essential component of postwar aid programs, 2, 5, 82; gift of, as direct gesture of humanitarian aid, 202; high status in peasant households in Poland, 162–64, 177; importance for Brethren, 3, 78; importance for local economy, 85; milk yields of, 270n27; photographs with recipient families, 164, 164f, 185; treatment of, and milk quality, 123; women's responsibility for, 161–62
cowboy(s): American, 73–74, 75; origins of term, 73. *See also* seagoing cowboys
Cox, Harvey, 58, 138, 140
CPS. *See* Civilian Public Service
Czechoslovakia: Heifer Project and, 4, 209n15; UNRRA and, 1, 4, 106

Danish Red Cross, 139, 190
deaths, of UNRRA animals, 130, 150, 253n126; upon arrival in Poland, 143–44, 148, 150; during initial period after arrival in Poland, 154–55; during ocean crossings, 5, 106–7, 116, 117, 119, 122, 126, 127–30, 172–73, 250n64; during overland transportation in Poland, 167; seen as justified by greater cause, 130; during transfer to ports in US, 96, 99; during unloading at ports in Poland, 141–42
deaths, present-day live animal transport and, 198–99
Declaration of the United Nations (1942), 13
Denmark: relief cattle from, 191; relief horses from, 50–51. *See also under* Danish
Department of Agriculture (US): Bureau of Animal Industry, inspectors from, 95, 96; Livestock Branch of, 43; veterinarians from, at UNRRA holding centers, 97
diseases, among UNRRA animals: upon arrival in Poland, 142, 143, 145–50, 171–72, 173; discovery at US ports, 96, 106–7; horses' susceptibility to pneumonia, 115, 126, 128, 129; spread during shipping, 99
diseases, present-day live animal transport and, 197, 198
Displaced Person (DP) camps, 14
Dobrowolski, Anatol, 170
draft animals: and agricultural rehabilitation, 31; cattle used as, 89; horses as, 1, 50, 76; oxen as, 77, 85

Drury, Charles M. "Bud," 22, 160, 189

Ebey, Robert, 122, 126
Eby, Kermit, 37, 38, 48
ecumenicalism: and Heifer Project, 39, 41, 55, 69; and UNRRA, 46–47
education: agricultural, in Poland, 191; on board of UNRRA ships, 60, 133; at Civilian Public Service (CPS) camps, 67
Erb, Paul, 73
Ethiopia, live animal aid to, 1, 209n15
Europe: founding myth of, 77–78; liberation of, 12, 14; post–World War II recovery of, UNRRA livestock program and, 1–2; purchases of relief animals in, 50–51. *See also specific countries*

Fast, Henry A., 69
fertilizer: reliance on farmyard manure, 29, 77; shortages in Poland, 24
film(s): on food security, 28; Polish, on UNRRA aid, 161–62, 172–73; UNRRA promotional, 47
First International Declaration on the Rights of the Child, 82
food: as basic right, 8, 26, 32–33; in Churchill's statement on Nazi defeat, 12; as component of relief, 16; and political stability, 28; and postwar international order, 27; post–World War I deliveries of, 25–26; post–World War II aid policies, 26; shortages of, addressing in short term, 24–25; as weapon, 26, 49
Food and Agriculture Organization (FAO), 32, 81; on Poland's need for cattle, 192
food security: as FAO's goal, 32; film about, 28; long-term, UNRRA's Poland program and, 25, 28; pursuit of, as priority after World War II, 5; Russian invasion of Ukraine and issue of, 203–4
France, Heifer Project and, 44–45, 223n58
freedom from want: as fundamental right, 82; Hot Springs Resolution on, 29; Roosevelt on, 26–27, 28
French, Paul Comly, 65, 68
Friends. *See* American Friends Service Committee; Quakers
Friesen, Gerhard, 137

Gdańsk (Poland), 255n17; German Mennonites in, 56; port of, 130, 136, 141; seagoing cowboys' impressions of, 137–38, 138f; veterinary clinic in, 147–48, 149, 150

INDEX

Gdynia (Poland): port of, 130, 136; UNRRA office in, 21; veterinary clinic in, 147
Germany: American Dairy Cattle Company's shipments to, 25, 216n72; Displaced Person (DP) camps in, 14; Heifer Project shipments to, 193, 209n15
Getz, Paul A., 190
Gingerich, John, 128
Gingerich, Melvin, 71–72, 73, 122, 133, 140–41, 250n59
Gingerich, Owen, 72, 117, 119, 132, 133, 138
global cooperation: and relief animal programs, 5–6; and UNRRA, 13
government(s): new understanding of role of, 13, 36. See also Polish government
Grater, Ed, 125
Greece: Heifer Project and, 4, 43, 178, 209n15; loss of cattle during World War II, 43; UNRRA and, 1, 4, 45, 51, 91
Gregg, John P., 22
Griggs, Charles and Frank, 97
Guetzkow, Harold Steere, 71

Hamilton, Stanley, 102
Hays, M. E., 22, 118, 167, 186, 187
Heatwole, Kenneth M., 123, 139, 140
Heifer Project, 2–3; advertising materials for, 83–85, 225n76; and animal welfare, 106; appeals for donations, 83–84, 100–101; Brethren's assessment of, 181, 183, 188, 192–93; BSC and, 2–3, 38, 39, 52, 64–65, 192; cattle breeds used by, 86; Christian ethics and, 47–48; collection/holding centers, 104–6; contacts between donors and recipients in, 180, 182–83, 185–88; donations to, 100–104; ecumenicalism and, 39, 41, 55, 69; and European rehabilitation, 33; executive directors of, 61, 231n63; follow-up visits with placed animals in Poland, 182–88; goals of, 78, 106; incorporation of, 193–94; logic of, 38–39; Massachusetts Society for the Prevention of Cruelty to Animals and, 98; number of animals delivered by, 4, 193; origins of, 3, 36–38, 81; partnership with UNRRA, 3–4; and "Passing on the Gift," 38–39, 180–81, 191, 221n25; placement of animals in Poland, 102, 178–80; and Polish government, 177–78, 181–82, 191, 192; Polish scholarship on, 19; in post-UNRRA period, 189, 190–92, 193; and principle of political neutrality in aid distribution, 38, 48; shipments to Greece, 4, 43, 178, 209n15; shipments to Poland, 4, 10, 87, 177, 201; shipments to Puerto Rico, 40–41, 102; success of, 193; UNRRA livestock program compared to, 100, 179, 180, 182
Heifer Project International (Heifer International), 3, 41, 185, 194, 207n7
Helstern, Russell, 125
Hendrickson, Roy F., 43
Henson, Edwin R., 43, 68
Hershey, Lewis Blaine, 66
Hertzler, Daniel, 132, 254n146
Hirschmann, Ira, 20
Hitler, Adolf, 5
Holderman, Earl, 228n6
Holle, H. A., 82
Hoover, Herbert, 26; American Relief Administration (ARA) under, 25, 26, 80; on children as victims of World War II, 82
horses: on board of UNRRA ships, 114–15, 115f, 116; challenges of caring for, 124–26; cost of, 42, 50; deaths on board of UNRRA ships, 116, 117, 119, 126, 127–29, 130; delivered to Poland, UNRRA livestock program and, 4, 31, 88, 90–91, 149f, 161, 201, 208n14, 242n85; as draft animals, 1, 50, 76; elite status of, 88; as essential component of postwar aid programs, 5, 8; from European countries, as relief aid, 50–51; as key to agricultural production, 5, 87–88; killed during World War II, 1; losses during UNRRA operation, 130; Polish farmers receiving, 158, 158f; and postwar rehabilitation of agricultural societies, 7, 8, 28; in postwar US, surplus population of, 93, 131, 242n4; shipped to UK, during World Wars, 92; slaughtered for meat, upon arrival in Poland, 143, 144; susceptibility to respiratory diseases, 115, 126, 128, 129, 130, 148; unhealthy, fate upon arrival in Poland, 143, 147–48, 176; unloading at Polish ports, 141–42, 143f, 146f, 147f; in UNRRA livestock program, 1, 76, 172; used as breeding stock in Poland, 152; working conditions for, Polish Communist government's regulation of, 174, 175
horses, Polish: breeding programs, 90; historical importance of, 89–90; preferences for, 90–91; prewar population of, loss of, 24, 30, 31, 88, 89

INDEX 305

Hot Springs conference, 29, 30, 32
Hulme, Kathryn, 110
human-animal studies, 210n25
humanitarianism: animal welfare and, 17, 173, 176; vs. charity/philanthropy, 18; Communist, 174; evolution in understandings of, 16–17; as heterogeneous project, 202; images of suffering children in fundraising campaigns, 47, 224n72; vs. missionary work, 58, 230n37
humanitarianism, mid-century: bold ambitions of, 202; Christian ethics and, 7, 9, 45–48, 134; Civilian Public Service (CPS) camps and, 67; different expressions of, 6; peace churches and, 8, 35; role of animals in, 5, 7, 10, 194, 202; role of seagoing cowboys in, 10–11, 58, 201, 202–3
Humanitarian League, 17
human right(s), fundamental: food as, 8, 26, 32–33; idea of, 26
Humphrey, Hubert, 49
hunger: approaches to alleviating, 32, 70; interpreted as consequence of government decisions, 36; malnourishment and undernourishment, 27, 29; milk seen as solution to, 78–79; plant-based solutions to, 194; and social instability, 5, 25, 26. See also starvation
hunger relief, soup kitchen model of, 26
hunger studies, field of, 27

Iceland, relief horses from, 50
inspections: AHA, 97–98, 106; at ports, 106, 107; UNRRA vs. government, 95, 96
International Humanitarian Bureau, 176, 268n81
internationalism: liberal, Christian ethics and, 48; vs. nationalist imperatives, 18; new, 13. See also global cooperation
International Maritime Organization, 199
Israel, cattle shipments to, 226n92
Italy: Heifer Project and, 4, 209n15; mules shipped from, 51; UNRRA aid to, 1, 14

Jan Sobieski III (King of Poland), 89
Janzen, Dave, 125
Japan, Heifer Project shipment to, 193
Japanese Americans: donations to Heifer Project, 102–3; as seagoing cowboys, 60

Kaczmarek, Mieczysław, 166
Karczewski, Wacław, 169–70

Karski, Jan (Jan Kozielewski), 29–30, 89
Kaufman, Edmund G., 69
Keller, Will, 142
Keys, Ancel, 70
Kopania, Antoni and Adam, 183–84
Kosch, Lewis F., 68

La Guardia, Fiorello: Christian rhetoric used by, 45–46, 224n62; on UNRRA, 3, 189; visit to Poland, 161
Lane, Arthur Bliss, 51
Lanzmann, Claude, 30
Łaptos, Józef, 19, 208n14, 247n7
Laski (Poland), Institute for the Blind in, 185–86
League of Nations: and First International Declaration on the Rights of the Child, 82; milk championed by, 80
Legg, Stuart, 28
Lehman, Herbert, 3–4, 26, 82, 188, 189
Levinson, G. Ben, 50
Levinson, Sol, 50
Levinson Livestock Company, 50, 226n92
Lewandowski, Antoni, 185
Libby, Paul, 250n64
Liberty ships, 110; animal loss rate on, 130; length of return trip for, 111; number of attendants required for, 112
Liepert, Jerry, 125–26, 252n98
Lintner, Henry, 50
Lintner, Robert: on animal condition upon arrival at ports, 107; report on UNRRA livestock program, 207n1; on seagoing cowboys, 44, 230n33; on UNRRA fleet, 247n7
live aid, use of term, 5
live animal maritime transport, modern-day, 196; conditions for animals on, 196–98; future of, 199; loss rates on, 198–99; number of animals on, 196; UNRRA livestock program compared to, 2, 199–200
livestock handlers. See seagoing cowboys
loans, for purchase of UNRRA animals, 154, 155
Lublin Committee (Polish Committee of National Liberation), 21
Lutz, Harold T., 70

MacDonald, Archibald, 106
malnourishment, 27, 29
manure: accumulation on board of ships, 115, 116, 126–27, 197; as fertilizer, 29, 77

INDEX

Martin, James, 252n103
Massachusetts Society for the Prevention of Cruelty to Animals, 98, 99
Matecki, Tadeusz, 175, 176
Mays, Benjamin, 60
McCollum, Elmer V., 81
McNett, Harold, 56, 57, 119
Men and Hunger (report), 70–71
Mennonites, 34; beliefs of, 34–35; Civilian Service Program (CSP) and, 69; and conscientious objection, 65, 66; German, in Gdańsk, 56; operations in Poland, 241n73; pacifist stand of, 63; relief aid during Spanish Civil War, 39; relief aid during World War I, 64; seagoing cowboys, 2, 56, 58, 68, 72, 229n17
Menshikov, Mikhail A., 22, 189
Merchant Marine, UNRRA ship crews and, 61
Methodists: and Heifer Project, 39, 101, 182; and NSBRO, 65; seagoing cowboys, 68
Metzger, John D., 192–93
Metzger, Thurl, 181, 189–90, 193
Meyer, Albert J., 58
Meyer, Arthur D. (Art), 120–21, 125, 128, 137, 185, 228n5, 250n59
Middle East, live animal exports to, 196
Mikołajczyk, Stanisław, 21, 31
military draft: peace churches' position on, 55, 62–63, 64, 65. *See also* Conscientious Objectors
milk: adulterated/spoiled, 79–80; availability on ships, lactating cows and, 122; and children's development, 82, 83–84, 87, 191; deliveries of UNRRA animals to Poland and, 160, 161, 202; as essential relief product, 1, 8, 38, 78–79, 80, 82, 85; government-funded programs for children, 81; human consumption of, history of, 79; importance for rural households, 85; nutritional science and popularity of, 80–81; nutritional value of, belief in, 2, 78, 79, 80, 81, 87, 204; nutritional value of, challenges to, 194; pasteurization of, 80; photos of Polish children drinking, 83, 83f, 163–64, 164f; Poland's deficit of, 163, 192, 202, 264n22; shortage during Spanish Civil War, 36; as solution to postwar hunger problems, 78–79; on UNICEF logo, 87, 240n57
Miller, Orie O., 65
Miller, Paul, 193

mines, unexploded: in Baltic Sea, 117–18, 135; in Poland, 23, 183; in Ukraine, 203
Mock, Virgil, 102
Morton, Nelle, 60

national interests, vs. internationalism, 18
National Service Board for Religious Objectors (NSBRO), 65, 232n77
Newport News (Virginia), 49–50
New Windsor (Maryland), BSC center in, 52–53
New Zealand, and live animal transport, 199
Nunemaker, John, 124, 251n80
nutritional science, 27, 29, 80–81, 82

Odessa (USSR), UNRRA deliveries to, 136
Oliver, J. B., 141–42
Orr, John Boyd, 81, 238n34
Osóbka-Morawski, Edward, 22
Oswald, Walter, 72
Our Folks (film), 261n123
oxen, 77, 85

pacifism: peace churches and, 35, 63–64, 67; seagoing cowboys witnessing war's destruction and, 138; UNRRA and, 67
pastors, on UNRRA ships, 72
Pato, T. A., 172
Pawlus, Stanisław, 158
peace churches, 34, 35; and Civilian Public Service (CPS), 66–67, 69, 101; collaboration among, 8, 65, 69; common origin story of, 34; communities of, 56; and conscientious objection, 55, 62–63, 64, 65; and Heifer Project, appeals for donations to, 100; pacifist stand of, 35, 63–64, 67; relationship to state, 35, 64; and relief aid, 8, 64–65, 69; relief work during Spanish Civil War, 3, 36, 39; seagoing cowboys from, 2, 55, 56, 68, 108, 229n17
The Peasants (Reymont), 162–63
photographs: of animals, in Polish recipients' letters to donors, 185; of Polish children drinking milk, 83, 83f, 163–64, 164f; of seagoing cowboys, 186–87, 187f; of wartime ruin, 100–101
Piłsudski, Józef, 90
Poland: agriculture of, precarious condition of, 23–24, 88–89, 137; animals received through UNRRA livestock program, 4, 160, 161, 201–2, 208n14; animal welfare

INDEX 307

in, 173, 174–76; charitable groups working in, 190; emerging Soviet control over, 20, 22, 135; food aid after World War I in, 25, 26; Heifer Project animals allocated to, 4, 10, 87, 102, 177–80, 201; importance for US geopolitical interests, 4, 20; postwar, seagoing cowboys' impressions of, 136–41, 138f; as primary beneficiary of UNRRA livestock program, 1, 4, 20, 137, 201, 208n14; Recovered Territories in, 10, 155–56, 261n123; special relationship with horses, 89–90; territorial changes after World War II, 24; UNRRA aid program in, deliveries of, 135–36; UNRRA aid program in, value of, 6–7, 209n20; UNRRA animals' arrival in, 141–50; UNRRA animals' overland journeys in, 150–51; wartime losses/suffering of, 20, 22–24, 137. *See also* agriculture, Polish; horses, Polish

Polish citizens: in Displaced Person (DP) camps, 14; gratitude and affection toward UNRRA, 160–63; loans taken by, 154, 155

Polish Committee of National Liberation (Lublin Committee), 21

Polish government: Communist, suspicion of foreign charities, 191–93; Communist takeover of, 21, 171, 172; control over distribution of UNRRA aid, 165–68; criticism of UNRRA aid distribution and, 168–71; criticism of UNRRA animals, 10, 172–73; in exile, 21, 30; Heifer Project and, 177–78, 181–82, 191, 192; and land reform, 152, 156, 260n98; sale of UNRRA goods/animals by, 152–54; shifting views on UNRRA, 10, 160–63, 171–72; and UNRRA animals after arrival in Poland, 144, 151–52, 258n61

political neutrality, in aid distribution, 15, 21, 38, 48

ports, Black Sea, and UNRRA deliveries destined for Poland, 135–36

ports, Polish: branding of animals at, 142, 170; infrastructure problems and labor shortages at, 141; inspection of animals at, 145–46, 148f; unloading of animals at, 141–42, 143f, 146f, 147f; UNRRA deliveries to, 136

ports, US: accidents at, 112–13; animal welfare standards at, AHA on, 112; Heifer project animals shipped from, 104; inspections of animals at, 106, 107;

transfer of animals to, 94–95; UNRRA and benefits to, 49–50

Puerto Rico: Civilian Public Service camp in, 40; Heifer Project shipments to, 40–41, 102

Quakers (Society of Friends), 34; beliefs of, 35; and conscientious objection, 65, 66; pacifist stand of, 63–64; relief aid during Spanish Civil War, 3, 36, 37, 38, 39; relief aid during World War I, 64; reservations about relief work, 71; seagoing cowboys, 2, 68. *See also* American Friends Service Committee

railroad companies, UNRRA and benefits to, 49–50

Rajchman, Ludwik, 87, 100

reconstruction, UNRRA and goal of, 16, 43

Recovered Territories, in Poland, 10, 155–56; resettlement of, 156–57; UNRRA animals distributed to, 157–58, 158f, 161, 165

Reed, Ollie E., 41

rehabilitation: essential role of animals for, 5, 7, 8, 28, 30, 31–32, 42–43, 194; UNRRA and goal of, 3, 16, 20, 31, 32, 38

Reiff Miller, Peggy: on age of seagoing cowboys, 230n33; on animal loss rates on ships, 130; on Dan West, 220n16; on first "seagoing cowgirl," 231n59; on HP and Birobidzhan, 226n92; interviews of seagoing cowboys, 109, 247n3; on origins of term "seagoing cowboy," 236n125; on peace-church background of seagoing cowboys, 229n17; picture book by, 251n80; on UNRRA ships' schedules, 214n45

relief: components of, 16; milk as essential component of, 8, 38, 78–79, 80, 82, 85

relief animal(s), use of term, 5

relief work: and benefits to American companies, 49–51; Brethren and, 35–36, 64; and global cooperation, 5–6; Mennonites and, 39, 64; peace churches and, 8, 64–65, 69; Quakers and, 3, 36, 37, 38, 39, 64, 71; and US global leadership, 48–49; after World War I, 25–26; after World War II, 15, 26

Reymont, Władysław, 162–63

Rockwell, Norman, 28

Rohrer, Glenn, 137

Romania: and maritime live animal exports, 198–99; and UNRRA deliveries, 135–36

308 INDEX

Rooks, Lowell Ward, 12
Roop Farm, 104–6
Roosevelt, Franklin D.: on Four Freedoms, 26–27, 28, 32, 66; meeting with Karski, 29–30, 89
Root, Kathryn, 228n6
Ross, James M., 97, 98, 106
Rowett Research Institute, 81
Rowland, E. S., 132
Royer, Byron P., 62, 116, 126
Russia, Bolshevik: American Relief Administration (ARA) operations in, 25–26; Mennonites' relief work in, 64
Russia, invasion of Ukraine, 203–4

Sabin, Donald R., 22
Salt, Henry, 17
Samuels, Gertrude, 46
Sawyer, Warren D., 127, 139
Schrock, Mark, 193
seagoing cowboys: accounts/diaries of, 106, 109, 134, 247n3; additional relief work in Poland, 139; advertisements for, 55, 56, 57, 58, 229n16; ages of, 57, 230n33; American spirit and, 74–75; animal deaths and, 127–28, 131; appearance of, 74; average number per ship, 111–12; Christian ethics and, 57, 58–59, 60, 62, 72–73, 74, 75; from Civilian Public Service (CPS) camps, 67–68, 69, 234n92; Coast Guard certification of, 61, 62; Conscientious Objectors as, 8, 55, 63, 67–68, 211n13; crews of, assembling, 71–73; dangerous work environment of, 117, 125–26, 127–28; diversity within, 2, 56–57, 59, 60; donations to Heifer Project, 103; experiences on board of ships, 113–14, 114f, 116–28, 120f, 199–200; impressions of postwar Poland, 136–41; mechanization replacing work of, 196; moral health of, concerns about, 73, 140; motivations of, 58, 230n34; New Windsor (Maryland) as first stop for, 53; origins of term, 73, 236n125; from peace church denominations, 2, 55, 56, 68, 108, 229n17; physical exam of, 60–61; qualities required to become, 54–55, 57, 58–59, 272n57; recruitment of, 2, 3, 6, 43–44, 52, 55–62; religious devotion aboard ships, 131–32; return journeys/leisure time of, 132–33; role in mid-century humanitarianism, 10–11, 58, 201, 202–3; vs. sailors, 133–34; speaker series by, 53; supervisors of, 54,
71–73, 118, 119, 123, 132; thank-you cards sent to, 61, 231n64; vs. typical cowboys, 74; as unique international actors, 6; from University of Minnesota Starvation Experiment, 70; visits to animals placed in Poland, 184–87, 187f, 188; wages of, 44, 53, 54; women as, 61, 194, 231n59
Seeds of Destiny (film), 47, 51
Selective Training and Service Act (US), 65
Senger, Marvin, 231n63
shipping industry: modern live animal transport, 196–99; after World War II, 50
ships, UNRRA, 109–11, 247n7; accumulation of manure on, 115, 116, 126–27; animal births on, 122, 250n64; animal deaths on, 5, 106–7, 116, 117, 119, 122, 126, 127–30, 172–73, 250n64; conditions for animals on, 114–17, 115f; design of, criticism of, 116; feeding of animals on, 117, 118, 119–21, 120f; loading of animals onto, 112–13; mechanical problems and accidents involving, 117–18, 126; religious services on, 131–32; retrofitting to accommodate live animals, 109, 110, 126; ventilation problems on, 116–17, 129, 197; winter sailing by, and hardships for animals, 126, 129, 173
Shoah (film), 30
Shultz, Lawrence W., 58, 184
Smeltzer, Ralph, 183
Smith, Dwight, 57, 113–14, 137–38
Smith, H. R., 126
Snyder, Daniel, 184
Society for the Protection of Animals (Poland), 174–76
Society of Friends. *See* Quakers
Sopot (Poland): holding stable at, 151; veterinary clinic in, 147
soup kitchen(s): model for, 26; in Poland, seagoing cowboys volunteering at, 139
Soviet Union: and agricultural destruction in Poland, 23–24, 137; confiscation of Polish horses by, 30, 31; emerging control over Poland, 20, 22, 135; Heifer Project shipments to, 193, 226n92; Polish provinces annexed by, 155, 156
Spanish Civil War: peace churches' relief work during, 3, 36, 39, 48; West's experience during, 36, 37, 81
SS *Alfred DuPont*, 193
SS *Beloit Victory*, animal loss rate on, 173
SS *Carroll Victory*, 49
SS *Cedar Rapids Victory*, 111f, 250n64; horses on board of, 115f

INDEX 309

SS *Clarksville Victory*, 112, 257n49
SS *F.J. Luckenbach*, 45, 110, 125, 186
SS *Frederic C. Howe*, 125
SS *Lahaina Victory*, 123, 173
SS *Mexican*, 110, 132
SS *Morgantown Victory*, 139
SS *Mt. Whitney*, 110–11; animal loss rate on, 130, 173; Heifer Project animals on, 178; number of attendants on, 54, 112; religious services on, 132; veterinarian's report on, 129
SS *Norwalk Victory*, 141
SS *Park Victory*, 132, 142
SS *Robert W. Hart*, 58, 120, 178
SS *Santiago Iglesias*, 178, 184
SS *Stephen R. Mallory*, 71, 117, 119
SS *Virginian*, 45, 110, 136
SS *Wesley W. Barret*, 128
SS *William S. Halsted*, 102, 117, 178
SS *Woodstock Victory*, 112; Heifer Project animals on, 178, 181
SS *Zona Gale*, 106, 116
starvation: fear of, in postwar period, 23, 24–25; University of Minnesota Starvation Experiment, 69–70, 235n102
Stine, Ora W., 61–62, 102
Stine West, Carol Maxine, 61–62
Styron, William, 250n64
supervisors, on UNRRA ships, 54, 71–73, 118, 119, 123, 132
Swedish aid groups, in Poland, 190
Szczecin (Poland): UNRRA deliveries to, 130, 136, 155, 166, 253n132; UNRRA office in, 21; veterinary clinic in, 147, 150

Tanski, Witold, 185
Throckmorton, Dillon, 182–83
tractors: horses compared to, 50; UNRRA deliveries to Poland, 88–89, 241n73
Truman, Harry S., 14, 46
Truski, Josef, 184

Ukraine, Russian invasion of, 203–4
undernourishment, 27, 29
United Kingdom: Animal Welfare Act in, 199; as contributor to UNRRA, 14; dairy farms in, expansion in interwar period, 80; horses shipped to, during World Wars, 92; relief horses from, 50
United Nations: and commitment to religious tolerance, 66; Conference on Food and Agriculture (Hot Springs conference), 29, 30, 32; first agency of, 13; First Council Sessions of, 20. *See also* UNRRA
United Nations International Children's Emergency Fund (UNICEF), 87, 240n57
United States: dairy farms in, expansion in interwar period, 80; geopolitical interests of, Poland's importance for, 4, 20; global leadership after World War II, 48–49; horses in, surplus after World War II, 93, 131, 242n4; as largest contributor to UNRRA, 14; postwar prosperity of, 49, 93, 131
Universal Declaration of Human Rights, 32–33
University of Minnesota Starvation Experiment, 69–71, 235n102
UNRRA (United Nations Relief and Rehabilitation Administration), 1; achievements of, 13–14, 18; Agricultural Rehabilitation Division, 43; beneficiary countries, 1, 4, 14; and benefits to American farmers/companies, 49–51; Christian ethics and, 7, 45–47, 73; Contributed Supplies Branch, 100, 244n36; critical assessments of, 18, 22; directors of, 12; Displaced Person (DP) camps operated by, 14; ecumenicalism and, 46–47; financing of, 14, 46–47; folding of operations, 190; and Food and Agriculture Organization (FAO), 32; image-making by, 163–64; literature on, 18–19; long-term food security as goal of, 25, 28; member countries of, 13; Ocean Shipping Division, 42; origins of, 12, 13; pacifist stand of, 67; partnership with BSC, 3–4, 6, 7, 8, 9, 41, 43–45, 189, 223n55; Polish gratitude and affection toward, 160–63; and political neutrality in aid distribution, 15, 21, 38, 48; priorities of ("three Rs"), 15–16, 38; Public Information Office, 83; and recipient governments, control over aid distribution, 144–45, 152–53, 179; rehabilitation goal of, 3, 16, 31, 32, 38; reports on Poland's agricultural crisis, 31; tasks of, 13–14, 15; Technical Committee on Agriculture, 43; types of aid distributed by, 14; and voluntary agencies, 15
UNRRA Guard (Straż UNRRA), 168–69
UNRRA livestock program: and animal welfare, 96–99; assessments of animal suitability and quality, 94–96; BSC and

logistical support for, 33; cattle in, 86, 87; deliveries to Poland, impact of, 160, 161, 201–2; and desegregated crews, 60; distribution practices in Poland, complaints about, 165–71, 266n54; donations to, 100, 244n37; fleet of ships, 109–11, 247n7; Heifer Project compared to, 100, 179, 180, 182; horses delivered to Poland, 4, 31, 88, 90–91, 208n14, 242n85; initial hesitation regarding, 41–42; justification for, 3; logistical challenges for, 96, 112, 116; loss rates, 130, 150, 253n126; vs. modern-day live animal maritime exports, 2, 199–200; monitoring of animal placements in Poland, 182, 186–88; number of animals delivered through, 1, 4, 207n1; Poland as primary beneficiary of, 1, 4, 20, 137, 201, 208n14; positive evaluations of, 188, 189; and postwar European recovery, 1–2; procurement of animals for, 43, 93–94, 100; rehabilitation goal and, 3; transfer of animals to ports, 94–95, 96; transportation costs, 109; and veterinary supplies, contributions of, 149. *See also* animals, UNRRA; ships, UNRRA

UNRRA's Poland program, 19–22; chiefs of mission, 22; and complaints about aid distribution, 165–68; deliveries of aid, 135–36; international field staff of, 189, 214n49; Polish historiography on, 19; selection of aid recipients, 151–52; value of, 6–7, 20, 209n20

vaccinations, of UNRRA animals, 95, 107
Vachon, John, 82; meeting with seagoing cowboys, 186–87, 187f; photos of Polish children drinking milk, 83, 83f, 163–64, 164f; in UNRRA delegation to Poland, 90
veterinarian(s): and design of retrofitted ships, 109; Polish, inspection of arriving animals, 145–46, 148f; at ports in US, 106, 107; recruitment for UNRRA livestock program, 43, 223n51; at UNRRA holding centers in US, 97; at UNRRA mission to Poland, 32, 130; on UNRRA ships, 54, 118–19, 122, 128–29, 249n52
veterinary clinics, in Poland, UNRRA animals sent to, 147–50, 172, 173, 177
Victory ships, 110; animal loss rate on, 130; length of return trip for, 111; number of attendants required for, 111–12

West, Dan: appeal for donations, 83–84; on Christian ethics and Brethren aid projects, 47; experience during Spanish Civil War, 36, 37; and Heifer Project, 3, 36–38, 39, 40, 81; and partnership with UNRRA, 41; and "Passing on the Gift," 180–81; as "visionary," 37, 221n18
West, Kenneth L., 62
West, Philip, 48, 101
White, David H., 185
Wilder, A. G., 32, 88, 90, 130
Wild West, in Poland, 155, 261n123. *See also* Recovered Territories
Willoughby, George, 142, 257n49
Wine, Jacob, 106, 114f
Wiszniewski, E., 93–94, 184
Witkowski, Ł., 172
women: in postwar Poland, 140; responsibility for cows, 161–62; seagoing cowboys, 61, 194, 231n59
Woodbridge, George, 4; on conditions for animals on ships, 115–16; on number of animals delivered through UNRRA, 4, 207n1; on UNRRA fleet, 247n7; on UNRRA's Christian ethics, 46; on UNRRA's Poland program, 20, 209n20
World War I: conscription issue during, 64; and food shortages, 25; horses shipped to UK during, 92; peace churches and relief aid during, 64; relief programs after, 15, 25–26, 35; US exports of condensed milk during, 80
World War II: as battle for food and land resources, 5; children as victims of, 82; horses shipped to UK during, 92; livestock and agricultural lands destroyed during, 1; pledge not to conclude separate peace treaties in, 13; Poland's suffering in, 20, 22–24, 137; relief programs during/after, 15, 26; US prosperity after, 49, 93; winning the peace in aftermath of, 26, 28

Yoder, Elmer, 125
Yoder, J. Olen, 112, 116, 127, 138–39, 228n5
Yoder, Milo, 193
Yugoslavia, UNRRA aid to, 1, 4, 23, 51, 91

Zigler, Michael Robert (M. R.), 41, 65, 67; on Heifer Project shipments to Soviet Union, 193; and *Men and Hunger* publication, 70; on quality of heifers donated to Heifer Project, 101

www.ingramcontent.com/pod-product-compliance
Lightning Source LLC
Chambersburg PA
CBHW032032300426
44117CB00009B/1025